# Welcome to 13th Street

# My Side of Town

By

## Garry Allison

Publication Coordinator
Editor - Layout - Design
Carlton R. (Carly) Stewart

Occasional Paper No. 42
Published in celebration of the 2006
Centennial of the City of Lethbridge

## Lethbridge Historical Society
A Chapter of the Historical Society of Alberta
**P. O. Box 974**
**Lethbridge, Alberta, Canada T1J 4A2**

Cover wrap-a-round photos:

Upper - A view of Westminster school yard looking west as children play. The structure on the right is the main school building while the structure on the left is the building where other classes were taught; it was a well used annex.

Mid - Adams Park was a bare facade, which housed the beauty and excitement of Lethbridge Miners' Baseball for many decades. Note Galbraith School to the right of the photograph.

Lower - Staff of Supina Mercantile family of stores about 1932.

Left rear cover photo:- 1938 photo of an air show that was staged at the air port as it was then situated on the site where Mountview Dodge Chrysler is today. The water tower on the left was never used as it was designed and built for. When the tower was dismantled, the upper storage section was moved to a farm on Highway #61 a few miles west of Skiff, Alberta, for use as a granary, and still is on site in 2005.

This 2005 edition was prepared entirely on the Lethbridge Historical Society computers. Camera-ready page printouts were prepared for the printer. Printed and bound in Canada by Graphcom Printers.

First Printing
December 2005

**Library and Archives Canada Cataloguing in Publication**

Allison, Garry
 My side of town : welcome to 13th Street North / by Garry Allison

(Occasional paper ; no. 42)
ISBN  0-9684921-8-5

 1. Allison, Garry.  2. Lethbridge (Alta.)--History--20th century. I. Lethbridge Historical Society  II. Title.  III. Series: Occasional paper (Lethbridge Historical Society) ; no. 42

FC3699.L48A48 2006          971.23'4504'092          C2005-905662-2

# Contents

# Acknowledgements

Memories - mine and others - only go so far. In researching I used many different sources. Yet you must bear in mind, one of the reasons I was asked to compile this book by the city's Chief Archivist, Greg Ellis, was because there is no definitive written history of north Lethbridge, of 13th Street North, or any of the businesses, buildings or its people. This fact made it difficult to do research when so little information exists. None the less I did find a wealth of information from a number of sources, including Archivist Greg Ellis and of course the back issues and photos of The Lethbridge Herald. I must also acknowledge all the personal interviews with people like my father, Andy Allison, and others: Jack Lee, Nap Milroy, John Kobal, Ab Chervinski, Blondie Mihalik, Jim Perry, Everal and Joe Horhozer, Brent Seely, June & Jim Carpenter, Lil Wright, Nellie Seaman, Scotty Armitt, Cammie Randle, the Bissett family, Mavis Standing, the encouragement of: Avice Anderson, Frances Kaupp, Ralph Michelson, George Varzari, Betty Gal and many others quoted in this book, some of whom answered our public plea for assistance. There were also the writings of people like Steve Vaselenak, an old neighbour of mine, revered Lethbridge historian whom I worked with from time to time while with The Herald, the late Dr. Alex Johnston and others like Audrey Swedish and George Watson.

As well, I relied on a limited array of materials in the Sir Alexander Galt Museum and Archives, past interviews I did over the years while with The Lethbridge Herald, the Henderson Directory, and the Lethbridge Historical Society Newsletters and publications, and in particular Irma Dogterom. As well

I've gleaned materials from *The Bend, a History of West Lethbridge, The Pioneer Pemmican Roundup* history book, *Kishiki-Nikkei Tapestry*, the history of southern Alberta's Japanese Canadians and other area history books. The photographs come from private collections, the Lethbridge Herald files, the Sir Alexander Galt Museum and Archives and the Lethbridge Public Library. No credit is given for photographs, as I consider them to be from the public domain.

The following people read my manuscript while it was still in my hands: Mavis Standing, Avice Anderson, Irma Dogterom, Mary Allison and Lynne Davis.

The Lethbridge Historical Society wishes to acknowledge the assistance they received from: Greg Ellis at the Sir Alexander Galt Museum and Archives, Dave Dowey, Barry Snowden, Dianne Violini, Bill Lingard, Audry Swedish, John Fisher and Carly Stewart who has recreated this design and layout from my early draft.

The Lethbridge Historical Society also wishes to recognized the financial grant received yearly from the Alberta Historical Resources Foundation, a portion of that yearly grant is directed to this publication. The Society wishes to acknowledge the Lethbridge Miners' Library Board for providing a grant toward the costs. All these grants allow the Society to sell at a reduced rate to you.

Garry Allison
September 2005

# Introduction

The concept behind the creation of this book was to give you a look at 13th Street North through a historical, personal and human perspective. It is by no means a be-all end-all book about north Lethbridge, primarily because the main focus is on 13th Street itself, between the years 1909 and 1975. Neither is it an in-depth, all exclusive look at 13th Street, but rather a glimpse of some of the key businesses, people and institutions along the street through the first seven or eight decades of north Lethbridge.

It is written from my perspective, dealing with many of my acquaintances, family and friends and at the same time trying to take in other people's memories and views. I looked at some of the areas in depth - or at least, deeper than other areas. Simply put, you can't talk about 13th Street North without wandering a few blocks east or west to Galbraith or St. Basil's Schools, or to places like the 16th Street Lion's swimming pool and skating rink, or over to Staffordville. I merely touched on some areas, and actually ignored other areas of the north side, the latter including much of the Industrial Park. That's a world unto itself. The industrial area dates back to the 1960s, though the city actually bought 125 acres from the CPR in 1912, for an industrial area.

Publication of this book coincides with the 2006 Centennial of Lethbridge. This is very appropriate as the book is a celebration of a very important segment of this city, north Lethbridge and 13th Street North in particular.

Naturally, when dealing with some institutions, like schools, I ventured off 13th Street, and I also touched on other neighbourhoods, buildings and people off the main corridor, but all of which had some contact in one form or another with 13th Street.

When compiling information on 13th Street, at one time virtually the only main north-south artery in Lethbridge, you have to deal with the 9th Street Bridge and its impact; and you can't forget the fact the north side had the city's first commercial airport. The north side was also home to Canada's largest prisoner of war camp during World War II, and also home to many prominent, important and colourful citizens. Every one of these aspects are an integral part of the story of 13th, and the north side in general.

In 1911 there were 1,192 people in north Lethbridge, a figure which rose to 11,806 by 1961. By 1980, 21,158 of Lethbridge's 53,235 citizens lived north of the railway tracks and in 1985, when the city's population climbed to 59,901, 21,706 of those called the north side home.

A glimpse of this growth and some of the many people and businesses I have not mentioned, all of whom are part of the tapestry of 13th Street North from the Henderson Directory, can be found in selected years, from 1909 through 1975, in a separate chapter 'Where They Were' of the book.

In 2003, I enjoyed the privilege of being the Honourary Parade Marshal for the Whoop-Up Days Parade. As my family and I rode in the open carriage and passed under the subway onto the north side, I felt a welling in my eyes and a choking in my throat. I was a kid from the north side, who went to school at Westminster, attended movies at the Lealta, ate hamburgers at the Wonder Cafe, had my hair cut at Greggy's, played pool at Johnny's and attended baseball games at Adams Park, all as a pre-teen and teenager. Now, here I was, heading up the Whoop-Up Parade, returning to 13th Street North, my home as a youth. The feeling was overwhelming, proving that you never really leave the north side. It will always be My Side of Town.

My life's work until retirement was writing for the Lethbridge Herald. This has given me much to dig back through. As reporters we were encouraged to use standard terms, i. e. "The Herald" was to be used in all our writings plus we also used various other standards in our writing format: when a Street or Avenue is identified we used N. or S. for North or South. I have therefore continued using those standards.

I hope you enjoy reminiscing with me through *My Side of Town*.

# My Side of Town

Welcome to my neighbourhood.

I feel like Mister Rogers, but the fact is 13th Street North of the 1940s and 1950s, was my neighbourhood - albeit shared with hundreds and hundreds of others. It was the business block of the north side, my side of town.

The north side has always been special in Lethbridge. It was the side of the blue collar people, the backbone of any community, from the coal miners of the early days of the city, to the mechanics, bus drivers, bartenders, streetcar drivers, butchers, bakers and even soldiers and sailors. Few doctors, lawyers and uptown types lived on the north side in those early days.

Mine was a special era in Lethbridge's history, the 1950s, something right out of Neil Simon, with a Damon Runyonesque style. The north side of the 1940s and 1950s, and even earlier, was an ethnic blending pot. My group of acquaintances and friends crossed many a cultural line, from Chinese and Japanese, to Italian, Hungarian, Scots and English. And the business community along 13th Street North was no different, with names like Wong, Sorokoski, Kobal, Lee, Credico, Morrison, Mihalik, Johnson and others.

Today, 13th Street North is exactly 3.2 kilometres long, from the underpass, or subway, to 26th Avenue, where the city, in its weird wisdom, decided to do away with a straight-through street right on to Hardieville and out the north end of town. Today, you stop, turn and generally follow a confusing jog if you wish to continue on to Hardieville. It is 2.5 kilometres from the subway to Little Wigan, and the house of my birth, at 1806 13th St., and just over 1.35 kilometres from the underpass to the old Adams Park front entrance.

While north Lethbridge, in its early years, was made up of pockets of nationalities, be they Slovacks, Scots, Ukranian, or English, when it came to 13th Street itself, it was a pot pourri of people. No matter what era, as you travelled down the three kilometre long street, you discovered a broad mix of nationalities all working side by side along the north side business street, with names like Doughty, Hong, Supina, O'Sullivan, Green, Hurst, Binning, Ponech, Mihalik, Ingoldsby, Kregosky, and Smerek.

The north side also had a reputation. "The guys around the north side would tell people they lived on the north side and it starts getting tough at the subway, and they lived in the attic of the last house," Alvin Bissett said with a laugh.

In the city's early history books there's a continual reference to Westminster Road, which was 13th Street, north and south. With Westminster School identifying the north side, the south side designation was dropped.

"In those early times the North Western Coal and Navigation Co. gave names to the city's streets," said the city's Chief Archivist Greg Ellis. "The Westminster designation was named after the district of Westminster in London, which was represented by William Lehman Ashmead Bartlett Burdett-Coutts, one of the major shareholders in the North Western Coal and Navigation Co."

When Lethbridge began there was no north-south designation along 13th Street, or what was known as Westminster Road, which ran from the coulees in the south to the coulees in the north. However, on the south side of the railway tracks the road was 100 feet wide, while on the north side it was only 66 feet wide, for some unknown reason.

In September, 1910, streets bearing people's names were changed throughout the city to a numbering system. Galbraith Street, for example, became 9th Avenue and Westminster Road became 13th Street.

You could head down 13th North and find everything you needed, from fresh baking, beer, clothing, hardware and haircuts, to movies, lumber, groceries, fast foods, jewellery, meats, dry cleaning, radios and tires.

The street was almost book ended by two large family grocery stores, Supina's at the 2nd Avenue corner and Mihalik's at 7th Avenue. In between there were major businesses like the CPR and a hotel, along with cafes, churches - though they were in a different type of business - hardware stores, confectioneries, tire shops, and a super little theatre loaded with as much character as Bogart himself. There were butchers, bakers, druggists and later even one of those new fangled television stores, not to mention the city's strangest library, as well as baseball and soccer teams, often among the best in the province.

In back of the main artery, which took you from the underpass, beneath the CPR tracks, all the way to Hardieville, three miles away, were the homes of the people who made up my side of town. While all northsiders were looked on as one, by themselves and by those south of the tracks as well, it was really a multi-faceted community, a community of divided sections, not officially mind you, but realistically.

Those of us west of 13th Street, and south of 9th Avenue were kind of one group, with minor dividing lines in between. To us, the east side of 13th was someone else's turf. As well, 16th Street was another dividing line, and then there was Little Wigan and Hardieville areas, and those centered around Galbraith School.

There were cross-overs allowed, to be sure, but really you stayed and played on your home ground. You ventured east to skate at the outdoor Lion's rink, and swim at the Lion's pool, and you crossed 13th to attend both Galbraith and Westminster schools, and later the new Wilson Junior High - which is Westminster today, the original Westminster turned into a donut shop by 2000 . . . but I'm getting ahead of myself.

The fact was, northsiders were different. We went downtown for the "big theatres", like the Roxy and Capitol, and later Paramount, and you shopped at Eaton's - you'd never miss Toyland during the Christmas season, which actually began in December, not October. And, of course, if you made it to high school, it was a long trek south to the LCI. Winston Churchill High School, on 9th Avenue North, wasn't built until 1960.

But the rule of thumb to remember here was northsiders went south, southsiders never came north. I honestly don't remember too many southsiders coming north to shop or to swim or skate. They had their own pools and rinks, their own theatres, stores and schools. But, we went south to share their wealth, often travelling on the old streetcars.

Johnny Walker, Johnny Frouws and others would be negotiating the old rattling cars down the track, which turned around at 9th Avenue, to head back south, to the heart of downtown and 5th Street, then the bustling centre of Lethbridge. I'd buy popcorn at Bert's at 3rd Avenue and 5th Street South - who didn't? - and then head to the Lethbridge Hotel, where my grandfather, Robert (Bob) Allison, tended bar or to the Dallas Hotel, where my dad was a bartender. But, once again I digress.

The key to north Lethbridge was to walk 13th, and to know its people, its stories, the fun, entertainment, work and tragedies of the street. I'll take you on a walking tour of my street, starting right at the underpass, dividing the city into two distinct neighbourhoods. You left 13th Street South, and went down a severe dip, under the wooden underpass onto 13th Street North. You literally ducked into our side of town. Oldtimers will remember the underpass, not for

its entrance way to either side of town, but for the fact the storm sewer at the base of the underpass never could handle a rain that amounted to more than half an inch.

Many a picture can be found in The Herald of trucks and cars, water up to their windows, as they sat soaking at the bottom of the underpass. And there they'd stay stranded in that lake until the drains caught up to the raging water.

I'll mention here, there was another main access north, the old steel trestled 9th Street bridge, which took you over the railway tracks into Staffordville, the backdoor to 13th Street. But we'll talk about that later.

My grandfather, Robert Allison.

The north side also had an industrial park in 1909, albeit for only one business, and on the west edge of north ward, not the east. A brickyard, employing about a dozen men, was still operating in the early 1920s just north of the CPR Roundhouse. One of the buildings using bricks from the yard was the original four-roomed Central School in south Lethbridge.

Along 13th Street, as you dipped into the underpass you came up in the north side of town, and your first sight was a bustling CPR warehouse complex.

Alex Slawasky was just one of the workmen involved, in 1928, with the paving of 13th Street, in the vicinity of the subway, which has long linked the north side to the south. A steam-powered cement mixer made work a breeze as workers lay pavement with trowels between the streetcar tracks, which once threaded their way from downtown to 9th Avenue North, down the middle of 13th Street. The same year, Alex was part of the crew tearing up the old board walks and laying concrete sidewalks, and gutters.

In 1909 wooden sidewalks, built on the west side of 13th and the north side of 9th Avenue had been approved, at a cost of $2,000.

Lethbridge historian Irma Dogterom said, "as the wooden walkway planks came up, we kids went through the dirt below (the spaced wooden sidewalk boards), searching for nickels, dimes, pennies and perhaps even a quarter." A coin dropped through the boardwalk was, for all intents and purposes, lost. Now they were being freed, their destination likely candy stores and theatres.

Prior to 1912, traffic crossed over the tracks as it entered the northside. CPR trains, freight and passenger, were busy crossing 13th Street from both east and west, while cars and horse-drawn vehicles were crossing the same tracks heading north and south. To accommodate the traffic, which by 1912 included the new-fangled streetcars, a flagman was often found at the crossing to protect the vehicular traffic from the trains, or the other way around. Often that flagman was J.B. Skrankovich, who controlled everything from streetcars to pedestrians to allow the CPR passenger and work trains to rumble past. With the planning for the streetcars prior to 1912 the city engineering department decided there would be an underpass for the cars entering the north side, not a level crossing over the CPR tracks. A large turnout of people in North Lethbridge had protested a bridge over the tracks, wanting an underpass instead.

Alex Slawasky helping pave 13th Street in 1928.

Work on the streetcar lines began April 1, 1912 at the corner of 6th Avenue and 5th Street S. and seven days later a Civic Holiday was declared and an official sod turning held. The underpass was completed, with a new road, albeit dirt and gravel, to allow the trains easy flow across the top of the ever-increasing road traffic on the street underneath.

Through the years poor drainage always plagued the subway, and many a time a mini-lake formed under the bridge, with a car or truck floating around, water spilling into the windows and the driver soaking wet on the road, looking down with a forlorn look as his car enjoyed an interior and exterior rinse.

## Streetcar Rails Head North

Streetcars swayed, rolled and clattered along 13th Street North from 1912 through 1947. The Lethbridge Municipal Railway was really built to serve the visitors for the Seventh International Dry Farming Congress in September, 1912. One of the lines found its way north. The debt incurred for the 10 streetcars and maze of tracks was not paid off until 1957, 10 years after they quit running!

In its heyday the system carried well over a million passengers a year along the four main routes, most of it in south Lethbridge, linking the downtown core with the south side, north side, and Henderson Lake and exhibition grounds areas.

It only took a year to lay the track for the city's streetcar network, at a cost of more than $250,000. Besides the farming congress, one of the key roles the new rail system played was the linking of north Lethbridge with the south side of town, quite likely preventing a move by the north side to break away and take on its own identity.

The streetcars were born in controversy and died in controversy.

The Lethbridge Municipal Railway was about 12 kilometres long, serviced by a peak colour-coded fleet of 10 streetcars, adorned with coloured lanterns as route markers. The cars themselves were amber and cream coloured, the last one sitting just outside the entrance to the Sir Alexander Galt Museum and Archives. The city of 10,000 was served by the White, Red, Blue and Orange Lines, linking all portions of the city. There was a short-lived Yellow Line which tended to duplicate the Orange Line's south side route, running the opposite direction. Later there was an airport line added as well. The first line was the Blue Line, taking people from the Club Cigar Store corner in the heart of downtown, along 3rd Avenue South to 13th Street South, north along 13th Street to the loop at 9th Avenue North. This was the longest-lasting line, with the last run Sept. 8, 1947.

One of the original uses of the line was to carry coal miners to work in the north Lethbridge mines. But they still had quite a walk to No. 3 and No. 6 mine areas from the end of the loop on 9th Avenue North.

One of the early drivers, the late Johnny Walker, said the streetcars were numbered 1 through 10, with those 6 to 10 having four wheels, two at the front and two at the back. The other cars, 1 through 5, had eight wheels, a set of four in the front and a similar truck at the rear. The eight-wheeled cars tended to sway from left to right as they maneuvered the city's undulating track system.

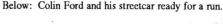

Below: Colin Ford and his streetcar ready for a run.

"The four wheelers went up and down on the track, but that wasn't too bad if the track bed was good," said Walker, who drove the 25-minute return trip northern route from 1945 to 1947. "The kids from No. 3 at the far end of 13th Street, would climb on and head for the horseshoe seats right at the back. Then they'd jump up and down and that really made the old cars bounce.

"I remember once when Bob Allison and I went over 30 straight days without a day off," said Johnny Walker. "We'd take the Sunday afternoon airport run and the evening north side route. Those old cars would go 30 to 35 miles per hour, you could wind them right up."

He said the cars had four motors when they came from the factory but city officials removed two of them to cut down on expenses. They also took out the expensive electric heaters, putting in coal stoves, which the drivers stoked diligently, keeping them full of coal and wood.

"They were cold," Walker said. "The coal stove was on your left side. One side of you would cook and your other side by the door froze. The passengers were none too warm either."

---

**Little Pay For Drivers**

Streetcar drivers were paid 45 to 50 cents per hour, working a nine-hour day, six days a week.

Walker remembered most of the old streetcar drivers, including: Bob Allison, Charlie Szabo, Nick Marks, Alf Smith, Bob Farrell, Bill Oliver, George Organ, George Wilson, Frank Rigby, Colin Ford, Clarence Maclean, Lloyd Tuckwell, Jim Maclaren, Bill Lee, Ludy Grant, Grant Horne, Dan Murphy, Laurie Davis, and two drivers named Merrick and Tilley. Streetcar superintendents included Bill Simons, Charles Castles and Jess Payne. Bill Cross and Bert Duncan were in charge of the tracks and Harry Carbert looked after the switches. Walker, Allison, Lee, Metcalfe, Frouws and others went on to drive city transit buses after the streetcars disappeared.

---

The first streetcar arrived in the city Aug. 8, 1912 and the first run, Aug. 17, was a trip by city officials over the entire track network. The first calamity occurred Aug. 21 when a temporary generator burned out due to overloaded cars heading to the exhibition grounds, bringing the system to a crashing halt. Service wasn't resumed until Sept. 12.

Streetcars had a stormy history in Lethbridge and by 1938 it was felt by many the expensive streetcars should be shut down. But the people of north Lethbridge didn't go for that idea. A vote Dec. 14, 1938 asking: Are You in Favour of the City Discontinuing Streetcars, was defeated 807 to 665. There were 157 spoiled ballots, enough to swing the vote. Five hundred southsiders wanted the lines closed, only 165 from the north side felt that way. The system began to seriously down-size in 1939 when two south side lines were closed, replaced by buses.

Walker said the outbreak of World War II saved the north side run. The government said streetcar lines were to remain in existence because they did not require gasoline which was so vital in the war effort.

The operation of the system was not without its problems, political and physical. In the winter snow and ice raised havoc with the rail lines.

"It was steel against steel and it didn't take much to get the wheels spinning," said Walker. "They'd get stuck a lot in the snow, but we always carried a shovel and a supply of salt."

During one winter blizzard a streetcar hit a flock of sheep on the fairground line run and killed about a dozen.

Stray animals were not uncommon sights on the tracks, but on Oct. 6, 1914, the first fatality involving a streetcar and a human being was reported in The Lethbridge Daily Herald.

At 7:30 p.m. the night before, near the Adams Park in north Lethbridge, Anthony Bolenka, a coal miner on his way home from No. 6 mine, walked behind a streetcar as it was backing up. Bolenka was pinned under the car, his leg partially severed. He died on the operating table at Galt Hospital a few hours later from shock and loss of blood.

Walker said every Halloween presented problems. The north side loop at Adams Park had a large, portable outhouse situated right in the middle of the loop, for passengers' convenience.

"It never missed . . . on Halloween night that outhouse would be moved onto the track," Walker said with a laugh. "Your light, as you turned on the loop, did not shine onto the track and you couldn't see. You'd come around and that toilet would be right there. You'd hit it and it would get caught up in the cow catcher up front."

Kids were forever pulling the trolley cable off the lines with a rope that dangled off the back of the cable said Walker. The driver would get out to fix the cable, a simple process of pulling the rope and guiding the pulley back onto the overhead cable. As he did this the kids would scramble onto the streetcar, unseen, and get a free ride.

Cars used to jump the track regularly and one just about went into Supina's and then the Miners' Library, said Walker. He said switches became a problem and bolts would have to be jammed in them to keep the cars on the rail as they turned. It wasn't uncommon for a switch to jump open in mid turn and have the front end of the car on a set of tracks headed down an avenue and the back truck going onto a track headed down a street.

The streetcars, which stopped every block along their route, ran down the middle of the street. They presented something of a traffic hazard, but vehicle traffic was light back then. Streetcars, though it was considered illegal, would often stop in the middle of the street to let passengers on or off the sleek cars.

"As time went on traffic got heavier and problems followed," said Walker. "I remember once, near Mo-Tires in north Lethbridge, a guy ran into the streetcar, right in the middle of the road. He told the police he didn't have a chance, the car he hit only had one light and was driving right in the middle of the road. He was stone cold drunk."

It was inexpensive to ride a streetcar, even as late as 1947, the last year the clattering electric rail-guided cars ran in Lethbridge. Yellow adult tickets were five for 25 cents or you could buy a book of 22 blue adult tickets for $1. Children's tickets were green and 10 for 25 cents.

Walker said the driver had to stand on a streetcar, though there was a stool available. The left hand was on the electric driving handle, which moved ahead slowly to start the steel-wheeled cars rolling. The air brake handle moved from side to side. On the smaller cars there was a crank handle for the hand-operated brakes. Often the pulley would bounce off the overhead electric wires during a run, but the driver simply got out, went around the back and maneuvered it back on with the pulley rope. The main power line would break fairly often and a crew came out from the car barns to repair it. It would take 20 to 90 minutes to get things under way once the crew arrived.

"Bob Allison and Bill Metcalfe both came to the streetcars from the city police force and in 1944 they went onto the buses together. I drove streetcars from 1945 to 1947 and then city buses for 10 years after that before moving into light and water reading and collection for the city," said Walker.

Only the north side regular route and four operating streetcars remained when Walker started driving. Only little No. 8 was running at the end he said. At the end of each day the cars headed for the car barns on 8th Avenue, between 5th and 6th Street South. The same barns were later used when the gas-powered city buses took over from the beleaguered streetcars.

"At the end the streetcars were in poor shape. They'd take the wheels off one, or a motor, and put them on another just to keep things going."

The last run was Sept. 8, 1947.

Bill Metcalfe came to know almost everyone in Lethbridge during his 28 years with the City. In his day he drove all the city bus routes at one time or another, including 4, 4A and 5 in north Lethbridge, and claimed he knew nearly everyone in the city. He started guiding streetcars around the tracks in 1944 and in 1945 left the streetcars for the buses, which he drove until 1971.

Drivers still around when Metcalfe made his first run included George Organ, Bill Oliver, Colin Ford and Frank Rigby, the latter three all going to work in the car barns when the streetcars stopped and the buses took over.

"I drove the last streetcar in July, 1945," said Metcalfe, who died in April, 2001 at age 94. "The streetcar only ran to the north side then, the other south side routes had closed down before I started. The north side run was the Blue Line."

A Pair of Bills, Bill Lee and Bill Metcalfe.

Metcalfe would pick up passengers across the street from the Club Cigar Store downtown, on the Galt Gardens southwest corner. The tracks went down 3rd Avenue and up to 13th Street and turned north to 9th Avenue, where Adams Ball Park sat. There, they turned and headed back south.

"Charlie Parry, the manager of the (Lethbridge and District) Exhibition for all those years, lived in the house right across from the ball park where we turned around," Metcalfe said.

The streetcar wasn't Metcalfe's first job with the city however. "My first job with the city, on my first night, consisted of Bob Allison walking me down all the back alleys in town checking door knobs," said Metcalfe, working his first night as a policeman.

His foot patrols each night took him through the downtown business district, all the way out to the government grain elevators, down 13th Street North to 9th Avenue and Matt's Taxi stand, and a walk back downtown.

Besides Metcalfe and Allison some of the other city policemen at the time included Jim Carpenter, Bobby Dunlop and Syd Wallis.

Metcalfe and Allison went on to drive city buses, Carpenter became Chief of Police, Wallis went to work for the city's recreation department and was often seen around the Lion's Pool on 16th Street North.

Metcalfe didn't like police work and spent only nine months walking a beat. March 1, 1944 he started driving streetcars.

In a word, Bill described the early buses which served Lethbridge as terrible.

9

"The first ones had just one door. They were all one-door Chevies, and everyone had to get off and on through the same door. You'd be swearing if you were at the back and had to get off at the next stop. In the winter the Chev was okay for the driver, he sat on the motor and could keep warm, the gear shift was to the rear of the driver and off to the side. Other than the gear shift they weren't so bad to drive.

"But it was cold for the passengers. In the summer it was pretty hot for the driver, and you always had the side window open for air, there was no fan, nothing. When I left they were just getting the air conditioning and good heaters like they have today."

The old buses would seat 20 people, but often carried up to 60, jammed in, front door to rear.

"When I was on the buses you couldn't wish for anything better with the people," he said. "If someone complained I'd tell them 'I'm never late, I'm just early for the next trip.' For some reason you couldn't get people to move to the back of the bus though, even after they had two doors. It was always kind of empty back there. I'd tell people, 'the back gets there the same time as the front, so move back please.'"

## Bridging the Tracks

If you were to take an aerial view of north Lethbridge in the late 1800s and early 1900s - which would have given you a place in history ahead of Wilbur and Orville Wright - you would have seen a smattering of what looked like tiny villages, and districts or what they used to call additions. There was the Village of Stafford, first known as No. 3 because it sprang up near the entrance to the Galt No. 3 coal mine in 1890 and by 1900 became incorporated as the Village of Stafford. Nearby were the Pierce, Hammerburg, Vare and Perry Additions - what would be known today as subdivisions. All these small settlements covered an area west from 13th Street, between 9th and 14th Avenues.

The area south of Staffordville, as residents called it, was mainly open land owned by the CPR, which spurred the railroad to assist the city in building the 9th Street Bridge, with hopes of opening the area up to settlement. The area included the old Wallwork home and a slough, appropriately known as Wallwork Lake.

Many civic leaders, and residents, felt the final location of the bridge was strictly for the benefit of the railway - which indeed it was.

Certainly the bridge would not assist the people settled along 13th Street, or those east of 13th. Those in Little Wigan, a row of houses along 13th, north of 9th Avenue, likely could have cared less. Little Wigan's name came about because most of its inhabitants were from Wigan, Lancashire, England, speaking with the tough-to-understand brogue of the Lancashires. Most of the men worked, not underground in the mines, but as mine technicians and mechanical staff, as they had in England.

As early as 1906 there was talk of a traffic link in the area, however the first idea was a subway, under the tracks. By 1909 talk had switched to the sky route, and the CPR was strongly pushing for the 9th Street route.

The proposed bridge over the ever-expanding CP railyards was designed to link the people of Staffordville to the downtown business core - and assist the CPR - and was given the stamp of approval by Mayor Elias "Shorty" Adams (1910-1911) and his council, at a cost of $86,000, the city to pay half. It was to follow an artery originally known as Coutts Street.

The bridge idea was bandied about during the 1911 election before it was finalized and construction began. At the same time the city was also looking west, with the towering high level bridge under construction as well. It was a bridge builder's dream - or nightmare - to be in Lethbridge in those years.

To aid traffic movement, with the parade of horse drawn drays and carriages moving north to south each day, a crossing was set up at Galt Street, and as the bridge proceeded, watchmen were in place night and day to assure no one took the new shortcut before it was ready.

Below: This 1930s test drive ended in a calamity on the 9th Street Bridge, almost falling into a black abyss.

The wooden-timbered bridge, with its metal girders, was opened, without ceremony, to traffic April 30, 1912. It was a grand day, but the world was unimpressed, still reeling from the April 13 catastrophe when the unsinkable Titanic went down.

The temporary Galt Street crossing was closed, blocked by freight cars, and all traffic was steered over the almost finished viaduct. However, teamsters and owners of new motorized vehicles did not fall in love immediately with the steep, long grade on the north section of the 1,100-foot bridge, nor the fact that there was a foot-high drop where the bridge met the road. Those traveling east-west along 1st Avenue South, past the CP station, were unimpressed as well with the potholes and litter created by the construction process.

At its completion Mayor George Merrick Hatch and his council were faced with an inflated bill, $110,000, of which the city owed $55,000. But it was too late to argue.

At the start the new structure was known by many as the Coutts Street Bridge, then it became Sage's Bridge, but was finally known merely as the 9th Street Bridge by the late 1920s or early 1930s.

Naming the bridge for Robert Sage, born in Perthshire, Scotland, seemed an honest and universal idea at the time. Sage, who came to Lethbridge in 1888 and died at age 72 in 1920, was originally a bookkeeper in the colliery office with the North Western Coal and Navigation Co., later the CPR, and he was also an early secretary for the A.R. and C. Library and Trading Room Association. After a series of other jobs in stationery and accounting, Sage, who was also a Mason, completed his link with both the railway and the city when he became the city's cashier, at City Hall, in 1915. It was a position he held until his death.

The bridge was narrow and there were more than a few accidents, a spectacular one coming in the early 1930s when a vehicle went out of control, darted between the girders, to hang precariously over the side, teetering above the train tracks below - there were no guard rails at the time. The late John Easton said the driver was a mechanic from Baalim Motors who was test driving a car for a customer. The old, mainly wooden bridge was rebuilt in the 1950s, with pavement added, serving as a very busy link for north and south until it finally fell to progress in 1984 under the National Salvage wrecking ball. It gave way to the overpass, part of the construction of the east-west Crowsnest Trail Corridor.

The old structure served everything from horse-drawn carriages and wagons in its early days, hauling everything from ice blocks and milk to vegetables and bread, to motorized vehicles of the new era. Often, those new fangeled vehicles had problems chugging up the steep north end of the bridge, an approach at least twice as long as the south slope. Come winter, whether the bridge was wood or later pavement, there were some great slides to be observed.

As kids we used to race down that north side slope at literally breakneck speeds. I picked up more than one sliver from a tumble off my old balloon-tired bike and I remember one day when a friend took a real bad tumble off his brand new three-speed and bore the scars for quite some time. Under the bridge was a real kids' playground, a web of interlocking wooden beams, ideal for secret hide-aways, places to smoke and talk of boys' things, and places to hide during war games. The war games, many times complete with actual BB-gun battles, were the extreme of our dangerous activities. But really, the almost uncontrolled bike races down the bridge were far more dangerous than BB-gun wars under the bridge and at the nearby Black Hill.

The bridge was our downtown link to the Roxy and Capitol Theatres, Bert the Popcorn Man, and the marvellous Eaton's Toyland at Christmas. It also marked the area where many a circus and midway entertained both north and south side, young and old alike.

Eddie Foychuk, son of a north side coal miner who went on to base his career around pitching fastball and was one of the very few fastball professionals in the country, remembered how as kids he and his buddies seemed to always be in trouble with the cops, especially when they went south.

"They were always after us kids from the north side," he said with a laugh. "They didn't like us because we were always in trouble. They couldn't catch us when they chased us because we had a deal we knew about and they never did figure it out. The old 9th Street bridge was still there of course, and at the bottom of the bridge was a manhole. We'd run from the cops, go down the manhole, and either head through the sewer system for the river bottom or go the other way to 13th Street.

"The cops couldn't figure out where the hell we would disappear to. Our trouble was just about anything, but nothing serious. We just had to play games with them. We had a lot of laughs . . . we never had no money, but we had a lot of laughs."

## Historic Firehall Gone

In 1909 North Ward boasted two lumber yards, two restaurants, two grocers, a general store, a drug store and the new No. 2 Firehall. Certainly one of the landmarks of 13th Street North - until 1970 when the wise city fathers ignored pleas to leave it as a historic site and ripped it down - was the two-storey, bright red No. 2 Firehall. The 24x50-foot hall, with its three big white front doors, and a small side door for the folks to enter the upstairs rooms, was built in 1909 at 128 13th Street, for a cost of $3,400. Topping it off was the moving over of the newly-refitted - from 1907 - horse-drawn hose wagon from the No. 1 firehall, built 10 years earlier. The hall also featured a 60-gallon chemical wagon, a ladder, seven men and six horses.

By 1962, with its large paved drive, white post chain fence, and small fir trees, the hall was a staple on the busy street. However, traffic was so heavy on 13th, a light was installed to stop the stream of cars so the engines could swing onto the narrow street without interfering with traffic. By 1970 the narrow, busy street was too much for the firefighters to handle and a new north side station was opened at 2825 5th Ave. N. An immediate order went out to demolish the old station, and within a short time a big piece of north Lethbridge history fell to the wrecker's ball.

No. 2 Firehall was an early north Lethbridge landmark.

When the hall was built there were a few houses across the street, but mainly it was empty. There was nothing on the west side of 13th south to the underpass and the many acres behind the hall were bare. The next building was more than a block to the north, but in a few short years it was a key spot on a busy street.

In 1970, Fire Chief William H. Short, who joined the city's fire department in 1911, called the grand old No. 2 Firehall "one of the few remaining relics of Lethbridge's early days."

---

**The Good Ol' Days**

The equipment at No. 2 Firehall included two fire engines, and an ambulance, a long way from the six horses, old fire wagon and 12 men back in 1909.

Looking back, Chief Short remembered how citizens would gather in the evening to watch the fire horses exercising. Six nights a week, at 8 p.m., a gong sounded and the horses would immediately move under their harness, suspended from the ceiling. The horses at north and south firehalls were gone by 1920.

---

Before demolition, it had been hoped the hall would be saved, finding a home at Calgary's Heritage Park. But it wasn't to be. It was also suggested the old hall could be moved and placed across from the Brewery Gardens and the Chinook Country Tourist Information Centre. But that didn't come to pass either.

Moving the old hall would not have been a new experience for the building, built in 1909. Its original location was about 200 yards south of its final site, and

set back a bit more off 13th Street. In 1916, the CPR needed more land for its freight sheds and service lines, and the hall was moved to the corner of 2nd Avenue, close to the street.

In early September, 1970, Marathon Realty had its way and down came old No. 2, making way for the final phase of the new Centre Village Shopping Mall, to be anchored on the east end by Sears.

The big Sears store pulled up stakes and headed south in 1988, to be replaced by Canadian Tire in 1989.

The mall also included a Macleod's store which gave way to Zellers, which greatly expanded the store. The mall was opened in 1970, with Smitty's, Shopper's Drug Mart and Razor's Edge the only remaining original tenants in 2003. Hans Isele of Smitty's, who oversaw a $50,000 refurbishing project in the late 1990s, won the Smitty's Pioneer Award in 2000 for the longest serving franchise owner in Canada.

With the demise of the No. 2 Firehall the crews and equipment moved to the new hall, many, many blocks away, on the corner of 5th Avenue and 28th Street North, the edge of the city's blossoming industrial park. As the doors closed on No. 2's life, fireman Don Carpenter took what was likely the last slide down No. 2's old brass fire pole, for the convenience of a Herald photographer.

In 1911 the men were on 24-hour duty, earning $60 a month, with an afternoon off every tenth day.

Married men were allowed to sleep at home, rather than at the hall, each night. By 1930, the men were working a two platoon system of 10 and 14 hour shifts.

That year No. 2 was redesigned to include three living quarters upstairs and a unit on the main floor. These barracks-like quarters, designed for the married men, existed through 1941 when a three-platoon system, of eight-hour days came into being.

The upstairs apartments were later rented to non-fire people, but they too had been phased out by the demolition date.

## WWII Prisoners

It is a fact, north Lethbridge played a vital role in World War II, not only in the numbers of men and women who served at home and overseas, but also as home to Prisoner of War Camp No. 133.

While world war raged in Europe, north Lethbridge, thousands of miles from the front, still managed to get a close-up look at the enemy. Lethbridge became site for an internment camp, Camp No. 133, located in the northeast corner of the city and operated from November 1942 to June 1946.

The camp was designed to hold 12,500 prisoners of war and cost $2 million to build. However, the camp overflowed at times with close to 15,000 PoWs behind wire during one short period, and you must remember, the city's population was only 14,000 during the war years.

The six sections of the camp each contained six two-storey barracks, a meal hall and administration building.

There were also two large recreational buildings, a dental clinic, mortuary, hospital and detention barracks within the camp boundaries.

There were four sets of barracks outside the wire compound, built to house the Veteran's Guard of Canada, the men of the First World War and some younger soldiers, and later returnees, assigned to police the camp.

The first prisoners arrived Nov. 28, 1942, many still wearing the tropical uniforms worn at the time of their capture in North Africa.

As it turned out, PoWs were a boon to the agriculture industry in the south. With most of southern Alberta's young men involved in the war effort in Canada or overseas, there was a shortage of farm labour. PoWs worked on farms and ranches, receiving only canteen credits as payment. But they eagerly volunteered for the relative freedom the fields offered. In 1944, there were 1,200 PoWs involved in the harvest and by the camp's evacuation in June, 1946 about 6,000 PoWs had been put to work on southern Alberta farms.

PoWs, though confined, lived well, receiving the same rations as Canadian troops stationed in Canada. Carloads of sugar, jam, and other rationed items were regularly brought into the camp, causing some resentment among city residents who were caught up in the rationing restrictions of the war. Shortages included everyday needs such as sugar, gasoline, butter and meat and the citizens were issued with ration books to cover their needs. Meat was scarce, except on some farms, many of which were self-sustaining.

The late Lloyd Roadhouse, who lived on 1st Avenue North, was one of the firemen on the three trains initially bringing prisoners into the city.

Below: Lloyd Roadhouse.

He said the prisoners were moved from a summer PoW camp at Ozada, west of Calgary, into Lethbridge. The Red Cross wanted the move made immediately. They did not want to see prisoners spending winter in tents when they could be in warmer wooden barracks. Those tents were mainly old condemned Canadian Army bell tents.

Most of the PoWs were from the North African campaign, taken when General Montgomery swept through north Africa in battles like El Alamein and Tobruk. Some, said Roadhouse, were 16- and 17-year-old boys.

"The first bunch we brought in were navy and submarine boys," he said. "Boy, did they goose-step past us when they were unloaded from the trains. They were the real Nazis. The rest were just regular soldiers and they lined up six abreast and simply marched in."

Trains were 17 to 19 coaches long and each one made a trip a day, leaving in the early morning and arriving about 2:30 p.m. at hour intervals. Roadhouse said many of the younger ones did not know what was happening and were worried. One young soldier threw himself around a guard's feet, pleading to know his fate. But that was the only real incident.

The trains drove right into the camp, with the guards opening the gate for the arrival and closing it behind when the last car was in. The trains were segregated from the main compound by high fences with barbed wire across the top. Guards at the camp were Canadian veterans from the First World War. The German Prisoners of War at Lethbridge were mainly a contented group.

It was 1946, the war was over and evacuation of the largest PoW camp in Canada was under way. Canadian soldiers were returning to southern Alberta from the front and German PoWs were passing them along the way, returning to Germany.

Turned out with fresh hair cuts and wearing their German Army uniforms, the prisoners were carried by CP Rail from the Lethbridge and Medicine Hat camps to Halifax. There, they boarded liners like the Mauritania and sailed for home, but not before being detained in England for more paper work.

The last of the German PoWs sailed from Canada's eastern shores Dec. 24, 1946.

One could see the lights of the PoW camp from my home in Little Wigan, across the open prairie, but I was too young to really know what it was all about. Many years later I was fortunate to interview many of the guards, prisoners and people like Lloyd Roadhouse, who had first-hand knowledge of the camp.

The one mile square PoW camp at Lethbridge stood empty as 1946 came to a close. All that remained were the memories of daily head counts each morning, the parading of up to 12,500 PoWs and the careful watch over them by 800 guards. Figures vary as to the highest number housed in Lethbridge, but with the moving in and out of PoWs in the early days it was estimated as high as 17,000 at one time or another, called the camp home.

Within a short time after 1946 the triple barbed wire fences of the prison compound were being torn down and converted to fences for farms and ranches in the area.

Colonel Carson McCormack had been the camp commandant until his death in 1943. He was replaced by Colonel E.D. Kippen. Each section of the camp had a Veteran Guard section leader, overseeing 36 barracks leaders.

The PoWs were fed in three shifts, with breakfast between 8 and 9 a.m., dinner from 11:30 a.m. to 12:30 p.m. and supper from 5 to 6 p.m. Everyone ate in the mess halls within their assigned section.

They were served in the manner of a large boarding house, with bowls and plates heaping with food set on each table. The PoWs served themselves. The rations given to the prisoners were the same as those eaten by the guards. It is said the average PoW gained 12 pounds during the first year in the camp. The men raised rabbits, kept beehives and grew vegetables to supplement their rations.

As a boy of 17, freshly recruited into the German infantry, Horst Niepel had no idea what was happening in Europe in June, 1944. Called up in April, he was stationed in Holland, at Arnhem, when the Allied Forces D-Day assault began June 6.

"There was some idea that something was going to happen, but we didn't know what," said Niepel a few years prior to his death.

Horst Niepel.

When the Allies hit the beaches of Normandy Niepel's unit was mobilized. It didn't take long to move them out of Holland and into Belgium, then France and finally near Caen. At the time Niepel had no idea what day, or even what month the move came. The soldiers didn't even know the time of day, let alone the month, he said.

He knew there was a lot of sabotage going on, both from the underground resistance forces and from within the German army itself.

"The 15-inch guns were getting 10-inch shells and the other way around," he said. "The Panzer divisions had no gas and ammunition dumps mysteriously blew up. After I was captured, when I got to the other side of the line and saw all the Allied ammunition piled up along the roadways I couldn't believe it. I knew then the end of the war was near."

Niepel saw very little fighting, none of the hand-to-hand variety where bayonets would be needed. He said they'd see some Allied troops in front of them, a ways off, moving about from time to time. But they tended to ignore them.

He and some others did capture American machine guns at times and would swing the guns around and fire back on their original owners. The noise was recognizable by the Americans and they'd think their own gunners were shooting by mistake. Instead of firing back they sent up flares trying to tell the gunners of their mistake. It was August, 1944 when Niepel was captured.

"During the night a couple of us went into some bush and it turned out there were a whole bunch of Yankees in there too," Niepel said. "They said, 'come in and sit down, the game is over.' We did."

It wasn't until Christmas of 1946 he was placed on a train for Halifax and the return trip to Scotland. There, he was kept in a work camp. He wasn't discharged from the camp and the army until 1949.

Born in a section of Eastern Germany, which the Poles took over after the war, Niepel really had no home to return to at the war's end. The few that did go back seemed to disappear.

"People there always figured you were a spy when you came back," he said. He lived in Scotland until 1951 and decided to return to Lethbridge to live. "I couldn't go back home and I knew the farms and places around Lethbridge so I decided to come here," said Niepel. "I won $1,500 in the football pool the week before I came and that paid my passage."

Below: A PoW work crew awaits assignment in 1945.

Ironically one of the north side homes he and his Scots bride Alfreda lived in was a portion of a large building from the PoW camp. The other portion was converted into another house across the street.

As a German prisoner of war Paul LaBusch worked on the Van Dyke farm near Nobleford, a long way from the 150 missions he flew with the Luftwaffe. He said during a visit to Lethbridge in 1995 his days as a PoW in Interment Camp 133 in Lethbridge were the worst of times, yet still full of the best of times. He arrived in southern Alberta after being shot down over North Africa by British guns.

"I became an English prisoner in January, 1942," he said. "I jumped out of the burning aircraft, coming down by parachute into the desert. As soon as I landed I just began walking. It was mainly through wasteland and it was there I came upon a British camp. I'll never forget, a British major gave me a cup of tea."

LaBusch was moved to a PoW camp along the Suez which was a collection point for German prisoners. From Suez he was shipped by boat to New York, not through the Mediterranean, but the long way around the southern cape of Africa and then northwards up the Atlantic to New York City. From New York it was a 3,000 mile train ride, in a passenger coach, to Internment Camp No. 133 in Lethbridge.

It was spring in southern Alberta when he arrived at Park Lake. He was held at a small hostel at Park Lake where he was on clean-up detail. Then it was off to the Ernest Van Dyke farm southwest of Nobleford.

"We could stay on the farm and it was feeling like home," said LaBusch. "Since then I've always had a connection with Nobleford."

After more than 50 years he was still returning to southern Alberta on a regular basis to visit the Van Dykes.

"We would get news of the war in the camp," he said. "Some clever German prisoners made their own radios. The prison camp was good times, strictly correct . . . but not all the time. Sometimes we got beer in the camp, in exchange for our German marks. Sometimes a Canadian veteran would sit on the steps with us and we'd talk. It was like a beer parlour."

When he arrived in southern Alberta after being shot down over North Africa, the first thing LaBusch did was toss his medals into Park Lake, where he was being held in a small tent camp. The war was over for him. "They are still in Park Lake," the veteran said with a smile.

When visiting southern Alberta he would often sit quietly on a bench at Park Lake, remembering. Thousands of miles from his home in Germany, LaBusch might have been thinking of the time he threw his medals, earned in the German Luftwaffe, into the lake. He might have been thinking of his summer working on the Van Dyke farm or of any one of the 150 missions he flew for the Luftwaffe. You do know he was definitely thinking of the years he spent as a prisoner of war in Interment Camp 133.

Cleve Hill.

**Red Bullseyes**

"In 1944 my father-in-law, Ed Anderson, from the Barrhill School area, got PoWs to work on his farm," said Avice (Frayne) Anderson. "Every morning, about 8 o'clock, he took his big farm truck to a sub-camp near Iron Springs to pick up about 12 men and two guards. The prisoners brought their own noon-time lunch.

"As was the custom on the farm, a mid-morning and afternoon snack was taken out to the workers in the field. Besides holding the freshly-made bread rolls, I steadied the huge coffee pot with my feet as we drove over the rough ground. At about 4 p.m. the men were loaded back on the truck to return to camp.

"I can still recall, as they headed away, the large red bull's eye on the back of each man's jacket."

There were four sets of barracks outside the barbed wire compound at Camp No. 133, built to house the Veteran's Guards of Canada, including Lethbridge resident Cleve Hill.

Hill was a sergeant with the 13th District Co. of the Royal Canadian Army Service Corps during the first half of the 1940s. Pretty well all the guards at the camp were World War I veterans. Some who signed up for World War II were placed in the guard unit, many due to medical problems. Also at the camp were 10 Service Corps people, including Hill.

There was a special CP Rail spur rail line right into the camp, right up to the supply depot, to facilitate the unloading of a freight car of beef each week as well as other products.

"The prisoners ate well, you bet they did," said Hill, who was the sergeant in charge of the food warehouse. "I heard many comments during my time there from civilians and guards wondering if our guys, who were prisoners of war over there, were eating as well."

The Germans had daily work parties to help get the food rations from the main depot to each section of the camp. The same parties also unloaded the trucks and freight cars. Hill remembers a German Sergeant Major, Kurt Stock, who was in charge of one of the work crews. Stock had served in the Luftwaffe and was shot down over London before being moved to Lethbridge.

"If you wanted anything done you spoke to him and he gave the orders to the work party," said Hill. "He was very well educated and spoke English well. He was an authoritarian. The Germans maintained strict army discipline within the camp."

There was little conversation between prisoners and Canadian military personnel at the camp, but Hill did speak with Stock from time to time and came to see a special side of this PoW.

The prisoners wore a type of uniform which looked like a jean jacket, with a big red dot on the back. The blue work pants had a red stripe down each leg. The red dot looked like a target said Hill.

There was certainly no abuse of the prisoners in the camp. In fact, the PoWs had more problems among themselves than with the Canadian Forces.

There were escapes from the camp, but nothing serious resulted. Lethbridge was too far away from Germany and on the flat prairie a PoW, with a big red dot on his back, was easily spotted. It wasn't too difficult to recapture escapees. Each morning there was a head count in the camp as the PoWs stood beside their bunks. The Canadians also had scouts they sent inside the wire at night to patrol the interior of the camp, unarmed, to look for escape tunnels and ferret out other problems. A few times they did find a tunnel being started under some of the perimeter buildings.

"You'd have to be pretty optimistic to dig a tunnel because the nearest buildings were none too close to the fences," Hill said with a laugh.

The fence system had a warning wire along the inside, a few metres back from the main fences. To step over the wire brought immediate attention from the guard towers spotted around the perimeter. It was said the main fences were electrically wired and if a mass breakout attempt had occurred the fences would be electrified immediately, said Hill.

"We stayed away from the camp; we were all scared of it," said Florence Seager, whose north side home was between the camp and the old north Lethbridge airport. "Some of the prisoners came to work at the cannery (Broder's, where Seager was employed) and we got to know a few of them. They would come over, four to six at a time, with an armed guard and when they were there they worked well. We saw them lots, but we really weren't allowed to talk with them too much. The ones we did get to talk with all said they were glad to be here in Lethbridge.

"I would never go over to the camp. Some nights it would be all lit up. They had those big search lights at the camp, but I don't remember them being on very much." Seager worked at Broder's from her mid 20s until retirement at age 63. She has fond memories of her days at the cannery, of the great basketball teams Broder's had, and of many of the players who worked at Broder's and played ball for the team.

Broder Canning Co. opened in the early 1940s, canning sweet corn, peas, beans and other irrigated crops grown right here in southern Alberta, often assisted by PoWs.

In the spring of 1950 demolition began on the PoW camp. By the early 1950s three businesses had already established themselves on the site, in the former stores and supply depot buildings - Manufacture's Distributors, Lumber Manufacturers and Magrath Woollen Mills. The entire camp eventually was eaten by the ever-expanding Industrial Park, an area City Fathers had envisioned as far back as 1912 when the city purchased 125 acres from the railway.

Soon after the war ended and the PoW camp became part of history, a whole new subdivision of wartime homes sprang up in the city, many on the north side, including portions of 12th Street and 12th Street A and along 8th and 9th Avenues, east of 13th. Adam Stickle was one of the many carpenters employed in the massive building boom.

## The Community that Wasn't . . .

It was 1912, and developers McKillop and Garfield of Toronto envisioned a massive housing development in north Lethbridge, bordered by 13th Street to the west, 9th Avenue on the south, 21st Street to the east (really a CPR spur line to Royal Collieries, one of many coal operation in the area) and 13th Avenue to the north.

Cutting diagonally across the development, which would create some off-centered streets, was to be Westminster Boulevard, an 80 foot-wide main thoroughfare. If you stood on the roof on the then brand new $85,000 Galbraith School and looked north, you would have had an overview of this dream, to be called Dominion Square. The development was to be serviced by the brand new streetcar system and have sewers, water, natural gas, telephone and electric lights. And it was only 1912!

Dominion Square was to have everything. What more could you ask for?

Well, sales for one thing.

The area was originally CPR-owned land and in 1912 was virtually uninhabited, as was much of the north ward. The idea was to sell the homes in the development to coal miners who worked in north Lethbridge mines. Problem was it was still too far to walk to the nearest mines and other areas of the north side were starting to be built, much closer to the mine sites, in unplanned ethnic-based communities.

North Lethbridge had always been around, right from the beginning of Lethbridge's incorporation in 1890, and it had an identity all its own. The Village of Stafford didn't become part of the city until it was annexed in 1913 and there were other little communities like Little Wigan, Hardieville and Westminster to name a few. The CPR main line dissected the city from east to west but it was joined north to south, mainly by Westminster Road, later called 13th Street, and the Sage Bridge, later called the 9th Street Bridge. That long, straight 13th Street ran from the coulees to the south of the city to the coulees to the north, much of these extreme regions outside the city boundaries. The road was 100 feet wide, narrowing for some unexplained reason to 60 feet when it crossed onto the north side.

The Westminster name for the street, and various other buildings and areas, originated from the Westminster District of London, England. There was a Westminster Park at 16th St. and 23rd Ave. North and Westminster School opened Jan. 1, 1906. Ninth Avenue North served as a boundary line and it ran right through the north side, from east and west, one of the few north side avenues to do that. It was along this dividing line Dominion Square was proposed.

Dominion Square was never sold. Miners didn't want it and certainly the mainly white-collared south side types didn't want to head north. Real estate had undergone a boom in Lethbridge in 1907 but, unfortunately for the Dominion Square developers the boom fizzled by 1913.

Two steel electric light standards marked the entrance to the square, on the diagonal boulevard which was to run northeast. As the Dominion Square dream slowly faded into the darkness, thanks in part to the tax man, the light standards wound up on the steps of Southminster Church in south Lethbridge, a fitting resting place for a dream.

Dominion Square sat virtually empty, except for the odd structure, until the 1960s when north Lethbridge development started to boom again, just about 50 years too late for the original developers.

Other areas of the north side did build up while Dominion Square stood empty.

### Staffordville

In 1890 the Galt company sank a coal shaft on the prairie level of what is now the western edge of north Lethbridge. The shaft, at that time, was outside of the city's official boundaries.

By 1900 the area around the new mine was known as the Village of Stafford, or Staffordville, after prominent businessman and mine inspector William Stafford. The village was north of 9th Avenue North and west of 13th Street.

The No. 3 shaft sunk by the company was at 6th Street and 9th Avenue, and the area later became known as Number 3.

The Galt company subdivided the land, about a mile east of the mine, into 90 one-acre sites bounded by 13th and 23rd Streets on the east and west and 5th and 7th Avenues to the north and south.

Those sites were offered for sale to mine employees, but sales were slow because most of the sites were too far from the mine site, where most of the residents worked.

The Pierce Addition however, closer to the mine, sold briskly. James Pierce had subdivided land much nearer the mine, dividing them into 40, one-acre parcels. An area west of the Pierce Addition, between 8th and 9th Streets, was also subdivided and combined with the Pierce Addition. It was the most populated part of the Village of Stafford.

Another 40, one-acre lots, the Perry Addition, was added in 1907 between 12th to 13th Streets and 9th to 14th Avenues. By 1911 the Vair Addition was added to the west, between 9th and 10th Streets. It was never fully developed.

Sewer, power, graded streets, water lines and garbage pick-up were non-existent in those early days. Outhouses, the wee hoose at the rear of each property, were necessary in each yard and water and coal was delivered by wagon. Almost from the start residents of the additions wanted to be part of Lethbridge, just across the CPR tracks. The city didn't want them however, due to the low assessment value of the village and the large population. To be sure, there was a certain amount of prejudice involved.

North Lethbridge residents, Staffordville people in particular, were a low economic class, mainly coal miners whose simple life didn't sit well with many in south Lethbridge. The south side was mainly home to the mine owners, doctors, lawyers and business people.

In 1903, F.S. Simpson of the Cranbrook Herald, wrote of Lethbridge: "It's a town of 3,000 spread over enough territory to hold a town of 100,000." Simpson went on to create The Lethbridge Herald in 1904 and in 1905 sold the fledgling newspaper to W.A. Buchanan.

By 1901 a miner's settlement called the Village of Stafford covered 250 acres. A Staffordville water debenture passed in late 1911 and $13,655 was borrowed for water mains in the settlement. The village's plans for further expansion in 1912, taking in much of north Lethbridge, spurred the city to seriously consider annexation. W.F. Wilson, chairman of the village, is credited with forcing the city's hand by moving to bring in most of the north side under the Staffordville umbrella.

### Annexation

In 1913 the Village of Stafford was annexed into the city, as the mayor had promised, turning all village property over to the City of Lethbridge. Early Staffordville councillors included names still familiar in north Lethbridge, such as the Sumners, Moodies and Vaselenaks.

As Staffordville established itself to the west, 13th Street North was taking on a new look.

Aiding annexation was the fact Lethbridge Mayor W.D.L. Hardie had promised annexation during his election campaign. He went on to serve as the city's mayor from 1913-1928. It is suspected the northside votes, those considered part of the city, came out strongly for Hardie, preferring the city annex Staffordville rather than be annexed themselves by the village.

It took the city from 1913 to 1915 to partially service Staffordville with electrical power and fire and police protection. Concrete sidewalks and sewer lines didn't come to the area until the early 1950s. Bus service was instituted the same year. Streetcars only travelled down 13th Street to 9th Avenue, and the line did not turn west. Staffordville residents had a choice, walk about 1.5 miles to the streetcar line along 13th, or 1.5 miles south over the tracks to downtown Lethbridge. That choice faced them daily until buses arrived in 1950.

No. 3 Mine was closed about the time annexation took place, but a new shaft, No. 6, was sunk in the Hardieville area. Most of the miners from No. 3 now faced work in No. 6, and some even had their small homes moved from the additions north to Hardieville. It meant a short walk to the mine instead of waiting for the company-operated transportation system.

At the same time the north side and south side areas were developing, people still resided in the Oldman River valley, some in elaborate homes, others in mere shacks. People lived in the valley right from the beginning of the city until the last ones were moved out in the 1960s.

Many worked the company mines, while other had small, private mines. Many of the valley names are still found in the city, including Sinclair, Gessinghouse, Shields, McNeely, Dickson, Hamilton, Weadick, Melvin and Rollingson.

## Murder Most Foul

Naturally the north side was not free from sin. The area has been the site of more than one robbery and murder through the years.

I can recall, as a 10-year-old, heading to buy candy at the little Chinese-owned shop along 13th, which still borders the CFCN parking lot, only to find it closed. Just minutes before my arrival an ambulance had carried off the owner - his blood stains still readily visible on the sidewalk - after he had been beaten and robbed.

Murders occurred as well, from time to time, and two of the more vivid ones came many decades apart.

Former City Police Inspector, Bill Plomp, vividly remembers the death of Janice Wilde, abducted from a Laundromat in the new Westminster Mall Aug. 25, 1978. The body of the 22-year-old - the head nearly severed after the assailant slit her throat - was discovered at the end of 13th Street, about where Uplands begins today.

"I got a clear fingerprint off the car," said Plomp, who retired in 1993. "We were working in conjunction with the Mounties on this case, and about two weeks later Randy Roo was tracked down and arrested by Saskatchewan RCMP. He was subsequently convicted of the murder and received 25 years in jail."

The December trial found Roo guilty and he was given a 25-year term with no chance of parole. In fact, a 1994 application for early parole was denied.

But Roo was given day parole in 2001, to live in a halfway house selected by the Correctional Service of Canada. The day parole was revoked when it was discovered he had fallen back into old habits - alcohol and heroin abuse. However, the parole board reinstated his day parole a short time later, determining Roo's level of risk had not elevated to the point where he was considered unmanageable in the community. However, it was later revoked for a second time.

The consequences for a 1911 murderer were far worse - for the perpetrator.

This north side murder led to the only hanging in Lethbridge in the old North-West Mounted Police barracks, which took up the block which now houses the city hall, old court house building, the Yates Theatre, the Lethbridge Senior Citizens Organization building, track and pool, the curling rink and the YMCA and today's RCMP Headquarters.

Throughout the years the Lethbridge Provincial Gaol was the designated death house for Calgary south, and 18 murderers filled their date with the hangman there, from 1912 through 1956. Prior to the jail's construction, Wasyl Chobator was hanged on Jan. 14, 1911, in a barn at the NWMP barracks.

In 1994, Berry Allan, then 86, a retired RCMP staff-sergeant, serving in Lethbridge from the late 1930s through 1951, said the hanging took place in the barracks hay barn, located about where the Fritz Sick Centre is today.

"According to what I heard, they dug a pit under the gallows to sustain the tension on the rope and make room for the drop," Allan said.

Chobator had murdered Alex Lazaruk, a fellow Austrian who also worked the north Lethbridge coal mines, in the dead of night somewhere between the No. 6 and No. 3 mines in the city. Lazaruk was shot with a revolver, and Chobator admitted to police he had committed the murder. After the trial he was an emotional wreck for about two weeks, sobbing much of the time. More than once he wished aloud that the victim's wife, involved in the case, would be hanged along side him.

> Chobator stood without a tremor, his eyes closed, as the black hood was placed over his head, and straps placed around his ankles, thighs and another pinning his arms to his sides.

About 6 a.m., 20 heavily-clothed fellow country-men of Chobator's, carrying lanterns and trying to keep warm in the winter morning cold, gathered outside the barracks perimeter to await the 6:25 a.m. hanging. A procession of the sheriff, provost-sergeant, the condemned man, four policemen and the hangman, a Lethbridge man wearing a hood with only small eye slits, walked the 150 yards to the gallows in the stable. A sleigh was at the ready in case the prisoner refused to walk, but it wasn't needed.

The last rights of the Greek Catholic Church were administered by Father Benedict Elceker, and then he left the barracks before the execution, not returning until it was over, meaning no priest stood alongside the condemned man on the gallows.

Despite his earlier nervousness, when he didn't want to put on a coat and shoes, wanting to walk to the gallows as he had slept, with shirt and pants and socks - he was handcuffed and a coat and moccasins were put on by force - The Herald reported that Chobator walked unassisted to the gallows and "ran easily, and unhelped, up the steps to the scaffold." The guards had to step nimbly to keep up.

As he stood there Chobator suddenly said, in a high-pitched voice audible to all: "Me no eata breakfast." He had been offered ham, eggs and coffee at 5:45 a.m. but declined to eat. Guards immediately pinioned the murderer, adjusted the noose and Sheriff Young gave the signal for the trap to be sprung. After the body was cut down, doctors examined the body and jurors viewed it.

The Herald account of the hanging said the body was placed in a coffin, packed in quicklime and buried in the seven-foot-square pit beneath the gallows. The law of the time stated the body must be buried within the grounds where the execution took place. That spot could be about where the Fritz Sick swimming pool now stands.

"The Lethbridge hangman was always known under the pseudonym of Mr. Ellis," said Avice Anderson. Ray Marnoch spent 36 years on the Lethbridge City Police Force. But his first contact with the seriousness of police work came as a Grade 3 student at Galbraith School. He and schoolmate Kaz Kaminski were heading home from school during the noon break when they heard a shot.

"At the time, in the early spring of 1942, Carl Fraser was away in the army," said Marnoch. "While he was away his wife Sophie, a mother of three, was being harassed by a member of the Veteran's Guard at the PoW camp. I guess he got pretty upset with her rejections of him so he shot her. The shooting took place in her back yard, just five doors down from the school, on 18th Street North. I lived on 15th Street, next to Kaminski's house, and you could see outside our backdoor right across the prairie to the school.

Ray Marnoch.

19

"We heard the shot and we ran in that direction, but there was already a bunch of others around. She was lying dead on the ground and the guy had taken off. We were all there before the police, but I didn't see much.

"A short while later our family moved to 1205 2nd Ave. S., next to three other Veteran's Guards, Percy Stone, Doug Barkley's father (Doug later played in the NHL for the Boston Bruins) and a fellow named Lunde. We later moved back north, to 1807 4th Avenue, and one of the girls we walked with on our way to the LCI was a daughter of the murdered woman."

Ray, born in 1933, died in July, 2004, leaving wife Edna, of 49 years, son Keith and daughter Sandra. The Ray I remember was a big, robust older schoolmate and later city policeman, joining up at age 20. No matter when you saw Ray he always had a smile and a story, whether it was when I was just a kid at school or he was walking the beat on 13th Street, or in later years when I was working with The Herald. You could ask Ray a name and he'd be able to tell you the history of that individual - and anyone that person came in contact with. While I've just touched on a few of the north side-related murders there's really no way anyone can begin to list the accidental deaths in north Lethbridge, be they in the form of vehicular accidents, lumberyard, streetcar, mine incidents, or home accidents. But it would be right to mention one of the earliest, if not the first, north side death.

## The First

It occured October 28, 1896, when a young unidentified boy lost his life in an incident involving a mine train. About 6 p.m. an A.R. and C. Co. railway switchman chased three boys off some water tank cars, just back of an engine as it left the No. 1 mine site heading north. At the railway wye, the engine was moving towards the No. 3 shaft when a yardmaster tried to put a lone boy off the car, but it was moving at the time. The water train inadvertently ran through a switch and in braking the yardman had to leave the boy. The train skidded along the wet tracks, slamming into a car full of rails. Some of the rails struck the water tank and the boy was caught below the hips, between the flying rails and the iron water tank, crushing his legs. He was rushed to Dr. Mewburn's house and then to the Galt Hospital.

The boy died the next day, but had he lived both his legs would have likely been amputated. "This should be a warning to young boys, and it is hoped that in the future the practice of them jumping off and on moving cars will be discontinued," a Herald editorial boldly stated the next day.

It may have stopped boys from hitching rides on railway cars - though not likely - but it certainly didn't stop them from hooking rides on streetcars or sliding behind buses on the thick winter ice while holding on to the bumper.

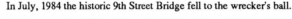

In July, 1984 the historic 9th Street Bridge fell to the wrecker's ball.

# The Fun Things

Every community needs to relax, to play, and to have fun, and north Lethbridge is no different. While the north side worked hard, it also played hard - as everyone should.

Along 13th Street you found a variety of entertainment, from movies to dancing and that dreaded form of relaxation and gambling, a thing called pool. The grand street was also home to the greatest of all entertainments, sports, with baseball and soccer the games of the day. Off the main thoroughfare there were other forms of entertainment, to the air shows at the old north side airport to circuses and travelling carnivals at Circus Flats.

## The Lealta Theatre

The Lealta was one of my favourite haunts, along with most of the northside theatre-goers. Owned by Cameron F. Doughty, with wife Emily taking tickets and later son Ken running the projector, the Lealta offered the best of the B movies, all those gangster-type films, the classic cowboy heroes like the Durango Kid, Gene and Roy, Monte Hale, Tex Ritter, Red Ryder, Hopalong Cassidy, The Lone Ranger, Wild Bill Elliott, Audie Murphy, and other stars of the day like Joel McCrea, Rod Cameron, Dean Martin and Jerry Lewis, the Bowery Boys and Randolph Scott. As well there were war movies, dramas and other fare not shown by the Famous Players movie houses downtown. The Lealta's ads - almost always one column wide by two inches deep, without pictures - appeared in The Lethbridge Herald, urging you to drop in and see Alan Ladd in Branded, John Wayne in Flying Tigers or Eagle Squadron with Robert Stack and Eddie Albert. You wouldn't see Walt Disney at the Lealta, nor the Cinemascope of the 1950s. Those were strictly downtown fare.

The Lealta wasn't the first theatre on 13th Street. Before the Lealta came the Monarch Theatre, which opened its doors Christmas Day, 1911, at 250 13th St. N., in the age of the silent films. The Monarch shut down several times along the way, and by 1915 had changed its name to the Regent. By 1917 the theatre building was vacant, and stayed that way until 1927 when the Moose Lodge took it over as their hall. But the Moose only stayed a few years and in 1933 Woods Exchange was the new tenant, lasting two years.

One door down, at 258 13th St., a new building went up, home to the Standard Bank, with room for renters on the upper floor of the two-storey building. In 1926 Standard gave way to the Bank of Commerce.

"I had an account at the Standard Bank," said Mavis (Harding) Standing. "I had a little bank book and you could deposit 25 cents at a time. I was about eight years old and it was 1922. When the Nazarene Church was raising money for its building fund I wanted to help and I asked my dad to help me write a cheque for $1 out of my bank account to give to the fund."

Scotty Armitt remembers a north side-based pipe band practicing downstairs in the old bank. The Lethbridge Caledonian Pipe Band was one of the first pipe bands in the city and it included the likes of Jimmy Stewart, Jim Goldie, Joe Patterson, Alec McCord and Johnny Martin and Roderick Patterson on drums.

Avice Anderson remembers the band practicing. "Their practicing took them to the streets, in full dress," she said. "When we kids heard them we would dash over to 13th Street and stand and listen to the 'kilties'."

Armitt said most of the early Caledonian band were north side guys. "In later years Roddy Patterson started up the Bonnie Doone Pipe Band, in the 1950s, with Bev (Allison) Paterson, Gordon Cargill, Bev Plomp and Gail Adamson as pipers and drummers included Al Hudak, Mel Willis and you Garry (Allison). They used to practice at his house and at Westminster School."

I remember sitting astride those long, low benches Westminster had in its gym, practicing the various drum rolls on the bench top, long before we finally received our snare drums.

The need for a North Ward theatre was again evident by 1938, and the Lealta opened it doors on Jan. 5 of that year, at 250 13th St., home of the old Monarch and Regent, sporting the first neon sign in North Lethbridge - there was a 10 a.m. matinee and an evening feature of, "You Can't Have Everything."

A drawing of the Lealta in 1981 by Lethbridge artist Arlene Bolokoski.

On Dec. 31, 1940 the theatre moved into the then vacated Standard Bank building on the corner, with the Doughty family living upstairs.

Buella Hall, Ab Chervinski's wife, used to sell tickets at the Lealta, well prior to their marriage, which was 52 years old in 2002. It was back when she was still in high school and needed a summer job.

Ab remembers running into Cameron Doughty occasionally at the horse races in Calgary, decked out with his Panama straw hat and big cigar.

"I believe the first show they had at the Lealta when it moved was the Dead End Kids, the one with Humphrey Bogart in it," said Ab. "They used to give away those semi-porcelain dishes to patrons and I still have some of those pieces downstairs. They'd get that stuff shipped in by the barrel load."

There are some who say there was an adjustable, tilting floor in the Lealta, but Ab said he never saw it. "I was in that building many, many times, before and afterwards, upstairs where the Doughty family lived and downstairs as well. I never saw a tilting floor."

To add an adjustable floor, in a building which already had a sturdy bank floor, would have been a major, and unnecessary expense, to be sure.

"In the winter of 1949 my mom and dad took my sister and I to the Lealta Theatre to see the movie *Red River*, with John Wayne," says Carly Stewart, longtime member of the Lethbridge Historical Society. "The film was shot, or processed in sepia tone, shades of browns. We came out of the theatre and my dad stopped us and told us to look around. Everything seemed brown! We had been exposed to the sepia tones for more than an hour and a half and our brains took some time to readjust to the normal colours."

The name Lealta was a derivation of Lethbridge, Alberta. The Lealta, which offered air conditioning as early as the early 1940s, catered to the ethnic population of the northside, with many a foreign movie brought in, including Chinese, Dutch, German and even a few special British offerings, like Bonnie Prince Charlie for the Scots. These special movies were usually Sunday evening, well before it was allowed to have Sunday movies because of the Lord's Day Act. But, the Doughty's beat the system with these special-service films for select groups.

There were also other "educational" films which didn't make it downtown, like the evils of sexual diseases, a special show you had to be 18 or older to see. But Mr. Doughty, always one to recognize devoted customers like Doug Sandberg and myself, did let us in to see the epic venereal disease flick, Bob and Alice. Perhaps that's why I was such a fumbling Lothario with the opposite sex - oh, that word had different connotations after that movie. The Lealta also featured Midnight Previews, which were well attended by the teen crowd, and the night workers coming off shift.

The 350-seat Lealta, really the north side's answer to the downtown Roxy, dominated the corner of the west side of 13th Street and 3rd Avenue. The east side of the street overshadowed the Lealta however, with the once proud York Hotel. The theatre had one of those recessed doorways and its marquee hanging out over the double-wide sidewalk. Playbills of the present shows - always a double feature - hung in the prime showcases in the recessed walls, while the showcases on the streets told the tales of upcoming features, like the Green Hornet or Tarzan and Mighty Joe Young.

The recessed entrance kept the patrons out of the wind as they were often jammed into the area in bunches waiting for the doors to open. On more than one occasion you'd round the corner on the run and ram smack dab into a huge policeman, wearing his buffalo robe coat, huddled in the shelter of the theatre entrance trying to beat a cold west, or north, wind on a cold winter night. More than once I bumped into policemen Ray Marnoch and Eddie Potts sheltered in the entrance-way, heavily gloved, with their earflaps down on their fur hats as they patrolled the 13th Street on foot, part of their beat. That was back when the police checked doors, did foot patrols, and knew every kid, and businessman, along the street.

**Movie man**

Cameron Fowler Doughty, died at age 73 in May 1966. He was born in Waterford, Ont. in 1893. After serving as a lieutenant in the Canadian army during the First World War, Doughty turned to insurance. He married wife Emily in 1916 and in 1917 the couple spent some time in Lethbridge before moving away. But, after 20 years in insurance, they moved back to Lethbridge, and went into the movie business in North Lethbridge.

Ralph Michelson was the city's Chief of Police from 1971 to 1985, and served on the city's police force from 1948 to 1985, including walking the beats in north Lethbridge. He remembers when walking was the policeman's tool, because the city force only had one car in the late 1940s.

"We kept in touch through a light system. The lights were high up on poles, one by the Alexander Hotel, another by the Dallas Hotel and one by the Arlington Hotel. You could see these poles from all the beats, but on the north side you had to be up in the No. 3 area to see the Arlington lights (about 9th Avenue North at that time). A red and green light meant the constable was to phone in immediately, while flashing red and green was for the sergeant and a green light meant the detective on duty had to phone the station."

The foot patrolman did just that, he walked. He checked every door handle and window on his beat and if there was a break-in, he had better know why, and also be able to find the guy who did it. If he was in a real hurry he'd flag down a passing car or a taxi. If he arrested someone he could bring them in by taxi, or if he was downtown he'd walk them to the station, not always an easy task. Rain, snow or hot summer nights, the beat cop patrolled Lethbridge streets and alleys. They wore ankle-length rain slickers and hats with protective neck flaps, or muskrat hats and long, shaggy buffalo coats in the cold.

"Those buffalo coats were warm, but they weighed about 40 pounds," said Michelson. "By the end of your shift your shoulders ached. When you walked those beats at night - and you covered the whole beat twice a night - you'd be walking down a quiet, dark alley and a cat skittering out from under a cardboard box could sure scare the hell out of you."

The Doughty family lived upstairs at the Lealta, the stairway to their apartment just to the left as you entered the lobby, the small, interior box office to the right. Their two windows fronting onto 13th Street were on either side of the triangular marquee with its vertical sign, all spelling out LEALTA. The foyer was carpeted and Mr. Doughty would wind people into the lobby in a snake-like row extending through the doors onto the street, as he and his wife waited until the stroke of 6:30 p.m. to start selling tickets to the 7 p.m. double feature.

I don't remember the Doughty's ever handing out any special prizes to we 10-12 year olds, but the theatre did have many a Dish Night, with female patrons receiving a free end-of-the-day glass bowl or candy dish and by the 1950s 22 k gold-trimmed Du Barry dinnerware, billed as "virtually free to ladies." These gifts came with their 25-cent admission - it was 10 cents for us kids, for the Saturday afternoon show, with its cartoons, a serial - usually a western and not the first-run feature you'd see downtown at the Capitol - and a featured film, be it Jungle Jim, Sabu the Jungle Boy or the Crimson Pirate.

"Doughty used to give you a dish each week, with your admission," said Phyllis (Bissett) Slovack, "and then the next time you came you got another dish."

Her brother Alvin also remembers the Lealta being used as a recreation hall for the young boys of the neighbourhood before its theatre days. The old bank was empty when the Bissett family arrived on 13th in 1934.

On purchasing the old Monarch building in 1938 Cameron Doughty refurbished the interior, adding "side sound effects" and cushioned seats for customers' comfort. The projector was a modern Homes model, and besides the Doughtys there were four staff to help patrons to their seats and operate the projector. The theatre was open every night, Monday through Saturday, with matinees Wednesday - remember when stores and offices used to close Wednesday afternoon? - and Saturday afternoons.

One of the great things about the Lealta, particularly in its latter years, and at the back of the theatre, was the fact that if you didn't have enough leg room two or three of you could just push the row ahead of you up a foot or two. You could stretch out, munch on your popcorn, your Mackintosh Toffee bar and drink your fountain pop. It was sheer luxury.

It was a thriving community gathering place through the 1940s and 1950s but by the late 1950s and early 1960s things were slow, slow indeed, as people headed south for the first run shows downtown, out to the Green Acres Drive-In . . . and worst of all they were staying home to watch a new phenomenon, television. In fact, right across the avenue from the Lealta, Jacks Radio had become Jack's TV.

As kids in 1956 we'd head off for a night at the Lealta, only to stop outside Jack's picture window and watch the miracle of television, free of charge. There, on Sylvania TV with Halolite, we could see the shows of the day, from I Love Lucy to Mr. District Attorney and, glory of all glories, wrestling. Many times we stayed glued to Jack's window and never did make it across the street to visit with the Doughty family.

The 16-inch to 21-inch screens had replaced the large Lealta screen, the comforts of home had replaced his fading, lumpy cushions and sliding rows of the Lealta. An era had ended and in 1963 Cameron Doughty closed his doors, remaining in the apartment until his death in 1966.

The Doughtys had two children, Kenneth and Phyllis, and were a solid part of the north side fabric. At 73, Cameron Doughty was laid to rest by Rev. John O'Neill, carried to his resting place by Bill Pratt, L.H. Clark, M. Hurst, W.R. Howell, one of his projectionists, Jim McLaughlin and R.A. Reed. Emily died in June, 1980, at age 93, after living for many years on the south side.

After the Doughtys had closed the doors on the Lealta, the building sat vacant for a spell, and then became home to a carpet store, a figure salon, a horizontal drilling outfit in 1975, which shared the space with karate king Blair Orr. Blair ran his Orr Karate Studio out of the Lealta for some time, leaving his mark on the story of 13th Street North.

Blair Orr, who took up martial arts in 1966, earned the North American kung fu championship, and multiple degrees of the black belt. He was a dominant fighter, with more than a half dozen gold medals in international tournaments, along with the North American full-contact light-heavyweight championship and the Canadian middleweight title.

"The biggest win in my career was the North American championship, and it was a good experience," said Orr. "It was followed up with a banquet, with me at the head table, at the Chinese Masons Hall in Vancouver."

In 1971 a large addition was made to the rear of the Lealta building, moving it right back onto the alleyway.

Blair Orr

### The North Side Library(s)

Reading was not ignored along 13th Street. We did have a branch of the downtown Public Library at 412 13th, later moving into the Westminster Shopping Mall when it was built in 1969. While I must confess I was a very infrequent visitor inside the 13th Street book hostel - my reading stage didn't start until after I married in 1963, and I don't know what that said about marriage - the little library did have a nice selection and certainly saved a walk over the 9th Street Bridge.

The North Side Branch of the Lethbridge Public Library opened under direction of head librarian John Dutton in 1957, and after a short stay in the new Westminster Mall, after its opening in 1970, the branch was closed in 1973, under head librarian George Dew.

The north side branch was mainly a children's library, and served a great purpose, until it was decided it was cheaper to have the kids head south than read in a special library in their own neighbourhood. However, I doubt it was closed due to the competition of another long-standing library a little further north along the thoroughfare - The Miners' Library.

A larger-than-life bronze coal miner watched the 13th Street traffic whiz past, day in day out, year after year until the Library closed in 2003. Dominating the parking lot of the Lethbridge Miners' Library the miner, created by Coaldale artist Corne Martens, was a

symbol of a way of life only a few Library members remember. In fact, the coal miners of Lethbridge's past are the very reason the Library exists. Dating back to 1895, the Library - a misnomer if there ever was one in the book-reading sense - had served both the city's coal miners and the community itself.

The City's Chief Archivist Greg Ellis said the Miners' Library was really part of a tradition of institutes, or libraries. "They sprang up across eastern North America in the 1830s through 1850s," he said.

"They were self-help institutes set up by working men to provide education opportunities so they could better themselves in life. The Miners' Library was very important to those who wanted to move into the upper echelons of coal mining."

The bronze miner once dominated the Miners' entrance, and now stands in the foyer of the Nordbridge Seniors Centre.

But to meet the Library theme the club did have some books, mostly on mining. Even to the end the club maintained a locked, glass bookcase with old books and sets of books, along with some of the memorabilia from the mines, like helmets, lights and belts.

"To my understanding it was the oldest continually operating club in Alberta, which was still the Northwest Territories back when it was formed," said past president Bill Gibson. A flood in the 1960s is blamed for the loss of all the records of the old club, and now, many historic facts are left to people's memories, passed-down stories and even rumours.

"Back in the 1920s they were trying to get a liquor license here and they called the club the Miners' Library so they could get a license," said Julius Peta who has been a library member for over seven decades, along with brother Frank Sr. "I ask you, how could they call this a Library. Hell, back then the majority of the coal miners couldn't read anything, let alone English."

In those early times beer was 10 cents a glass, monthly membership was 25 cents, and despite the fact these were hard-working miners, with the possibility of death a constant companion, profanity and gambling were both strictly forbidden.

**Pigeon tales**

Jimmy Brown

"Jimmy (Brown) used to be our milkman, when I lived on 12th St. C North in the 1960s," said Rose Rossi. "He'd give me and my friend (Adelle Eisler) and a whole lot of other kids rides from time to time on his wagon."

As the kids rode along, Jimmy would often talk about his pigeons. He'd take the two girls over to his coop and show off his collection of birds, explain all about them and even the difference between a Homer and a Modena, a bird originally named for Modena, Italy and popular today as a show pigeon.

One day, Jimmy gave the girls a selection of eight pigeons.

"We took them home to my place, and we only had a rabbit pen, so we kept them in there," said Rossi. "We thought it was so cool at Jimmy's coop, where he'd let the birds go and they would fly away, and then return home . . . so we tried that with four of our birds. We opened the cage and they flew off . . . but they never came back. They flew to Jimmy's house."

After this happened a few times, and the girls had to go back and forth to Jimmy's house to retrieve their birds, the pair were hit with a super idea.

"We tied some string, all rolled up on a spool, to the birds legs, and we let them fly," Rossi said with an embarrassed laugh. "As they flew we'd let out more string. Trouble was they flew up into the trees and wires and the string all became entangled in the branches, and our pigeons were just hanging there."

"I won't tell you what happened, but needless to say that was the last of our pigeons. We sure got into so much trouble over that, boy did we get it. I was never allowed to keep pigeons again."

Part of the Miners' clubhouse was originally the old Bailey Street School, a wooden structure with four-inch siding built on 16th Street North, between 5th Avenue and 5th Avenue A.

Once the school was closed, after an addition to Westminster in 1909, it served as a gospel hall, home for a choir and other uses, until 1917. That's when Charlie Peacock of the Library approached the school board. The school was bought for $700 and summarily moved, via horse-drawn skids, to the Library's site at about 733 13th St. N.

The bookcase in the Library contained a picture of the old school, with a similar architectural design to the old Hardieville School which still sits along 13th a few klicks further north.

"Old Nick Zuback said the Library members started taking donations to raise money and bought the school," said Peta. "They then had it moved to this present site."

Cammie (Campbell) Randle remembers when her grandfather lived just back of the Miners' Library, and her mother and father, who worked at the No. 3 coal mine, moved to a house on 15th street, next to Roy Meredith.

"I remember when the Miners' Library moved that school onto 13th Street, the Bailey School I believe," said Cammie, who started at Galbraith School in 1916, when cars first became the vogue. As a result her real name, Elizabeth, earned her the nickname Tin Lizzie, so mother Campbell started calling her Cammie - a derivative of Campbell - and as a 94-year-old she is still known as Cammie.

"I was a kid when they moved the school onto 13th Street for the Library. Before that the miners had a little library on 12th Street C North, about 10th Avenue. I don't know why they called it a library, but I do know a lot of the miners would bring books over to trade with others. At the same time, a lot couldn't read English at all.

"Matt's Grocery was just across from the Miners' and Matt Kropiniak also had a taxi service, to haul the miners to Hardieville and the other mines before and after work, and for regular taxi service as well. Matt's also had a wonderful package of ice cream, for only 25 cents," said Cammie.

Frances Kaupp recalls visiting the Miners' Library and being impressed with the large collection of Zane Grey books they had. (Proof there was some reading material available after all.)

"The coal miners also had a band as I recall, and included John and George Petris," said Francis.

At the start, said Peta, it was the men of No. 6 coal mine, which employed more than 600 at its peak right in Hardieville, who had the exclusive membership of the Library. By the time No. 6 mine closed in 1934 other miners were being allowed into the club and when No. 8 mine closed in 1957 the Miners' Library had more than 1,000 miner members.

For me the Library has a few special meanings, including the fact Jimmy Brown was a long-time member and a long-time friend of my family. Jimmy did marvelous work in the Library's name over the years. As well my grandfather Robert Allison was a Library member.

Jimmy Brown was a mainstay for the Miners' Library for many, many years, assisting uncountable people and organizations to secure financial assistance from the Library for various projects. As well, he was one of the city's most popular milkmen, working both the north side and the south side.

Miners' members love for the outdoors goes back to the soccer and baseball days and the times when family picnics were the order of the day. "In the 1930s the Miners' used to rent a train, some 25 coaches long, for picnic excursions to Medicine Hat and the Crowsnest Pass," said past-president Gibson.

At the beginning, the Miners' Library was strictly a men's club, no women were allowed. But that changed after World War II. In those early days the Library featured showers for its members. The big coal mines had showers for their men but some of the smaller mines didn't, said Peta. As well, many men preferred to ride down to the Library on the mine bus after work, have a shower and a beer or two before heading home.

"The miner's wives used to curse the Library a lot in those early days," Peta said with a laugh. "Back then the Library only sold beer, while today they sell everything. Finally, after the war, the women were allowed to come into the club."

The club members were very involved in sports in the early days, with the soccer and baseball teams. Their skills with a shovel and an axe were often surpassed by their skills on the soccer pitch and ball diamonds of the southern part of the province, and they won a number of provincial championships as well. "The only thing the men had back then was the mine, so the Library became their social club," Peta said.

The final Christmas celebrated by The Library.

Julius Peta spent much of his life working the coal mines of Lethbridge and district, and is one of the longest serving members of the Miners' Library, with more than 52 years of membership.

When No. 8 Coal Mine opened in west Lethbridge in 1937, Julius Peta walked from Hardieville to the mine site, atop the coulees on the west side of the Oldman River, every morning for 30 straight days looking for a job. Coal mining was what he did. It was in the family. His father, Frank Peta Sr., worked the Commerce, Diamond City, No. 6 and Chester mines. Chester was east of the old Social Credit Mine across from Diamond City.

Those were hard times, and settlements like the mining communities of Hardieville and Shaughnessy had barrelled water, usually kept in front yards, and filled two or three times a week by a delivery truck.

"This was water for washing and household use, delivered by Mr. Koshiman," said Peta, who worked the Hardieville No. 6 mine, No. 8 mine and other mines from the 1930s to 1957. "The water and the service was $3 a month. Back then there were a lot of houses in Hardieville with no lights, and you bought coal oil for 25 cents a gallon. That would do for a month. The electricity bill was $1.25 for the same time, so you saved a $1."

The Library honoured its long-time 50-year-plus members a few years before its closure. From the left, front row, are: Ralph Vedres, George Mihalik, Nap Milroy, Ray Berglund, Fred Beddington, J.B. Deak, Bert Mezei, Connie Wing, and Steve Zsovan. In the rear, from the left: Frank Wince, Alex Vigh, John Koskoski, Harry Gorda, Bill Kucheran, Frank Gorda, Billy Gibson, Leonard Dodd, Joe Horhozer, Alex Koshman, and Julius Peta. Also honoured, but not pictured were Frank Peta Sr., Ittalo Ruaben, Nick Onofrychuk, Albert Hing, Sonny Slavich, Jim Demster, and Abe Wall.

Peta said the Hardieville mine officials were pretty good, as far as officials go. The miners' wives were allowed to pick up chunks of coal from the mine site, in buckets, for home use, and no one said a thing.

With the water problems, the mine allowed the kids to shower and wash up Saturday mornings and the wives in the afternoon, with husbands holding sheets and blankets in place for privacy. As for the miners themselves, they showered after every shift, but their work clothes, left at the site, were seldom washed. If they were, they were thrown on the shower floor and the miner stomped them as he showered. After all, they were going to get coal-black dirty again the next shift. There were also showers at the Miners' Library for the men.

To secure his job at No. 8, Peta walked over each morning until he was finally hired, when one morning Bill Crawford told him to come back the next day, he had a job. Once on the payroll there was a mine bus for transportation. Peta said Matt Kropiniak operated the mine bus in 1934, before No. 8 opened, and the miners called it Matt's Taxi. Later the miner's union bought and operated their own bus service to the various area coal mines. The bus route included stops at the Miners' Library, Hungarian Hall, No. 2 Firehall, and the old Arlington Hotel as it headed across the river each and every shift change.

"No. 8 bus drivers included Floyd Lloyd, Alex Sipos, John Boychuck, Anthony "Smoky" Pearson and spare driver was Steve Voytko," said Peta. "Coal is how Lethbridge started. If there was no coal here there'd be no Lethbridge. It was a hard life, but part of our history, and generations to come should know about it."

The Miners' Library had a very strong impact on the overall community. Among those benefiting from Miners' Library generosity have been the University of Lethbridge, Sir Alexander Galt Museum and Archives, the picnic area at Pavan Park, George Vaselenak Park, the Handibus and city social programs. The Library also handed out $10,000 in scholarships each year and was a major shareholder in the Lethbridge Hurricanes of the Western Hockey League.

"We had also had a strong political influence for getting things done on the northside through the years," said Gibson.

Library members enjoyed an active social club, dinner shows, dances, pool tables and even making floats for the Whoop-Up Days parade.

The Library likely held the original tailgate parties at fair time. For years Sundown Hank and his chuckwagon stationed themselves on the Library's parking lot, flipping flapjacks and making coffee at parade time each summer.

Many, many miners and members made the Miners' Library what it became in the community, and in the late 1990s the Library honoured some of its oldest surviving members.

Following is a list of 50-year-plus members the Library honoured on that night, with their year's service to that time: Ralph Vedres 51, George Mihalik 56, Nap Milroy 52, Ray Berglund 54, Fred Beddington 52, J.B. Deak 66, Bert Mezei 51, Connie Wing 60, Steve Zsovan 51, Frank Wince 53, Alex Vigh 52, John Koskoski 54, Harry Gorda 52, Bill Kucheran 54, Frank Gorda 55, Billy Gibson 51, Leonard Dodd 51, Joe Horhozer 62, Alex Koshman 52, Julius Peta 67, Frank Peta Sr. 68, Ittalo Ruaben 63, Nick Onofrychuk 54, Albert Hing 52, Sonny Slavich 53, Jim Demster 52, Abe Wall 52.

An entire way of life for hundreds and hundreds of miners came to a quiet close Jan. 13, 2003, when the Miners' Library closed its doors, in financial ruin.

## Miners' Library Sports Scene

While the original intent of the Miners' Library was to serve the men of the coal mines, it progressed well beyond that in its more than 100-year history. In the early years, sports were important and the Miners' sponsored, and supplied players for some formidable soccer and baseball teams. Through the heyday of the two sports, the teams put the Miners' on top of the sporting podium. In the 1930s, 1940s and 1950s names like Yanosik, Kucheran, Deak, Tarnava, Onofrychuk, Seaman, Luciani, Vaselenak and many others carried the Miners' banner.

The city owned the Adams Park ball diamond, where the baseball team played, and the soccer pitch back of the right field fence.

"I remember one time when George Yanosik threw a ball back to home from left field," said 62-year Miners' member Joe Horhozer. "It flew over the backstop, out of the park and broke the window in Matt's store across the street."

As early as 1927 and 1928 the Miners' baseball team was dominating the scene with players like Jack Randle, George Yanosik, Andy Pisko, George Swedish, Lloyd Gurla, Fredo Luciani, Joe Honesko, John Lawson, Al Freed, George Petrunia, Joe "Boiler" Chollak, and Steve Smerek. In 1934 Mikey George, a midget who owned a barber shop across from the Library, was the team's bat boy, and players included the Onofrychuks, Fred and George, as well as Ernie and Ollie Luciani and Andy, Alex and George Yanosik.

In 1936 the Miners' won the first Alberta senior baseball championship and they repeated in 1937. They recorded 36 wins and 12 losses in 1936 and were 39-7 the following year, earning them a spot in the Lethbridge Sports Hall of Fame.

When I started delivering newspapers for The Lethbridge Herald in the early 1950s, I was absolutely bursting with pride when I realized one of my customers was none other than Clarence Yanosik.

By 1954 Yanosik was practicing law with Max Moscovich and was married, living on 12th St. C North, right across from a future Boston Bruins star in the NHL, Autry Erickson.

The Miners Baseball team of 1927-28 included, from left in front: Eldo Luciani, Jack Randle, George Yanosik, Andy Pisko, Lloyd Gerla, George Swedish, and Maggie Romanchuk; middle, from left: Fredo Luciani, Joe Honesko, Bob Dunlop, Al Freed, George Onofrychuk, John Lawson and Joe "Boiler" Chollak. In the rear, from left, are George Petrunia, Daddy Petrunia and Steve Smerek.

The 1936 Miners Baseball Club, front from left: Rigo Toccoli, manager Edlo Luciani, Ken Ringland, Ollie Luciani, President Andy Pisko, and Eric Dolighan. In the back, from left: Ernie Luciani, Fred Onofrychuk, George Onofrychuk, Joe Haniesko, George Petrunia, Howard Teel, Steve Smerek and George Yanosik. Not in the photograph are Alex Yanosik, Dutch Holman and Art and Jack Lewis.

28

"At least once a month, I still drive through Staffordville, where I lived and grew up as a kid, and look at the house I was born in. There was nothing north of 10th Street back then. In 1938 my dad built a house on 12th Street C, and that's the house I lived in when I got married. I still drive down that street every once in a while," Yanosik said on his retirement as a judge.

Judge Clarence Yanosik

Yanosik played with the Lethbridge Miners, really a northside baseball dynasty in the 1930s, 1940s and into the 1950s, but found it hard to crack the lineup. The early Miner stars included his father George, and later stalwarts like Ollie Luciani, Mike Seaman, Rigo Toccoli, Hector Negrello, Steve Smerek, Fred Onofrychuk and Matt Slavich.

"In 1949 my father and I started the Lethbridge Reos Baseball Club, and the next year we called them the Lethbridge Cubs," said Yanosik. "The Reos had a lot of young players and Todd Haibeck sponsored us, from Reo Mercury. The Cubs were together from 1950-1954, with the backing of a lot of city businessmen. From 1955 to 1957 I played for the Miners again, and in 1958 with the Lethbridge Warriors. The umpires back in the Miners' and Reos' days included Henry Viney before he went to Calgary and Mel Friend, who only had three fingers on his right hand, the one he called strikes with."

Concerning his playing days, the judge said he could hit well, but his arm wasn't worth a darn. He did everything left handed, including hitting, but for some reason, threw right handed. His batting average however, was always in the .300s and he could power the ball out of the park, given the right pitcher was on the mound.

"I didn't like lefthanders though, especially if it was Matt Slavich," he said with a laugh.

The Honourable Mr. Justice Clarence George Yanosik was born in his grandmother's north side home, with the aid of a mid-wife, in No. 3, a small residential area just north of the former No. 3 coal mine site, in what is now the Staffordville area. It was 3 p.m., April 20, when George and Anne Yanosik welcomed their new son.

"My grandparents on both sides of the family came from the northeastern part of what was Czechoslovakia in the late 1890s, and both sides of the family were coal miners, in the No. 3 and No. 6 mines. My father worked in the coal mines too, then at the Garden Hotel, as bar manager. In 1952, he and his brother Alex bought the Carmangay Hotel."

They operated the hotel until the early 1960s when George bought the Warner Hotel, which he ran for 15 years. George died in 1985, a year after his wife passed away, but both lived to see their son appointed as a judge, Sept. 24, 1969 at age 43.

Some may feel Judge Yanosik could swing a heavy gavel during his 30 years on the bench. But, his swing was nothing compared to how he could swing the lumber in his younger days on the city's baseball diamonds. A headline in a June, 1957 Lethbridge Herald underlines just how potent the young lawyer, and soon to be judge, was with a bat, boldly stating: Yanosik Tops Loop Hitters. The good judge, still a young lawyer back then, had been to bat 38 times as a member of the Lethbridge Miners, had cracked out 18 hits and three home runs, for a league-leading .473 average.

Yanosik was playing with some pretty fair talent in 1957, including the likes of Jocko Tarnava, Earl Ingarfield, Vic Stasiuk, Les Colwill, Frank Deak, Johnny Klem, Mitch Stzaba, Steve Odney, Bill Kucheran, Wes Rice, Jerry Kjeldgaard and Bert Nyrose to name just a few of the stars.

"He might not tell you about some of the longest balls ever hit out of Lethbridge ball parks, because he hit them," said his long-time friend and fellow teammate on the bench, Justice Laurie MacLean. "He could sure hit them out of the park."

The late Mike "Mitchie" Seaman remembered one of the strangest games the Miners ever played, in Bow Island. The Miners' refused to take the field until all the snakes were killed.

"Steve Smerek, nor anyone else, would go into the outfield until someone killed a seven-foot snake out there," the first-baseman said. "A farmer came out of his car, caught the snake, grabbing it by its tail and with one flip snapped its spine."

Mike Seaman played three years for the Miners before heading overseas with the Calgary Highlanders for World War II. It would be another eight years before he rejoined the team.

"I played first base all the time because I was tall and had the reach. I don't know what my average was as a hitter, but I was the top batter two years in a row, so I guess it was over .300. I was a good hitter and had about eight or nine home runs a year."

The right-hander belted two home runs in Brooks in one game, blasting the ball into the rodeo bucking chutes in back of centre field. Other teams in the league back then included Bow Island, Medicine Hat, New Dayton, and George Yanosik's south side rivals, the Reos.

Seaman played with many of the same Miners of Yanosik's day, as well as with Stan Chervinski, Ollie Luciani, Steve Arisman, Joe "Honey" Honesko, Fred Onofrychuk, Norm Petrie, Hec Negrello, Matt Slavich, Art Lewis and Steve Smerek.

The Miners, who would travel to games in one of the mine buses, used to get a five cent chocolate bar and a five cent pop between games, as payment for Sunday doubleheaders.

The old Miners soccer teams of the 1920s to the 1940s, were dandies as well, and won the provincial championship on more than one occasion. The 1923 Scott Cup championship team included men like Robert Allison Sr. - my grandfather - Bob Livingstone, Dave Allan, Bill Linning and Dave Campbell.

The city's minor soccer association was well supported by the Miners' Library and the Library sponsored ball teams, including the Miners team in the American Legion League until the club's demise. The Library spent a lot of money supporting the city's minor sports systems and also played host to charity golf tournaments, the city dart league and fishing derbies. A number of years back Val Tarnava created the Miners' Library Fish and Game club, where everyone who bought a Miners' membership became a member of the club. The club also held an annual awards night for its anglers and hunters and sponsored a fishing derby for the kids each summer.

## Adams Park

Adams Park, all 10 acres of it, was first developed by city workers as a flat playing field, ploughed and seeded with grass and trees in the spring of 1910. The land had been bought from the Alberta Railway and Irrigation Company in September, 1909, in a deal which included the acquisition of Henderson Lake. The Adams area, named in honour of a former city mayor Elias "Shorty" Adams, took in blocks 167 and 168. A water main and irrigation ditch ran alongside the property.

In 1910, when Adams Park first saw the light of day, the city council consisted of C.B. Bowman, William Oliver, George M. Hatch, later to become mayor, D. King, Robert Sage of Sage's Bridge notoriety, later to be just the 9th Street Bridge, and Arthur Frayne. The mayor was Elias "Shorty" Adams.

"It was suggested on council they name the new park in North Lethbridge after my father, calling it Frayne Park, because he was the only north side member of council in 1910," said Avice (Frayne) Anderson. "My dad lived along 4th Ave., between 13th and 15th and that original Frayne house is still there. He declined the honour and the council then decided it should be named after the mayor, hence it became Adams Park.

"The streetcar used to turn at Adams Park, and that was about the only time I'd ever see it, because we kids would ride the streetcar right up to the turn-around, as far north as it would go, and then back to our stop because it cost the same amount of money as getting off early. Right across from Adams Park where the streetcar turned was Dominion Square, with a big concrete block declaring it so. There was one lone house right there on that corner, and the lady used to come to mother's for tea all the time.

"I do know when Nick Supina had that big soccer team of his, that's when they built the big walled fence around the soccer field."

Adams was a super place, a gathering spot on week nights, but mainly weekends, for sports fans throughout north Lethbridge, with a baseball field right on the corner and a soccer field adjacent to the right-field fence.

In 1918 North Lethbridge United played soccer at Adams, on a dirt field - it wasn't until late 1932 a grass pitch was created. Ted Radley, a star with Supina's for many years, once said of the Adams' dirt pitch: "Dogs buried bones in it, and I knew every gopher by name."

One of the premier teams in 1923, calling Adams home, was the Callies, which included players like Al Walton, Jim McNabb, Jimmy Dunlop and Albert Pink.

In 1932 Supina's was undefeated on the Adams' dirt pitch and went on to beat Edmonton in Mewata Stadium in Calgary for the Alberta championship, playing on the grass. Supina's, sponsored by Nick Supina at a cost of $30, scored 43 straight goals that year before anyone scored on them. In the provincial championship match in September, they beat the Edmonton Radials 4-2.

Players included Norman Gurr, Frank Hill, Jimmy McMahon, Alex Linning, Al Walton, Addie Donaldson, J. Gurr, with Ed Bruchet as the manager and J. Gibson and D. Dearie the trainers. Other players included Ted and Clarence Radley, Bill Knight, George Wilson, Jock Clark, Joe Lakie and George Sumner.

Below: 1911 Callies Soccer Team.

30

Admission in those days was 10 cents for regular matches and two bits for the big games. There was room on the bleachers for about 500 fans and drays would be pulled in for the really big games, and lined up along the sideline, for fans to stand on.

"An old fella named Willetts, and his wife, looked after the soccer field, and he lived right there, in a small house on the east end of the park," said Brent Seely, who lived just a few doors to the east of the Adams complex. "In fact his house was right at the entrance and you had to walk around it to get into the soccer field. The house, and the soccer field, were right across from a small wading pool, with a slide and fountain, kind of a mini-park, right where the First Dutch Reform Church now sits.

"We used to hop the fence at the back of the soccer field and climb up on the bleachers or the fence to watch the Miners baseball games, and that old Willetts would chase us away."

Seely said people must remember the heyday of Adams Park, with its ball diamond and soccer pitch, came well before there was television, and people spent a lot of time there.

He was a baseball fan, and his family, mother Leona and father Frank, even supplied room and board to one of the Miners' pitchers for three years, Freddie Friemuth.

"All the towns had clubs then, with the Wesleys at Granum and George Watson at Picture Butte bringing their teams in to play the Miners," Seely said. "I used to like seeing the barnstorming teams that came through and first saw Eddie Feigner, The King and His Court, at Adams. Also, the Lethbridge Nisei team played out of Adams.

"The first Little League games in north Lethbridge were actually played at Adams, right there in the Miners ball park. That was something to play there, and I might add that no one ever hit a home run out of there on the Little League teams."

Seely remembers playing with the Moose Royals, coached by Mel Friend, the city's health inspector and umpire for most Miners games, who lived right across from Adams, just off the little mini-water park.

It is likely Seely's life-long enjoyment of country music was spurred by his regular attendance at Miners games in the late 1940s and early 1950s.

"Eddie Ferenz, who lived just over on 12th St. C, was the PA announcer for the Miners and he'd always play Vaughan Monroe's "Ghost Riders in the Sky" before every game. You could hear them riding all over north Lethbridge every Sunday as "Ghost Riders" boomed out over the loud speakers.

"Eddie went on to be the Travelling Secretary for the Philadelphia Phillies in the Major League for many years." Just another northsider who made good.

Nellie Seaman, whose husband Mike went on to play for the Miners in the early 1940s before going off to war - and for a few years after - starring at first base,

remembers being around Adams Park as an eight-year-old.

"We'd go under the wooden seats, and they had big gaps in between the boards," said Nellie, who was born and lived for many years on 12th Street C. "We kids would get some sticks to poke people in the legs through those gaps, and laugh as they'd chase us away. When Mike, who was born on 12th St. B, was playing I went, but I didn't want to go there all the time. I had three little kids to raise (Bob, Barry and Tom)."

Besides playing ball for the Miners, Mike, after a few years at the Dallas Hotel, was the bar manager at the Miners' Library for many years.

---

**Another Gardens?**

"When I first remember Adams Park it was all nice and green, with red ash trails . . . and if they had left it alone it would be just like Galt Gardens is today," said Cammie Randle.

---

Memories of some of those Adams Park experiences remain vivid in my mind, and in the minds of many who watched baseball and soccer. You could often go to a soccer game - the field just the other side of the right field fence of the ball park - and stand on the back row and keep an eye on the baseball game at the same time.

Bill Kucheran at practice and Ed Frenenz

golfer Bobby Dunlop below:

For me, it was a thrill to go to games with my grandfather Robert Allison and watch people like family friend Mike Seaman play first base, and umpires Mel Friend and Henry Viney, both frequent visitors to my grandparents' home, and players like Johnny Klem and Clarence Yanosik and later Bill Kucheran.

My grandfather used to take me, as a five- to eight-year-old to the Adams Ball Park, just a few hundred feet north of the Miners' Library's door. I thought he was an avid reader, but it turned out that wasn't so. He'd drop me off at the ball game at times and tell me he was going to the Library to read. It wasn't until my grandmother asked me how my granddad enjoyed the game, and I said he was in the Library reading, that I discovered the Library was really a beer hall, not a place of quiet solitude to peruse your favourite Jules Verne novel.

Another piece of misinformation my grandfather gave me concerning the Miners baseball games, was the fact I didn't have to pay when I went with him . . . if I walked in backwards so they'd think I was coming out. Kids, of course, were free back then, and Sunday they couldn't charge at all, due to the Lord's Day Act, and silver collection was all you needed.

The Allison clan was a frequent visitor to Adams Ball Park and to the soccer pitch, with my dad (Andy) and granddad (Robert), and uncles (Bob, Alec, Jim and Stewart) as players, trainers and later fans. My grandfather was a trainer for quite a spell with the Miners. He was the trainer for the Miners football team when they won the Scott Cup in 1923 and again in 1925 when they took the Scott and Charity Cups and won the Lethbridge and District League as well. Players on the 1925 team included A. Tennant, W. Dunlop, J. Dunlop, D. Connor, J. Connor, D. Campbell, W. Anderson, E. Willetts, N. McColl, N. Gurr, M. McLukie and captain D. Allan. Some of the other faces on the 1923 squad were W. Earl, T. Hotchkiss. Billy Linning, E. McKenna, T. Walker and D. Legg.

Teams in the senior league back then included the powerful Supina's squad, a side which included my uncle Al Walton and the Radley boys, Alec, Ted and Clarence. I later worked with Ted for years at The Herald where he was the head bookkeeper and Clarence was our next door neighbour on 4th Avenue. There were also other teams like the Miners, ANAF, Arcade, Coalhurst and Commerce coal miners, the Callies, a Scottish side and an English team, St. George's.

Virtually kitty-corner from Adams Park was Matt's Confectionary, a favourite after-game place for players and fans. My father (Andy) remembered going to Matt's as a kid. Two decades later I was going there, and in the 1950s I passed Matt's on a daily basis as I delivered The Herald. Matt's had great ice cream, and an assortment of candy, books and other smaller grocery items.

Matt's, of course, was also across from the Miners' Library, and Matt Kropiniak operated the mine buses for years, at 25 cents a trip.

"You would go to the ball game and sit in the back row of the grandstand so you could see if any of the foul balls hit a car, or Matt's window during the ball games," my father said - and we did the same thing. "When the ball games ended the kids headed for Matt's and the men went to the Miners' for a beer . . . but you had to be 21 back then. The senior soccer teams also played during the week, and dad (Robert Allison, my grandfather) would come home from work from the mine, rush over to Cliff MacCallum, the barber, and get a quick shave before heading for the game. He was a full back when he played, and later the club's trainer."

The Miners' soccer field bleachers.

West side fence needed reinforcement.

MacCallum lived in Little Wigan and owned the Hub Cigar Store at 410 13th St. North. The Hub sold "old country" newspapers, set out every Saturday morning, along with cigars of course, magazines, other "men's" stuff, and a half pack of cigarettes for 10 cents and a full pack for 25 cents. When the Hub closed in the early 1940s, MacCallum moved his barbering business to the Dallas Hotel and set up his chair there for many years.

Cammie (Campbell) Randle was born on what came to be an ominous day, Sept. 11, but her birth was back in 1911 in Dunfermline, Scotland. In the spring of 1912, this nine month old and her family were living in north Lethbridge, in a little grey house in Dominion Square, just across from where the Adams Ice Centre sits today.

"Adams Park was a real nice open park when I was a kid. There was a small bandstand in it, and the Salvation Army band used to come over north and play each Sunday night. Then the city made it into a fenced baseball stadium, putting a big, dirty old brown fence all around it. I was about 12 or 14 when they put that fence up, and it cut off the view and the red shale walkways and the ball fields that were there before.

"It seems they cut the park in half, with a baseball stadium along 13th and a soccer pitch next to it to the east."

Her father, Archie Campbell, played soccer for the Callies before his death in 1922. The Callies was made up of a lot of Scottish players and an English team at the time included quite a few of the Holberton boys. In later years Cammie's husband Jack Randle - they were married in 1936 - played for the Miners, with the 1936 team including men like John Lawson and Bobby Dunlop. As a result, Cammie went to quite a few ball games to cheer for husband Jack and his Miner mates. (Lynn Davis of Diamond City said her uncle Bob Chiswick used to play for the Callies. He was English, so his teammates Scottishized him, calling him McChiswick).

"Jack, who worked at The Herald from 1923 to 1974, played before we were married as well," said Cammie. "The balls used to fly over the fence a lot too, right into our yard. My grandfather used to pick them up and then call the boys over to come and get them. At the football games I remember old Mrs. Dunlop and Mrs. Linning. They had two boys each on opposite teams and Mrs. Dunlop used to holler over at Mrs. Linning and ask if her boys 'had their porridge this morning?' They were always nagging at each other.

"I don't ever remember Adams having a covered grandstand, that was just for those on the south side."

Cammie remembered the early walkways in north Lethbridge, especially around Adams Park, they were black ash which was "awful." Then came red ash, from Diamond City and Commerce coal mines, followed by the wooden sidewalks and then concrete.

"Those wooden sidewalks were okay, but your dimes and nickels would go through the cracks if you dropped them on your way to buy rock candy from an Italian store along 18th Street," she said.

"Sunday afternoons you could hardly walk down 13th Street because everybody was heading for Adams Park for the baseball or soccer games," said Phyllis (Bissett) Slovack. "The streetcars were full as they headed north, and then after the games they were full heading south down 13th. The streetcar turned around at the north end of Adams. But, fact was, most people preferred to walk down 13th when going to and from the ball games."

Outside the ball park, and across the street, was a little wading pool, and Scotty Armitt, born Halloween night 1925, recalls Charlie Dearie as being its caretaker.

"He'd fill it with fresh water in the morning and drain it down at night," said Scotty.

Adams had sun-hot bleachers and never did get lights for night baseball, like Henderson Stadium did in south Lethbridge, but it was the jewel of the north side for many decades.

Alvin Bissett remembers many a day on those bleachers. Like he said, they were called bleachers because you'd go to the ball game and sit there all day in the sun and bleach.

Adams ballpark was torn down in 1963 to make room for a large green space and the Adams Ice Centre, out where centre field and the back of the soccer stadium used to sit. The ice centre opened Sept. 30, 1962, built at a cost of $258,000.

Below: A lonely dog kept his eye on Adams Park, as seen from the home-team dugout angle, in the off- season in the 1950s.

Above - Adams Park soccer field east fence is braced for the west wind.

Right - Adams Park baseball diamond visiting team's dugout.

Below - Adams Park baseball diamond home team's dugout.

Below left - Mike Seaman.

Below right - The caretaker for the Adams ball field and soccer pitch lived inside the soccer area, along the 8th Avenue side of the park where the Boys & Girls Club is today.

## Circus Time

The 9th Street Bridge, while well to the west of 13th Street was another key link to south Lethbridge, downtown in particular.

The flat area to the west of the bridge, and just slightly to the north of its meeting with 9th Avenue North, was known for years as Circus Flats.

There are records of the Barnum and Bailey Circus setting up on Circus Flats in the early 1900s, with parades over the 9th Street Bridge to downtown, to entice the circus goers north, Pied Piper style, to enjoy the animals and side shows.

June Glanville had married Jim Carpenter by 1933, but before that she remembers circuses and other shows being featured on Circus Flats.

"My mother took me to a circus there, an afternoon performance, when I was little. It had everything, tightrope walkers, and all the glitter, sparkle and kaleidoscopey you'd expect from a circus. I don't recall the name of the circus, but we kids were allowed to go and buy one thing only to eat, probably popcorn," June recalled.

My biggest memory of this area involved the Gayland Shows, in the early 1950s, when they had all the midway games, a few rides and best of all, a wrestling tent. The barker would set up outside on a platform, with his featured wrestler - in this case one Tiger Tomasso, also known as Dave Ruhl. Sound familiar you Stampede Wrestling fans? - and challenge all comers. The locals would climb into the ring, inside the tent, and win $10 if they stayed three minutes with the Tiger.

Tiger Tomasso.

It was a costly venture to pass into the tent, at least 50 cents for kids. And that kind of money was hard to come by, when your allowance was 25 cents a week, and the midway was in town for a week. You could always sneak in, but that could often result in a swift kick you know where if caught, or you would beg 50 cents from a relative . . . my older cousin Bill Wright paid my way in one day, and I knew he could have

beaten the Tiger, but he just laughed at the idea. Fact is, Bill would have taken him, this man drove for CP Freight and could unload fridges off the back of those CPR trucks without a dolly and carry them into houses.

However, there was one other way to get in free. Before each session the Tiger would demonstrate one of his masterful wrestling holds on anyone who dared to step up onto the platform. With the demonstration came a pass for one or two shows. Well, there we were, out front, Blair McNab and I, with no money. So I leapt to the opportunity, up onto the stage, and the Tiger immediately put me flat on my back and demonstrated to the crowd - much to my chagrin - the various painful aspects of the step-over-toe-hold. We got in free, though I limped in and Blair went in laughing. The Tiger was beating everyone, and soon no locals would take him on, and, if memory serves me right he took on local wrestling promoter Darby Melnyk, a much smaller man, and the Tiger did Darby harm.

The next night no one would fight the Tiger, even though Melnyk was back and wanted to climb back into the ring. It looked like it was going to happen, until a heavily-muscled black man stepped forward. Unbeknown to us at the time, it was another pro wrestler, known as King Toby, and the Tiger wanted no part of him. But the crowd insisted and the tent sold out. The Tiger fell prey to the King. Ah, sweet justice. We got our money's worth - in my case leg's worth - and the Tiger fell. It was years later that family friend Pete Shologan, known in pro wrestling circles as the Coaldale Cossack, told me all about those sideshow wrestling gigs, and how he and Dave Ruhl worked the circuit many a time, promoted by Darby Melnyk. It was, like wrestling itself, all a show.

But boy, in those early '50s, that was quite a show.

Pete Shologan knew the wrestling business.

The Gayland Shows also had rides, though not as many or as large as those during the summer Fair, and there was cotton candy, pop and even girlee shows, would you believe, right here in north Lethbridge? Unfortunately I cannot report first hand on those.

Mavis (Harding) Standing remembers Circus Flats for all its circus tents and a few rides. The circus would come into the north side area, unload, put up its tents and then load up its big-wheeled carts with lions and other wild animals and then gather its people and head south over the 9th Street Bridge for downtown to entice the southsiders north for the show.

"In 1944 or 1945 the circus set up near the International Harvester building, and this time it was mostly rides," said Mavis. "I went on some of those rides with Wilf Perry and when we came off them I sure was sick, and my husband just laughed."

Avice (Frayne) Anderson said noon hour at Westminster School used to be from 12 to 1:30 p.m. "There was plenty of time for us to watch the parade, go over the 9th Street bridge and then get back to school. Some of the boys got jobs watering the animals for the circuses."

Scotty Armitt said it was common for the kids to play hooky at Westminster and Galbraith when the circus and midways were in town. Then they'd not show up at home for lunch or supper and parents would make their way to Circus Flats and were soon seen dragging their wayward kids home via an ear, or by the scruff of their neck.

"I remember Clyde Beatty was there once and so was Mable Stark, a lady lion tamer," Scotty said.

He remembers the circuses costing a nickel or a dime, and most set up a merry-go-round and a small Ferris wheel along with the tents for the animals and side shows.

Adam Stickel was in his late 30s in 1948 when a circus came to Circus Flats. "They unloaded the elephants and walked them down towards 13th Street to exercise them," he said with a laugh. "I helped hammer in pegs for the big tent, along with others, and we all got free entrance to the circus for our work. They had all kinds of different people doing tricks. One guy climbed way up high, then stood on his head, feet straight in the air, and slid down a long, angled wire to the ground. The elephants also did different tricks."

Margaret Schile recalls seeing the Barnum and Bailey elephants in the early 1930s. She was staying at her aunt's house, Fred and Teressa Kane, along 4th Avenue North. "We could see the circus from her house and they would walk the elephants along the railroad tracks, 6 or 10 of them at a time, and we'd watch from my aunt's upstairs window. We never did get to go to the circus, we weren't that rich. But we enjoyed seeing them walk the elephants in the big open field by the railway tracks."

Ab Chervinski said Barnum and Bailey and the other circuses would put up posters on the big billboards along 13th Street, one where North Lethbridge Hardware eventually built and another just north of where the Dairy Queen sits today. He remembers how all the boys would go over to the Flats to help put up the circus. They'd all throw their caps in a big sack and they'd get them back from the circus people, with a free pass, when the work was done.

Florence Seager would walk all the way from 21st Street North to 9th Street to attend the shows at Circus Flats. "Despite that walk, I know I enjoyed the circus very much," she said with a laugh. "In the late 1920s some had a merry-go-round, but not always."

## Fun of a Different Sort

You can't talk about a historic area, with more than a century of history, and not at least ask about ghosts.

"There have been reports of occasional house hauntings, but really, there are no accounts of north side ghosts," said the city's Chief Archivist Greg Ellis.

However, there may be an opposition player or two who took the field against the Miners' ball team who may have wondered a time or two if, indeed, there were Angels in the Outfield.

Nick Zubray wasn't a ghost, he was a real presence in the city, but was often assigned mystical qualities. Nick was a well-known Hardieville area sportsman, and many knew him as The Ankle Express. Nick was a longtime promoter of boxing and wrestling during the 1940s and into the 1970s. He was friends with another top north side sportsman, wrestler John Katan, and worked with the Coaldale Cossack, Pete Shologan, a time or two.

"Nick could sing like an angel; he had a very good voice," said Ab Chervinski. "I knew Nick and as well, I once saw the great John Katan wrestle one of the best, Whipper Billy Watson."

Nick Zubray.

One of Zubray's last promotions in Lethbridge featured Canadian boxing legend George Chuvalo, against a guy called Stanford Harris, out at Exhibition Park. Chuvalo won in three and fight fans got what they wanted to see.

## TV comes to Town

In 1955 CJLH-TV ushered in the modern era in Lethbridge, using its northside tower to beam Don Slade, Sandy McCallum, Norm Young, Bill Matheson and others into homes throughout the city. It was called CJLH-TV, the CJ for one of the owners, CJOC radio, and the LH for the other owner, Lethbridge Herald. H.P. (Hugh) Buchanan, then publisher of The Herald, was the president of the station and Norm Botterill, from CJOC, was the managing director.

One of the most popular Lethbridge singing groups was the Country Capers, from left, Donn Petrak on guitar, the singing Potts sisters, Sharon, Betty and Shirley Ann, Herb Urano on bass, Remo Baceda on fiddle and vocals, vocalist Eddie Potts and Joe Horhozer on accordion.

CJLH began broadcasting Nov. 21, 1955, as a CBC affiliate with 40 per cent of the programs coming from the mother network. It wasn't until 1976 that CJLH became an independent broadcaster. More than 4,000 people visited the station during the open house sessions the first 10 days it was on the air in 1955.

Early viewers won't forget Bill Matheson with his weather watch - many feel Bill was the best weather person the city ever had - viewed on their 21-inch black and white TV, selling for $569.95 at the time. Viewers were also glued to shows off the network like Howdy Doody, I Love Lucy and Wayne and Schuster. There were local shows like TV Corral, a one-hour program featuring Elmer Peck, Curly Bob, Art Dietrich, Eddie Dietrich and Neil Hood. And who can forget Blair Holland and son Padget on Channel 7 Ranch?

Those early years also spotlighted the Country Capers with Eddie Potts, the singing city policeman, his sisters Betty, Sharon and Shirley Ann, Donn Petrak, Herb Urano, Remo Baceda and Joe Horhozer. One of the top children's shows in Canada featured Georgia Fooks and sports fans delighted to Sportlight Quiz, hosted by Matheson with Don Pilling and Al McCann as regular panelists, and a guest star each week.

Bill McCamley and Vic Reid were among the early engineers at the station and Harry Higa and Roy Hopkins were on the control board. Brent Seely started live in the electronic media as a cameraman at CJLH and well-known western sculptor Corne Martens was a mainstay in those early days, working the camera and designing sets. He was an award-winning set creator, including a set for a fashion show, with Elisha Rasmussen, where everyone appeared to be in miniature. Ron Joevanazzo, a Lethbridge boy, spent his entire career behind the scene at the television station.

As well, Barry Bergthorson, got his start at CJLH before going on to greater things, including working with actor-producer Peter Ustinov.

Those without television sets, particularly the younger folk, would gather outside stores to watch the new phenomenon. Jack's Radio and TV on the corner of 13th St. and 3rd Ave. not only had TVs running in the window, but outside sound as well. We kids gathered there for hours, and some of us even used to hang around outside Jimmy and Jack Lee's house on the corner of 4th Avenue and 12th St. B to look through the window - there was no sound - at this new marvel. Occasionally Betty would invite us in to watch a show or two. On Halloween, a five-minute glimpse of TV with sound as you entered the porch to receive your candy, was better than any candy treat.

Below: Brent Seely.

37

While CJLH was well away from 13th Street, the city's second television station, CFCN, located itself right on 13th Street, almost kitty corner from Martin Brothers, and next to Mihalik's.

CFCN was originally located on 20th Ave. S. and Mayor Magrath Drive when it first came to town in 1968, but moved to its 13th Street location Nov. 5, 1973. It entered the local market Sept. 3, 1968, with its first newscast sponsored by Hoyt's Hardware.

## They liked to Dance

There are many fond memories of Burgman's Hall at 418 13th.

"Dick Burgman was both a boxer and a wrestler," said Scotty Armitt. "He used to take the kids downstairs at his dance hall and teach them how to box from time to time. One time, old Mr. Jarvie came out to watch and he didn't like what he saw, so he knocked old man Burgman right on his you know what.

"Cameron Doughty's wife, Emily, from the Lealta Theatre was a Burgman."

Armitt said Burgman's Hall was home to many Masonic Lodge dances, as well as other clubs and lodges of the day.

In later years McCaffrey's Drugs moved into the lower level of the hall and among the early delivery boys were Scotty and Gerald Reid.

"Steve Leonard was a pharmacist there, and later Paul Pheirson came along," said Scotty.

Joyce Davies was too young to go to the dances at Burgman's Hall when she was growing up in north Lethbridge. But, as an eight year old she and her friends would put on lipstick - to be removed with water from the outside tap before going into the house - and go to Westminster playground. The playground was right across the street from the dance hall, and the girls would hide behind the trees and watch the dancers come and go and catch a glimpse through the upstairs window.

"Burgman had a pool hall up there as well," recalls Alvin Bissett. "I used to go up there with Brian Wardman."

Florence Seager, who lived across from the old north side airport as a child, used to pass Dick Burgman's large brick house on the corner of 19th Street and 5th Avenue, as she walked from home to 13th Street, often stopping to talk with the dance hall proprietor.

"He was a very particular man; he wanted everything to be just right," she said. "We'd go to the dances at Burgman's Hall and dance our heads off. People used to rent the dance hall all the time, for things like weddings, and we'd meet there for the Vasa Lodge as well."

The Vasa Order of America met in the Scandinavian Hall on 12th Street C, between 2nd and 3rd Avenues, for many years as well, said Florence.

Vasa helped support the elderly and those in need and encompassed all members of the Scandinavian community, be they Norwegians, Fins, Swedes or whatever.

"We had dances galore at the Scandinavian Hall, with good music too," Florence remembers. "The Alberta Ranch Boys came and played there and some of the guys in the Lodge had a band as well."

Burgman's brick home as it looks today.

Mavis Standing laughs when she talked of the many dances she attended at Burgman's Hall, even though she wasn't allowed to go. "We'd push up the bedroom window and climb out. Then we'd run across the Westminster School grounds and go up to Burgman's," she said. "Boy did I get it when I'd get back home. I remember Burgman as a big, rough old man, but I was only 16 when we went there."

Margaret Schile was about 15 when she first went to Burgman's: "Mostly they had live dance bands and I remember guys like Remo Baceda played there quite a few times."

Cammie Randle used to head to Burgman's to dance in the 1930s, but didn't enjoy it too much. "There used to be such terrible fights there, so we quit going. We went over south to the Trianon and listened to the Alberta Ranch Boys. I do remember Mr. Burgman would round up all the boys in the area and teach them how to box, downstairs from the dance hall. The boys were always coming out of there with black eyes."

## And They Called It Pool

There was a pool hall along the street, Acme Snooker, between 2nd and 3rd Avenue run by Bill Willetts' father, Bill Sr. This hall operated from 1947 to 1975 in the old Hart Hardware building, before giving way to Tom's Trading Post. The hall had that old pool hall atmosphere and was a serious place to play, along the lines of the grand old Arcade downtown. Many an hour was spent playing poker pool or snooker, with some of the hot sticks belonging to Tommy Yip and "Shakey" Earl.

Bill Willetts Sr., William if you care to be formal, ran the pool hall, just north of Supina's, where he worked for some time before turning to pool. He and wife Edna had a son, Bill, an always laughing character who was not above a prank or two, and daughters Jeanette and Darlene.

"Willetts Pool Hall also had a taxi service and Ethel McKenna was one of the drivers," said Scotty Armitt. "Jim McKenna, the old fire chief, was her brother-in-law."

When I delivered The Herald along a two-block portion of 13th Street, from 7th Avenue, starting with the Ponechs, to 9th Avenue, where I headed west for three blocks, two of my earliest customers were Johnny Credico and then little Mikey George just a few doors to the north.

Johnny had a barber shop and a small pool hall in the same little concrete block shop across from the Miners' Library, and the first place I'd hit after leaving Ponechs and passing a large open section - later to become a strip mall.

Johnny came from Italy in 1949, where he had learned the trade of barbering at the tender age of 13. In fact, he made pocket money during the four-week boat ride across the Atlantic by cutting fellow passengers' hair. After cutting hair downtown for a couple of years in the old Garden Hotel, Johnny built his barber shop-pool hall along 13th Street, taking advantage of a bustling trade from residents and Miners' patrons, most of whom in those early 1950s were still making their living in the coal mines in the Oldman River valley.

I remember Johnny as a smiling, friendly, though kind of tough guy, and on more than one occasion spent my Herald wages - from delivering newspapers and after I started full time at The Herald in 1957 - in his shop, both for haircuts and pool, though I must admit mostly it was the latter which drained my coffers. Johnny was as good with a cue as he was with his clippers.

Some of those coal miners stayed loyal a lot longer than I did, many in their 80s and 90s still dropping in at Johnny's a half a century later for a trimming - not at the pool table, but in the barber chair.

The tools of his trade, the old hand clippers, straight razors and pointed scissors, as well as the modern electric clippers stand silent now, with Johnny leaving the business of cutting hair to others in 2002, but my memories still remain of that little shop where you could get clipped in two ways, in the pool hall and in Johnny's antique barber's chair.

"There used to be a pool hall run by Pete Briosi, in what we call the new Lee Duck Cleaners building," said Ab Chervinski, "Then the pool hall became the Wright's Bakery, and they did the baking right in the back. David Wright went on to become a big wig in the newly forming Social Credit Party."

As a 14-year-old going to the LCI, Mavis (Harding) Standing used to walk past the pool hall. "The pool hall guys would be hanging around outside, boys like Pete Larko, Matty Petros, the Homulos boys and others, and I'd hurry past there as fast as I could to avoid a confrontation. Right next door to the pool hall was Bing Wo, and later Jack Wong had a store in there."

### A Special Place

Just down the street from Circus Flats, along what is now Stafford Drive, was a place we called the Black Hill, an old coal mine slag heap, which was well away from the nearest wartime homes back then, and a place for day hikes and picnics, and war games and cowboys and Indians.

One of my 4th Avenue neighbours, Neils Kloppenborg, gave me a photo years later he had taken of boys playing on that slag heap, and those boys certainly could have been any of our gang - me, Pete Maloff, Doug Sandberg, Bob Stevenson or maybe even Mel Willis and Marvin Tamava from those mid-to-late 1940s days when we hung together on 12th Street B North.

Pictured below are some young lads - these could be my pals and I at play.

# Churches *and* Schools

Religion has always found a home in north Lethbridge, albeit in a variety of Houses of God. Northsiders have always had a strong religious base, with an array of churches through the years, many denominations still maintaining a presence in north Lethbridge.

There was a strong Catholic presence from day one, due mainly to the heavy influx of central European coal miners, part of the Roman or Greek Catholic persuasion. With the influx of English and Scottish miners the Anglican faith established a strong north side presence as well. Naturally there were many other denominations and church buildings sprang up not only along 13th Street, but throughout the North Ward.

Church buildings date well back in North Lethbridge, and though it was just a boarding house, Rev. James Robertson didn't mind conducting the first Presbyterian Communion in north Lethbridge in Nov. 1885. The boarding house was located on what was known as the Bank Head Road, an old driveway to Stafford coulee.

In this book we are looking at the Churches which were established along 13th Street, with an occasional detour, but the focus always remaining on 13th.

Here is a brief glimpse at some of the other denominations, by no means an all-inclusive list, but one giving an idea of how many different religious groups have located north of the railway tracks, especially in the early years of the North Ward.

There are records of a Greek Catholic Church at the No. 3 mine, back in 1906 and St. Peter's and St. Paul's was established across from St. Basil's School in 1922, said to be the second Catholic Church built in the city.

Rev. C. B. McKinnon established a Baptist Church on 5th Ave. in 1909 and in 1910, under John Fozard, a Baptist Mission was started at the same location.

Rev. W.W. Bryden held sway at a Presbyterian church meeting in the Redding Hall at 1315 5th Ave. N., with the first service held in 1910. Westminster Methodist Church, under Pastor Alfred A. Lytle, was established on the corner of 8th Avenue and 13th Street in 1912.

By 1918 Rev. Charles M. Neve had a Pentecostal Mission at 1723 5th Ave. N. In 1976 the Norbridge Community Church, operated by the Evangelical Church of Canada was established in North Lethbridge.

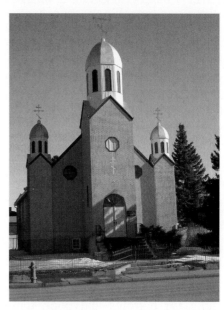

Ukranian Greek Orthodox Church at 13th Street and 7th Avenue North.

In 1936 Rev. Bidault was the parish priest at the Catholic Church in Hardieville. The church was later pulled by a Caterpillar tractor, owned by George Stank, and moved to Coaldale under McAdoo and Van Horne Moving. Unfortunately the church caught fire and burned while still parked along the roadside after the move.

Through the 1940s the Gospel Hall's doors were open to worshippers at 205 13th Street.

The Parish of St. Vladimir's Ukranian Catholic Church, an impressive structure readily visible from the Crowsnest Trail as it passes over 13th, first appeared at 715 13th back in 1955. The Jehovah's Witnesses established themselves in 1960 along 13th Street, their Kingdom Hall sitting at 125 13th. The Witnesses moved to a new Kingdom Hall, at 1510 Stafford Drive North on the corner of 18th Avenue, about 1986.

The Buddhist Church has long held a presence on the corner of 13th Avenue and 13th Street. The Buddhists have been established in the city for more than 50 years.

In 1978 the Church of Christ purchased the old Bethel Baptist Church at 716 23rd St. N., under direction of its minister, Jim Chapman. In 1979 the Park Meadows Baptist Church was dedicated Nov. 18 under Rev. Merrifield.

In 1985 the Hungarian Presbyterian Church was to be found at 10th Avenue and 10th Street North.

About the only church which didn't head north in those early days, at least with a building of their own - this is prior to the 1960s - seemed to be the Church of Jesus Christ of Latter-day Saints, the Mormons. After holding meetings for some time in the gym of Wilson Junior High in the early 1960s, the church built a chapel along 23rd Street North, creating a home for the North Lethbridge Ward in 1967.

"When I was in Grades 2, 3 and 4, we kids went to Primary classes in the old Westminster School," Alvin Bissett said about the early days of the LDS Church in north Lethbridge. "Later we used the United Church hall for our meetings. We also went to the United Churches for Mission Band, similar to the LDS Primary, a little Sunday school type thing during the week. As well, the Church of the Nazarene was just east of the York Hotel and we'd even go there during the week, to watch movies from Africa and other countries about their missionary work and we didn't have to pay to get in. We'd go to these other churches for entertainment and to learn about them, and we received a well-rounded education. Remember, there was no television back in the 1930s."

St. Vladimir's Ukranian Catholic Church has been on 13th Street since 1954.

There were, and are, many other denominations, fellowships, Reformed churches and Bible groups which met on the north side through the years. My memories now deal mainly with the churches along 13th Street North.

Former Lethbridge Herald Managing Editor, Bill Hay, who ruled the editorial roost when I first joined The Herald in 1957, wrote an extensive history on churches in Lethbridge, back in 1966. Most of his three-page feature dealt with the first established churches in Lethbridge, all of the originals on the south side, though some were along 2nd and 3rd Avenue South, relatively close to the north side devotees.

He wrote of the co-operation among many of the early church leaders and the sharing of congregations, men like Presbyterian Charles McKillop, Anglican E.K. Matheson, John Maclean of the Methodists, and Father Van Tighem, Catholic.

It was 1886 to 1888 and the North Western Coal and Navigation Co. was offering church lots to the various denominations where buildings quickly sprang up.

Miners would often attend services conducted by Rev. W.P. McKenzie, a Presbyterian, held in the Stafford home in the Oldman River valley. Van Tighem also celebrated Mass in the Stafford home.

August 1885 saw the first service held on the prairies, above the valley floor. It was a Methodist service held in the billiard room of the original Lethbridge Hotel.

Having worked with Bill Hay for decades, and having high respect for the late editor, I feel no qualms in stealing from his epic in The Herald. "It was Oct. 11, 1885 that John D. Higinbotham, pioneer druggist and the city's first postmaster, conceived the idea of a Sunday School, and this really marked the beginning of the Presbyterian Church in Lethbridge," my old mentor wrote. "One month later the first Presbyterian communion service was taken by Rev. James Robertson, who later became the superintendent of missions for the west. The service was held in the Boarding House, situated on the old driveway to Stafford's Coulee, north of the CPR tracks."

There you have it, the church has headed north.

All the first church buildings went up south of those tracks, however soon the Presbyterians, Methodists, Roman Catholics, Anglicans and Baptists were establishing themselves north of the tracks. Early in the century the Greek Catholics had a building near the No. 3 Mine.

In 1907 a board meeting in Wesley Methodist Church dealt with establishing a north side Methodist church. The Methodists bought the Greek Catholic building, and some lots along 13th Street, at the corner of 5th Avenue.

"The opening of Westminster Methodist Church took place May 10, 1908, Rev. James Allen of Toronto preaching in the morning and a student, Alfred A. Lytle in the evening," Hay wrote. "At the annual conference held that year in Medicine Hat, the newly-ordained Lytle was stationed as pastor of the new church in north Lethbridge."

In 1909 a subscription of $1,850 was raised to build a parsonage, just to the rear of the church along 5th Avenue. The grand old home remained until 1960 when church expansion created the need to tear the parsonage down.

Hay spared no words in praising another Herald employee, the business manager John Torrance, who dedicated himself to the youth of the church via the Westminster Sunday School and creation of The Hustlers, a church group for boys encompassing religion, sports, music and other activities.

By 1916 war was raging in Europe, but Westminster Church was decorated for the Christmas program all the same. In the early hours Christmas Day, a Sunday, an overheated stove set the church ablaze. In a very short time the congregation was without a home, though most of the furnishing had been saved from the fire. St. Andrew's Presbyterian Church, now established in north Lethbridge two blocks to the north, invited their Methodist brothers and sisters to join them in worship.

"It was June 1917 when the two congregations became one under the ministry of Rev. E.J. Hodgins," writes Hay. "This was the forerunner of church union which was to see these two denominations, right across Canada, united in 1925. The church became known as the North Lethbridge United, and following the national union, First United Church."

First United Church as it was in 2004.

During the years together, even before officially coming together under the United Church banner, the women of the two churches had worked hard for the Red Cross during the WWI years. With the union the Ladies Aid continued to serve, changing their name in 1925 to the Women's Association. At the time there were two groups, a Junior and Senior Association. In 1962 the name changed to the United Church Women, combining women's association and the missionary society, dating back to 1917.

With the Depression of the 1930s and declining membership, it became difficult to maintain the church building and hall, now refurbished, along 5th Avenue. In 1937 the 7th Avenue church was sold to the Roman Catholic Church, and soon sold again, becoming the Eagle's Hall, which was torn down in 1966.

The church prospered at 5th Avenue and 13th and, on Good Friday, March 31, 1950, a new sanctuary was added to the First United corner. A few years later an even larger addition took place, and the once new sanctuary became the church hall.

In writing of the Presbyterians, Bill Hay said the move was fathered by the Knox Church congregation of South Lethbridge, and in 1909 Rev. Walter W. Bryden was named to work on the north side.

"The people gathered in a building known as Redding's Hall (1315 5th Ave. N.), where services were held," writes Hay. "Later, Bailey Street School was used, located at 16th St. N., near 5th Avenue. A church building was started in the spring of 1911, erected by voluntary labour (at 13th Street and 7th Avenue North with seating for 400). The old Scottish style of architecture was followed and featured the pulpit over the entrance and pews facing the front of the church. The new structure was named St. Andrew's."

The building was there and ready for the fire-razed Westminster Methodists in 1917.

In 1922, a second Catholic Church was built in north Lethbridge, St. Peter's and St. Paul's, a Greek Catholic Church on the corner of 12th Street B and 6th Avenue. The old building has undergone many additions and face lifts and still serves the community today.

## Strong Catholic Presence

In 1901, a third of the northside residents were Roman Catholics, while the entire city at that time was one third Presbyterian.

The large Catholic numbers on the north side are certainly the reason behind St. Basil's School opening in 1914, and the fact the North Ward had a Catholic Cemetery dating back to 1889, when St. Patrick's Cemetery was consecrated on June 22 atop the rolling coulees on the southwest edge of Staffordville. Property for the cemetery, at the west end of 6th Avenue was donated by the North Western Coal and Navigation Co., and was reserved for Catholic burials - except for a small corner in the back northwest corner, on a downward slope, reserved for Chinese residents of the city. The early names were written in Chinese.

St. Patrick's Cemetery was associated with St. Patrick's Parish, the first in this area of southern Alberta. Likely the most prominent names to be found in the cemetery are some of the men who died in the Coalhurst mine explosion of Dec. 9, 1935.

Many of the markers in the older sections of St. Pat's Cemetery are wooden, most of them long gone and many of those remaining are unreadable. The old section was known as the miner's cemetery to most of the people, and many of the inscriptions were in European languages. During a clean-up of the old cemetery in 1961 the Lethbridge and District Oldtimers Pemmican Club, and Room 21 of Hamilton Junior High, erected a monument between the old and new sections of St. Pat's in memory of those laid to rest prior to 1910.

## A New Church on 13th

St. Basil's Church, on the corner of 13th Street and 6th Avenue North celebrated its 50th anniversary in 2000.

"God, our father, We thank You for 50 golden years of celebrating Your love in St. Basil's Church. We ask You to continue to bless and protect Your faithful people who dedicate their lives to serving You. St. Basil, who cared for those in need, pray for us." This prayer was written in 2000 by the Grade 4A students at St. Basil's School to recognize the half century of St. Basil's Church.

The church, along with the school about two blocks to the west, was named for St. Basil, who lived from 329 to 379 A.D. Basil was one of 10 children and went on to become the Archbishop of what is now south-central Turkey. He led the fight against the Arians, who claimed Jesus Christ was neither divine nor eternal. Basil was known for never surrendering. He was always moving forward and demonstrating that perseverance is just another word for success. Sainthood was bestowed long after his death.

During its 50 years, St. Basil's Church has been home to seven priests, the first being Father Michael Harrington who went on to become the Bishop of Kamloops. Father John Dunbar was his successor and he was followed by Fr. James Killen. From 1966 to 1971, Fr. Gaston Marien made his home at St. Basil's, replaced by Fr. Edward Flanagan, who stayed until 1984 when Fr. John Maes arrived. In 1989 Fr. Inno Cambaling was the director of the parish and in 1995 Fr. Eric Nelson arrived at St. Basil's. "His Excellency Francis P. Carroll, Bishop of Calgary, blessed and laid the corner stone for the church," said Betty Gal, a life-long member of St. Basil's Parish. "The building has certainly changed through the years, with new lighting, the side altars were changed, the basement has been renovated, offices added to the north side of the building, the stained glass windows cleaned and replaced, the stairways were expanded and the church has been made handicap accessible, with ramps and an elevator. If those beams in the sanctuary could talk they could tell you a lot of stories."

Other members of the anniversary committee included John Cicman, Jenny Feher, Mary Ellen Johnson, Yvonne Kunyk, Lilliane Lastuka, Val Lazzaretto, Diane Lewicki, Marlene Makel, Bernice Pavan, Helen Ruston, Susan Storey, Jacquie Stroud, Helen Tendler, Anna Travaglia, Cathy Whelpley and Helen and John Zajac.

Gal said the church has had two brushes with disaster, in regards to fires, but believes divine intervention stepped in, because nothing happened. One of the altar boys was lighting candles for the Blessed Sacrament and the wax from the burning candles dropped on the table cloth below and started smouldering.

"Father Marien smelled the smoke and came out to see what it was," Gal said. "The boys were busy lighting the other candles and didn't notice it, but

Father quickly got things under control. At Easter, in 1999, a server placed a candle too close to a potted lily and the paper around the plant caught fire. But someone saw it and it was put out. It must have been divine intervention both times because nothing came of either fire."

St. Basil's has dominated the corner of 13th Street and 6th Avenue North for more than half a century.

Along with the physical improvements through the years the church has undergone changes in other areas, including no longer saying the mass in Latin, formation of the Knights of Columbus and the addition of girls as altar servers. "It was during Father Maes' time the altar girls have come in. He said it was okay because he couldn't find enough boys for the job. Today, there are more girls than boys," said Betty.

That first service in 1950 was a special, serene experience, as well as a chilly one Christmas Eve 1950, when the faithful parishioners of the not-yet-completed St. Basil's gathered for the first Midnight Mass in the new building. The roof was almost completed. It wasn't solid enough to keep out the chilled drafts or even the snow.

"There were huge, wet snow flakes coming through the roof, descending like angels upon the people," said Gal. "The choir had to protect their song sheets from the snow. It was a special night."

Construction had begun in the fall and by Christmas the top floor was on and the roof finished enough for the Mass to be held. People had to stand, all except the elderly, because there weren't enough seats.

"Not one person left before Mass was over, despite the snow flakes which fell like angels and then quickly disappeared when they landed," said Gal.

Father Michael A. Harrington, from Blairmore, officiated at the first Mass, assisted by ushers Art Dorigatti, Mike Mudrack, Cyril Filchak, Tom Sobuliak, Steve Salansky, James Lynn, John Chumik, Alex Currie, Joe Arisman and Mike Petrunia.

Now a north side landmark, St. Basil's was home to 1,260 members in 2000, not too many more than in 1949 when serious discussions began about building a church. The property was acquired and building of St. Basil's Church began.

Until the building of the church, St. Basil's school was often used for Mass for resident north side Catholics.

"Before St. Basil's Church was built we were under the jurisdiction of St. Patrick's, on the south side," said Gal, whose father Steve came to north Lethbridge in the early 1930s to work in the coal mines, later to farm and then work for the city. "A priest would come north once a week and hold Mass in St. Basil's School, but we were always walking over the 9th Street Bridge to church at St. Pat's."

Gal attended St. Basil's School, which went to Grade 8, whose teachers included Sister Sylvester, Sister Mary Margaret, and Alberta Clarke.

Once it was decided a north side church would be built a committee was struck, headed by contractor Art Dorigatti, also a parishioner, along with Irvine Bruchet, Andy Gyulai, Steve Vaselenak, Lawrence Filchak, Andy Yanosik and James Lynn.

When that first Christmas Mass was completed the workers took over again and by March 10, 1951, a year to the day the parish was officially formed, regular service began in the new church.

---

**Among Those Who Served**

Past presidents of the men's society included Art Dorigatti, Tony Yackulic, who spent many years with The Lethbridge Herald, John Babick, Lou Troman, Jack McCallum, Joe Skrukwa, Fred Sparks, Bill Jackson, Victor Credico, Con Van Buuren and Joe Chenger.

---

"The church was built by the parishioners, in all kinds of weather, pounding every nail," said Gal. "The bricks were laid by the men of the church too, and it was all done under the direction of Art Dorigatti. The ladies of the parish cleaned the church. Dennis Rosetti said his father and brother would threaten to throw him off the roof when they were building the church because Dennis wasn't pounding nails fast enough."

The only delay came when a railroad strike held up the arrival of the bricks for the upper section of the church. The members raised money for the building and one of the special projects, carried out mainly by the women, was hoeing, trimming and topping sugar beets on nearby farms. The money earned went directly to the building fund.

"John Babick would pick the women up, and some men too, and drive them out to the beet fields to work," said Gal. "They went out in any kind of weather, and it was hard work."

The blessing of the church took place Sept. 20, 1951 and in July the church bell, named Our Lady of Lourdes and Fatima, had been blessed.

A special memorabilia display for the anniversary included a 1923 Catechism and an 1898 Hungarian Prayer Book. Parishioners also created a 50th Anniversary Quilt, in the shape of a church, with a rising sun in back. The quilt panels were made up of a series of symbols, and formed a peak on the roof to symbolize the seven sacraments. Symbols included the cross, fire, a lily, three joined triangles for the Trinity, the sun, a fish, the staff of Jesus the shepherd, and keys, symbolizing Christ is the key to the kingdom of God.

"The quilt has the church name and the years the parish has existed sewn into it," said Gal. "The symbols were added to embrace our Christian faith and they represent what we believe as Catholics."

St. Basil's Church serves as a history of the members of the Catholic faith of north Lethbridge. Many prominent city and northside business people, including construction contractor Art Dorigatti and retailer Nick Supina, called St. Basil's home, as did city alderman and educator Steve Vaselenak. John Hegedes, a two-time Emmy Award winner, in 1996 and again in June of 1997, for sound editing, was also a St. Basil's member.

"All of the Alberta Ranch Boys band were members here," said Gal. "Remo Baceda was our choir master for many years, and Curly Gerlock, Buck Waslovich and Joe Horhozer all sang in the choir. The only Ranch Boy who wasn't in the choir was Lou Gonzy, but he was a St. Basil's member."

The Alberta Ranch Boys date back to 1937 and were heard nationally on radio for many years and played a big part in the early days of television in Lethbridge, with the first TV station being built in north Lethbridge.

The society of men began in 1951, with 42 members and helped cater to many of the annual events, from the church carnival, held in an open area adjacent to the north side of the church, and now a small shopping plaza. Even we Protestants were welcome at the carnivals. It was a great place to spend your nickels and pennies as a kid. It didn't seem to matter what your religion was, it was simply an event on 13th Street, and everyone was welcome.

"They were the forerunners of the Knights of Columbus, No. 1490, and were the backbone of the church," said Gal.

"They were the men's group for the parish. The Knights of Columbus 1490, a Catholic fraternal service organization, has always been active in our parish. They serve as ushers, Eucharist ministers, readers, greeters and altar servers and as coffee hosts after the morning Masses. They sponsor breakfasts and are an integral part of the parish."

The Catholic Women's League is also very active at St. Basil's and in 1950 instigated the beet field work to raise money for the building of the church.

"They took anyone in the parish who was able to work the beets," said Gal with a laugh. "If you were standing still they grabbed you. They were formed in 1950, on a motion by Sue Demers and seconded by

Helen Sobuliak. Mary Parfitt was the first president. She was 104 years old when she died in 1996."

Mary Parfitt's husband Maurice helped create Henderson Lake Park, back in 1911, with a pick and shovel and a lot of elbow grease.

Mary, who was born May 2, 1892 at Pincher Creek, died just a handful of days short of her 105th birthday. She was one of Lethbridge's pioneer school teachers, serving many years at St. Basil's School, and at her death was the last surviving member of a family of 17.

"Mother taught many grades at St. Basil's and was my teacher in Grades 3 and 4," her daughter Alice Thom said shortly after her mother's death. "She was also the first president of the St. Basil's Catholic Women's League, and was there when they built the church."

Besides Alice Thom, Mary's daughters included Kathleen Wilkinson, Helene Byrne, Francis Webb, Geraldine Parfitt and Jock Carpenter a longtime director of the Interfaith Food Bank. She was predeceased by son Maurice in 1922. At her death, in 1996, Mary had 38 grandchildren, 50 great-grandchildren and 10 great-great grandchildren.

## Others had an impact as well

"The history of a church is a history of its people," said Fred Bosma, who as a 15-year-old, was part of the forming of the First Christian Reformed Church in Lethbridge.

Called in the Dutch language by a small one column by one inch advertisement in The Lethbridge Herald, about 25 Dutch immigrants met March 13, 1949 in the old YMCA building on 4th Avenue South in Lethbridge.

The driving force behind creation of a church within the city was Rev. Peter John Hoekstra of Nobleford, a man who also left his mark on Christian Reformed Churches in Brooks, Taber, Medicine Hat, Vauxhall, Calgary and Lethbridge.

The official organization took place Nov. 9, 1950, under the direction and leadership of the Nobleford and Iron Springs districts. Early services were held in the Dutch language until about 1954.

"P.J. Hoekstra, who accepted the call to become what we call a home missionary, was the father of the whole thing," said Bosma, whose father Andrew and mother Lankje, along with his two brothers and three sisters, were part of the original church in the city.

"The first services were held in the old Y building, and from there we moved around the corner when more people came, buying the old Christensen Funeral Home, just north of the back of Southminster United Church, and next to Trimble Tires. By 1953 we had outgrown Christensen's, which the church had bought for $14,000, and we built on the north side, just off 17th Street, where we stayed until 1991."

The north side church was built through volunteer labour, under direction of Chris Withage, one of the founding members and a foreman for Oland Construction at the time.

"There were so many volunteers they sent some of them home," said Bosma.

Pastor P.J. Hoekstra.

Hoekstra served the Lethbridge congregation for two and a half years, preaching his final sermon in January, 1953 before being transferred to Calgary.

In 1991 the church went through troubled times, with a large percentage of the congregation breaking away from First Christian Reformed over doctrinal differences. The smaller group left the north side chapel and for a while met in the auditorium of Immanuel Christian School.

"Then we bought the small church on 8th Avenue and 14th Street North," said Bosma. "The spirit of the church is best expressed when you have togetherness. It seems when a church becomes large it becomes impersonal. Through the years the strength of the church, by and large, has been expressed by the women. It has been amazing, they are the backbone of the church. Women sense instinctively a need in a family, or in another woman; they are the soul of the church, the very fibre of the church. Through the 50 years it is remarkable the role they have played in the heart and soul of our church."

> "The amazing thing about the building of the church here was the people were poor, but whatever they had, they shared. They'd come to church for the morning services, eat lunch together and stay for the afternoon services."

From 1949 to 1954 at least 400 families from Holland made their way to southern Alberta. One of those was the Bosma family, Andrew and Lankje and their six children.

"Many of the families came from the cities of the Netherlands to work the sugar beets of southern Alberta, with no clue at all about farming," said Andrew's son Fred. "All mainly came to work in the sugar beet fields, as labourers. Some of the farmers sponsored the immigrants, with a guarantee of a minimum of a year, but they liked you to stay for two. In those days you hoed beets and topped them by hand. Man, it was manual labour. We first came to work for a family near Coaldale. We all worked the fields; my family were all beet workers."

At the time the Dutch people were coming into the area there were three Christian Reformed Churches established, in Nobleford, Granum and Burdett. There was no church in Lethbridge. Pastor Hoekstra saw the growing need for a First Christian Reformed congregation in the city, feeling the post-war immigrants were in need of spiritual guidance and strength. The initial idea was to gather all the new immigrants from Holland together.

The people coming into the south had survived the Great Depression and then the Second World War which ravaged their country. They were coming to Canada looking for a dream. Part of that dream was the need for their church to follow them. Bosma's father, like many others, had been part of the underground resistance during the war, harboring Jews and assisting downed Allied fliers find their way back to Britain.

"These people had gone through a decade and a half of strife and war, and I think a lot of them were spiritually disillusioned at the time," said Bosma, a retired teacher with Immanuel Christian School. "They were asking themselves, 'what have all these difficult years really solved?' A lot of them were following a dream, period. They had a rosy picture in their minds of opportunities here when they came, but it didn't always work out. One man had been an accountant, a bookkeeper, in Holland and had no clue at all what a sugar beet looked like. It was a hopeless cause for him. After a year, many moved on from the beet fields, to Calgary, Edmonton, or the lower mainland and Vancouver Island."

A poster in the foyer of the First Christian Reformed Church on 8th Avenue somewhat sums up the feelings of the new arrivals: "We cannot become what we need to be, by remaining what we are."

Rev. Andrew Joosse is the First Christian Reformed pastor now, one of many stalwart pastors the church has enjoyed through the years. Rev. D.J. Scholten followed Rev. Hoekstra, and was the first to live in the parsonage next to the new northside church. Following him were Rev. Andrew Kuyvenhoven, J. Vriend, L. Mulder. P.W. DeBruyn, J. Tuininga, James Joosse, and Rev. Stewart.

The Christian Reformed Church in North America started in Holland, Michigan in 1857 and included a seminary and college in Grand Rapids, Michigan, where Bosma later earned his teaching degree.

The first congregation of the church in southern Alberta was formed in Nobleford and Monarch 100 years ago, in 1905.

In 1904 Dutch immigrants were moving into southern Alberta, around Granum and Monarch, the year before Alberta became a province.

Some of the early families coming in included the Withage, ter Telgte, Emmelkamp, Venhuizen and Feller families. With help of the congregation from Manhattan, Montana, a church was established in Canada, and Sunday, May 14, 1905, the first congregational service was conducted at the Postman home in Monarch. On May 20, 1909, the First Christian Reformed Church in Canada held its initial services in its church in Nobleford.

## A Dream Fulfilled

In September, 1962, Immanuel Christian School opened in north Lethbridge, just west of Stafford Drive and north of 5th Avenue. Opening day saw three teachers greet the 63 Grade 1 to 5 pupils to the new school. As each year passed a grade was added and in 1966 the first Grade 9 class graduated.

In the fall of 1971 a kindergarten program began and in 1976 through 1978 Grades, 10, 11 and 12 were added, one grade each year, making Immanuel Christian a bonafide high school.

Henry Heinen, a past administrator at Immanuel Christian School, said most Christian Reformed Churches established in southern Alberta also formed localized Christian school societies, with the express aim of starting Christian day schools for the children of the church. Groundwork for a Christian School Society for the church was laid in the mid 1950s.

"The church councils usually never got directly involved but certainly were encouragers to get the ball rolling," said Henry Heinen. "Many of the early immigrant pastors were in the forefront of this movement and became directly involved in helping to organize the school societies and write the constitution. It is to Pastor emeritus Andrew Kuyvenhoven's credit and strong vision that he was instrumental in getting the school societies of Granum, Nobleford, Iron Springs, Taber and Lethbridge together to have them start thinking about joining forces and starting one school, together, in Lethbridge. Not all the people were of one mind. Some favoured strongly to start a Christian High School while many, if not most, of the more recent immigrants favoured an elementary school, with possible junior and senior high expansion in the future."

Below: Immanuel Christian Schools into another construction phase in 2003.

Heinen said there was a high school society in existence at the time, which owned property in the Wal-Mart area. Iron Springs also owned property in Picture Butte and even had a building moved onto the site, so were reluctant to join with Lethbridge when the school opened in 1962. They did join in 1963 however, and their children came into Immanuel Christian that fall, in year two of the school's operation.

Under Pastor Kuyvenhoven, the Society for Christian Education in Southern Alberta was formed and registered, a constitution written, debated and adopted. In May, 1958, property was purchased, about six acres, from the city for $11,000. About a year later a bid of $8,000 was made to purchase an old building off the Commonwealth Air Training Base at Claresholm. It was rejected. But, in April, 1961, the bid was upped to $13,276 and was accepted.

The Constitution and by-laws of the Society were incorporated under the Societies Act, July 31, 1961. Heinen said further amendments were adopted in 1968 to accommodate the Canadian Reformed people in and around Coaldale.

"This group formed its own local school society and was guaranteed membership on the Board - main board it was called - and the Education Committee," Heinen said. "All other local Christian Reformed Churches also retained their own local Christian school societies and each society was guaranteed a minimum of two members on the central or main board. That system is still in effect today, with Lethbridge having four board members."

The first chairman of the Board was L.F. (Bert) Konynenbelt of Nobleford, who served from 1961-1964 and again from 1977-1982.

The board's first priority was acquisition of a school building, and the bidding process began on the Claresholm air base structure.

"This was a structure consisting of two wings, containing 10 classrooms and deemed surplus by the federal government," Heinen said. "With our bid accepted in 1961, the society now owned a building, but it was 40 miles west of Lethbridge. Actual moving cost, as quoted by the mover, was $7,000.

"There was public criticism in Lethbridge, via The Herald, about city council allowing an old building to be moved in. Some considered it an eyesore. But the building was moved to its present site and connected with a central, flat-roofed addition housing the furnace for the east wing, staff room, kitchen, principal's office and bathrooms. Volunteer labour was used to complete 'construction' of the new school. There was a lot of enthusiasm and hard work to effect this vision, as the people struggled to establish themselves in a new land. They built their homes, their churches and their schools, in that order. They were convinced that is what the Lord expected them to do because of what they believed as Calvinists, promised at the baptismal font, when their children were baptized, and the pastors preached the need for Christian day schooling from the pulpits."

Heinen said the new school, even though it was the old H-wing, was concrete evidence of a vision of faith put into practice, "and the people felt blessed, that so soon after immigration after the Second World War, their venture of faith was on its way."

The doors were opened in the fall of 1962 with three teachers, John and Marilyn Nieboer - John being the first principal - and Trix VandenTop.

"The building filled up more quickly than anyone could have anticipated, with the addition of the junior high grades through 1963 to 1965. The combination classes soon became single classes and during the 1966-1967 school year all rooms were used, one being the library," Heinen said.

In 1975-1976 a six-room, senior high wing was added to the west of the junior high wing and in 1977-1978 another large addition was added, including a regulation gymnasium with full basement, home economics facilities, a band room and eight classrooms. The next year, the first grade 12 class graduated. In the fall of 1995, the original old H-wing was replaced.

## The Little Church on 12th St. C.

St. Mary's Anglican Church dates back to the active coal mining days before 1910. Many miners, who had come from England to work in No. 3 mine, lived in Little Wigan and sought out an Anglican Church, close to their homes. They found a home in a small building in the area of 9th Avenue and 13th Street.

St. Mary's began as a mission in 1906, but before the mission hall's construction, backed by several prominent St. Augustine's members, Anglican services were held in the home of Mr. and Mrs. George Moore. The first building, designed to hold 75 people, was located on the southwest corner of 9th Avenue and 12th Street North. The first services were conducted by lay readers, one of whom was Ben Martin, a founder of Martin Bros. Funeral Home.

Below: Peaceful tranquillity of St. Mary's Church.

In 1910 the church building was moved to the southeast corner of 6th Avenue and 12 Street C North, where it still sits today. Very soon a new church was built next to the original, with the first services held in December, 1912. The original chapel became the Parish Hall.

The first vestry was elected March 28, 1910. Rev. W.V. McMillen divided his time between St. Mary's serving as rector of St. Cyprian's Anglican parish on the south side, before it merged with St. Augustine's. With the growth of its congregation, plans went ahead for a new St. Mary's Church, with C.R. Matthews one of the key planners. Rev. C.H. Popham succeeded Rev. McMillen and remained with the congregation until 1916.

Avice (Frayne) Anderson remembers the windows of the church as having red, yellow, blue and green panes, but a big hail storm in the late 1920's broke most of the glass.

"Gone were the beautiful colours when white glass replaced the shattered panes," she said. "The ladies of the parish, the Women's Auxiliary, helped with church work and the young girls joined the Junior Women's Auxiliary. I was a member of the Juniors. In January, 1928, I was given a Bible which was inscribed: Presented to Avice H. Frayne by the St. Mary's Women's Auxiliary for perfect attendance and good conduct during the years 1926, 1927. It was signed, January, 1928, W.T.H. Cripps, Rector.

"Mrs. Taylor was the lady who directed our activities. We put on plays and held 'Teas' to help raise funds to buy accessories for the church. As I grew older, I attended the Anglican Young Peoples Association. Around this time the Parish Hall was enlarged when a kitchen and a stage were added on the east end. Now there was room to put on plays and the WA Ladies were able to hold suppers. They were well attended as I can attest."

The church had a bell in its bell tower, with a long rope hanging down. This bell was rung to let everyone within ear shot know services were about to start. "Oh, how I had longed to give that rope a pull!" said Avice with a laugh.

When Thanksgiving approached each year members of the congregation decorated the church for an annual Harvest Festival. Sheaves of wheat and oats, corn, pumpkins, and many other vegetables, as well as large lumps of coal, were place near the front interior of the church.

"The pulpit was decorated with bunches of grapes by Mrs. Swingler, a task she did for many, many years," said Avice.

St. Mary's was the oldest church in the city still serving the same religious denomination when it closed its doors in 2004.

## A Special Presence

For more than half a century the Buddhist Church has been part of the north Lethbridge history.

The book *Kishiki-Nikkei Tapestry,* a history of Japanese Canadians in this area, details not only the history of the Buddhist Church but of the Japanese people themselves and their contributions to the culture in this area dating back to the Second World War.

A meeting of 30 Buddhist faithful was held in December 1948 in the lunchroom of the Broder Canning Co., the first such meeting since the war's end.

For the next little while the church was struggling to find a permanent home. The first Obon service was held July 31, 1949 in the Rainbow Hall and on Jan. 31, 1950, the first Hoonko service was held at the Labor Temple Hall.

Buddhist presence along 13th Street.

On Nov. 19, 1950, a meeting in the chapel of Christensen Funeral Home established the Lethbridge Bukkyo Fujinkai and Suma Uyemura was elected president. March 10, 1951, Rev. Shinjo Ikuta, Rev. Yutetsu Kawamura and the newly-appointed nisei minister Rev. Ensei Nekoda led a service in the Rainbow Hall. By May 1952, it was decided to raise funds for a permanent home. After purchasing the land at 1303 13th St. N., construction began in September 1952, with some key funding through a mutual financing association. There was also a carnival at the Civic Sports Centre, raising more than $1,000 for the Building Fund, and a second carnival was held May 19, 1953. Lord Abbott Kosho Ohtani of Nishi-Hongwanji performed the sod-turning ceremony for the new building Nov. 9, 1952 while visiting Lethbridge during a North American tour. The shovel he used has been encased and is displayed in the guest room in the church. Jan. 30, 1955, the first service held in the new building was the Ho-onko service, though the church was still under construction.

"April 1, 1956, the members held a special commemoration service, Kyosan Hoyo, for the completion of the building with an 'engei kai' (variety show) afterwards," translator Masako Kikuiri said in the book. "Remarkably, the congregation did not borrow a large sum of money to build a church. The fact is, except for specialty trades such as plumbing and heating, the work was done almost exclusively by volunteer labour, the memory of which, is still held in great respect."

A temple shrine was ordered from a Kyoto butsudan maker, arriving in the fall of 1957.

By February 1962 a 1,320 square foot addition was completed. In September of 1964, the Lethbridge Japanese Language School became affiliated with the Lethbridge Buddhist Church.

March 19, 1972, the Kyosan Hoyo Service was held to commemorate the 25th anniversary of the church.

Through the years the church underwent many changes, as a church, and even extending to giving up its popular food booth at the Lethbridge Exhibition in 1988, all detailed in the tapestry book.

A memorable moment for the church occurred in 1984. In 1982 Rev. Kawamura retired, and two years later he was appointed a member of the Order of Canada, honouring his pioneering work for Jodo Shinshu Buddhism in Canada.

In 1992, the Lethbridge church and Fujinkai hosted the Annual General Meeting of the Buddhist churches of Canada and the 10th annual Buddhist Churches of Canada Women's Conference, another landmark for the church. The 13th Street church received a boost in 1992, when the Picture Butte Buddhist Church closed its doors and the 44 members joined the Lethbridge Buddhist Church.

As Kikuiri writes in the *Kishiki-Nikei Tapestry*: "The members were secure in the knowledge that despite all the strife and tribulations, the church was strong enough to survive and even prosper . . . Throughout the 1980s and 1990s, the Lethbridge Buddhist Church enjoyed a period of stability and continuous growth."

## They Were United

It was at a board meeting held in Wesley Methodist Church in November 1907 when the idea of holding services north of the CPR tracks was first discussed. Early the next year arrangements were made for the purchase of a Greek Catholic church building near the No. 3 Mine site, and some lots on 13th Street and 5th Avenue were secured.

Westminster Methodist Church opened May 10, 1908, Rev. James Allen of Toronto, preaching in the morning and a student, Alfred A. Lytle, at night. Later, at the annual conference in Medicine Hat, the newly-ordained Lytle, was named as pastor of the new church in north Lethbridge. To facilitate the new minister and his wife, a parsonage was built in 1909, along 5th Avenue - the new First United Chapel, built in 1960, sits on the spot, along the alleyway, where the parsonage once stood.

First United Church, at least the structure, has had a varied history. It started life as a coal mine building and was converted to serve the congregations of three different churches for the first half century. The original old wooden structure finally fell to the wrecker's ball in September 1960.

The hall was a church sanctuary from 1908 to 1951 before switching to a Sunday School room, the Boy Scout Hall and gathering place for church plays, concerts and youth activities. To the back of the building was the manse, or home for the minister, and it too fell in 1960 as a massive rebuilding project took place.

It has been a long and intricate history for First United Church.

Below: Excelsior Male Choir, 1913 - Though many names are lost to history, at the top, second from left is Jim Jaemeson and next to him is Billy Lamb and Alec or Bob Johnson, who ran the Red and White Store. In the middle, second from the left is one of the Gurr boys and in the front, second from left, is the druggist W.H. McCaffrey, Rev. Frances, and on the far right William Stott.

Just across the alley from the manse was the home of Tom Wardman. Like most of the Wardman family he was a longtime CPR engineer, in those early glory days of steam.

In 1908 the hall, then sitting along 6th Street and 9th Avenue North, was purchased from one of the north Lethbridge coal mine sites and moved down to the corner of 13th Street and 5th Avenue. All this for a cost of $1,055. A sign was added to the building, declaring it the home of Westminster Methodist Church. The congregation gathered each Sunday, to sit on planks strung between kegs and boxes, and it had a platform and a pulpit up front. The same year painting and repair work took place and benches and chairs were set up so the people could intently listen to Rev. Lytle. In 1909 the manse was built for the good reverend, at a cost of $1,850.

One of the members of the congregation back then was Mrs. Robert Kergan, Annie Laurie, mother of Bill Kergan, and still active in the church when the restoration took place in 1960. Another of those early members was Clara King.

All was well, until Christmas of 1916 when a fire destroyed the front part of the church, leaving the congregation without a home. At the same time, the Presbyterian Church, just to the north on the corner of 7th Avenue, had no minister, so the two congregations came together in 1917, moving into the old St. Andrew's Church on 13th Street, just past Galbraith Street, and calling themselves North Lethbridge United Church.

The first congregational meeting of the United Church of North Lethbridge was held May 18, 1917 at St. Andrew's Church. More than 200 people were on hand to hear Rev. Ferguson, Superintendent of Missions for the Presbyterian Church from Calgary. It was the initial meeting of the combined Knox and Wesley congregations.

In the 1920s the church had an active Canadian Girls In Training program, known as CGIT, and the group included Phylis King, Mona Walton, Martha Kergan, Marjorie King, Verna Gray, and was overseen by Rev. T.O. Jones.

Shortly after, in 1925, the United Church of Canada was formed and the church took on the name, appropriately so, of First United Church. They sold the St. Andrew's building in 1937 and moved back to the old hall on 5th Avenue and 13th, which had been restored and was being used as a meeting hall. During an anniversary celebration in 1937 it was noted that a feature of the ministry of Rev. Francis was the Men's Own organization, which met every Sunday afternoon, as the men sang lustily and listened to inspiring addresses.

"We went to First United when I was young," said Cammie Randle, 91 at the time, and a former choir member at First United. "But I was baptized at St. Andrew's, which was where Martin Brothers is today. Those two churches later joined up to be First United. I also remember going to many a United Church picnic in the summer out at the Experimental station."

In 1950 a new sanctuary was built and the old hall became the Sunday school and youth hall. The minister wasn't forgotten either, and in 1958 a manse was acquired at 1105 14th Street North.

The new sanctuary, built in 1961, went up where the old manse and hall once stood, and the 1950 sanctuary addition followed the footsteps of the old hall and became the Sunday School and activity hall.

Below: Award-winning First United Church Choir of 1927 included, in front, Nora Jackson and Janet Larson. Second row, from left: Mrs. Soady, Mrs. Delay, William Stott, director Mrs. Fred Jackson, Rev. King, Mrs. McIlvena and accompanist Ethel Larson. Third row, from left: Fred Jackson, Annie Laurie Leitch, Susie McIlvena, Margaret Jackson, Molly Walton, Hilda Morris, Blanche Olander and Nigel Hall. Fourth row, from left: Joe Lackenby, Olive Jackson, Mona Walton, Grace Livingstone, Erika Olander, Edna Olander, Lorraine Christie, and Wilf Pearson. In back, from left: Norman Taylor, Arthur Jarvis, Mr. Taylor, John Rae, Jim Livingstone, Jim Goldie and Fred Delay.

CGIT group of 1921, with Emily Mitchell second from left, an unknown girl, Elizabeth Stott, Mary Mitchell, Mona Walton, unknown, and Rev. T.O. Jones.

A fine example of the 1930 Hustlers of First United Church.

First United choir leader for many, many years was Lily Jackson, and Ethel Larson was the organist. In 1937 the choir earned three shields at the 1937 Lethbridge Music Festival, which pleased Rev. Irwin a great deal. Among the choir members were Nig Hall, Fred Jackson, Blanche Olander, Jean Taylor, Marie Cameron, Belle Riley, Daisy and Lucy Hunt, Elvina Wright, Kay Cowell, Mona Walton, Janet Larson (the school system's music teacher) Lorraine McIlvena, Annie Laurie Kergan, Peggy Kergan, Nora Jackson, Grace Livingstone, Janet McIlvena (who conducted the school music radio broadcasts), Joe Lockenby, Jim Jamison, Joe Lowther (who had carried on his singing from the Westminster school choir) John Rae, Jim Livingstone, Arthur Jarvis and Tom Smith. Often, Nig Hall, Mona Walton, Gerdina (Dena) Cole and Arthur Jarvis would combine for a quartet presentation.

"Lily Jackson was the choir director, and it seemed she had the job forever," said Elizabeth Stott, whose father William always took the role of Santa Claus in church productions. "Fred Jackson supported his wife very much. She always put on a Christmas Contata as a fundraiser and her choirs always went to provincial festivals and Fred was always there to assist. He had won a car in a raffle and we used to go to choir things in that car. In those days, when the choir went on trips to Calgary or Edmonton, they had to drive over dirt, and later gravel roads, not pavement like today."

Elizabeth's parents used to be part of the Westminster Church adult Bible classes before the church became First United.

And speaking of singing . . . First United's new church chapel, 1950s variety, was the site of my one and only public singing appearance. It seems the choir was putting on a special concert and I was in about Grade 7 at the time. They were seeking volunteers and I volunteered to sing, with friend Laurence Jones. Now Laurence was a great guy, but the blunt truth is he sang as bad as I did. The only thing you could say for our rendition of Jimmy Boyd's "Tell Me A Story" was, we did know the words. Being a church audience, therefore having Christian standards of forgiving, they applauded at the end. I dare say, because we were finished they were clapping - with joy. Later at home, my mother, a 50-year veteran of the First United church Choir, took me aside. She explained it was nice to volunteer, but under no circumstance was I ever, ever, ever to sing in public again.

Many of the same 1937 choir names could be found in the First United Sunday School class of the early 1920s, taught by Miss Andrea Matson, a well-known north side name. Students included Isa Stewart, an aunt of mine and mother of the Dorren boys, Ron and Bryan, of electrical business fame in this city decades later, and others like Elizabeth Jarvie, twins Bessie and Nina Seargeant, Marjorie Anderson, Elizabeth McNab, Chrissie Horne and Elizabeth Morris.

From the outset the church took aim at youth and John Torrence, a young newspaper man, was set apart as a missionary to the youth of north Lethbridge. He dedicated himself to excellence from the day

51

Westminster Church opened. Under his direction the Sunday School became one of the model Sunday Schools in Alberta with the achievements of his youth Hustler classes legendary.

"I started with the Hustlers about age 10, but they ranged up to ages 20 and even 22 and 23," said Nap Milroy, who was a Hustler in 1934 and 1935. "My brothers Robert and John were in the older group and I was with the younger boys. It is hard to explain what the Hustlers were, but it was done through the church and old John Torrence was the original organizer. It centered around Sunday School and sports. They met on Sundays, apart from the church, and it wasn't a Sunday School class in the real sense."

It was 1929 when a group of young boys were officially organized into a Sunday School class to be known as the Hustlers. By 1939 The Hustlers numbered close to 100. John Torrence was the founder of the boys' club, under direction of First United Minister Rev. W.H. Irwin, but Torrence had been working with the young boys since the creation of the United Church.

Such was the devotion to the groups that Alf Bartlett, a charter member, recorded a consecutive record of eight years of perfect attendance in Sunday School. Other early Hustlers included Robert Anderson who went on to become a Boy Scout leader with First United in the 1950s, James Hunter, Peter Ribalkin, Jack Lakie, George Mansen, Norman Cruickshank and Robert Raikes.

"We went to Sunday School every Sunday because, if you missed a Sunday, you couldn't play basketball or soccer during the week," said Andy Allison, who at 93 at the time of the interview, was the oldest living Hustler. "Our basketball team included Bobby Dunlop, Bill Christie, Joe Lakie, myself, Theodore Wilson, Ivan Thompson and Bumpy Allan . . . he only had one leg. Hod Seaman was one of the referees, and he was a bug man (insect research scientist) at the Experimental Farm at the time. John Torrence helped teach us basketball and every church in town at that time was part of the league, along with the YMCA."

The league was sponsored by the Inter-Church Athletic Association, with six teams.

---

**Welcome Mr. Premier**

In 1931, none other than the Premier of Alberta, J.E. Brownlee, graced the Hustlers' anniversary banquet head table, and the boys prepared a short ditty to welcome him:

Welcome Mr. Premier, how do you do?
Proud to have you here with us, honoured too,
We're very glad you've come our way,
We hope you'll come some other day,
The Hustlers sure will welcome you.

---

Even into the new century, one of Andy's most cherished possessions was a small gold medal, from the 1925-1926 league championship game. In the game

they beat Knox Church 18-17 and he said he scored 17 of the team's 18 points. He even recalled, with some relish, how they held the LDS team to a mere four points in one game.

Torrence used to say the idea behind Hustler sports was every boy had the opportunity to play, and he'd select a variety of sports. In 1930 Robert Armitt, Herb Hamilton, Jim Martin and Norman Cruickshank, wearing the purple and gold of the Hustlers, ran in The Herald-YMCA Road Race, with Robert finishing fifth. Runners like Ernie Holberton, Wally Anderson, Mark Lowther, Jack Russell, Don Marshall and Joe Lowther were among the many others who brought pride to Torrence and ministers like James Whitmore.

The Hustlers also walked south, to the YMCA, on a weekly basis for gymnastics, dodgeball, and swimming.

Top swimmers of the 1930 included Alf Bartlett, Art and Richard Smith. The boys also participated in softball and baseball and for the non-athletes there was a club orchestra.

The focus of the Hustlers, of course, was religious training, and perfect attendance was recognized each year. As well, Bible Study tests were important and in 1930 boys like Lloyd Bruce, Norman Cruickshank, George Mount and Jack Lakie were among the leaders.

John Torrence was called the father of the Hustlers, said Bud Belle.

"John always said, if anyone of the boys needed someone to talk to they could come on down to The Herald and see him there. He was quite a guy," said Belle, who came to Lethbridge, and the north side when he was 12 years old. "The Hustlers were a Sunday School group mainly, coming together for special dinners each year, attending Sunday School and participating in sports, and they even had an orchestra. We would go to Sunday School in the church hall on 13th and 5th Avenue and then march up to the church on 13th and 7th for church services."

Below: Popular First United Quartet of Arthur Jarvis, Dena Cole, Mona Allison, and Nig Hall.

Belle said the Hustlers had several sports teams and would go to places like the YMCA to play basketball. "A lot of us didn't have money for the Y, but maybe it was John Torrence who paid for us to be at the Y, he was that kind of guy. His idea behind the Hustlers was maybe to keep the boys together, to keep them off the street by giving them things to do. I don't know when the Hustlers ended, but I think it was the war years that broke things up."

When asked what the Hustlers should be, one of the boys said a Hustler should be clean-minded, a good sport, should study the Bible, and attend Church and Sunday School. Another felt the Hustlers should be known as a bunch of helping, willing boys.

Torrence himself told the Hustlers they "had the greatest thing we can enjoy together - the friendship, and spirit of helpfulness brought about by a common purpose." Torrence went on to say he enjoyed being with the young, calling them the real people.

He put a lot of emphasis on perfect attendance, and gave yearly awards to those who never missed a day.

At the 10th anniversary in 1938 he praised Alf Bartlett, an original Hustler who, as a youth and as a leader, had eight years of perfect attendance.

Sports was another emphasis of the Hustler program, and in 1937 the junior football club won the city championship, with players like Ken Tilly, James Sloan, Robert Anderson, Steve Pedersen, Frisco McCormack, Jim Campbell, Alex Marshalsay, Sid Whitman, Jack Tennant, Andrew Moodie and others. There were runners like Robert "Scotty" Armitt, Herbert Hamilton, James Martin and Norman Cruickshank, hockey players, including future world champion Lethbridge Maple Leafs: Hec Negrello and Nap Milory and inter-church basketball stars. There were boxers too, including Jim Culver.

Bud Belle, born in 1915 and a Lethbridge resident since 1927, was a Hustler, and a northsider. He remembers walking the old wooden boardwalks up Little Wigan as he passed the Saxon, McNeely, Hackett, Sumner, Webb and More homes along 13th Street.

"I remember the trains that ran across the prairie from the main yards along a spur line up to the No. 6 coal mine," said Belle. "That train caused many a fire on the prairie as the coal-burning steam engine travelled right up to Hardieville. We used to walk to Galbraith School, way out in the middle of the prairie.

There was an old Catholic Church northwest of Galbraith, all by itself on the prairie. We'd walk past Miners' Park on the way to school and duck in through the fence to smoke before going on to school. I went to Galbraith, my kids did and even some of my grandchildren have gone to Galbraith. Straps were popular back in my day, and I recall two boys who skipped school to hop a freight, and when they got back to school, boy did they get that strap."

Living in the heart of coal miner's homes, including neighbours like Mike Douglas who went on to become one of the city's top golfers and Ed Bruchet of junior hockey fame, Belle was conscious of the plight of the miners. He remembers the fateful night in December 1935 when the Coalhurst Mine disaster hit.

"We hung around Matt's taxi all night listening to news of that sad event," he said.

Belle also remembered funny times, like when a bunch left the Miners' Library after a night of beer drinking and carried off the Library's outhouse, leaving it in a field. He also remembers the horse-drawn barrel-shaped wagons, with covers on the top, that came in the night, the drivers cleaning out the outhouses in the back of each yard.

Fire hit the small Westminster Church on Christmas Eve in 1916.

"Through heroic efforts much of the furnishings were saved but in a short time only the four walls were left standing," Herald Managing Editor Bill Hay wrote in his story. "The congregation was without a church. In response to an invitation from St. Andrew's Presbyterian church, two blocks to the north, Westminster joined with them in worship and they, being without a minister at the time, Westminster's Rev. J.B. Francis ministered for the next months to the joint congregation."

During the Great Depression the church moved into the old Westminster hall, which had been salvaged from the fire, and the St. Andrew's Church sold. In 1939 it was sold to the Roman Catholics and it was subsequently sold again, becoming the Eagles Hall.

Even back in 1922 the First United Church Choir was an award-winning group. In front, from left: Mrs. Leitah, Mona (Allison) Walton, Martha Kergan, and Olive Jackson. Middle row, from left: Mrs. Martin, Mrs. McKay, Jean Lakie, Erika Olander, leader Mrs. Fred Jackson, unknown, Janet McIlvena, unknown, Mrs. Jones, and Mrs. Hoult. In the back, from left: Blanche Olander, Bob Hume, William Stott, Mrs. McIlvena, William Hoult, Jim Goldie, Rev. T.D. Jones, Fred Jackson, Nigel Hall and Eva (Hargreaves) Hall.

## Vassey's School

St. Basil's School went up in 1914, between 6th and 7th Avenues on 12th St. B N., just a block north of my grandfather's house. While I attended Galbraith - for a month and a half - and later Westminster and Wilson, because St. Basil's was literally part of our play area, I was quite familiar with the grand old brick structure, and in particular caretaker Joe Szabo who used to put the run on us from time to time when we were messing around too near the building and not on the soccer or ball fields. I got to know the school's long-time principal quite well, Steve Vaselenak, also a prominent city alderman for many years, who lived immediately across the street from me on 4th Avenue in the 1950s and 1960s. He was born Oct. 15, 1908, the youngest boy in a family of 15, son of Michael Sr. and Anna Vaselenak.

Vassey, as he was known to everyone, and wife Emily were great folks and she and Steve had three children, Dianne, Delbert and Joan. Emily was a long-time friend and care-giver to Grace Dainty in her later years. Miss Dainty was the city's first school nurse, from 1917-1929, and rode her bike, dressed in her nurse's uniform, to and from city schools in the 1920s and 1930s. Miss Dainty also operated a maternity hospital on 15th Street, at 239 in 1910 and 244 by 1913, and a general hospital from 1918 to 1923, the only one ever on the north side. She was also matron of the children's shelter in 1905 and was a registered nurse at the Galt Hospital. She retired about 1932, but continued to care for those in her neighbourhood. Upon her death she left $50,000 to the school board, and a generous donation to St. Mary's Anglican Church. Miss Dainty died, at age 97, in 1975.

Steve Vaselenak had a long association with St. Basil's School.

A Grade 1 student in the fall of 1914 was Emil Stephen Vaselenak. The six-year-old had started

school at St. Aloysius Convent in south Lethbridge, but in late November was transferred to the new St. Basil's, where he stayed for 56 years. He'd walk over to St. Basil's from Staffordville, often taking shortcuts under and between the railway coal cars along the spur line between the school and Staffordville. In later years Vassey said about 50 families lived in Staffordville, three quarters of them of Slovak origin. St. Basil's main core of early students came from the Staffordville area.

Steve came to St. Basil's as a teacher in 1928, and by 1932 he was principal, and was still in place for the school's 50th anniversary in 1964, finally retiring in 1970. Before becoming a teacher at St. Basil's, Vassey was one of the first students, in Grade 1 under the guidance of Laura Roy.

You could say St. Basil's consumed Vassey's life. St. Basil's first principal was Mother Mary Edith of the order of the Faithful Companions of Jesus.

In 1933-1934 the staff included Vassey, of course, Mary Parfitt, Edna Mae Bernard, Alta Flock, Margaret Lacey, Telita Comessotti, and Marion Clarke.

In 1946 Vassey showed his versatility as he coached the St. Basil's boys to the senior football championship with the team including the likes of Howie Yanosik, who went on to a long career in pro hockey, a future Lethbridge Native Son hockey star Steve Arisman, and a future city Fire Chief, Lawrence "Nobby" Dzuren.

Alberta Clark, who would go on to run a riding stable near downtown Lethbridge, taught at St. Basil's from 1933 until her retirement in 1973. A lover of music, her Grade 4 class won the Bowman Shield four times during her tenure.

Like all schools of the era - Galbraith, Westminster, Central, et al - St. Basil's had high ceilings, stairwells on each side of the main hall, tall windows, and varnished wood floors, and an upper level gym. Naturally back then, especially in north Lethbridge which was the heart of the coal mining community, it had a coal fired furnace.

The school turned out some of the city's finest, including at least five students who went on to become priests, and the likes of L.S. Turcott an Alberta District Court Judge, former Lethbridge Herald City Editor Mel Hinds, many a school teacher and principal, and athletes like George Rodzinyak and Johnny Vaselenak.

Vassey was principal of St. Basil's until he was replaced by W. Ruff in 1970. But the old educator didn't walk away from education, making his debut on the Separate School Board in October 1971, serving as chairman of the board in 1977, 1978, and 1979, his final year of continuous service on the board.

St. Basil's, which allowed north side Roman Catholics to forgo the walk to St. Aloysius Convent School on the south side of the tracks, was the first separate school in north Lethbridge, opened Nov. 29, 1914. The next, St. Paul's on 12th Street A and 11th Avenue, wasn't built until 1954, at a cost of $111,623 by Bird Construction.

Principal Steve Vaselenak surrounded by one of his early classes.

St. Basil's was Steve Vaselenak's private domain, having a presence in the school from the time of its opening as a student, through becoming a teacher then becoming the principal in 1932 at age 23 to his 1970 retirement. His teaching career began in 1928, at $1,000 a year.

---

### How'd She Do It?

Speaking of my friend Stan Romaniuk, his sister Irene was something we never could understand as school-hating youth of the day. In 1948, Irene received an award for perfect attendance, and never being late for school, not even once, and never being absent while attending Westminster from Grade 1 through 8, 1940 to 1948. And, to make matters worse, she never missed a day at the LCI either. That's 12 years perfect attendance. My friend Stan did not live up to his sister's standards.

---

Vassey was proud of his Slovak ancestry, which tied him in with many northside originals. Twenty Slovak families arrived in north Lethbridge about 1895, the men heading for the coal mines. Writing a special article for The Herald in 1985, Vaselenak pointed out his father, Michael Vaselenak, had been sent to Pennsylvania to recruit miners.

"These 20 families formed the nucleus of the Slovak Community established later, adjacent to the No. 3 coal mine. It became known as Staffordville. Many of their descendants still live in Lethbridge and area and many worked in the mines, some at 14 years of age, and one I know of at age 12. Some pioneers took out homesteads before Alberta became a province in 1905.

"Some of these early (prior to 1900) pioneers were: Andrukovich, Begalli, Chumik, Dorchak, Duda, Dudas, Grisak, Hanisko, Homulos, Kosko, Lagurski, Luchanski, Maras, Morris, Negrey, Olshaski, Pahara, Petras, Kohut, Kotch, Kostelnik, Petrunia, Pisko, Popson, Rebar, Rossecki, Slovinski, Staysko, Seaman, Sweda, Stetz, Supina, Yackulic, Yanosik, Yorko, Zemani, and Zuback.

"Their children attended St. Aloysius Convent and later, when others came from Upper and Lower Slovinski (villages) in Austria, they attended St. Basil's School which welcomed its first pupils in November 1914. I was one of those pupils who transferred from the convent."

In those days the city's residents distinguished an area by ethnic origin and religion. Most continental Europeans settled north of the railway tracks while the British represented 80 per cent of the people living south of the tracks.

Though not on 13th Street, St. Basil's did play a major role in the lives of the North Ward. The soccer field offered us the opportunity to play baseball, soccer and even our north side version of cricket. It was also the place Joyce Sandberg learned to drive - almost. She managed to miss the goal posts, but climbed the small hill and hit the Sandberg fence after she shot through the goal posts, head down searching for the brake pedal.

The guys of the area, including our regular crew, and others like Roy Sandberg, Jack Reid, Tommy Wheeler, Stan Romaniuk, Mel Willis and Syd Slaytor used to play cricket, with baseball bats and tin cans for wickets. It actually became more popular than baseball for a time.

Frances Kaupp still has her report cards from her days at St. Basil's School, and is especially proud of the Grade 6 card, with almost all H's.

The Salansky family was one who benefited when St. Basil's Church was built, in 1950, and Frances was married there in 1952, to Clem Kaupp.

"The parishioners built a lot of that church themselves," said Frances. "My dad, Steve Salansky, hated heights, but there he was up on the roof. 'Someone's got to do it,' he said. He went on to join the Knights of Columbus and was an usher at the church as well."

## Westminster School

In the late 1880s the ratepayers of North Ward were demanding a school and finally, in Aug. 1891 the North Ward School was built in an area later known as 1315 5th Ave. N., about where the Moose Hall now sits. The school was for lower elementary kids and the older students still had to trudge south to Central School, built in 1896.

The new North Ward School was heated with a central pot belly stove and drinking water was ladled from an old 10-gallon whiskey barrel. The barrel was replaced by a 10-gallon beer keg in 1898 and filled twice a week by the Hyssop Brothers water wagon as it travelled along its residential route in north Lethbridge. Right outside the school irrigation water flowed past in a ditch which extended south past a blacksmith's shop, in an area destined to become the eastern edge of the Westminster School playground.

The North Ward School, a one-roomed edifice, was built in 1891, about where the Rainbow Hall stood. Today the Rainbow Hall is known as the Moose Hall. I recall a time back in the late 1950s when the Rainbow was to be the venue for a very important speaker, Tim Buck, the communist leader well-known in the Crowsnest Pass. Working at The Herald at the time, a bunch of us were talking about taking in the speech,

just to see what all the excitement was about. Reporter Joe Csaki however, came back into the composing room to warn us not to go. As it turned out, few others did, and the RCMP was on hand to take names and license numbers. I don't know if they mailed them south to Senator Joe McCarthy and his Communist witch hunt or not.

In 1942 and the following year as well, the Pemmican Club of Lethbridge welcomed in the New Year with their gala ball at the Rainbow Hall, the only time the ball has been held in north Lethbridge.

The North Ward School cost $1,050 to build and was designed for elementary-aged students. Senior high schoolers had to travel south, across the tracks. In 1905 a two-roomed addition was added to the original framed structure, but it was soon evident a bigger school, Westminster, was needed. By January 1906 Westminster was up and open, named for the street on which is stood, Westminster Street, which became 13th Street in 1912.

Avice (Frayne) Anderson, a lifelong city resident and historian, said Baroness Angela Burdett-Coutts was a shareholder in the North West Coal and Navigation Co. operated by the Galts - the towns of Burdett and Coutts are named after her. As well, her husband William Ashmead Bartlett was a member of the British parliament for the riding of Westminster. "Westminster Road was named for him," said Avice. "In 1905 the city decided to build a new school and C.H. (Charles) Harding sold Lot No. 37 to the School Board for a mere $225. He was my uncle and he owned the land from 13th to 15th Streets."

On the east end of the property there was a blacksmith's shop, which later was sold to the city, with the land, for the rest of the Westminster School grounds. The new school was a four room brick building and the bricks were probably made at the Brick Yard, as were the bricks for Central School.

Below: Stately Westminster and its Annex to the south in the early 1940s.

The Westminster Choir of 1927, was the best in the entire city for Grades 7-8 at the Festival. Front Row, from the left, Joe Lowther, Billy Bastien, and Cecil Swingler. Second row, from left: (standing) Dora Sloan, Margaret Dougall, Edna Good, Jean Milroy, Gladys Bateman the teacher and conductor, Mavis Harding, Avice Frayne, Ella Findlay, and Annie Whitfield. Third row from left: Hilda Gurr, Helen Kucheran, Margaret Leitch, Barbara Mason, Ella Trowhill, Florence Bartlett, and June Glanville. Fourth row, from left: Frances Bogusky, Dorothy McCaffrey, Freda Carter, Mildred Little, Ethel Ingoldsby, Mary Edwards, Edna Marshall, Alice Oberg, and Freda Moorhouse. In the back, from left, are: Gladys Kucheran, Annie Homulos, Edna Neilson, Annie Slemko, Margaret Alfrey, Jean Lynd, Peggy Parsons, Edna Gerbrandt, and Nellie Bowker.

Opening Ceremonies for Westminster School were held Jan. 2, 1906 and the first principal of the school was Harold G. Long, a Lethbridge Herald executive. He was with the school until 1907 and when he resigned R.R. Davidson took over. Then came Mr. Brandow, Mr. Ritchie, H.H. Bruce, J. Watson, C. Larson and William Wishart.

"The old North Ward School was sold to J.M. Redding for $800 and became known as Redding Hall," said Avice.

Westminster opened Jan. 2, 1906 at a cost of $9,750. Mayor George Rogers was on hand for the Westminster official opening, as was Harold Long, Dr. Walter Stuart Galbraith, a city pharmacist who was encouraged to become a doctor by Dr. Frank Hamilton Mewburn, the city's mayor from 1899-1905. Galbraith, who also served as mayor, in 1907, suggested a good motto for the new school would be "Integrity, Intelligence and Industry".

The event attracted pupils and parents, who took in the marvels of the imposing brick structure with its fine wood floors and wainscotting. The blackboards were called splendid, and the airy, well lighted rooms were the envy of parents who were schooled in much less ideal conditions. Those on hand were told only two rooms on the lower floor would be used and the second storey would be kept for future expansion.

An addition was added to the east side of Westminster in November 1909 and the gymnasium was built in 1911. Other editions followed in 1926 and 1957. Before the 1909 addition was completed on Westminster, another two-room wooden school was built along 5th Avenue A and 16th Street North. They called this the Bailey Street School because in those days the streets were named, not numbered. That school building was soon empty and was sold in December 1917 and moved to 13th Street and 7th Avenue where it became part of the Miners' Library.

The Bailey Street School was built in 1908 on the east side of 16th Street, between 5th and 5th Avenue A. to handle overflow kids and was used periodically as a school until 1914.

Hardieville School, at 3225 13th, was opened Jan. 12, 1912 to serve Hardieville students. The northern-most community was named for William Duncan Hardie, the city's mayor from 1913 to 1928.

"The Westminster gymnasium was a separate building on the southwest corner of the school ground right along 13th Street," said Avice. "It was originally used as a gym, but in 1922 it was partitioned to make two class rooms. Years later the building was leased out to the Lethbridge Collegiate Institute for a home economics class. Just down the street to the south, there was a wood-working shop, set up in a converted garage, for the LCI boys. In the fall of 1936 the building was still being used for home economics classes. Dick Burgman, of Burgman's Dance Hall, built that little building, and he also built his brick house which still stands on the northwest corner of 5th Avenue and 19th Street North.

"As I recall Burgman's Dance Hall was upstairs (in what became the McCaffrey Drug Store) and our St. Mary's Anglican Church group used to rent that hall for Christmas parties. The hall was also rented for a school room at one time. I know this because my brother George attended school there in 1922 or so."

In 1928 another addition was put on the west side of Westminster School, consisting of four classrooms and an office.

An auditorium was created in the basement and gone was the Teachers' Door, which Avice remembers racing to open, as young students, to have the honour of holding it open for the teachers. Imagine such a thing happening today!

It was March 1944 before the School Board purchased the extra land to the east for the playground and Charles Harding's brick house, at 1401 4th Ave., was demolished to make room for a larger play area for the Grades 1-8 students.

"Charles Henry Harding used to deliver coal, with a horse and dray, when he came here in 1888, and by 1906 was a city alderman," said Avice. "Philip Harding had a large blacksmith's shop on the property, and I have a picture, taken in 1914, with my mother and father Edith and Arthur Frayne in front, and at back there's the shop. The signs on the roof say: Plow Work by Sharp; Buggy and Delivery Wagons; and Auto Springs and Bodies."

"The blacksmith shop was originally between our house and Verna Gray's house and then they built a new shop on the property, along 14th Street," said Mavis (Harding) Standing, whose father sang in the United Church Choir about 1918. "It was about 1944 when we sold the entire property, with the house and shop on it, to the school division for the extending of the Westminster playground."

Another addition was built in 1956, extending the school eastward. It consisted of a music room and a gymnasium complete with a stage. The old basement gym floor had severely warped by this time, and in one corner looked like it had waves. The saga of Westminster and its changes finally ended in 1968 when the school and land was sold to make room for a shopping centre. Wednesday, May 1, 1968 the pupils were transferred a few blocks east to Wilson Junior High - now it is known as Westminster School.

Jake Walton, heading for the golf course.

Westminster was the first of the big schools built in north Lethbridge, an anchor on 13th Street for much of the first half of the century, opening its doors in 1906. It was a grand old school, much like the aforementioned St. Basil's. Every morning you answered the bell, lining up down the hallways, and up the stairs, all facing the main wall, with the clock, the flag and principal Jimmy Wishart holding court. We'd sing the national anthem, and often "The Maple Leaf Forever", and we'd recite the "Lord's Prayer" to start the school day off right. As a young Grade 1-2-3 student, lining up in that monstrously large school I was totally intimidated, so much so I was certain the words to the "Lord's Prayer" were really: "Our Father WISHART in Heaven, hallowed be Thy name . . ."

Jim Wishart's father, John, was born in Scotland in 1862 and came to Canada in 1906, with his three children. A fourth, Jim, was born in Lethbridge. John Wishart worked for the Hudson Bay Co. and later as a city weed inspector.

Jimmy Wishart was one of the few who taught me what little I know about spelling. He had some great little rules for those trick words.

I don't get principal and principle mixed up "because you must always remember, the principal is your pal."

Comfortable was easy: "Just think of two foreign movers at the door, telling you they've come - for - table". Lieutenant was a cinch using my old principal's system - "The landlord said to the renter, 'lie - u - tenant'. And then there's depot, where the cook on a train said to his helper, "Hand me de - pot." It was a cinch to spell with Jimmy.

My days at the school coincided with those of Jim Smith, the janitor, a fine, fine man. One of the earlier janitors at Westminster was Jake Walton. In 1939, a few years after my mother's death when I was in Grade 1 at Galbraith, my father later remarried, to Mona Walton, Jake's daughter, so my linkage to Westminster is a special one.

When recess came at Westminster, the bell saw the boys go out the front door, the girls out the south door, and never to cross the imaginary line on to each other's side of the school yard. The boys played softball every recess and noon before school. Now remember, Westminster was Grades 1 through 8, so the "big" boys always held sway. The idea was for one of those big fellows, like Ray Marnoch, Chris Ramage, Con Grisak or Joe Roadhouse to try to blast a home run over centre field and through principal Jimmy Wishart's window. It seems to me, I remember Ray Marnoch completing that awesome feat.

These were also the days, the 1940s and 1950s, when the school employed travelling teachers, like Miss Janet Larson who taught music - "sing the scales Garry, don't say them!" - art teacher Effie Reid, school nurse Miss Agnes Short, who for many years was accompanied by Dr. Edmund Cairns on school visits. She retired from medicine in 1975. Agnes was 78 when she died.

Born in 1916, Short lived for many years in the No. 1 firehall, her father being Fire Chief William Short. Agnes chose a career of nursing and in 1949 was the head nurse for the city's public school system, a position she held until 1964 when she became director of nursing for the health unit in the city. Her nursing days with the schools brought her in contact with the diseases of the day; diphtheria, polio, scarlet fever and tuberculosis. Besides nursing she had an interest in the Eastern Star Lodge, Southminster Church and the Lethbridge Horticultural Society.

The physical instructor was George McKillop. Naturally Mr. McKillop, a man with a soccer background, knew my grandfather, Robert Allison, a great soccer player and later trainer with championship Supina teams, so he expected me to play the game well. He'd seen my dad Andy, and uncles Bob, Alec, Jim and Stew all excel at the sport, now he had the next generation. Boy, was he disappointed.

George McKillop was the son of Rev. Charles McKillop, the city's first Presbyterian minister in 1886.

George McKillop served in the First World War and upon his return, with the rank of major, joined the Lethbridge school system as cadet and physical education instructor, a position he held for 42 years until his retirement in 1962. With his position McKillop travelled to Galbraith and Westminister schools, and the south side schools in the public system, directing the physical education program.

In 1965 he was named the city's Sportsman of the Year and was inducted posthumously into the Lethbridge Sports Hall of Fame.

One of the games we used to play in the Westminster downstairs gym, with its severely warped floor, was something called chicken fighting. He'd lay down mats - they looked like old army mattresses, or pally asses as my father called them - and then he'd line up two boys, usually a big one against a small one, and they'd hold their left foot behind their back, hop around on one leg, like a deranged chicken, and try to drop the opponent to the mat. It could be a hard-hitting affair and was much more fun than soccer.

One of the other positions universal to all city schools, Westminster included, was that of truant officer. Two in particular spring to mind, Bill Kergan and Billy Lamb. Walter Billy Lamb, along with George McKillop, was hired by the school board. I never did get to met Mr. Lamb, other than to have him pointed out on the streetcar by my mother, but grew to know and like Mr. McKillop. The other truant officer and I did become acquaintances however.

Billy Lamb died in 1948 and Bill Kergan was appointed the city's truant officer for both public and separate schools, a job he held until 1957. In 1904 Lamb was working on the railroad, as a conductor on the old narrow gauge line from Lethbridge to Coutts. Then came his days with the school board, and he held the position as truant officer from 1911 until his death. In the early days he would regularly show up at schools, or homes, on horseback. Along with his chasing down kids skipping school - in those early times most absences were because the parents kept the kids home to work - Billy Lamb was a Lethbridge Herald society reporter in 1906, and was a member of the City Police Force in 1926.

Bill Kergan

Bill Kergan and I visited many a time in regards to my not wishing to attend classes during the hours prescribed by the city. As well, I knew him from First United Church, kitty corner to Westminster, where he sang in the choir with my stepmother, Mona, her sister Molly and others like Nig Hall and Janet Larson. Kergan had a dramatic, deep baritone voice and his renditions of "Old Man River" and the "Lucky Ol' Sun", rendered in the church hall during a Saturday night concert, remain with me today.

Bill went on to serve the city well, as an alderman and a public figure fighting for the little man. He was a man I always respected and there is some irony in the fact that this man, who lectured me as an elementary school truancy afficionado, would become a relative long after his death. My eldest son Jason married Sherida Kergan, Bill's great-niece.

Bill resigned as truant officer in 1957, replaced by Albert Dickson, who was replaced by George Watson in 1961. Joe Lakie held the position from 1974 until the position's termination.

Recess was also taken up with an array of games, from marbles - our school's marble champion one year was Tuffy McLaren. If memory serves right Tuffy lost the city championship to Kai Yip, at the Civic Sports Centre, in 1952. This was before Kai, a two-time Canadian amateur boxing champion, saw the light and moved to 15th Street North - to Red Light-Green Light, and of course baseball on the smaller field, away from the big boys aiming at the principal's window. There was also a large playground area with a giant slide. After watching Dale Bastura fall off that slide and crack his head open above his eye, I could never make it all the way to the top, and had to back down the ladder against the stream of kids filing up.

Teachers like Mrs. Vaughn, Bokovoy, Kadlac, Glamack and Skully held court in the main school, while Mrs. Zeman's classroom, for Grade 3 students, was in the small building to the south of the big school, in a home ec building. This was the era of the strap, and Mrs. Skully had a neat little trick to encourage you to be on time - the last one into the classroom after recess, morning and noon, got a smack on each hand. She had an arm like a wrestler with all that exercise. I remember one time lining up for the strap from Mr. Wishart, likely for skipping school which is something I majored in, and I got the first laugh. He got the last. As the red-faced principal wound up for a mighty swing I pulled my hand back as the strap was about to make contact and he cracked himself a solid blow on his thigh. After some puffing and mumbling, he resumed his task, with my hand on the desk. There was no give and it stung twice as much.

Kai Yip, flanked by two other top north side leather throwers, the Brown brothers.

Westminster also had a school milk program, where those less fortunate were able to get a small bottle of milk each noon hour.

Lynn Davis (Easton) said "students who looked small for their age were given milk too. I remember one small, but feisty, girl who was very upset because drinking that milk every day cut into her time on the school's playground's equipment."

My family all worked, my dad as a bartender at the Dallas Hotel, my grandfather as a bartender at the Lethbridge, so I never did qualify for the free milk lineup, though I was small for my age. I did find myself in other lines though, like the yearly vaccination shots and for the mobile x-ray unit which would come around to check for tuberculosis. Those lines weren't nearly as good as the milk line. I remember one boy taking a look at the needle held by Dr. Cairns, assisted by Nurse Short, and collapsing right in front of me. He and I were both happy when, in 1952, Dr. Jonas Salk came up with the sugar cube-like tablet for polio, instead of the needle. And that TB x-ray was always a chilly experience, leaning against the cold glass, sans shirt, and outdoors in the mobile van, usually in the dead of winter.

School plays were a big thing in the 1940s and 1950s, and likely before and after. On one memorable occasion, a beautiful upper-grader whose name is lost to me forever, wearing a blue gown of course, wowed the Westminster-play audience with her rendition of "Alice Blue Gown".

I only spent six years at Westminster because they opened Wilson Junior High, just a few blocks east down 4th Avenue, when it was time for me to enter Grade 7. I never did get a chance to swing for the principal's window, though I doubt I'd have got the ball over the shortstop. One thing we did get at Wilson was something no other city school was getting at that time, hockey and skating at the outdoor Lion's rink, looked after by Mr. Paskuski, and swimming at the Lion's Pool. They were right on the Wilson school yard.

At Westminster we often played inter-school sports, be it soccer, hockey or fastball, and we'd all walk over to schools like Central or Fleetwood to play our south side rivals, or to the Civic Centre, packing our equipment, for the hockey games. The Music Festival each year - where I excelled in the choral speech section and stood in the back and moved my lips for the musical selection - saw us pack up all our music and such and march south, over the 9th Street Bridge, to Southminster Church.

In 1914, the Grade 3 class at Westminster, taught by Miss U.A. Flett, included Doris Stafford, one of the daughters of the original Staffords, one of the key families in the early days of Lethbridge. Other familiar names in that class included Leonard Shaw, Clarence McNulty, George Nibbs, Jim McGowan, John Riches, Albert Giles, Alfred Wescott, John Dougall, Edwin Skinner, Jim Kergan who was the brother of Bill Kergan later to become the school system's truant officer, Mary Walker, Agnes Jarvie, Sarah Cunningham, May Annetts, Ethel Dodd, Beth Wishart, Charlie Lewis, Alton Logan, Bessie Baird, Harriett Carter, Bessie Lange, Bessie Wilson, Eleanor Lindsey, Doris Jowatt, Annie Kerr, Ethel Larson, Iris Glanville, Barbara McDonald, Bill McNabb, Eric Cranston, Albert and Willie McEachren, Hugh Livey, Dick Coultry and Willie Emery.

Westminster had a reputation during the 1920s, for having quality choral groups, under teacher Gladys Bateman. The chorus was dominated by girls when it won the provincial shield in 1927, with only a handful of boys, including Joe Lowther, Billy Bastien and Cecil Swingler. Among the girls, with their white shirts and sailor collars were Dora Sloan, Hilda Gurr, Helen Kucheran, Jean Milroy, Margaret Leitch, Barbara Mason, Avice Frayne, Ella Trowhill, Mavis Harding, Florence Bartlett, Helen Findlay, June Glanville, Annie Whitfield, Frances Bogusky, Gladys Kucheran, Annie Homulos, Dorothy McCaffrey, Edna Nielsen, Freda Carter, Annie Slemko, Dorothy Little, Margaret Alfrey, Ethel Ingoldsby, Jean Lynds, Mary Edwards, Peggy Parsons, Edna Marshal, Edna Gerbrandt, Ruth Oberg, Helen Bowker, and Freda Moorehouse.

I've seen a picture, dated 1919, and the bright, smiling faces all belong to Grade 2 students at Westminster School.

In the first standing row, fourth and fifth from the left, are twins Betty and Nina Seargeant.

"Betty is the one with the curly hair and I'm the one next to her making goo goo eyes at the photographer," said 90-year-old Nina Kloppenborg with a laugh a few years before her death. "Betty's beautiful curly hair was the difference between us. My hair always looked like I was dragged through a hedge backwards. But we were extremely devoted to each other and we even had a type of ESP between us."

Many of the others in the picture have been lost in Nina's memory - almost. Though Nina remembers many of the names, she just can't match them with the faces as she once used to be able to do. She knows Ernie Pankhurst and Ron Peake are in the picture, along with Wilf Shreeves, Wilf Russell and Bill Kergan. Clarence Larsen, Ivan Thomson and Jim Stewart are also among the smiling little boys.

"All those boys were so mischievous, but I don't remember any being real trouble makers," Nina said. "A lot of them had nicknames, like Turkey Kergan, Goose Larsen and Chick Thomson. I remember in later years when the Thomson boy was up in a small plane and it crashed into the prairie, (in February 1931) across from the end of 12th Street North. He was killed. I remember how devastated we were, to have a boy from our class killed."

Nina (Seargeant) Kloppenborg.

Among the girls in the Grade 2 class was Isa Stewart, who worked for years at Eaton's and married Johnnie Doran. Another was Kathleen Donaldson, sister of Wilson and Addie Donaldson. Ena Davis, whose brother Laurie drove streetcar, was a short, dark haired girl.

On the male side, Ernie Pankhurst went on to serve the community as a butcher and store owner for many years, and Wilf Shreeves retired from a career in the Post Office. Bill Kergan, for whom the Kergan Centre is named, was also in the class.

"Betty and I were born in 1911, by the railway tracks, on Railway Row, where there was a long row of houses down by the old CPR roundhouse," said Nina. "Dr. Peter Campbell was in charge that night and mother said we were the first twins Dr. Peter delivered in Lethbridge. We never met another pair of twins until Grade 8 when Harry and Andrew Watson came in from

Picture Butte. Then it was special, two sets of twins in one class. We were born at home, with a midwife present. My mother said Dr. Campbell was removing his gloves and getting ready to leave when the midwife said, 'hold on doctor, there's another one here.' I was born a half hour later. We were always called Sooner and Later at home."

The Seargeant twins grew up on the north side, attending St. Mary's Anglican Church and Westminster School. Nina believes the Grade 2 teacher was a Mr. De La Maitre, a man who scared the wits out of the children. His students had to sit straight, with both feet under the desk. He was very strict, but she remembers him as a wonderful teacher.

"Our Grade 6 teacher in 1926 was Miss Agnes Kerr and everyone enjoyed her. In Grade 7 Miss Bateman was the teacher, a tall, angular woman and a fine music teacher. We loved singing in her class. One year she went to England for a holiday and she brought back a bunch of names of kids to write to as pen pals. Betty wrote to hers, Jessie Block, for years. Betty married Art Hostetter in 1934 and in 1960 they travelled to England and Betty met Jessie Block." Betty died in 1989, Nina in 2004.

Nina recalled a special school outing, about 1917 or 1918, when her school class was marched two by two south on 13th Street and across to the 9th Street bridge and onto the train station's large wooden platform to greet the Prince of Wales.

"We had our little Union Jack flags to wave at David, Prince of Wales, who was standing on a flatbed on the train waving back to all the kids."

Nina married Niels Kloppenborg on Christmas Day, 1941. They spent Boxing Day together and Niels returned to the Royal Canadian Air Force, stationed in Clinton, Ont., where he worked in the radar depot. He returned to Nina in March but the couple was then separated from March 1942 to the end of October 1945. Niels finished off the war with the RCAF in photo recognizance. His post-war work life was spent with the Dominion Research Station in Lethbridge. A lover of the violin, Niels played for many years in the Lethbridge Symphony Orchestra. He was also an avid outdoorsman and an accomplished photographer and was a long-time member of the Lethbridge Fish and Game Association. He operated the club's target range, near Pavan Park in the north end of the city's Oldman River valley park system, for many years before his death in 1993.

The school had earned a reputation as the 1930s began for its girls' basketball program, under Miss M.J. Carruthers. Her 1930-31 junior team included Jean Gogan, Nora Trenholm, Agnes Shorthouse, Helen Jooreas, Greta Sundquist, Ethel Bartlett, captain Elaine McIlvena, Bessie Gardiner and Hazel Bodgener. The Galbraith School Cup-winning seniors of 1931-32 included Isabel Arkinstall, Winona Taylor, Jessie Tulloch, Lillian Smeaton, and Trenholm, Jooreas, Bartlett and Gogan off the junior team the year previous.

Old Westminster School had a smaller building on the south end of the property and in 1924, when Avice (Frayne) Anderson was in Grade 4 it was known as The Gym, and served as a gymnasium when Avice and Nina Kloppenborg attended Westminster in the 1920s. In later years the building served as a classroom, and among the classes there was the Grade 3 groups of Mrs. Zeman in the late 1940s and early 1950s.

In her book, *Where Was It? A Guide to Early Lethbridge Buildings*, Irma Dogterom said the Physical Culture Building - home to Mrs. Zeman's classroom as far as I was concerned - was built in 1912 as a proposed school drill hall. Sometime within the next 18 years, a boys' technical arts education program was held in the building and by October 1934 girls from the LCI were spending a half day a week there, for domestic science instruction - cooking and sewing I guess.

"I attended Westminster from kindergarten to Grade 8 and the school only had eight classrooms," said Avice. "It was filled to over-flowing and even the gym (the Annex) had to be used for two classrooms in 1923 and 1924, with Miss Flynn's class in the west half and the Opportunity Class, with Mrs. Cameron, occupying the eastern classroom. When the annex became the domestic science department it was complete to the last word. The boys' section was well equipped with anvils, a forge, a machine shop and woodworking room equipped with a motor-driven lathe. Things went very well until World War I broke out in 1914. Then, due to financial conditions, classes were cancelled in the spring of 1915. Some of the equipment was sold and the rest was put in storage. The building then became the High School, and was later named Bowman School.

"It was not until the fall of 1934 that restoration of the boys' technical and girls' domestic service course took place. Where to hold them? The LCI had no room to spare so the school board looked around and found some buildings in north Lethbridge. A building along 13th Street which had been used as a garage was rented for the boys' workshops. Equipment purchased in 1912 was brought out. The girls held their classes in the old gymnasium for a while, or as it was then called the Westminster Annex."

The boys studied motor mechanics, woodworking and electricity.

At least one of the two rooms in the old annex building had become a classroom for an over-crowded Westminster by the time I was in Grade 3, in the very late 1940s.

North side resident Bert Bosch, whose son Clark went on to become principal of Winston Churchill High School in 2004, said the Technical Arts building stood north of where Gergley's Glass sits today, and he remembers Fred's Barber Shop being across the street and down a bit because that's where he got his red hair cut.

"He (Fred) was an old war vet, from the First War, I believe," said Bosch. "Our teacher was Doc Liebe and his son Chuck was in our class. Chuck was later killed in an airplane crash. Larry Cook, the Post Master's son, was also in our class. This was about 1948 and I was in Grade 8 at Westminster. I remember the lights in the building were hung by chains, those fluorescent lights. We had brass tags with a number on them, and when you checked out a tool you left that tag with your number in its place. We had just about all the wood-working tools, the big sanders, planers and lathes."

Bosch said he headed south for high school, which was still in Hamilton School then, for Grade 9, but still came back over to the arts building for shop. They'd walk over once a week for the class.

"I believe they taught everyone in town in those two buildings back then, the girls in one, the boys in the other, all for different classes. Shortly after the LCI opened and had its own shops, the arts building closed. Dr. Liebe went over to LCI to teach wood shop."

Elizabeth Stott was proof positive the technical school wasn't for boys only.

"I went to the wood-working shop along 13th, taking night classes from Dr. Liebe," she said. "I had a friend who made a table and I wanted to be able to do that, so I went to the shop. Dr. Liebe took the end table I made, to see if it was plumb, and he picked it up and tapped it on the floor, and the whole thing collapsed. He felt so bad he cut me out another table, but I never finished it. That was in the 1940s, when I was teaching at Bowman School."

Right: - A view of the newly built Westminster School, overlooking some of the homes it served.

This LCI Tech Class of 1945, a lot of them northsiders, walked north from the LCI to 13th Street North for tech program classes each week. Front, from left, are: Andy Andreachuk, Ernie Afaghanis, Alvin Bissett, Gord Pankhurst and Ted Venables. Next row, from left, Arian Pontarollo, Bill Myers, Bernard Charles, and Ray Pascal. Third row, from left: teacher George Watson, Frank Aiken, David Hogg, Charlie Cockerill and Brian Wardman. In the rear are: Charles Walkniotz, Syd Holberton, Walter Dietrich and Dan Kearney.

Anyone who ever spent time near Dr. Liebe will never forget some of his favourite lines: "Smoosch, smoosch, like a baby's bum!" when referring to a finished wooden creation, and the best of all, "No smoking in the pee pee!"

The Tech served the high school boys five days a week.

For Alvin Bissett it wasn't much of a walk, just over from 419 12th Street B, and Brian Wardman was just across the street from him.

"Sometimes though, we had to go to class at the LCI and then walk back to the tech," said Alvin. "Tech was five days a week, either in the afternoon or mornings. There was electricity from Mr. Ryder, mechanics from Forester and wood-working from Dr. Liebe. The tech was there as early as 1934 that I know about and until the LCI built its own shops with expansion in 1952 or thereabouts."

The old technical building was at 319 13th and was replaced by Victory Equipment, which pulled out in 1958 for a large Mo-Tires expansion.

Alvin's sister Audrey attended Westminster and walked across the school yard to the girls' vocational school where Verna Gray was one of the instructors. She learned cooking, housekeeping, sewing, how to make a bed, ironing and other household chores during her years at the vocational school.

"I remember we did things like sewing, like how to make an apron, and other things like that," Audrey said.

When I was in Grade 3 at the Annex building it had two separate rooms. It was in one of these rooms we used to sit as a Grade 3 class and listen to Janet McIlvena with the school radio broadcast each week. McIlvena, in whose former home Nina Kloppenborg lived in the late 1940s and early 1950s, was one of the city schools' music teachers and had a radio show in

the 1950s, Sing and Play. These Alberta School Broadcasts were listened to by students in the classroom, including Mrs. Zeman's Grade 3 class, of which I was a member. The building came down when Westminster itself was torn down in May of 1968.

Verna Gray, who lived at the east end of the Westminster school yard, was a school teacher, receiving her public and high school education in Lethbridge and graduating from Normal School in Calgary.

She was employed by Lethbridge School District No. 51 for 47 years, 32 as a Home Economics instructor, many of those years in the small annex at Westminster and later at Wilson Jr. High School.

Gray and McIlvena belonged to the same women's social club, which met at homes of its north side members for more than 50 years. Also part of the club were Mona Allison (Walton), Nessie Knox, Dorothy Wardman, Ethel Gruenwald, Mary Webster, Blanche Lang (Olander), and Bertha Davies. A visiting member was Molly Walton (Gronberg), Mona's sister who lived in Whitefish, Montana. The Club met at members' homes each Tuesday night for more than half a decade and for breakfast every Easter.

In a 1989 letter, Kathleen Brown (Ethel Gruenwald's daughter) remembers how the club members were known as "The Girls", and the link went into the second generation, with one of Kathleen's early playmates being Joan Wardman, Dorothy's daughter.

"Verna Gray taught me home economics," Kathleen added. "We used to live at 329 12th St. B and Bertha Davies lived just behind us. I remember The Girls used to hold an annual breakfast the morning of Good Friday, after their ritual walk."

Janet McIlvena (McLeod).

Kathleen married Keg Brown, who used to own the Bowladrome on 7th Street South. His brother Murray worked as an editor at The Herald for many years before his death in 1975.

Janet McIlvena McLeod moved to Lethbridge in 1910. She studied music in Toronto, and returned to Lethbridge to teach music and become Supervisor of Music for the public schools of the city. Early in her career she was a member of First United Church choir, but became choir leader and organist of St. Andrew's Presbyterian Church in 1927. She was a key figure in the city's Music Festivals, both as a competitor and an official and in 1930 was instrumental in organizing the Lethbridge Music Festival and its affiliation with the Provincial Competition. In 1951 she approached the Kiwanis Club to have them take over the operation of the festival. The Janet McLeod Memorial Kiwanis Scholarship is still offered in recognition of her efforts.

She also directed other choral groups in the city and conducted many local radio music programs as well as having her own CBC School of the Air broadcast for more than 20 years. Janet McIlvena (McLeod) died early in life in 1951.

The concrete basement of the big brick Westminster school was where washrooms and storage area and furnace rooms existed, and in later years a classroom and a small gymnasium, with a badly warped floor were used. The basement holds a scary memory for Nina Kloppenborg.

"It was about Grade 5, and we had a bulldog go mad on the school playground," said Nina, who ran to the basement to seek shelter away from the rampaging animal. "I thought I'd hide in the bathroom, but there were no doors on the cubicles. So I was just standing there in the open and the dog was coming down the stairs. Mr. Walton lassoed him with a rope though just as he was coming down, and that saved me."

The Girls: Front row, from left, Nessie Knox, ?, Janet McIlvena, and ?. In back, from left, ?, Dorothy Wardman, Blanche (Olander) Lang, Mona (Allison) Walton, Molly (Gronberg) Walton, Verna Gray, and Mary Webster.

Jake Walton was the long-time caretaker at Westminster and lived on 4th Avenue North, just two blocks from the school and two doors west of where Nina and husband Niels would later live, after World War II ended. The Kloppenborgs moved into the old McIlvena home in October of 1945, after Jake Walton had died, but only a few years before his daughter

Mona, and her new husband, Andy Allison, were to move into the old Walton house. Nina, whose father served in the Boer War, grew up at 413 12th St. N., close to her father's railroad job. The Kloppenborgs moved into the McIlvena home because the Dieppe housing project in southeast Lethbridge was too slow in developing. The couple were expecting their first child and a home was a priority.

Anne was born in September 1946. The couple had three more children, John, Kathy and Robert.

When Nina attended Westminster, and the practice remained through the 1950s, the girls awaited school opening and enjoyed recess on the south side of the school. The boys held sway on the east side of the playground, never the twain to meet even though there was no fence separating the two distinct groups.

"We played jacks and the boys played marbles," Nina said, marvelling at the way some of the girls could balance jacks on the backs of their hand and still snatch the ball. She also recalls the class outings, one in particular in Grade 8 when the class went down to the Oldman River valley.

"About a half dozen of those audacious boys in the class climbed the high level bridge, and then threw their caps down on us from the top," Nina said. "The principal was there, I think it was Art Hostetter, and we girls just stood and watched in awe and wonder. He watched too."

After completion of her schooling in Lethbridge it was on to Calgary for Nina Seargeant, where she earned her teaching degree. Her first teaching job, in 1930, was at a school between Benton and Acadia Valley, the one-roomed Carlyle School. After a series of other small schools, she found herself at Galbraith in 1939. Her principal was Jim Wishart, who would later be principal at Westminster where Nina's school life had begun. She taught at Galbraith until 1942 when the war forced cutbacks.

When Westminster closed it doors in 1968 Jimmy Wishart was still the principal, and teachers included Lamberta Evans, Avice Anderson, Phyllis Jensen, Bea Nixon, Nettie Wiebe, Kathy Kahn, Jack Fulwiler, Ellen Thurlow, Avis Hunt, Betty Howell, Edna Fern, and Jean Marie Gregg. School nurse was Dorothy Gooder, after whom the school across from Galbraith was named, catering to the handicapped. Head caretaker was Keith Myers.

Two staff members, Jimmy Wishart, who'd been principal for 20 years, and Avice Anderson, had also been students at Westminster School.

Numerous other school and civic officials attended Westminster through the years, including John Watson, principal at Allan Watson School; Joe Lakie, principal of Fleetwood School; Clarence Larson, principal of Lakeview School and Lethbridge Fire Chief Wilfred Russell.

All Westminster pupils and teachers were transferred to Wilson Junior High which was vacant and it took on its new name, Westminster.

An era ends as the final staff of Westminster poses outside the school in 1968, in back, from left, head caretaker Keith Myers, Avis Hunt, Lamberta Evans, Ellen Thurlow, Avice Anderson, Betty Howell, Barbara Willowby, Phyllis Jensen, Edna Ferne, Bea Nixon and caretaker Mrs. Schneitzer. Front, from left, school nurse Dorothy Gooder, Nettie Wiebe, principal Jim Wishart, Kathy Kahn, vice-principal Jack Fulwiler, and Jean Marie Gregg.

Westminster was demolished in 1968 to make way for a shopping centre, anchored by a Safeway Store. Not too many years later the Safeway store too was gone, replaced by a clothing store and then a bowling alley. The Westminster Mall has served many patrons through the years, the most recent those who like Tim Horton's Donuts. Chinese food, fish and chips, a laundromat - which, in 1978, was the scene of one of very few north side murders - book stores, banks, a library branch, and other shops have all been regulars in the mall.

In 1953, Wilson Junior High School opened, at a cost of $355,000, taking the Grades 6 through 8 students from Westminster. Those of us west of 13th then walked just a few blocks east, to the new school, which was officially opened by Alberta's Minister of Education, Anders Aalborg. The school was named for George F. Wilson, a school board trustee from 1933 to 1953, four of those years as the board chairman. Another loss for Westminster, besides its junior high-aged students were teachers like Mrs. Vaughn and janitor Jim Smith.

Reg Turner was the first principal at Wilson Junior High School at 5th Avenue and 16th Street North, and a few years later, when they built and opened Winston Churchill High School on 20th Street and 9th Avenue North, Turner became their first principal. Winston opened Jan. 19, 1961 and was named for Sir Winston Churchill, the wartime prime minister of England. Today's Winston Churchill High School, on 15th Avenue and 18th Street North, incorporates V-shaped concrete features along the front of the school commemorating Churchill's famous two-finger V for Victory sign so popular during the war years. And just to keep you confused, the 1961 Winston Churchill

School is now Wilson Junior High, and the old Wilson is now Westminster - the Westminster site is now a donut shop.

Turner was born in Bargoed, South Wales, into a miner's family, but was saved from going to work in the coal mines by passing the entrance examinations into secondary school at age 11. At 16, he became the youngest person in his district to win a scholarship to university, all expenses paid. He attended the University of Cardiff where he completed his BSc in mathematics.

Reg Turner

After teaching school in Wales for two years, he and wife Ena emigrated to Canada in 1930, landing in Claresholm. After attending school in Calgary he went on to teach in Carmangay, Bow Island and Trochu and he also completed his B Ed degree at the University of Alberta. By 1942 Turner was teaching physics at the LCI.

Becoming a public figure, Turner was elected to city council in 1946 and served until 1960, where he was active on various commissions and committees, including the Planning Commission, the Land Sales Committee, and the Police Commission. He also worked hard to establish the Regional Hospital.

In 1953, he became the first principal of Wilson Junior High School, the only secondary school on the north side at the time, and when Winston Churchill High School was built in 1960, he was again chosen as the first principal. While there, Churchill became nationally recognized as one of the leading schools in the country.

Turner was also an avid fisherman and golfer as well as an expert bridge player. At one time he was a driving force behind creation of a golf course on the northern edge of the north side, aimed at youth, but the plan fell through.

Reg Turner died in 1980.

## Galbraith

For families in the coal miner's district called No. 3, the opening of Galbraith School in 1912 meant their children finally had less distance to travel to school each day. But they still had quite a walk to school.

No. 3 was a neighbourhood along 13th Street, between the communities of Little Wigan, along 13th Street and 18th Avenue North, and Hardieville. Galbraith School, at 1801 8th A Ave. N., was still blocks away from the closest house almost a century ago.

The late Stan Hargreaves, whose father was a coal miner at Hardieville, lived in No. 3 in 1912.

Born in Lancashire, England, Hargreaves came to Lethbridge in 1909 at age five. He had been attending the Bailey Street School until Galbraith opened.

"We were in there all right, right at the start, my sister Eva and I," said Hargreaves, 93 at the time. "I went there two or three years and then moved over to Westminster because we moved."

Hargreaves, who worked at The Herald for 50 years, retiring as foreman of the stereotype department, recalls the new school being quite isolated. The nearest house to the south was three blocks away and a house on 13th Street was the closest to the west.

"It was sort of out there, all alone . . . To the east and north there was nothing. I do recall we took our lunch to school. It was still quite a walk home and back at lunch time. Adams Park was up about that time too, and the football field was there as well."

The school was designed by the Widdington brothers and built by Lussier Construction Co. at a cost of about $75,000. It was named for Dr. Walter Stewart Galbraith, mayor of the city in 1907 and a member of the school board from 1904-1912 and school division doctor from 1934-1939. Galbraith, born in Guelph, Ont. in 1866, came to Lethbridge after an invitation by pharmacist J.D. Higinbotham. Galbraith died in 1939.

He and wife Tillie had four children, Ruth, Francis, Eileen and Jean, who later became a teacher at Galbraith, as well as other city schools.

Critics at the time said the three-storey school was larger than needed. Others said it was as perfect as a school could be. The school was built of brick and white stone quarried at Fort Macleod. The basement had two large play areas, one for boys, one for girls. There were four classrooms with cloakrooms on the main floor with a teachers' room. The principal's office was on the second floor, with four classrooms as well. Up top, with majestic round windows, was a large gymnasium and storage area with two changing rooms off each side. The school boasted maple flooring throughout.

By 1918 the skeptics were proven wrong and an additional classroom was opened and 40 new desks arrived in 1919.

Much of Galbraith School's 1912 appearance remained in 2003, at least on the south exterior of the old school.

Another classroom was opened in 1922 with the basement windows frosted over and blinds fitted to stop the children from gazing at the growing north ward.

By 1941, 30 lots were purchased to expand the playground, and 10 years later the playground expanded again.

Galbraith and Westminster Schools' coal furnaces were replaced by gas in 1948. In 1962 expansion was needed again, with 10 rooms, a gymnasium, stage, library and music room added for $210,000.

The work included window replacement, wiring, lighting, washroom and stair upgrading, all in the old building. Further upgrading took place in 1977 for another $212,000, with work on the heating system, two new classrooms, washrooms in the basement, an art area, science room and work on the roof.

Some of the city's most prominent names in years to come attended Galbraith including Joe Lakie, former professional hockey players Vic Stasiuk and Autry

Erickson and Olympic gold medalist Billy Gibson. The 1913 students included people like John Linning, Joe Szabo, Dolly Saxon, Peter Zasadny, Oliver Sumner, Alex Radley, Clara Melling (who would become my Aunt Clara with my birth in 1941), Ernest Willetts, John Kommar, Tom Logan, Robert Dow, Dora and Edith Harris, Albert and Richard Brown and Agnes Wright, all longtime north side names. In future years you would find names on the rolls the likes of Jean and James Goldie, Steven Swedish, John Ponech, Jerry Arnold, Harvey Nyrose, Roy Beddington, Garry Brown, Annabelle Johnson, Brent Seely, Reg Arnold, Robert Heaton, Peter Stasiuk, Eugene Lehto and Lyle Trockstad . . . and oh yeah, me too.

One of the city's early bread men, Jack Scott, lived near Galbraith. In 1915, at age 13, he started to deliver bread in both north and south Lethbridge. Scott eventually bought the City Bakery and moved south.

A lady who now only comes to my chest, but used to tower over me when I went to Galbraith for two or three weeks in Grade 1, will always be remembered. After all, she was my first crush. I only spent a few weeks in her classroom, but I still remember Miss Erla Keyes, all these years later. And the memories are good ones.

It was 1997, the next time I would see Erla (Keyes) Sanderson - known to me as Miss Keyes. She was still as I remembered her as I entered Grade 1 at Galbraith School, loving and caring.

There we were, about a half century later, sitting in the living room of her Nobleford home, overlooking the tailored flower garden and yard and the grain fields beyond, looking through old photos of Galbraith teachers and classes she taught, in 1946, 1947 and 1948.

At the time I was there, you could also find Miss Agnes Short the school nurse, principal Clarence Larson, and teachers Jean Zeman who later taught me in Grade 3 at Westminster, Janet Larson the music teacher, truant officer Billy Lamb and Helene Parfitt, Bessie McCully, Gladys Rollag, Ethel Hawthorne, and Alice Gaetz.

We talked of lining up in the hallway at the start of school each day to recite the "Lord's Prayer" and sing "God Save the King" and "O Canada". Erla also remembered the janitor.

"Mr. Chapman . . . we called him Chappy. But he was a terrible crank, always sweeping the broom into your feet if you were in his way. But he kept the place clean," she said.

Miss Keyes was only at Galbraith three years. She married in 1948, spent some time in Saskatchewan, and came back to teach at Nobleford in 1950 for 20 years. Not Grade 1 though, she graduated to the higher grades.

Her scrapbook had a picture of the old Galbraith school, set out in the middle of nowhere. There was also a shot of Ken Wilkie and a Herald clipping of Elizabeth Adams, one of her favourite students, as she graduated from the LCI.

"A lot of the kids at Galbraith came from No. 3, a coal mining area to the west of the school," Erla said. "They had quite a walk. Galbraith was way out there. We even had horses in the school yard. One of the sports kids (she thinks it was Billy Balla) got kicked by a horse out in the field one time."

Miss Keyes, now Mrs. Ed Sanderson of course, used to coach Grade 7 and 8 girls' basketball. She remembers playing all the other city schools, but never beating Fleetwood, coached then by Anna Kunst.

When George McKillop came to the school to teach physical education he took his classes up to the gymnasium on the third floor.

"The end lines for the basketball court were the walls," Erla said. "The ceiling was so low. There were an awful lot of ceiling balls each game. We also had our Christmas concerts upstairs in the gym. Galbraith was a lovely school, as schools went at that time."

Her Grade 1 classroom was on the main floor, the first door to the left as you came through the front doors. The teachers' room was straight ahead. It was two full flights of stairs up to the gym.

"If you were in the gym with the Grade 1 class and the firemen came for a fire drill, it was quite a circus getting them down those stairs," she said. "The Fire Shield was a big thing then, given for the best fire drills. I think we won it at least twice in the three years I was there, and maybe three times. It was a real big thing."

The 1947 staff at Galbraith included, from left, school nurse Agnes Short, principal Clarence Larson, Mrs. Parfitt, Jean Zeman, Bessie McCully, Gladys Rollag, Ethel E, Hawthorne, Alice Gaetz, Erla (Keyes) Sanderson, Janet Larson and school truant officer Billy Lamb.

We talked about Billy Lamb, the truant officer and how he brought hookey-playing kids back to the school. He was later replaced by Bill Kergan. We talked of the cloak rooms, where there were no lockers, only hooks for coats and the floor for boots and lunches.

Most students brought their lunch back then she said.

Erla remembered Alice Cleaver, whose brother Billy was in the Boy Scouts with me, as we perused a class photo and the late Eugene Lehto, recalling how he hated school. She picked out Bob Hogg's picture too, and she wished aloud that she'd written all the names on the back.

Those were the days when schools had no libraries, no frills.

"School was a lot different then. Those were the days of the 3 Rs and no field trips. I'm glad I'm out of teaching now. I taught a lot of kids and I taught with love, with a hug now and then. You can't do that now," Erla said with a laugh.

One of my buddies growing up was Roy Beddington, who we called The General, a quiet, always smiling nice guy from day one. I last heard from Roy in 1997 when he sent me a letter, and by then he had retired from a 37-year career with the Canadian Armed Forces.

In his letter he spoke of many north side memories, starting with MY Miss Keyes.

"Those good old Galbraith days. . . I was in Miss Keyes first class, having started school at the tender age of five in 1946," Roy wrote. "I must admit that I too was in love with her. I think it was common with every other kid in her class, but none-the-less she was always my special teacher. Never again through the subsequent 12 years of schooling did I experience such a feeling for a teacher.

"It is great remembering the monstrous layout of that old brick building out in the middle of the prairies. I can still recall George McKillop's consternation at being unable to teach me to do a proper forward roll. . . how I dreaded the mat and that part of gym class up on the third floor. Also there was the frustration of poor Effie Reid in art class being unable to get my colours correct. What a relief it was to find out many years later that I was, in fact, colour blind. Vindicated at last. I also seem to remember having to endure the compulsory downing of a small quarter pint of pasteurized milk (usually warm) each morning. I think we had to bring a nickel to pay for it, but I'm not sure. I know I was a bit relieved when the milkman didn't show up from time to time.

"Galbraith was a good school and although it was hard initially to start making friends when we moved to 12th Street, and my new place of learning at Jim Wishart's Westminster, I have no misgivings about the experience, for it was at Westminster I really think my formative years were to take off. It was there I met, and grew up with, the group of boys and girls that were to form the core of my relationships of my childhood.

Students gather outside a relatively new Galbraith School in the early 1920s.

"There were guys like you Garry, Bob Sanford, Rick Steadman, Gary Kelly, Dan Gyulai, Al Hildebrandt, Brian Carpenter, Glen Howell, Kaz Sawada and Marv Tarnava. This was our 12th Street gang, and we all lived on 12th, or 12th A, B, or C, with some on the Avenues, between 2nd and 6th. That was pretty well the limits of my immediate enclave and I pretty well confined my day to day activities to that area, which also included my paper route."

The General went on to talk about the good time to be had down the Oldman River valley and in the coulees, and fishing at Alexander's Bend or hunting in the river valley. He fondly remembered the games played along the railway tracks and the 9th Street Bridge. He also remembered the catwalk under the High Level Bridge.

"I remember going to Sunday School at First United, across from Lou's Confectionary where we'd always lose part, or all, of our collection-plate money at the candy counter," Roy wrote. "One of my memories of those Sunday School days took place in the old basement where we were attending Bible Class and the person in charge said that we were going to form an executive to run our little club. I can still remember, with great embarrassment my blurting out, "I'll be the general!" Everyone collapsed into fits of laughter at my faux pas. But it was you Garry who made it stick, and I was thereafter The General, or just General, whenever in your company. It was the best nick-name I ever had . . . but it's just as well it didn't stick."

After all, The General did join the army. He rose through the ranks, from Sapper to Chief Warrant Officer, to commissioning as a Captain, the rank he retired with.

"It was four promotions short of my goal, but a good career none-the-less," he said.

With the army Roy toured Canada, the Arctic, Europe and Australia, a long way from his roots, planted so firmly in north Lethbridge.

# Working People

No neighbourhood is complete without its working people. Indeed, you could say the people who ran the businesses along 13th Street, and in other areas of north Lethbridge, were the backbone of the community, the sinew which bound the community together.

The working people numbered in the thousands, and unfortunately only a handful are mentioned, hopefully the key people and businesses. But fact is, anyone who worked along 13th, be they an employee or a business owner, made a contribution to the varied quilt of people and business that was 13th Street North.

Join me as we walk down 13th Street, heading north from the underpass, and talk about some of the key businesses through the years.

## Macaroni

It was 1949-1950 before Catelli found its way to 13th Street. Oh, there had always been a macaroni factory on the north side, between 13th and the wooden 9th Street bridge, linking the northside to the downtown area over the expansive railway tracks, dating back to 1913. That's quite a run for Lethbridge-produced pasta, from 1913 to the plant's closure in 2001.

In 1945 Catelli took over the old pasta factory and in 1950 the Catelli operation was greeting people as they passed under the subway. In 1948 Catelli was producing about four million pounds of pasta a year, a figure which had increased to 40 million pounds in 1991.

Catelli moved into the spot where Bird Building had held sway. Bird moved down to 200 13th St. and the pasta people took over the first business plot on the north side, on the westside of the street as you passed under the underpass.

Back in 1911, the old woolen mill, nestled near the CPR roundhouse, in a no-mans-land, backed by the railway tracks to the south and open fields to the north, was being refurbished, and caught the eye of people from the Columbia Macaroni Factory, which wanted to move from Fernie, B.C. to Lethbridge. A two-year lease was signed and the pasta factory began operation.

City historian Alex Johnston wrote in *Lethbridge - A Centennial History*, that it was likely the Marinaro brothers, at the end of the lease in 1915 who moved to a new factory they built at 150-158 12th St. A N.

"When they moved in they must have changed the name of the business from Columbia Macaroni Factory to Marinaro Macaroni Company," writes Johnston.

In 1950 a family moved into Lethbridge, the Santoni family, from Italy, with a new group of kids for north Lethbridge, and lived in the old factory, converted from creating pasta to housing people.

The macaroni factory became known as Catelli Macaroni Products Corporation Ltd. it was relocated to 13th Street, the first business to greet you as you passed under the subway. In 1984 it became part of the Borden Group, the world's largest pasta manufacturer, and in late 2001, it was announced this long-time north side landmark was closing.

As an aside, here's a tidbit for you about pasta consumption. Italy leads the way with 160 pounds per person a year while Canadians eat about 15 pounds a year.

With the moving of the factory, the old brick structure was converted to an apartment complex, with at least two families living there, including the Santoni family. The building was managed by Alfie DiSabato.

Below: The macaroni factory looks forlorn in 2002.

One of those new boys moving into the old factory in 1950 was Corrido Santoni, who in later years distinguished himself as a top-caliber basketball referee in college, university and high school leagues. In those early days young Corrido, who spoke only Italian when he came to the city, enjoyed the Frog Pond (old Wallwork Lake), a slough just to the east and north of the factory. The pond was a favourite of kids from the area, a region which took in 12th Street to 12th St. C and north up to about 6th Avenue. The groups would gather, make rafts, get wet, catch pollywogs, play war, cowboys and Indians and throw mudballs, snowballs and even rocks.

Being new to the region, the Santoni boys - Corrido, 9, and twins Danny and George - were soon tested, with a rock fight involving a group of us. And in the end it was Corrido who reigned supreme. From then on Corrido was all right with us, after all he and his brothers won the rock fight.

Margaret Schile, born in 1925, said the kids of her day used to stalk the frog pond and catch floppers. "Floppers were what we called ducks before they could fly," she said. "We'd catch them and take them home to eat . . . that's when they tasted best."

Pietro Santoni arrived in April of 1950, established himself here and sent for his family, wife Ester, the three boys and daughter Rossi, who arrived in December 1950.

"The building had apartments up top and down below there was a warehouse for storage," said Corrido. "There were stairs up to our apartment, with three bedrooms, a big one for my brothers and I. I also believe B-Line, a trucking outfit, was right across the street, along 2nd Avenue. We only lived there for about two years at the very most, and then moved further north to Stafford Drive. My dad worked at Catelli for a while, but he couldn't take the inside work. He enjoyed working outside, and left Catelli and went to work for the city. I remember I wasn't used to the climate here and walking to St. Basil's School was a real chore for us, even though it was just a few blocks. We just weren't used to the cold. We had lived in northern Italy, in a village called Ville de Monte, in the mountain region. I've been back there six times since we came here."

The fact Corrido knew no English at all was tough on him at school - "I didn't even know what Hi was" - but right after the Christmas break, at the start of 1951 he was in school, in Grade 1, despite being 9 years old. Soon he was picking up the language and was moved quickly through the grades to Grade 4.

"One of my teachers, and I thank her to this day, failed me in English and made me learn it properly. That was Alberta Clark, the horse lady. (She had riding stables in southwest Lethbridge at the time)," said Corrido. "We'd play at the Frog Pond a lot, that's where I learned to skate. It would freeze over in the winter so we'd skate on it . . . we'd also play road hockey along 12th Street A, between 3rd and 4th Avenues. In the summer we'd build rafts and collect frogs and stuff from the pond."

Corrido, who now speaks perfect English, is retired from the city's Community Services department and was one of the volunteers during the 2001 Alberta Seniors Games in Lethbridge.

It seems, what we called the frog pond, once had a real name. The frog pond once was known as Wallwork Lake, in the early 1900s. Even then it was a favorite for kids, as a skating pond, and for the summer forays we enjoyed in the 1940s and 1950s, rafting, and frog collecting.

"During the Depression years many men in north Lethbridge were unemployed," said Avice (Frayne) Anderson. "To fill in their time, some of them took to digging, not in their garden, but in their basement. A lot of the early houses were built on a surface foundation. There were no full basements, just a small hole under the kitchen, usually reached through a trap door.

"The Depression was a good time to enlarge that hole because the men had little else to do. My dad was one of those who dug a basement during that time. But what to do with all the dirt? Many, many loads were taken to the old lake (frog pond) bed. In fact, so many loads were dumped there a lot of the lake dried up. I used to see those piles of dirt as I walked west along 4th Avenue."

In my time, the late 1940s, those rounded piles were still evident around the small pond. Wallwork Lake was likely the first named area in north Lethbridge, and dates back to the arrival of the Wallwork family from Lancashire, England. Father Nathan arrived first in 1883, bringing his wife, daughter and son James out to be with him three years later. Both Nathan and James were part of major contributions to the prairie landscape.

Nathan worked on the construction of the telegraph line from Dunsmore to Lethbridge, and then on to Fort Macleod, while James, who arrived in town with his mother and sister via the old Turkey Trail narrow gauge railroad, was an integral part of the construction of the high level bridge in 1909. He hogheaded, or drove, the engine carrying steel and other material onto the bridge during its construction. James began his career with the CPR in 1902, and by 1905 was an engineer, finally retiring in 1939.

Nathan, who died in 1909, was around this area during the Riel Rebellion and purchased 80 acres of land north of the railyards in Lethbridge, from the Galt Company in 1885. The land stretched a quarter mile east of 13th Street and a half mile north from the rail yard.

Now here's where history takes on two stories.

In one tale, centered in 1886, Nathan and Rachel Wallwork arrived in Lethbridge and purchased 80 acres of land. They built a home on what is now 13th Street, at 131, said to be the first house in north Lethbridge, where daughter Amy was born.

But, according to the Pemmican Club's history book, *Roundup,* Nathan Wallwork's wife Rachel, son Jim and daughter Ellen arrived in the city in July 1886, at midnight, and had a two-room house waiting for them just 75 yards north of the stone cairn of the high level bridge.

Rachel quickly made the little house a home, with curtains and elbow grease and was soon welcoming members of the Blackfoot Confederacy, and others who came out of the river valley to the top of the hill, into her home. Daughter Amy was born in 1887.

In a Herald interview many decades later, Nathan's son Jim, who was born in Bury, England in 1874, said his father bought eight (not 80) acres of land from the Galt Company in 1888, covering an area a quarter mile east of 13th Street and a half mile north of the railway line. As soon as the house, on 13th between 1st and 2nd Avenues, was completed the family moved in.

They expanded their dairy business to more than a dozen cows, and Jim delivered the milk via horse and buggy, at 10 cents a quart in winter and 12 quarts for a dollar in summer.

Then in a historic piece written for The Herald in 1952, Mrs. J. McCaugherty said Nathan built what some say was the first house in north Lethbridge, in 1886, a two-room structure east of the freight sheds. Amy Wallwork was born in 1887 in the house, then a lonely structure north of the tracks. The home area included a huge market garden and a small dairy business. Nathan had more than a dozen milk cows, and sold milk to the townspeople. Young James was delivering the milk, becoming the city's first milkboy, using a horse and buckboard, the milk carried in large containers and doled out in quarts and even pints. In winter, it was 10 cents a quart, and down to 12 quarts for a dollar in the summer. The livestock was watered at Wallwork Lake and drinking water for the family was hauled from a standpipe, north of the old 1st Ave. S. location of the Lethbridge Iron Works. James, back in 1891, was known as Smoothie, and played soccer and lacrosse on various city teams.

Amy Wallwork

The farm was eventually subdivided into what they called the Wallwork Addition, divided into plots by C.A. Magrath, with the streets named for members of the Wallwork family.

The questions surrounding the various tales come down to eight or 80 acres, and did they live in a small house by the coulees first (which would have been the first house in north Lethbridge) or immediately build a house along 13th?

No matter what, the Wallworks were an integral part of the early north ward, back when the sternwheelers still ran on the Oldman River. Riel was still a concern and railroading was in a major growth stage. James was a bit of an adventurer, extending well beyond delivering milk. He became an apprentice mechanic with the Alberta Railway and Irrigation Co. but by age 23, in 1898, he was off to the Klondike in search of gold. He was soon back in Lethbridge, working as a fireman on the narrow gauge line between Lethbridge and Montana, owned by the Galt family. By 1902 he was with the CPR, the striking achievement of working on construction of the high level bridge still ahead of him. James died at age 83, in October 1959.

Amy Wallwork, who would later marry CPR conductor Michael Tolan, was the third white child born in Lethbridge and the first born in north Lethbridge. She was born Dec. 8, 1887 in her father's north ward home, the first birth in the first house in north Lethbridge - perhaps.

In a 1960 Herald article Amy remembered her father also having a farm near Bow Island and how she'd go along on horse and buggy rides into Grassy Lake, a trip of 50 miles return, just to send a money order.

One of the oldest houses in Lethbridge's northern area was where 9th Avenue now sits, at 1267 in fact. The tiny home is still standing and was said to be built in 1887 by James Perry Sr., on Perry's 40. James Perry, and at least one member of the Perry family lived in the home until 1983, with the exception of 1962-1965. The No. 3 Coal Mine and Staffordville were to the west and Hardieville almost straight north. Perry had bought the original 40 acres, where the house was built, for $5 an acre.

Lettice Perry came to Lethbridge in 1885, and lived in the little house, where the Perry family remained for 97 years. She was a coal miner's wife, who arrived pregnant, with several small children in tow. Her first home was a cave in the side of a hill, waiting for her husband to build a house well north of the railway tracks.

### The Freight Sheds

The CP Express Company, set up between the No. 2 Firehall and the railway tracks, extended back hundreds of metres. Its long sheds held the freight brought in by the trains. The freight was then loaded onto the CP trucks and carried right to residents' homes.

One of the people employed by CP Express was Leonard Robinson, better known as Rocky from his hockey playing days with the Lethbridge Native Sons. Rocky did the back-breaking work of delivering everything from refrigerators to towels for 41 years. Besides his hockey days, Rocky also coached Pony

League Baseball and was inducted into the Lethbridge Sports Hall of Fame in 1991. Rocky died, at age 74, in April 2002.

Ironically, after they both moved to the south side, Rocky's next-door neighbour was Bill Wright, another long-time CP Express delivery man.

I'm going on a personal quest here for a minute or two, concerning Bill Wright, the most robust, pure man's man I ever knew. What limited knowledge I have of fishing and bird hunting I learned from him. What little knowledge I have of riding horses and being around those foot-stomping, arm-biting beasts I learned from him. He was a huge man, super strong, the ultimate outdoorsman. His words and instructions to me as a young kid were gospel.

I marvelled at his strength as I saw him lift refrigerators off the back of the CPR truck he used to drive or carry huge sacks of grain or bales of hay around the farm with ease as if they were 10 pounds not 150 pounds. I marvelled at his ability as he totally dominated a horse that was beyond domination.

Bill Wright, who died in May 1994, opened the door for me to experience farming first hand, to help seed a field, rake hay, stack bales and feed chickens and other assorted farm animals. He introduced me to the world of rodeo and some of the people who starred in that marvellous world.

Being around Bill Wright was a kid's dream. It was like a youngster admiring and looking up to a gunfighter in the old west. He was a man's man. There were no faults in him, no chinks in his armour. I only saw in him the image of a hero. Looking back I'm sure he had his frailties. All humans do. But those are unimportant to a boy when he's learning what life is all about.

Bill Wright

He'd share thoughts and stories about everything from horses and fish to that then unknown world of girls. I hung on his every word. Images and ways I have to this very day were moulded more by Bill Wright than almost anyone else with whom I had contact. My main contact with Bill Wright was as a youngster, as an impressionable youth growing up, walking beside a genuine hero. The impressions he left with me will last forever. He lives on in me and even through my kids who didn't get to know Bill Wright. He lives on through them because much of what I have passed on to my kids, through my ways and my thoughts, was taught to me by Bill Wright.

"When we got married in 1946, after Bill returned from the Navy during the war, he worked in the CPR Freight Sheds," said Lil Wright. "He worked the night shift back then, unloading the cool freight cars when the CPR had huge meat cars coming in each day, with the sides of beef hanging from hooks on the roof of the cars. It was hard, heavy work. As a kid he had worked for a while at Supina's, where many north side kids worked at one time or another. Later he was on the delivery trucks, and he worked with guys like Rocky Robinson, Charlie Batsford, Ormie Mead and others whose names I can't quite remember, like Ernie and a guy named McIntosh. Their trucks would line up at the loading docks each morning and head out on routes throughout the north side and south side, to businesses and to homes."

Gordie Kay, Mickey Kovacs and Chuck Purdue worked at the freight sheds and on the trucks as well, unloading the rail cars into the warehouses and then onto the delivery trucks and from there out to the people.

"Everything for southern Alberta came into those freight yards in those days," said Alvin Bissett. "There were miles of side tracks and dozens of sheds to store everything you can imagine as it was unloaded and loaded."

The sheds were a maze of long buildings, with miles and miles of spur lines emerging from the main rail lines in the large Lethbridge yards. The lines serviced all the sheds in the freight yards, and also spare lines for standing rail cars. There was also a spur line which left mid-way down the main yard, just east of the 9th Street Bridge, turning north along what would now be 12th Street, on its way to the No. 6 Mine. Another spur turned off this line at 6th Avenue, moving west to the No. 3 mine site. At the eastern end of the main yard another spur line turned north again at 20th Street.

The line turning north at 20th Street headed out to Royal View and the mine in that community near the coulees, in Township 9, east of where Pavan Park sits today.

"They actually had a little hotel there and a fairly busy community," said Irma Dogterom of the Lethbridge Historical Society.

The Royal View Mine operated under a number of names and opened in 1904 before being abandoned in December 1912. The mine employed 200 at its peak.

"Charlie Coyle worked at the freight sheds, and a Mr. Stanko," said Scotty Armitt. "Jackie Eagan was a secretary there and her father, Bob Turnbull, was a CPR man for many, many years."

## Supina's

Supina's Mercantile was also a family affair. Nick Supina was the sole owner, but brothers John and Steve stayed on with the store almost as long as Nick. While Nick ran the overall operation, as well as the Klever Dress Shop and Nick's Men's Wear (managed by Doug Priestly) downtown, Johnny managed the warehouse and Steve managed the grocery department.

Billy and Anna Supina were there at the start and along the way, Nick's daughter, son, wife and the children of many of his customers went to work at Supina's Mercantile.

Everal Horhozer, Nick's daughter, still has the original hand-written agreement from March 1914, when her father started in the grocery business. Nick's father, Michael, operated a small grocery store on the corner of 15th Street and 3rd Avenue North, and Nick bought a half share in that business. The letter of agreement stated, in part, that his dad had sold "half interest in his store at 3rd Avenue and 15th Street to son Nicholas Frederick Supina, including stock, fixtures, horse delivery rig and harness and other articles on the premises. The business is to be called Supina and Son Mercantile Co."

Nick Jr. was born Dec. 19, 1881 and was four years old when he arrived in Lethbridge with his family, from Czechoslovakia. Donah Everal Hill and Nick Jr. were married June 7, 1922 and Donah used to help out in the little confectionary on 15th Street, and later in the big store on 13th.

"I was born at 127 15th St. N., in 1927," said Everal. "My grandpa (Michael) had a horse and buggy at that old store and then my dad had many buggies and horses after he moved to 13th Street in 1922."

In 1909 Michael Supina had a home on 13th and by 1917 Supina and Son was in operation at 230 13th,, with Mike living at 234 13th. During that era the Bellevue and Supina Cigar Factory was operating a short distance west of where the Supina store stood. Perhaps that's why Nick always gave away cigars to his customers when they paid off their accounts.

The horse and buggy was still needed in the 1930s, and the books show Nick Jr. had two horses, worth $100. That same year he sold two for $25. In the late 1930s he also had a car, valued at $442.

Joe Horhozer, who would later marry Everal Supina, remembers Tommy Chumik coming to the Horhozer home on 7th Street up No. 3 to pick up their order and young Joe would ride back with him to school.

"Most of the people back then didn't have telephones and my dad sent out delivery wagons in the morning to take the orders of our regular customers. The drivers would come back to the store, fill those orders, and deliver them in the afternoon. In the 1920s and 1930s telephones were rare on the north side, but you knew who the people were who had phones and in an emergency you'd run a block or so to their house to use the phone. At one time up No. 3 only the Natolini and the Birdie families had telephones. Also back then, a lot of north side people didn't speak English so dad would make certain the driver spoke the same language as the people he was serving. It's funny, my dad was Czechoslovakian, but he seemed to favour the Scots. He dealt with the Scotsmen a lot because he liked them and maybe that's why he was so supportive of their soccer team."

Nick Supina had a long association with one of the best soccer teams of the 1930s and 1940s, not only in Lethbridge, but the province as well, featuring many a Scottish player, and some Englishmen. It was managed by Addie Donaldson and coached by soon-to-be Lethbridge hockey legend Ed Bruchet. Nick watched his Supina's soccer team win the Alberta Cup in 1932, going through an undefeated season to become the first city outside of Calgary and Edmonton to take the Cup.

Players included Norman Gurr, Frank Hill, Jimmy McMahon, Alex Linning, Al Walton, Addie Donaldson, J. Gurr, with Ed Bruchet as the manager and J. Gibson and D. Dearie the trainers. Other players included Ted and Clarence Radley, Bill Knight, George Wilson, Jock Clark, Joe Lakie and George Sumner.

Al Walton

Nick Supina was a complex man, very strict and demanding with his family, a boss who expected a day's work for a day's pay, a rather poor, but compulsive gambler, a trusting, compassionate individual, and a non-drinker, unlike his father.

"I worked at Supina's from 1946 to 1947, before I went on to nurse's training in Edmonton," said Frances Kaupp (Salansky), who was born in 1929.

Frances lived on 18th Street and 1st Avenue A North and her dad, Steve, was a railroader. She said he brought one of the first Dayliners into Lethbridge, from Medicine Hat.

"We always lived right along the railway track there on 1st Avenue A, near where they built the underpass, across from Harvey Gowan and the Singletons,"

Frances said. "When dad went to work he'd go past the house in the train and toot the horn. There were a lot of railroaders in that area, including the Roadhouse, Osecki and Dave Watson families. When I worked at Supina's I remember old Nick Supina always looked kind of like a grumpy old bear . . . but he had a heart of gold. I guess he was a bit of a gambler, but I enjoyed working there. For Christmas he'd tell us, 'go pick something out of the store you really want'. That was the era nylon stockings first came out and that's what I picked out. When I left for nursing school the staff gave me a zipper briefcase for my notes. I still have it.

"Nick carried a lot of people during the Depression in particular. At one time, during the war years, my mother phoned in an order, but it never got delivered to us. It was filled and sent out, but none of the boys knew where the delivery went. But Nick refilled that order, with something extra. I remember when I was there Mrs. Supina worked in ladies wear and her daughter Everal was there as were Annie and Johnny Supina. The butchers included Ernie Pankhurst and Leo Grotollo."

Living down along 1st Avenue A it was only natural to shop at Supina's, but the Salansky family also shopped at Kobal's. Mihalik's was too far north for them to walk.

"Anne (Kobal) had a pretty nice little store there," said Frances. "We also walked a little further north to Credico's Bakery, but talk about a treat, it was to go there and get an ice cream.

"Dad did a lot of kind things. Every Christmas Eve he would go down to the store, all by himself, and pack up hampers with turkey, groceries and candy and deliver them himself to those who needed them in north Lethbridge. He didn't want anyone to know about what he was doing. He also gave a lot of needy kids a job."

Everal had a long first-hand association with the Supina's store. "When I was 14 my dad put me to work in the store, about 1940. Whatever the other kids were doing on a Saturday, I wasn't with them, I was in the store and my brother Nick had to go and weigh out potatoes for the store, in 10 and 20-pound bags. He just hated that. I worked from when I was 14 to 18, and then I went away for school. But every time I came back home for the holidays, I worked in the store. Once a year we did go for a holiday, for 10 days, to Portland and Spokane. But as soon as we returned we were back in the store.

"Dad was strict and we had to be at work on time, right at 8 a.m. He would walk to the store every day from our home on 15th Street and then he would walk up town to the men's store and women's wear store he had downtown. One day, when I was 15 I believe, he was late coming in, which wasn't like him at all so I went out to look for him. I found him in the gutter right in front of the store, he had slipped on the ice and broken his hip. He wasn't the same after that."

Nick made a point each spring to head for Montreal, on a buying trip, to buy the latest in fashion for the clothing departments, and his two south side stores.

Supina's had just about everything you'd need for one-stop shopping, from a large butcher shop, to men's and women's clothing and a full grocery department. The only thing it didn't have was a hardware section.

**Cheerless Christmas**

Everal laughs as she tells how Nick would receive bottles of alcohol each Christmas from salesmen who serviced the store, and how many of the staff would stand by in shock as he poured the contents down the drain.

Below - In 1934 the Supina Soccer team won the Alberta championship with players like, in front from left: George Anderson and John Truman. Second row, from left, Clarence Radley. President Robert Ashcroft, Nicholas F, George H, George Sumner and Jack Lakie. Third row from left, J. Gibson, Davey Watson, J. McMahon captain, George Wilson, Scotty Sinclair, Alex Linning, John Clark, Addie Donaldson and C. Dearie.

Supina's prices were very competitive for the times and while they were right there with most other stores of the era, reading the old ads is somewhat of a shock for shoppers today. In January 1937 Nick Supina placed a two and a half page ad in The Herald, attracting people to his Giant Clearance Sale to get rid of overstocked items. Such a sale should take place today. You could get Heinz ketchup for 21 cents a bottle, two pounds of chocolate eclairs were 39 cents, two pounds of jelly beans were 26 cents, three dozen family-sized Sunkist orange juice cans were 45 cents, salmon was 10 cents a pound, you could get two whitefish for 25 cents, pork spare ribs were three pounds for 19 cents, a case of Country Kist corn was $2.39, or 10 cents a can.

On the clothing side, a man's suit was $9.95 with extra pants $2.95 and fur felt hats were 95 cents. Dress socks were five pairs for 98 cents, as were work socks, and ties were on for 29 cents. Ladies' silk crepe dresses were 99 cents and Rayon bloomers 29 cents. Men's work shirts were $1.49 and ladies' shoes $1.89.

Things had changed a bit by 1942, but not much. Prime Rib was 30 cents a pound, boned and rolled, and sirloin or T-bone roasts were 32 cents a pound and for 35 cents you could buy two pounds of pork sausage.

Remember the Big Little Books? . . . well they were 15 cents and marmalade was 30 cents for a two-pound jar. Cheese was 35 cents a pound, Clark's soup was 90 cents a dozen and you could buy men's lined horsehide mitts for $1.

Everal's husband, Joe Horhozer, was in the butcher shop for two years. About the same time Jack MacCallum was the department manager and others included Fred Baceda and Bill Hleuka.

"I was there for two years and one day I told Nick I was going to marry Everal . . . and he fired me," Joe said with a laugh.

Joe had no trouble getting a job though, hired on by Enerson's, one of the sponsors for the popular Alberta Ranch Boys, a western band where Joe was the accordionist.

It was 1949, and on their wedding day, Saturday, Sept. 3, Everal still had to work.

"When I got off at 6 we went right over to St. Patrick's Church on the south side, which was still a basement back then, and we were married at 7 o'clock," said Joe.

Everal too, laughingly recalls the big day. "I kept working in the store after we were married, and I worked in it right up until dad closed it in 1963. When I finished school I worked steady from then on in the ladies department. My father didn't want me to go east to study merchandising, which would have been a good thing as it turned out. In those days the saleslady went right in the dressing rooms with the customer, helping them try on the items they'd selected."

Supina's always had a large staff, and in 1934 The Herald ran a photo of the staff lined up outside the store, which included the butchers; Jack MacCallum, Bill Clark, Leo Grotollo, Henry Piepgrass, and Ernie Pankhurst. Then there was Steve Supina, Mike Petrie, Doug Priestly, Johnny Supina, Andy Watson, Jimmy McKenna, Tom Chumik, Steve Hanisko, Ann Supina, Edith Berkley, Helen Petrunia, Harry Kerr, Nick Supina, Lloyd Gerla, Mary Kostelnick, Peggy Parsons, Elsie Filmer, Syd Upton and Elsie Frayne.

Nick, who served as a war finance worker for many of the wartime Victory Loan Drives, was always enlarging the store, stacking the goods higher and higher, and getting in the latest in work-wear needs. He was proud many of the coal miners and CPR workers came to him for their work clothes, as well as their groceries.

Nick would allow his customers to run a tab, with many a northsider having a bill at Supina's, some paid off every pay day, others at the end of the month, and some not at all.

"When you paid your bill you got a big bag of candy and the men got a cigar," Everal said with a laugh. "Many people dad carried through the Dirty 30s and the war years took a long time, but they eventually paid their bills. But, when the store closed, and you looked back through the books, you could see my dad carried oh so many people, and many of them never paid. Many still owed him, at least thousands and maybe as much as a million if you added it all up."

The store closed in 1963, and was soon replaced by Howard's Furniture. Though Supina's was still doing fairly well it was heavily impacted by the Safeway stores, and Nick also liked to play cards, a game at which he was never too successful.

Some customers stayed loyal.

Everal tells a story of how young Bud McLean was in the car coming down 13th and his mother suggested they shop at the new Safeway. Bud's father was indignant, chastising his wife and telling her how Supina's had carried them in tough times, and they were shopping only at Supina's.

Nick Supina kept some secrets from his family, and one of them was his mounting gambling debts, which eventually led to the closing of the store. He did not have a great head for his accounts, though he ran a tight ship inside the store and met the customers' needs.

"As far as real estate was concerned, he was a poor businessman," said Everal. "He had a chance to buy the York Hotel in the 1940s, and he turned it down. They wanted $15,000."

Nick Supina died in 1975, at age 84, wife Donah died in 1995 at 92 years of age.

Everal said her mother was 18 when she married Nick Supina, and had worked as a young girl cooking for the huge threshing crews each fall.

In later years Donah had a reputation in north Lethbridge as being a psychic, and a good one at that, reading cards and telling fortunes.

"Mother could not only tell the future, but made the people feel good about things at the same time," said Everal. "Mother was also a charter member of the Benevolent Order of the Royal Purple and Eagles Lodges."

With Nick's death in 1975 many tributes poured in, one of the most poignant from James Pere Jones, the minister of Knox Presbyterian Church in Guelph, Ontario, and a former neighbour of the Supina family in north Lethbridge. He said with the death of Nick it was another change for what was once a very happy, congenial neighbourhood along 15th Street, where the families lived. He was also aware of the role the Supina family played in the well-being of that neighbourhood.

"He was certainly a good man in many, many ways, one of which was that he befriended our family in those difficult days of the '30s," the minister wrote. "I recall, as a young boy, being able to go to the store and being able to bring home groceries after they had been written up on the bill - a bill that was paid when funds became available. And I remember my mother and father, when paying the bill, Mr. Supina always gave a cigar to my dad.

### Unforgettable store

Florence Seager, who came to the north side in the 1920s, can't forget Supina's.

"You'd order chops from the butcher shop when the driver came to your house to take your order, driving their horse and wagon. Then he'd deliver those chops in time for dinner . . . right on the dot," she said with a laugh. "You just placed your order and they'd send it out, all the way up to 21st Street where we lived. It sure was handy."

"I can see Mr. Supina even yet walking among the counters of his store, straightening up the peaches or the oranges, shifting the loaves of bread, settling the clothing in the racks, greeting his customers, befriending them and helping them."

Rev. Jones had memories of the horse and wagon that delivered groceries along 15th Street, and the vacant lot next door to the Supina's home where the kids played ball, and time after time it was Nick Supina who tossed the ball back after it had gone over the fence.

"All of us used to play in the alley behind the house, the Richards and the Lazaruks," Jones wrote. "I remember how in those days, when the chickens were killed for the store, and the blood would be spattered about as they shook themselves, how pails of hot water were brought for taking the feathers off."

Rev. Jones felt the Easter weekend of Nick's death was a fitting time for him to "finish his earthly pilgrimage".

"Mr. Supina was very much a churchman. I remember many, many Sundays as I was walking to worship, Mr. Supina would walk along the same path as

well. We would take the route that led along First Avenue, under the 13th Street bridge, across the path alongside the Caterpillar Tractor lot and the old arena. Eventually we would part as he would go to St. Patrick's and I would walk further on. There was even a time when I attended worship at St. Patrick's with him and Celia Lazaruk. These are all good memories of a very wonderful past."

Nick was more than a business man, he was also a life member of the Elks Club, Chinook Club and a member of the Knights of Columbus. He also served on St. Michael's Hospital board, alongside fellow north Lethbridge store owner Andy Mihalik.

Many young northsiders worked for Supina's, including my father, Andy Allison, who came to Lethbridge as a youngster in 1918.

"I delivered for Supina's some," he told me shortly before his death at age 92. "I worked for them on weekends, Friday after school and all day Saturday. I had all the heavy work, hauling sacks of chicken feed and oats. I was only 14 at the time and I'd take deliveries out to the No. 3 mine area, with a horse and buggy. In those days everyone seemed to have a cow or two in those isolated houses. Renee Fox used to take a herd of cows over the tracks by No. 3 in the morning, to a grazing area at the top of the coulees, and bring them back in the evening, taking each cow to their individual homes where they were supposed to go."

There were a lot of butchers along 13th Street in that era, and perhaps all the cattle, housed in north side yards, was part of the reason. Andy remembers a butcher shop, owned by Swingler, just north of the Lealta Theatre. Past 7th Avenue, across from where Martin Brothers now sits, an English fellow had a butcher shop, and then there were the Gurrs, and Barnaby's, just across from Westminster School.

"There were three Gurrs, and Alf was a butcher," said Andy. "They were set up next to Pete Credico's Bakery. Alf was the oldest, and another brother, Norman, used to play soccer for the Miners."

For Phyllis (Bissett,) Slovack Supina's was a cluttered store, a mix of men's and lady's wear, meat and groceries.

"It was the junkiest store in the whole world," Phyllis said. "You'd walk in there and it would be like a dungeon . . . they had everything in that store, and all the big shots shopped there. I remember once when I bought a red sweater, for $2, and I paid for the garment with that old Bible Bill Aberhart script money which my grandfather had given me. When I think about it now, that sweater was really ugly. There was a little house on the corner, just before Supina's store, the Kirby family home. She worked at CJOC for years."

### The House of Labour

My personal memories of the Labour Club surrounded the years 1951 to 1956, much of that time spent as a newspaper boy for The Lethbridge Herald, my route running from 7th Avenue to 9th and from 13th to 12th Street B.

Two landmarks are now gone, the short-lived Labour Club still under construction here in foreground, and the old North Lethbridge Airport hangar in the background

We used to pick our papers up at The Labour Club, winter and summer, rain or shine, and head north to start the route, often joined by my helper Rick Petrie, who later worked with me at The Herald as an apprentice printer for a few years before his tragic death in a traffic accident. Tom Waterfield, a former city milkman, was the man who doled the papers out to us each day, Monday through Saturday. The papers would be delivered via Herald truck, driven by Hank Forward. He'd count them out, route by route, and off we'd go. Paper boys like myself, Doug and Roy Sandberg, Ray Rowland, Jack Smeed - who became one of the city's top bowlers - Wayne Doolittle, Wayne Clark, the Pish boys, Ken Ball, Jack Dietzen, the Allan brothers, Jerry Barnaby, and a slew of others went through the Labour Temple doors each day, and out to work. Seems to me I had just about 110 papers and made about $5 a week - so much for working out of the Labour Club, home of the union rank and file and the place for fair wages.

When the Second World War ended the labour movement in the city bought The Gospel Hall, a church on 13th, across from the No. 2 firehall, with the idea of building a permanent home. Major city unions found a home in the Labour Temple as it was then known, under the management of the Lethbridge and District Labour Council.

The main floor of the club was home to the different union offices, board room and the main ballroom, where we picked up our newspapers. There were also full kitchen facilities for banquets and other functions. Built by Bird Construction Ltd., the building was designed by Meech, Mitchell, Robins and Associates.

I can remember Harry Boyse, the secretary-treasurer of the trades council, being around the club most days we went in for our papers.

The Labour Club had a history on 13th well before the Labour Temple was built. Labour unions date back to 1906 in Lethbridge, with the original offices downtown. But soon the council headed north, setting up in the basement of the old Bank of Commerce building on 13th Street. They built their own hall about 1925 or 1926 at 240 13th, raising much of the funds from a dance. By 1946 they had two locations, at 240 and the Trade and Labour Council offices across the street, in an added-on hall next to the old Terry's Tire Shop. Part of the new hall was formerly the officers' mess at the PoW Camp, and was set up on the 13th Street site, for about $10,000.

Terry's Tire and Auto Shop had held down the corner of 2nd Avenue from 1938, with owner Barry Ingoldsby living upstairs and the old glass-encased gas pump out front. He finally sold his land to the union people. In 1959 the club bought the old Terry's shop for expansion.

"I met my husband at Ingoldsby's garage on 2nd Avenue and 13th," said Mavis Standing. "I was going to high school at the time and Edna Good, Annie Hargreaves and I used to walk past the garage every day. We'd stop and flirt a bit with the boys. My husband-to-be worked for the telephone company and was at Ingoldsby's doing some work for a few days and I'd stop and talk with him as we walked to and from school."

Two years after buying the tire shop the union folks bought the land to the north, for a parking area. Construction of the new building began in 1964, at a cost of $155,000, financed by the sale of shares to the union workers. The old Temple with its additions disappeared.

The new building was called a monument to labour, and indeed, according to Chamber of Commerce President G.W. Lomas, "a monument to all Lethbridge citizens". The new building served as a meeting place for various labour groups, but also catered to social functions and other non-union-related activities. The Lethbridge Labour Club, organized under the Societies Act, operated the building as a separate entity of the Lethbridge and District Labour Council, under president Dave Cooper.

This 1968 championship Labour Club fastball team featured numerous north side stars, in front, from left: George Magilla, Marvin Moser, Tom Yip, Harry Nagata, Monty Kendall, Brian Murkin, and Richard Chollack. In back, from left: Terry Rhodes, Jerry Areshenko, Ed Carpenter, Wayne Nesbitt, Frank Tuttle, John Kobal, Bob Setaguchi, and Roy Adachi. The batboy in the middle is Jerry Areshenko Jr. Missing is Andy Konno and Stan Snider.

There are those who would say unionism and religion had a lot more in common than just an old building site. But as far as buildings went there seemed to have been a direct link between north side religion and unionism. The Labour Temple property was once the Plymouth Brothers Mission, from 1929 to 1938, and then was known as the Gospel Hall from 1940 to 1946.

The old Labour Temple was acquired by the city in 1980, and was renamed the Bill Kergan Memorial Centre, still serving as headquarters for many ethnic and community groups.

In 1980, the Labour Club built a $3.5 million, 64,000 square foot edifice on the old airport land, just west of where the old airport hangar used to sit. The club only lasted a few years before going bankrupt and closing its doors Jan. 1, 1989.

The building fell to the wrecker's ball in 1993.

### The York

In its day, The York Hotel has had at least two official names, been a respected hotel, home to a restaurant, pharmacy and even a doctor's office, but it has also become known for other things. There have been strippers, a girl and her tiger and only a certain clientele will remember the infamous ping pong ball girl, who did things with a ping pong ball you don't even want to think about.

In September 1914, two years after the World Dry Farming Congress in Lethbridge, a new brick hotel - the brickwork done by Richard Burgman who ran Burgman's Dance Hall just a block and a half further north - opened its doors on the corner of 13th and 3rd Avenue. It was known as the King's Hotel, or King Hotel, either one a bit pretentious don't you think?

"I was in the York (King's) Hotel a few times as a kid," said Avice (Frayne) Anderson. "It was originally a hotel with single rooms to rent, but later they created some housekeeping rooms by cutting a hole in the adjoining wall and making a passage from one room to the next. This was about 1926. I was selling something, and I was going down the hall knocking on doors. I'd knock on some door and a person would answer, then I'd go to the next door and knock again, and the same person would answer. It was one of those housekeeping suites."

June Carpenter, wife of late Lethbridge Police Chief Jim Carpenter, had some memories of the York as well, through two 14-inch Chinese decorative brass plates hanging on her living room wall.

It seems Jim was walking his north side beat one night coming down 13th Street, and as he passed North Lethbridge Hardware, owner Pete Chumik was taking stock, about 11 p.m. at night. Jim waved as he walked past and minutes later stepped into the lobby of the York to warm up.

"The hotel had a big brick fireplace across the corner in the lobby . . . it was quite a nice hotel at one time," said June. "The owner and Jim got to talking. Jim saw these two plates over the fireplace and asked him if he'd sell them, and how much they would be. 'More than you can pay,' came the reply."

The owner then told the future chief of police, if he'd find him a big, sturdy ashtray which no one could break for his lobby, so people wouldn't flick cigarette butts into the fireplace or on the carpet, he might think of selling the plates. Well, Jim took off out of the store, right back to Pete Chumik's place. He asked the hardware store owner if he had a big ashtray, and Chumik dug out a large brass ashtray, with a little piece knocked off the stand.

"Jim bought it for $5, and rushed back down to the York and plunked it down," said June. "The guy couldn't believe his eyes, but he gave Jim both those plates in exchange for the ashtray."

78

B.B. McCarty awarded the contract to build his Kings Hotel, in May of 1914, to Hostson, Leader and Goode. It was the same year St. Basil's School was going up a few blocks to the north and west, along 12th St. B. McCarty promised his would be the finest hotel in the city.

The Herald said the three-storey hotel would have a full basement, with a fancy brick exterior. The frontage along 3rd Avenue would be 110 feet and along 13th, 95 feet, with the main foyer at the corner of the street and avenue, designed by architect E.E. Carver.

Opening of the grand new structure was celebrated by 50 invited dinner guests, enjoying "one of the finest meals laid on a table anywhere," according to The Herald. Among the dignitaries and speakers were Mayor William Duncan Livingstone Hardie, John Gilmore, president of the North Lethbridge Businessmen's Association, future mayor George Hatch, and of course, McCarty, builder H.J. Goode and Hotel Manager Thomas Underwood. Assisting the new manager would be J.K. Hislop and F.J. Colpman, day and night clerks respectively, and a chef appropriately named King, direct from serving as the second head cook at the CPR Hotel in Vancouver.

Furnishings for the hotel were supplied by Bawden Brothers and Wilson Furniture Co., with the 51 rooms, each featuring a weathered oak desk, a brass bedstead with a 120-coil spring and fine felt mattress, a wardrobe and antique oak dresser. Every room faced outside, which meant excellent ventilation.

According to The Herald again, the hotel was neither the King or the Kings, but the King George, and "without a doubt one of the finest hotels, not only in the south, but in the province". But no matter what its official name was, the Kings was a grand spectacle.

The dining room featured more oak, with eight large artistic tables. The lobby was said to be homelike, with a large old-fashioned fireplace. A tour of the building convinced the Herald reporter the hotel "was not built for its bar alone". But, truth is, the bar is the mainstay of virtually any hotel. The basement was home to a billiard room, sample rooms where travelling salesmen both stored and displayed their wares, along with the laundry room and the boilers.

Rooms in the grand edifice went for $2 a night, or as Underwood preferred, $30 for a full month, not only for the room but board as well.

"Juris owned the Kings in the 1920s and 1930s and a fellow by the name of Wolfman had it, as the York, during the war years," said Ab Chervinski.

"The Conklin Shows, which used to set up northwest of the 9th Street Bridge in those days, used to have slot machines. They'd give blankets and stuff like that away to the winners. I had two of those slots at home, in the garage. I had gotten them from my stepbrother when I was about 16, along with a whole bunch of tokens. I sold one for $25 and later, during the war, Wolfman told me he'd take the other off my hands and

sell it up north. When he came back he told me he had sold the machine, telling me, 'I got rid of it for you.' But he didn't say what he sold it for and I received no cash for the deal. He said he really had done me a favour, saving me the trouble of explaining to the police what I was doing with a slot machine."

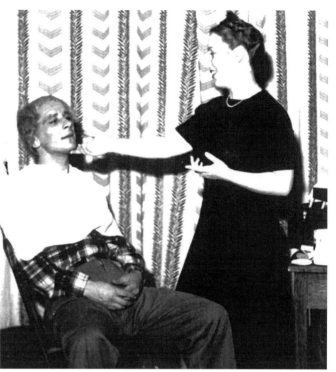

Ab Chervinski, being made up as Scrooge for a theatre production.

Chervinski said the York served more than just boarders, beer drinkers and room renters.

"During the Depression years they started a Leisure Time League at the York, in the back. It was a place for young people who couldn't find a job to hang out . . . just like the YMCA in a sense." Chervinski said. "Instead of robbing someone or just getting into trouble the young people went to the York to play cards and games, but there were no meals. Mrs. Lonsberry and Miss Bateman did a lot of work there and Bob Moodie, quite a horseshoe thrower in later years, was quite active helping the boys who attended the club."

Phyllis (Bissett) Slovack said she was a baby in 1925 and her parents lived at the Kings, in the small apartments, for a short while when she was a baby. The small apartments were merely adjoining rooms. She said the hotel was also used as a recreation hall for young men, teaching boxing and other sports.

By the last half of the 1930s the hotel, like the country itself, fell on hard times. The hotel was closed.

"It was empty by 1937 or 1938 and we kids used to throw rocks through the windows," said Phyllis with a laugh. "I wasn't the only one, all the kids did it."

After the war the hotel was owned by Joe Bush and Johnny Shaw, then came Syd Pechet whose family was into the hotel business in a big way, with oldest son Mitch playing for the Montreal Canadiens.

"When Syd had the hotel Matt Tarnava was on the front desk for years and years," said longtime northsider Scotty Armitt. "Other owners I knew included the Royer brothers, Ron Chervinski and Alvin Popowich.

"Before the Kings got its liquor license the First United Church used to take over the first floor on Friday nights for their church dances," said Scotty. "There was a gymnasium downstairs, with showers, put in to help the local kids out with boxing and other training for running and things. My brother George, Ernie Holberton, Johnny McColl and other runners all used to train there back in the 1930s. The boys would run from the hotel straight down 3rd Avenue to the old brick yard, down into the coulees and up the Laundry Hill on the south side, back over the 9th Street bridge and back to the hotel.

"My father always used to tell me the Prince of Wales opened the Kings Hotel in 1914, and different people have said that is why, when they changed its name to the York Hotel about 1940, they chose York because it was also Royal. The Kings was a good hotel in its day," Scotty said. Records, however, show the Prince of Wales wasn't in Lethbridge until Oct. 3, 1919.

Scotty Armitt

Mavis (Harding) Standing, who still lives two blocks from the York, said coal miners used to be the best customers for many years, picking up their pay cheques at work, cashing them at the Standard Bank, and then crossing the street to the York.

In 1936 the vacant hotel was full of some great stuff, including a huge array of fixtures from doors to door knobs, locks and bathroom fixtures. Again, it should come as no surprise this drew the attention of those who preferred the five-finger discount when shopping. A thief was caught, arrested and given a year's suspended sentence for walking off with a full-sized bathtub, a sink and some bathroom fittings.

But the hotel structure remained, and by 1940 had reopened as The York, the fittings all back in place.

In a tourism brochure of 1952, The York, though it had no beer license at the time, bragged about its 40 rooms to let, at $2 a night and up. A similar brochure in 1967, featuring city hotels, listed The York with its 40 rooms without bath, and six rooms with bath. There were four double rooms, the rest singles. The hotel also included a dining room/coffee shop and banquet facilities for 65 people, as well as having the all-important liquor license.

The York coffee shop was a place seldom visited by the youth of 13th, but it was a handy spot if you were waiting for the Lealta to open on a Friday or Saturday. You could grab a quick burger and fries and shake - did teens ever order anything else? - and then head off for the show right across the street. But, you seldom left until you had poured the salt into the sugar dispenser and refilled the salt shaker with sugar.

The hotel also had a pharmacy, operated by Bill Skelton, who lived along 4th Avenue North at the time, next to the Lee family, who owned Lee Duck Cleaners. Lil Wright, whose side fence bordered Skelton's back yard, said Bill, in 1951 or 1952, gave her a brand new ointment, Ozonol, to ease the pain of a cut she received from breaking a prized beer mug, owned by Alan Tyrer.

Don Standing was one of Bill Skelton's delivery boys, when Skelton's Drug was part of the York Hotel, back around the late 1940s and early 1950s. About the same time there was the Pisko Drug Store north of the Williamson Block.

In 1985 the newly-remodeled York included a barber shop, coffee shop with homemade pies and Ukrainian food, and the Silver Fox Pub.

Francis Kaupp (Salansky) recalls the days when Dan Royer had the York, and the introduction of Sunday brunch.

"It was really quite nice in there," she said. "They had a wonderful brunch, and I particularly remember the large, whole salmon, with salads and all the trimmings. My mother sure liked that salmon."

By 1997 the once proud hotel was condemned, only to be restored two years later, and in 2004 it was undergoing yet another major face-lift.

"Just down from the York, in the late 1920s and early 1930s, Aunt Aggie Parks had an auction market, or more of a flea market I guess," said Scotty Armitt. "She'd pick up and deliver, with an old horse and wagon. There was a small building and a very big yard loaded with lots of junk."

Margaret Danty and her family lived on the corner across from the York, then came Dodd The Tailor.

Scotty said the only name he remembers for the fellow who ran the tailor shop across the avenue from the York in the 1930s and 1940s was Dodd the Tailor. He does however, remember a taxi service working out of the York, North Side Taxi, in the 1970s.

Mavis Standing remembers Dodds Tailor Shop as a tiny store just north of the York, between the avenue and O'Sullivan's garage, with the owner's name Walter Dodd.

"My dad, who came to Canada in 1888, used to have his trousers shortened there," said Mavis. "There was also a small house in there, and it later all became part of the North Lethbridge Motors."

## Let Them Eat Meat

Joyce Davies Rasmussen Scott remembers "oldman" Swingler always being in a long, usually bloody apron, with a big bushy moustache. There were also four boys, Cecil, Willie, Joe and Harry.

Swingler's butcher shop, with its sawdust freshly spread on the floor each day was right up to the sidewalk, while their house was next door, but set back a bit with a small front yard.

---

### 4 and 20 Blackbirds . . .

"Mrs. Swingler also made pigeon pies for my grandmother, Martha Matthews . . . with the pigeon's feet sticking up from the crust. She's get the pigeons out back and then make up a pie or two. I grew up eating things like that, as well as tripe, brains, tongue and head cheese. I never did like blood sausage though."

- Joyce Davies Rasmussen

---

"I'd be about six or seven years old and I'd walk all the way over from 12th Street A and 6th Avenue to Swinglers, with 25 cents my mother gave me to buy veal chops for three adults and me, and get bones for the dog," said Joyce. "Imagine buying that today for 25 cents.

"As I remember it, Swinglers actually killed the animals right in back, in sort of a court yard and stable area. They'd butcher the animals back there and cut them up in the basement area. To this day I can still see Mrs. Swingler bouncing a bloody pig's head in her lap, on her bloody apron. I suppose the idea was to entertain us kids looking on. This is the same Mrs. Swingler who sang in the St. Mary's Church choir. I'd go downstairs where Mr. Swingler would be making sausage or cutting up the meat and read through their stack of the Daily Mirror newspaper from London. It was a great read. The Swinglers also had two big police dogs, Vic and Zar. One day I put my arms around one of their necks and he bit me, taking a V-shape piece out of the end of my nose."

Phyllis (Bissett) Slovack said Mrs. Swingler used to walk from the store to St. Mary's Anglican Church regularly, where she also served as the church janitor. She also raised the pigeons for her pies right in the back yard of the house and shop on 13th.

"All our parents used to buy lard in cans in the 1920s and 1930s and we kids would collect these cans, or tin buckets if you will, and take them to Swingler's," said Ab Chervinski. "They'd give us money for those little pails and off we'd go to the show.

"Kearn's Shoe Repair was near Swingler's, and he was a very smart old cobbler. Norma Charles once took a pair of skates to him, where the blades had separated from the boots, and he put them back together for her. He charged her two bits (25 cents)."

Swingler's house was set back off the street and the business was attached to it.

"Mrs. Swingler felt all girls should be taken out of school and taught to look after the home," said Phyllis (Bissett) Slovack. "Harry, Willy, Cecil and Joe were her boys, and she used to fill them up by feeding them suet pudding. Joe was killed overseas in the war."

Swingler's was first known as Westminster Meat Market, dating back to 1912. The store was gone by 1942 however, though Mrs. Swingler was still living in the house in 1952. Adnitts also had a meat market on 13th at one time, between 3rd and 4th Avenues, with Curly Baird as the butcher. Noy Barnaby had a meat market into the 1950s, across from Westminster School, helped out by son Jerry and daughter Carol.

## Motoring History

Across the avenue from the York Hotel, in the early era when the York was the Kings, sat a house and then Dodd The Tailor, both eventually overtaken by North Lethbridge Motors, later to be Mo-Tires.

"I met my husband (Matt Slovack) there," said Phyllis (Bissett) Slovack. "He started in that business working for Frank O'Sullivan, who owned the original North Lethbridge Auto Wreckers before the Roelofs. O'Sullivan was a heavy construction fellow. He had tires and a welding and a body shop, but was also into heavy construction and had a house-moving unit. He also did a lot of mechanical work. O'Sullivan later sold to Henry and John Roelof. My husband Matt taught John and Henry the radiator business. John later opened up a radiator shop downtown, and O'Sullivan went to South America to build bridges for the government."

Frank O'Sullivan had a house just north of his shop and further along 13th to the north was the Tech School, from about 1934 to 1954. When O'Sullivan sold out to the Roelofs, the wrecking yard evolved into an auto-based business. O'Sullivan's was the original auto wreckers and eventually evolved into Marshall's, which first had a home in south Lethbridge before moving out to the eastern edge of town. O'Sullivan's, said Ab Chervinski, was a wrecking yard where many a kid used to play, and hold smoking sessions as well, hidden away from family members.

Phyllis Slovack met her husband at O'Sullivans, when she was 14 and a half. Four years later they were married and living across the street from the garage, from 1934 to 1939, when they moved off 13th to 12th Street B North.

Phyllis remembers the two watchdogs North Lethbridge Motors would let out at night for protection of the lot, an English Bulldog called Bubbles and a German Shephard. Her family had a dog called Major, a Heinz 57 variety said brother Alvin Bissett, and Major used to fight the two watchdogs, and win. Major also used to raise havoc with a squirrel stole, worn over a lady's shoulder with its head hanging down the back.

Mo-Tires Ltd. has been in business for about 66 years along 13th, and has been doing tire retreading for 62 years. The company continues to be a city family company maintaining customer service as a key to its long term success.

In the 1990s a third generation of the Roelofs family was involved in the business, with brothers Brian, Glen and Jim all taking an active role in various positions with the company. The business was originally started in 1937 by Henry J. Roelofs Sr., Henry J. Roelofs Jr. and John Roelofs. Soon after the business started Henry J. Roelofs Sr. passed away and Henry J. Jr. bought the remainder of the business from his brother John.

By 1940 Mo-Tires was into retreading, with the urging of the wartime prices and trade board. At the time, due to the war, tires were in short supply. Retreading was a way in which the country could conserve its supply of raw materials and recycle existing tires. Retreading has been a big part of the business ever since. The company estimates it had retreaded more than 360,000 tires by 2000, saving these tires from heading for the city's landfill.

In 1951 the Tire Shop building was built. At that time, the business was still known as North Lethbridge Motors and Auto Wreckers. In 1966, Brian Roelofs, son of Henry J. Roelofs, joined the firm as the new acting General Manager. At the same time the company's name was changed to North Lethbridge Mo-Tires Ltd.

In 1967, the company's operations were housed in the 13th St. location including the retread plant. Today, the company's auto centre remains in the old location, but in 1974 Mo-Tires built a new truck tire service centre and retread plant at 2830 5th Ave. N., about the same time Jim Roelofs, Brian's brother, joined the staff. Ralph Shipley joined the staff in 1971 and became manager of the Truck Centre.

In January, 1988, Henry J. Roelofs, co-founder of the company passed away and Brian Roelofs became president, with Dave Roelofs secretary-treasurer. In 1989, Glen Roelofs joined the family firm to make all Henry's family except Marilyn Gall, who is a school teacher, active in the business.

## Kobal's

Like the much larger Supina's Mercantile just a block and a half to the south, Kobal's Grocery had its beginning in a small store on the corner of 3rd Avenue and 15th Street North. As well, the other large grocery and mercantile along 13th Street, Mihalik's, to the north of Kobal's, played a role in the store's beginning. Kobal's Grocery began life about 1938, on the corner of 15th and 3rd, two blocks east of the York Hotel.

"We were there about two years, but the owners didn't want to sell, and there was a property along 13th owned by Wo Fat I believe, under Henry Yee's name," said Johnny Kobal. "The person who got my dad (George) started in the business was Andy Mihalik. My dad was the choir master at St. Peter and St. Paul's Church on 12th St. B and Andy Mihalik was a member of the church's board. When dad wanted assistance in starting a business it was Andy who got him going."

Before going into business for himself, George Kobal had driven a horse-drawn delivery wagon for McGavin's. Kobal's was a full-service grocery and confectionery, and at one time even had booths with a soda fountain and ice cream bar, but George soon took it out. One of the store's early butchers was Ernie Pankhurst, who had also worked for Supina's and later had his own butcher shop in north Lethbridge. Harold Waldron was also one of the butchers in those early years. The last 25 years or so of the store's life, Kobal's was out of the meat business, mainly because dealing with the packing houses and paying for the shipping became a major expense.

"We just couldn't afford to bring hanging beef in," said Johnny. "Some of the delivery guys through the years included Al Hepple with City Packers and Fred Popovich, Phil Tommy and Martin and Joe Snopek. We had all the confectionery items, like candy and pop, and a full stock of groceries. We were open 8 a.m. to 10 p.m. Monday through Saturday and opened after 10 a.m. Sunday, when church was over at St. Peter and St. Paul's."

The Kobal family, George, wife Anne and son Johnny lived at the back of the store, which had two bedrooms, a living room, kitchen and bathroom. Upstairs was the home of Jim and Jean Smith, for about 30 years. Jim was the janitor at Westminster School just a block and a half north and later the first janitor at the new Wilson Junior High, three blocks to the east. In 1947 George Kobal died and wife Anne then took over full operation of the store, literally devoting her life to the business until it was closed in 1995, after 40 years on 13th Street.

"It was just me and mother in the store for many years," said Johnny. "When I came home from school (at St. Basil's until Grade 8) I did pretty well what had to be done in the store. My grandmother (Mary Pinchak) moved in after dad died and she pretty well raised me while mother ran the store. Mother spent most of her life in the store and the only vacations she had is when she had to go into the hospital. Her last vacation came in 1951 when she went to Spokane. She did enjoy it though. Early in her life she used to be a house cleaner and she enjoyed the store much more, mainly because she was a people person."

Anne Kobal died at age 79, July 1, 1995. She was not a trained bookkeeper but did have her own particular style of keeping records. Son John said it wasn't fancy, but it was accurate.

Johnny, a long-time city employee before retiring, was also known to southern Alberta sports fans as a hockey referee and a baseball umpire. He worked as a linesman at the Sportsplex in the Western Hockey League for many years and from 1978 through 1979 was on the world scene in baseball. He was chosen to go to Italy, representing Canada, in the world championships. He also did a few Pioneer Baseball League Games.

One of the games in Italy he remembers in particular was in Bologna, between Cuba and Japan, won by Cuba 3-2. Johnny also worked the Canadian Little League Championships, receiving a standing ovation from all the teams at the wind-up banquet for his high calibre of umpiring.

Kobals - a second hand shop in 2003.

In its last few years the Kobal store was losing money, but Anne insisted on keeping it open. Through the years she had allowed many northside families to run a tab at the store, and while most came in and paid the accounts off, at her death there were many unpaid accounts.

"There was a stack we could have retired on if they had been paid," said Johnny. "Those bills stacked up over the years and they ran into hundreds of thousands of dollars owing her." Many of the accounts were destroyed when storm drains in the basement backed up and wiped out the files. The basement was a storage area for the grocery upstairs, with most of the shelves made from the wood of the old-style orange crates, broken down for shelving after the oranges were placed in the produce section of the store above.

The store did have many paying, steady customers who came in daily and weekly for their groceries. Some would charge up through the week and then pay their bill each Friday on pay day.

"We had a lot of good customers like that," said Johnny. "We had a good core of regular customers, but through the years some would move to the south side and they never came back north to shop. The Ruslings, who lived on 22nd Street North were good customers. He was a brick layer and every Friday they came in and bought their week's groceries for years and years. The DeCostes were regulars, and others like Bolokoski, Gonzy and Chenger families and Mrs. Deak were loyal customers as well.

"Swingler's had a meat market for years, where Luigi's is now, and they did their grocery shopping at

the store. Next door to us was Bill Hales, a shoemaker, and he was a customer too. We did deliveries at one time, and I used to deliver on my bike, Ron Dorren used to deliver groceries on his bike for my mother back in the 1940s.

"His parents, Johnny and Isa, shopped at the store too. Then we hit the mechanical age and my mother had to get a car. My uncle, Mike Pinchak, would deliver by car for us, and his brother too."

As you stepped up the two small, about one-inch high steps, into the store and opened the door, a bell rang in the back, and out would come Anne Kobal, ready to serve. She did hate to make the trip from the back to the front counter for a couple of kids who only wanted to spend two or three cents, but she always did.

"We lived upstairs for many years, over what became Kobal's Grocery," said Phyllis (Bissett) Slovack.

"The store was vacant for a while then the Douglas Beauty Shop was in there. In 1937-1938 Bill Lemar had a jewelry store down there and Bill Hales had a shoe repair shop with an apartment down the side and another apartment at the back. Billy Lamb's daughter lived in that apartment at the back for a while with her husband and two kids."

When war came Phyllis' brother Alvin remembers looking out the window and hearing The Herald paperboy walking up and down 13th hollering "Extra! Extra! Germany invades Poland".

"Henry Pickering used to do wood carving, you know, the kind that looks like a basket weave, and it would be open inside and he'd carve a little ball in there which ran back and forth as you tilted it," said Audrey (Bissett) Kesler.

"We lived right in the back and he lived in the Kobal apartments too."

Just north of the Bissett apartment complex was the A and B Confectionary, with an upstairs apartment complex.

"It was quite a place upstairs," said Phyllis. "It had a lot of rooms upstairs, but all the rooms opened onto the hallway, and people who lived there had to go into the hall to change rooms, from the kitchen to the bedroom. It was loaded with bedbugs and the kids would squish them on the wall. There was also only one bathroom, for a whole bunch of people who lived up there. One day McCaffrey's was giving away free samples of Ex-Lax, and I got a bunch and gave it to the kids who lived up there . . . as chocolate. Boy that hallway was busy!"

"The Bissett family had a cow when they lived above Kobal's, and George milked it," said Phyllis. "There was a little shed out back, and we'd keep the cow there and milk it each day. I can remember one weekend when we had 29 quarts of milk at our house, for the six kids. Milk was 10 cents a quart, but $2.90 was a lot of money then, and that's why we had the cow.

# Hardwares

Peter Chumik used to work for Hoyt's Hardware in his younger days and was quite a ball player. It is said, during the 1929 championship season celebration for the Hoyt's Softball Team, winners of the Southern Alberta Men's title, Pete and a fellow-Hoyt's employee doctored the victory punch. Both were fired, for it seems B.B. Hoyt was not only a temperance man at home but a past president of the city's Temperance organization. To add to the irony of the whole affair, the softball trophy was sponsored by the Lethbridge Hotel, which rumour would have it, had a beer parlour on the premises. We assume B.B. kept the trophy anyway, though apparently not his employees.

"Hoyt's had a hardware on 13th, north of Kobal's, and later Carload Pete (Chumik) took it over," said Mavis (Harding) Standing. "About 1950 or so I worked there a bit, and Vonda Chmelauska also worked there at the same time. Originally, I believe Pete was in the Burgman Block, downstairs. That's when Vonda began there. Alex Linning used to be Santa Claus for Chumik's during the Christmas season when I worked in the store."

Malvina and Joseph Chmelauska came to the Nemiscam area in 1928.

Vonda Danielson, with daughter's photo in back.

They had married in Lithuania and had honeymooned in Canada, with the idea of returning home in 10 years. But the Dirty 30s hit and they never did go back. Joseph, who didn't speak English at the time, worked as a farm labourer before joining the CPR. Because of his job the family moved to Lethbridge, when daughter Vonda was in Grade 4.

"I was born in Nemiscam and I have very fond memories about living there," said Vonda, as she tells of nudging snakes, snaring gophers and running barefoot along roadways.

Anyone who bought appliances, fine china, lingerie or other items in Lethbridge, either at Pete Chumik's North Lethbridge Hardware, the downtown Hoyt's or Eaton's, will likely remember Vonda. Her love for fine china still exists, and she prizes a set of Wedgwood dinnerware she has.

"I was in sales for many, many years, I just loved to sell," said Vonda, who started the Bride Book tradition at Hoyt's. "Old Carload Pete (Chumik) always told me again and again, 'the customer always comes first'. I really believed in that when I was working."

Vonda and her late husband Dean Danielson, have a daughter Brenda, who was the right-hand assistant for years for Father Keon at Assumption Church. She has gone on to become a head nurse in a London, Ontario hospital and the mother of two.

There have been many other furniture stores along the main north side thoroughfare through the years, some there just for a while, others lasting much longer.

Across from where St. Basil's Church stands, at 546 13th Street, Fred Rodgers had a furniture store during the 1920s.

"He was very English and his good friend Percy Perry had the Jersey Dairy in town," said Mavis. "Across from the furniture store, on the avenue, was the Kerr family and Watsons, along 13th, was a big family with nine sons."

Scotty Armitt recalls Galenkamp Furniture on 13th Street, between 5th and 6th Avenues, in the late 1930s and into the 1940s. He said Galenkamp would make all the furniture for sale in the store.

In 1913 William Hart - not the famous movie cowboy - and Dave Patterson operated Hart Patterson Hardware Co. The store was at 418 13th until 1917 and moved to 246 by the late 1930s, as Hart Hardware. By 1946 Acme Billiards was in that location. There were suites above the Hart Hardware as well as the old Hennesey and Wilson store, which dated back to 1917. Next to these big buildings was a house, home to a music teacher whose daughter was Margaret, remembers Mavis. She said a brick house came next, just off the street, and Mr. Bruce, principal of Westminster lived there, before he moved to the 1500 block on 4th Avenue.

Below: Hart Hardware in 1922, at 246 13th St. N.

"Hart Hardware was a nice store, as I recall," said Phyllis.

Ab Chervinski recalls how Olanders, another popular furniture/hardware store along 13th, would pass out plates to its regular customers at Christmas time, each time they made a purchase. Olanders had a long run, from 1914 at 524 13th until the advent of the 1940s.

One of my early hardware memories centres on Morrison's Hardware in the 1950s, with their sons Bud and Hugh. Ab Chervinski remembers Morrison as a "chubby fellow with a moustache," and adds that just up the street from Morrison's Hardware was the Candy Kitchen and Peta Clothing Store. Frank Peta has his law office in the same area today.

The Morrison Hardware was in a building later home to Lyle's Hardware. During most of the 1960s two of the finest people 13th Street was ever home to, Bob and Eva Deimuth took over the hardware for a few years. Both had deep roots in the hardware business, with Pete and later Lyle Sproule, when he operated Lyle's Hardware for a time.

## The Wright Way

Wright's Bakery established itself in a store destined to become the second home of Lee Duck Cleaners. The bakery, just south of 4th Avenue, was in operation from 1933 into 1940.

"I used to go and help Vera Wright," said Audrey (Bissett) Kesler. "Vera wrapped bread, and there was another daughter Grace too, and their brother Bill."

Grace (Wright) Jensen worked in the bakery with sister Vera when she was 12 or 13, right after school. There was also two other sisters, Ellen and Francis.

"The family left for the store in the early morning - the baker was making the bread early - and I would go off to school, at Central. Then I'd go over to the bakery and wrap the bread after school to sell over the counter so people could have fresh bread for supper. I worked until 9 o'clock," said Grace. "My older sister, Vera, helped a lot too. One time we got in a new bread slicer and she cut her finger off using it. There was just Vera and I who worked in the store, our brother Bill was too young to help. A man called Vince was the main baker with an assistant named Viney. My dad, Dave Wright, and his brother Albert owned the bakery, though I know my uncle didn't have too much to do with it. My dad eventually sold out to Weston's in Calgary in the 1930s, and then he went to work for them. Uncle Albert went on to become a Social Credit MLA."

The bakery turned out bread - three loaves for a dollar - cookies, cakes and other treats.

At the time Grace worked in the shop the family was living on 7th Street South, but her dad eventually moved back north.

"We used to live on 3rd Avenue North, just down from the Kings Hotel, next door to my grandfather, Charlie Wright," said Grace. "Next door to him was Art and Lilian Giles. Lilian was my dad's sister. Also on that street were Josie Larson, David Hodge on the corner and Jockey Monroe across the street. Ethel Ingoldsby was to the west of us, on the north side of the street.

---

**Apple picking time**

Both Bill and Grace served for four years in the Canadian Navy during World War II. Bill was on the HMCS Huron and Grace was in charge of the Officers' Mess at King's, in Halifax, then at an officers' training school at Digby.

"Bill would come visit me when he was in port and we'd go along the Annapolis Valley, picking apples up off the road," said Grace with a laugh.

---

"The Albert Wright family lived on 19th Street and Mrs. Wright taught music as well," said Ab Chervinski, who lived at 230 16th St. N. at the time. "Mr. Wright (Albert) was involved in the early days of the Social Credit Party. That area where Albert lived included other families like the Fossards, Jarvie, McNabb, Albert Park and Dick Burgman was up on 19th Street.

"There was also a Gilmore Bakery along 16th Street and 2nd Avenue. The Bodgeneer Dairy was right across the street from us, and we were there quite a few years, around 10 or so years before the dairy closed around 1930. The Gilmore Bakery, which made breads and special items like raisin bread, was further down the street and they later sold out to McGavins. My step-brother and I worked there for a time."

Chervinski's step-brother was Ed Synik, and he had two step-sisters, Stella and Jeanette. As well, the Chervinski family included Margaret, Roberta, Albert, Elizabeth, Mary, Helen, Sophie, Ralph, Rose, and Adam, or Ab as he's been known much of his life.

"We won a prize at the Lethbridge Exhibition in the 1930s for having the biggest family," said Ab. "We went into a side show to see all the strange animals and the guy asked my father if we were all his children. When my dad said yes, the guy said: 'Just stay here, I'll bring the animals out to see you.'"

## Chinese found a North Side Home

Chinese families were prevalent on the north side, and some of the business blocks on 13th Street bear Chinese names. Chinese citizens however, were not always welcome on the north side, and were even segregated to a specific area of the south side, known as Chinatown, which still has some of the traditional old shops.

In 1907, during the Christmas season, a Chinese restaurant was wrecked by a racist mob, following a heated argument with an unruly customer. The RCMP were called in to quell the ensuing riot. Within two years, north Lethbridge ratepayers were asking that no Chinese laundries or restaurants be allowed on the north side of the tracks. By late 1910 feelings were so high that a city bylaw was passed restricting Chinese laundries and businesses to west of 4th Street South, which was also the home for the city's brothels. The bylaw only lasted until 1916 however.

I can honestly say, when I went to school, at Westminster and later the new Wilson Junior High School, racism was virtually non-existent at least from my standpoint as a kid, though I know some adults had different views; with the Chinese kids mixing easily with we Scots, the English, Hungarian, Japanese and many other European nationalities. That was the great part of my side of town, we were a true melting pot.

One of the longest surviving businesses along 13th Street North was Lee Duck Cleaners, dating back to its early days as a tailor shop and cleaners. Originally set up at 402 13th Street, from 1918 through 1945, the business moved across the street and down a store to 330 in 1945, where it remained until its closing in 1979, when Park Neilson Cleaners took over from the Lee family.

Jack Lee, son of the originator of Lee Duck Cleaners, Duck Lee, said the 402 13th St. shop was a tailors and cleaners, set up in a two storey building with an attic.

"We used to live upstairs, and the attic was where my bedroom was," said Jack, who drove the cleaner's delivery van for years. "My father had a shop in Vancouver too, on Hastings Street and I was born in 1924. I didn't come to Lethbridge until I was one or two. When my father first came to Lethbridge he was an apprentice tailor with a man named Ridpath, before he opened his shop. The shop was dry cleaning and tailoring, right from the start, and in later years we still did repairs."

When Jack was four, his father took him back to China, to be schooled in Chinese and to learn the Chinese culture. Jack returned in 1939, getting out of Hong Kong just before it fell at the start of the Second World War. He was 14 when he returned to 13th Street, and was sent to school just cross the street and down a block, to Westminster.

"I went to Westminster for four years when I came back, and had to start in Grade 2 . . . every three or four months they'd move me up a grade," said Jack, who didn't speak any English when he returned to Lethbridge, so school was quite a culture shock.

Duck Lee and his wife Soon Yet had eight children, losing one son and one daughter, raising Jimmy, Harvey and Jack and daughters Margaret, Jean and Betty. Most of the kids attended Westminster School and the three boys all worked in the business. The girls worked only on a part-time basis. In its heyday the business also included four other staff members.

Jack worked there much of his life, except for three years in the Canadian army, serving in Belgium, Holland and Germany the last seven months of the war. Returning home, Jack spent more than two decades in the militia, the Royal Canadian Engineers and the 18th Field Regiment.

Lee Duck's was the only dry cleaners on the north side, and one of the earliest ones in the city. It was one of the few 13th Street businesses which catered to both north side and south side clientele.

"In dry cleaning you used solvents, and with laundry you used water," said Jack. "When we first started up we used gasoline in the dry cleaning, which wasn't too safe. This was before varsol came into play. I don't know how many times things caught fire in that shop."

Duck Lee wanted to expand by the end of the war years and decided the original building just wasn't up to it, and after a major fire he moved across the avenue. About the same time he bought the family a new home, just two blocks west on the corner of 12th Street B and 4th Avenue. The new shop had a counter across the front, and all the machinery in the rear, on the main floor. The basement was home to the boilers. As a little kid Joyce Davies remembers walking past the original Lee Duck location next to the Credico Bakery.

"We'd go past and old Mr. Lee Duck would be sitting in the window, operating the Mangle (a large pressing machine) almost every day."

"At 402 we were right next to Pete Credico and his bakery, and when we moved there was a vacant lot on the corner (later Western Plumbing would build there and for a time an Alberta Government Liquor Store was based in the huge building), and next to us, on the south was Jack Wong's Confectionary," Jack said. "Through the years the family made a living . . . my dad survived the Dirty 30s, while at the same time not many others were making a go of it. We also delivered all over the city, because we had a driver who worked cheap - me. My father died in the 1950s, but the business kept on."

Mavis (Harding) Standing was about eight years old when she saw the original Lee Duck Cleaners burn.

The original three-storey building was on the corner of 4th Avenue, located in what was later Credico's Bakery. It was 1922 when she watched the blaze from the bedroom window of the family home across the street, in what became the Westminster School yard. Lee Duck's soon recovered and set up a new shop just a few doors south across 4th Avenue, along 13th.

"It was 1922 and I was at home in bed with Typhoid Fever," said Mavis. "I looked out the window and saw the cleaners was on fire. My dad (who served on city council in 1906) was outside our house hosing down the roof with our garden hose to put out any cinders which blew over from the Lee Duck fire. The flames were a very pretty colour.

"Our house was the first brick house built in Lethbridge, but it was torn down when the city bought our property to expand the Westminster School grounds. When Lee Duck's burned down you could sit in the window of our four-roomed cottage and see through the gap in 13th Street all the way to the 9th Street Bridge, with nothing in the way. There was nothing until an area we called the High Line, a CPR spur track that ran just back of the macaroni factory, past the International Harvester Building and up to the coal mines past the Little Wigan area to the north. In the winter, at night when it would be storming or the snow would be blowing, my father would put a lantern in our window so the miners getting off the rail cars in that area could have a guide across the prairie to 13th Street. Those who lived south of the mine would often ride the cars back to the railyard after their shift to save themselves a walk."

Across from the Lee Duck home on 4th Avenue was the Sherman home, on the north east corner of 4th Avenue and 12th St. B. The house dates back to the early 1900s and included some barns, operating at the time as the Levellie Livery Stables.

Levellie Livery could be found on the Sherman property for a very short time. William Levellie came to Lethbridge from Welland, Ontario in 1910 and for less than three years ran a livery on the corner of 4th Avenue and 12th St. B North, before his death in September 1913. He was survived by his wife and daughter, and was predeceased by a son in 1912. Levellie, 42, was said to be a community spirited man, though he had a very short history in north Lethbridge.

For many years the Sherman family called the little house home and the family included daughter Bette (Slovak). "My grandfather, Donald McNab, was an alderman in the city in the 1920s and he was also a member of the Alberta Legislature, under the United Farmer's Party banner. He only served an interim position, to fill a vacated seat. I don't think he was ever elected again, as a strong labour man, even back then, well, it just didn't float."

## Baking and Ice Cream

About where Higa's Jewellery now stands at 13th Street and 4th Avenue, you used to find Pete Credico's Bakery.

"Wow! what a bakery that was," said Bette (Sherman) Slovak. "I have never tasted bismarks as good as his, not ever! In the back of the bakery Pete had an ice cream parlour and in the 1940's I remember a juke box. All the teens hung out there. We must have driven him crazy punching in the same old songs over and over. He didn't seem to mind us . . . He was a fine man.

"Pete Credico had a fancy spot where you could go in and have a milk shake," said Avice Anderson. "You'd go in after he'd been making bread or buns and there was all those wonderful smells and flour in the air. That bakery was there in the '20s through the 1940s."

June (Glanville) Carpenter also fondly remembered the ice cream in the bakery store, with its old ice cream tables and those round, wire ice cream chairs at the back of the shop.

"We would spend a nickel on one of his lovely jelly doughnuts and then have ice cream," said June. "Pete would often let you make your own milk shake . . . if he thought he could trust you not to put in eight scoops of ice cream."

"Pete Credico was part of the National System of Baking, and no one made better donuts," said Ab Chervinski. "The kids would rush over from Westminster to buy them, and enjoy the little soda bar in the back. Jack Credico was a city policeman, but his sister helped out at the bakery."

Alvin Bissett believes Nick Credico was the father and the first owner of the shop. Then later Pete ran the bakery. "Their apple turnovers were wonderful . . . I used to steal them sometimes," he said with a laugh. "Camille Bridarolli had the bakery for a while after the Credico family left. Bridarolli lived down on 12th Street C, in the 600 or 700 block."

## Cutting It Close

Nestled in a small building just south of McCaffery's, across an open lot from Morrison Hardware, was Bill Kregosky's Barber Shop, known as Greggy's,

You could read the comics of the day, magazines like "Field and Stream" - Greggy was an avid angler - "The Saturday Evening Post" or "Sport". The shop was full of men's talk, of men's smells, from the shaving cream to aftershave and even cigar smoke. There was Wildroot Cream Oil, Brylcream and other smelly stuff that was sprinkled on after each haircut, making your trip to the barber shop even more special.

"Greggy was my dad's first cousin," said Frances (Salansky) Kaupp. "I remember Greggy used to go down to Cross-Coulee, where we had a farm south of Raymond, and swim across the reservoir. He was quite a swimmer. He used to cut my hair too, and I hated it. He'd give me one of those little girl Dutch cuts, just like my mother told him to do."

Greggy was also a wood carver, and had some great carvings on display along an upper shelf above the mirrors in the shop, a fish and a ball player as I recall.

You didn't make appointments back then, you just dropped in, sat on the chairs and read as you waited. Once in the chair, adults or kid, Greggy would chat away about fishing, sports and even tease the younger patrons about girls.

Greggy's was a man's shop. I remember even my mother respected the sanctity of the shop, and if she needed my attention, or wanted to give the money to Greggy that I'd left at home, she'd just poke her head into the shop, not cross the threshold. Women just didn't belong in a men's barber shop back then.

My haircut of the day, through the early 1950s, was a brush cut or crew cut, called a buzz today. As I recall, while Greggy was a great barber, no matter what I told him I wanted, I received a crew cut. But, as I got older, 15 or so, the style changed, with the duck-tail coming into vogue. Later I added a twist to that with a crew cut on top and a duck-tail, with the long sides at the back and around the ears.

"Greggy was just a barber, but he did sell tobacco to the men who came into the shop on Saturday night for the poker games . . . and to some others who came into the shop," said Kathleen, widow of the popular 13th Street barber regarding his selling tobacco in the shop. "Greggy only had one chair, and he'd take his lunch to the shop each day, stopping long enough around noon time to finish it up before going back to cutting hair. His hobbies were fishing and wood carving. He did all those carvings, on display on that upper shelf in the shop. In those days barbers didn't work Sundays or Mondays, but he was sure busy the rest of the week."

Ab Chervinski said it was his father who taught Greggy how to barber. He also said McCallum's had a barber shop, and operated the Hub Cigar Store, just to the south of Greggy, with Fred Ward as one of the barbers.

"Ward barbered a bit, but mainly he was a member of the Veteran's Guards who worked at the PoW camp," said Ab.

Joseph Chervinski and Peter Stanko, said Joe's son Ab, were the first barbers in north Lethbridge, set up downstairs in the old Standard Bank.

"This was in the late teens sometime," said Ab. "After cutting hair for years my dad went to work in the coal mines about 1920, as a machinist with the J.J. Hamilton Coal Co. He gave up barbering after that, but he's the man who taught Greggy how to cut hair."

Another of those early barbers along 13th was John Pilchak, at 258 13th in 1920. Joseph George, Mikey's brother, was up and running in 1934, where he and his brother held sway for decades.

John Jooreas had a number of locations along 13th, being at 330 in 1925 and at 410a by 1929, a spot filled by Greggy from 1932 to 1972. Scotty Armitt remembers when Cliff McCallum operated the Hub, which sold cigars, magazines, cigarettes and other types of tobacco, and pop. The shop also included a barber's chair.

"Greggy's shop came along after the Hub, and Greggy bought out the barber portion of the store," said Scotty. "The Hub and Greggy were right next to each other for a while."

There were other barber shops along 13th, including Little Mikey George's shop across from the Miners' Library and Johnny's, just south of Mikey George's a few buildings. Johnny's came complete with a pool room.

Johnny's closing - with Johnny's death in 2003 - had a few tables in a cinder block building, and offered some quiet games, even with Johnny himself.

Just a few yards north was Mikey George's little old shop, which included a small soda counter and a pinball machine or two back when I was delivering newspapers in the early 1950s. It also had a juke box, and it was stocked with country and western music. The first time I heard Webb Pierce was on that juke box and he was singing Honky Tonk. It only took a nickel then to play the juke box, and, in this case, Brent Seely had put the nickel in the machine.

"Wayne Clark and I used to go over to Mikey's each week and pick up the records for just a nickel apiece when the service guy came in to change them, taking out the old hits and putting in the new ones," Brent remembers. "I used to have a stack of 45s this high (hand out by his waist)."

Fred's Barber Shop was right next door to Greggy's, and while Greggy's was simply a walk-in with the door on the street, to get into Fred's two-chaired shop you had to go up five or six stairs, in somewhat of a porch.

For many years the Seely family, Frank and Leona, daughter Karen and son Brent, lived on the upper level of Fred Ward's shop, at the back end of the building, with their own private entrance along the side between the barber shop and Credico's bakery and up the wooden stairs at the back. Between the two buildings 10 to 20-foot icicles would form in the winter months due to lack of exposure to the sun. The other five apartments had a common stair well at the front. The apartments were basically one room, though the Seely's had two, with the bathroom for all, down at the end of the hall.

"Fred was about 6-foot-two, a tall skinny guy, and he married a midget lady," said Brent. "They lived on the main level, at the back of the barber shop. I always got my hair cut by Fred; I think my mom would have killed me if I went next door to Greggy's."

Credico's was right next door, to the south, and the bakery was often a must-stop place for sweet rolls, donuts, buns or bread, said Brent.

On the other side, going north, was Greggy's and Steve Mezei's Shoe Repair. The shoe repair shop always had a smell of leather and shoe polish, with the burr of the foot-operated stitching machine, a fascinating place for kids to stop. Seely also remembers the BA Service Station on the corner of 4th and 13th, across from Fred's, and south of the old Westminster teacherage/classroom/industrial arts building.

"Who can forget the old Firehall, Supina's or going to Kobal's Grocery?" said Seely. "There was the blacksmith just around the corner from us, on 4th Avenue to the west. You could spend hours standing in there watching him. I mostly remember the darkness, the blackness of the place, and the smell.

"Just past the Lealta Theatre, owned by Mr. Doughty with that big cigar, was Tom Kerrison's Second Hand Store. I'm not sure why, but we called him Grandpa Kerrison and I remember he had a beautiful singing voice. They lived in the back of the store and we would go there Christmas Eve and we'd sit around and he would sing. That was nice. My friend Jim Standish and I would often sleep over at Grandpa Kerrison's place. . . He had all those old second hand beds up along the balcony of the store, so we slept on them."

Ab Chervinski said Kerrison's daughter married Jerome Platt, who went on to become a member of the

Alberta Sports Hall of Fame as one of the province's best runners, out of Taber. Platt sometimes ran with the Armitts, John McColl and Emery twins who trained across the street at the York Hotel for a while.

Jerome Platt

"Across from us there used to be a farm equipment dealership," said Seely. "I remember all those V-shaped things piled up along there. We always shopped at Supina's when we lived above Fred's but then when we went further north it was Mihalik's. In those days you could charge your groceries and pay for them on pay day. Right up there too, across from the ball park, was Matt's Confectionary, for candy, pop and stuff. As I remember the north side back in the 1940s and 1950s, it was made up of little pockets of communities, everything revolving around your own neighbourhood. That may also be just because of our age and the fact we think we were different. One thing we all had was that 9:15 curfew, sounded each night over those old air raid sirens. You were in real trouble if you weren't home within minutes after it sounded.

"From growing up on the north side I certainly remember the streetcars and the little Oriental fellow with a market garden out by Hardieville who used to deliver fresh produce by horse and buggy . . . those horses the milkmen had knew the routes better than their drivers. We'd often go up on the 13th Street underpass and watch the cars going north and south and try to identify them as they came through. That's when cars weren't all alike, like they are today. Then there was the 9th Street bridge, and that easy access to downtown because you could cut right across a lot of open fields to get to the bridge back then.

"Across from Westminster there was the Johnson Red and White Store, run by Alex and he had a daughter named Betty and son Sandy. They lived right across the alley from the store. Also along the 12th St. C area was the Mogus family, and Al Hepple just a block or two north. Also, across from the blacksmith and across our alley when we lived above Fred's there was the Withage home, which I thought was a mansion with its nice manicured yard and beautiful house."

It was in the Withage's side yard where two miniature churches were built in the 1950s, later moved to unknown sites, at least unknown to me.

Shortly after the war ended the Seely family moved even further north, to the new Wartime houses along the 8th Avenue area just east of 13th. That meant Brent, who had started his schooling at Westminster, transferred to Galbraith. In Grade 7 he became part of the original Grade 7 through 9 graduating class at the new Wilson Junior High, ironically straight down 4th Avenue if you walked out the front door of Fred's Barber Shop.

"Back then, 8th Avenue was the end of the world," said Brent. "There was nothing north of us, except Galbraith School out there all alone on the prairie, and some houses along the west side of 13th Street. When they finally opened that old Dominion Square area it was way out in the boonies. We were in some of the first homes out there, between 13th and 15th Street and up to 10th Avenue."

It was in this region where Seely and other neighbourhood kids would gather, in the mid- 1950s, on the street in front of the Waterhouse home to watch that new fangled television through the living room window, even though the picture was mainly snow much of the time. It wasn't too long after that Seely was working at CJLH-TV as a cameraman, later moving in front of the camera, behind the microphone, on the sports desk and then on to CJOC for a career in radio, culminating with retirement in 2002 as the station's vice-president and general manager.

## McCaffrey

North Lethbridge residents had access to one of the great healing ointments of the time, and Gwen McCaffrey's collection of memorabilia included a tiny bottle, with a faint ointment odour. The bottle dates back many, many decades, to an era when W.H. McCaffrey, and later son Jack, made and sold McCaffrey's Compound Healing Ointment.

"Grandfather patented the ointment," said Gwen. "It was a good healing ointment. My husband Jack used to make the mix too, but he finally stopped towards the end, just before the store was sold. It was the best healing ointment I've ever known. I wish we still had it today."

The ointment was available at McCaffrey's Drug Store, along 13th Street, between 4th and 5th Avenues. It was good for burns, cuts, cold sores, ulcers, cracked lips, the itch and other ailments. The last remaining bottle was salvaged from the final clean-up, after the store was sold in 1978.

Gwen McCaffrey, Jack's widow, salvaged some of W.H. McCaffrey's old prescription books, his original early pharmaceutical scale, utensils, bottles and a mortar and pestle. William H. McCaffrey bought an existing drug store on 13th Street North in the early 1900s, just a few doors south of where the present building stands which housed the final store at 418. The original shop was known as the W.P.J. Alexander Peoples Drug Store.

"The north side was a going concern then and people were hoping 13th Street would eventually be built right out across the river to Picture Butte as it continued north," said Gwen. "It was the only drug store for many, many blocks around in those early days."

W.H. lived about a block and a half from the store, on the corner of 12th St. C and 5th Avenue, in a stately, verandahed home, the McCaffrey house. Jack and Gwen were married in the home in 1945, but they lived on the south side.

W.H. McCaffrey also set up the first sub-station Post Office in Lethbridge, in his drug store, in 1918. Besides stamps, W.H. sold only drugs during those early years. Things did evolve to beauty aids, magazines, and various other health and body-care related items as the years passed, but nothing like the super-drug marts of today.

Jack McCaffrey received the first Air Mail letter delivered in Lethbridge, Jan. 15, 1931.

When Jack McCaffrey graduated from pharmaceutical school in 1938 he opened up a drug store on 6th Street South, next to Cameron's Ladies Wear. Later, he moved the store into the Oddfellows Building, on 5th Street. When W.H. retired Jack moved north, about 1956 or 1957. He ran the store and the Post office until he retired in 1978. Jack died two years later, at age 66. One of the long-time employees of McCaffrey's was the late Paul Pheirson, a soft-spoken man always willing to help a customer.

"Paul was there when I first came here," said Gwen. "He was very good in the store."

The store, with its old walnut and glass-cased counters on the main level, included an elevated area at the rear of the store for the druggist. There was also a second storey, which had a lot of uses through the years, serving as everything from a native friendship centre to the home of The Garbutt Business college for a few years and later a design lighting studio. Garbutts began in 1909 and before it closed in 1967 it had occupied numerous locations in Lethbridge, including the Masonic Hall and the upper level of the then new Woolworth building.

In the 1930s and 1940s the upper level of McCaffrey's 418 address was a happening place. It was home to the Burgman Dance Hall, a place people came to dance, many of them Veteran's Guards, relaxing after their trying hours at the PoW Camp to the east. Later Garbutt Business College would move into the hall, replacing the band music with the rhythm of the typewriter.

My mother, Lily Melling (Allison) was one of the many graduates of Garbutt's and served for years in the accounting department for Woolworth's. She was the head girl in accounting but had to quit her job when she married my father, Andy, in 1939, who worked in the Dallas Hotel, almost right across from Woolworth's front door. Back then, Woolworth's only hired single girls. Gain a wedding band, and you were gone.

Mavis Standing remembers the original McCaffrey store, which was just south of its final spot, having rooms upstairs. One of the residents was Hilda Joule, who married Fred Harding, Mavis' brother. Hilda died on the couple's sixth wedding anniversary.

Ab Chervinski recalls the back of McCaffrey's Drug Store more than the front, and with good reason.

"We'd go out back and check their garbage for comic books each week," said Ab. "With the comics that didn't sell, the store would rip the cover off and mail it back to the company for a refund. They'd then throw the comic book, without its cover, into the garbage. That's what we'd go after in the barrels out back."

Joyce Davies said with a laugh: "One Halloween we stole the back gate off McCaffrey's house and chopped it up and used it for firewood, burning it in a big bonfire."

## Red and White

"I remember going into the Red and White store from Westminster, and if you worked it just right Mr. Johnson would be gone for lunch," said Joyce Davies. "He'd have an assistant take over for him when he wasn't there and when you bought five cents worth of candy from the assistant he'd fill the bag right up . . . when Mr. Johnson was there you'd just get what seemed like a sprinkling of candy on the bottom of the bag."

### Bill-payers Rewarded

"When the miners got paid they'd go to the Red and White and pay their bill, and Johnson would always have a bag of candy for the kids," said Scotty Armitt.

Before World War Two, Jimmy Yip ran the Canadian Cafe just south of the Red and White Store owned by the Johnsons, said Scotty Armitt. He said the Red and White store had a barn out back, for the delivery wagons and the horses needed to pull those wagons.

Mavis (Harding) Standing said John McGillvery used to deliver for Johnson's Red and White in 1938. "Times were tough back then and my husband had gone to Vancouver to look for work. We were on relief, getting $20.10 a month and $10 of that was for rent. Christmas was coming on and on Christmas Eve the McGillvery boy arrived from the Red and White with a big box of groceries for us. I had never ordered those groceries, but they were sent from the store courtesy of the Oddfellows Lodge. That parcel had everything in it, and I just cried my eyes out. Until then I had no idea of what we were going to do for Christmas. I sold a bag of flour for $1 and bought two toys, one for each of my children."

In 1917, Alex Johnson and A. Williamson went before city council and then the District Court of Appeals, on behalf of the North Lethbridge Ratepayers Association. The businessmen were appealing what they called the city's unequal business assessments, between the north and south sides of town. They said business property on the south side of the tracks had their assessment reduced to 56 per cent of the 1913 figures, while those on the north side were reduced to only 73 per cent. They also said sales of some lots along 13th Street were bringing $250 a lot.

Judge McNeill traveled in from the district court in Fort Macleod to hear the appeal and ruled against the pair. City Assessor Meech told the judge he felt the assessment was equitable, and cited three cases of business property along 13th bringing a return of at least eight per cent on the investment, after expenses. He said the lot where the Standard Bank stood brought $3,000, with the average assessment along the street being $1,500. McNeill, in his ruling, said the evidence showed the assessment was most equitable and dismissed the appeal.

Hennesey and Wilson operated a clothing store near McCaffrey's at the time and Alex Johnson and his brother John had the Red and White grocery store.

"When I was little, my grandmother and I would walk all the way from Little Wigan down to Johnson's (between 4th and 5th Avenues) on the boardwalk along 13th to pay our bill," said Lil Wright, who was born in 1924. "I remember he'd always give me a treat when she paid, jelly beans. I don't think Mihalik's was open at the time and I believe my grandmother shopped at Johnson's because he was an old Englishman and my grandparents were from Lancashire. When I got married (1946) we went to Mihalik's, and later when we moved to 12th St. B, just off 4th Avenue, we went to Supina's mainly."

For a time, next to the Red and White in its early days in the 1930s, was a fish and chip shop operated by the Soady family.

## It Dressed People and Burgers

One of the special places, at least for me, along 13th was the Wonder Cafe operated by Lou Hong. Lou's was a combination small grocery store, candy and ice cream store and cafe with wooden booths at the back and a long counter along the 5th Avenue side of the store. When my dad remarried, after my mother's death in 1946, my step-mother, Mona Walton, was a bookkeeper for the Juniors and Imperial Women's Wear stores in downtown Lethbridge, so for lunch on many a school day I'd get 50 cents - actually she dropped the 50 cents off with Lou and I'd just go in and order. I'd get two hamburgers, single of course, and a pop for that 50 cents and then dash back across 13th to Westminister in time for the afternoon bell. Lou also sold snuff, those little round tins of Copenhagen chewing tobacco, which sold for 30 cents. Interesting that something you were going to chew and spit out cost more than a hamburger.

---

**Remembering Lou**

"When I was about 16 I used to work for Lou at the Wonder Cafe." said Audrey (Bissett) Kesler. "I'd help sell groceries, fry hamburgers, make tea, did the dishes, coffee and milkshakes. Lou was very nice, a real friendly fellow. Lou liked to drink coffee, but he liked to add a little rum to it once in a while. He used to live downstairs, at least until his wife came over from China.

---

My grandfather Allison used to give me three dimes almost every day to run down to Lou's and pick up his supply of snuff. He didn't have to say a word, just pass the dimes, and off I'd go. Like any bartender in the 1940s and 1950s he had a huge supply of dimes. It was custom for all patrons - with the odd cheap exception - to flip a dime on the bartender's tray when he delivered the glasses of 10 cent draft beer.

My granddad, at the Lethbridge Hotel, and my Dad at the Dallas, always came home with a pocket full of slightly damp and beer-smelling dimes.

"We'd be open early and I can remember we'd be open until 10 p.m. or later on certain nights to catch the crowds coming back from the hockey games at the old arena on 2nd Avenue South, to buy smokes, milkshakes and pop," said Audrey (Bissett) Kesler. "One of my jobs was to roll all the change Lou had in those paper wrappers. I'd sit in the old wooden booths at the back and roll the change, which Lou used to gather in old coffee, tobacco and jam cans, and have all over the store. I still have some of those tiny nickels they used to have at one time, which Lou said I could keep because they didn't fit into the rolls."

"I'll tell you one thing about the Wonder Cafe few people know," said Scotty Armitt. "When Christmas came during the war years Lou Hong would make up parcels of cigarettes, candy and stuff and send them overseas to the boys who were in the service who used to be his customers before the war. That was pretty special."

Before Lou Hong came along about 1940 with the Wonder Cafe, the building was home to Ontkean's Lady's Wear, and later an array of shops, including a grocery store and coffee shop. Then Sawilla Home Improvements Ltd. held down the corner, until mid-2005.

"The front entrance was the same, with the show windows on each side the big middle door," said Mavis Standing. "There were hats, purses, dresses and things. I was only about 10 or 12 at the time, so this must have been about 1925. It was there a long time."

Armitt said one of the Ontkeans was Michael, who went on to be a TV star, in The Rookies, and appear in TV and regular movies.

Florence Seager, born in 1912 and a north Lethbridge resident since 23 months of age, fondly remembers Ontkean's Dress Shop, in the mid to late 1920s, and the fact McCaffrey's had a Post Office, a very convenient attraction for north side letter writers.

"Ontkean's was a very nice shop, and it was busy all the time," said Seager "Everything they had was real nice; I don't know why they closed the store."

When Ontkean's moved their business downtown, the little store became a grocery, first owned by the Piskos and then by Don Arnold, said Ab Chervinski. Then, Lou Hong and the Wonder Cafe came along.

Ab, whose uncle married an Ontkean, said international television and movie actor Michael Ontkean was a distant relative of the dress shop family, and came by his interest in acting honestly. "Orville Ontkean used to write some of the Wayne and Shuster radio scripts," said Ab.

## A Maple Leaf's Store

Sorokoski's Grocery was a tiny store, narrow but long, at 544 13th St., which included, among the groceries, a slot machine and punch board.

Isidor Michael Sorokoski was born in Poland in 1886 and came to Canada in 1910. He and wife Helen had four sons, Frank, Stanley, Victor and Karl.

In 1923 Michael bought a small store at 544 13th Street, assisted by brother Tony while Michael continued to work with the CPR. Tony lived at the back of the store for a while but soon left to farm near Athabasca.

In the early days of the store the brothers had a slot machine and a punch board, but when Michael took over full-time the machines left. Michael got rid of the now illegal gambling machines in 1926 - the punch board was a large card, with tightly rolled mini-paper sheets with the prizes on them, to be selectively punched out with a pin by the buyer. The full attention of the store then fell on groceries and confections and Michael set up a delivery service, as far away as Coalhurst and Coaldale.

"Mr. Sorokoski used to deliver groceries, from his store, in a rubber-tired, horse-drawn wagon, and he did this wearing a derby hat," said Ab Chervinski.

Frank often delivered to Coalhurst, by horse and buggy each Saturday, over gravel roads.

Writing in *The Bend*, a History of West Lethbridge, Frank Sorokoski said the store received much of its supplies in bulk, with cheese coming in 50-pound wheels, coffee and sugar in 100-pound bags, as did the peanuts. The store refrigerator was a large ice box, with 100-pound blocks of ice to keep things cool.

During the Depression the store had relief chits and ran credit, the farmers paying off at harvest time and the coal miners whenever they earned a pay cheque. The family also received chickens, eggs, hogs and other foods at times as payment.

Among the senior Sorokoski's helpers were sons Victor and Karl, working the store when it became too much for their parents to handle, as they virtually left the store in the early 1950s, moving to 1313 6th Avenue North. In 1960 Michael died, wife Helen following in 1978.

Son Karl made a name for himself on the world hockey scene as one of the goaltenders for the Lethbridge Maple Leafs, world hockey champions of 1951.

The Leafs, on their road to the world championship, played 62 games, lost seven, tied four and won the rest, at one time putting together a 44-game winning streak, all this from Dec. 17, 1950 through April 18,1951. Karl was in goal for 22 winning games and lost four, with one tie. He and fellow goalie Mallie Hughes both recorded two shutouts. In the six-game world tourney the pair allowed only six goals while the Leafs scored 62 times.

Above: Karl Sorokoski - below: Billy Gibson

The Leafs won the world championship March 17, 1951 in the Palais des Sports in Paris, France with a 5-1 win over Sweden in front of 17,000 hockey fans.

One of Karl's friends on the team was fellow northsider Nap Milroy, and later, after he moved in from Coalhurst, Hector Negrello. Other Maple Leaf northsiders included Billy Gibson, Don McLean and Robert McGregor.

The store was always caught between the large food stores along 13th, Mihalik's to the north and Supina's to the south, and a bit later Shop-Easy, right next door. Safeway and IGA finally killed the business.

Sorokoski's wasn't the lone small confectionery/grocery store along the three km long business section of 13th. You could also find Kobal's, four Chinese-owned stores, bakeries and meat markets. As well, there were small mom and pop grocery stores east and west of 13th, just a few blocks off the heavy-traffic route, serving the neighbourhoods in their immediate area.

## Big Business Arrives

The 1970s were a bustling time along 13th Street.

The largest development by far was the Centre Village Mall, though its official address was listed as 1240 2nd Ave. A N. Fact is, the busiest entrance to the mall is really off 13th and 2nd Avenue, though it could be argued the entrance by Save-On Foods is equally as congested. When the mall first welcomed customers it was only partially finished, and included at least one of its featured attractions, a huge Simpson's Sears store.

With completion of the massive project in 1972 the mall included Sears, Allstate Insurance, a chiropractor, MacLeod's store, Art Williams Travel and Real Estate offices, Tip Top Tailors, the Betty Shop, a bath boutique, shoe store, Smitty's, the Razor's Edge, Shoppers Drug Mart, Merchant Prince Emporium, Renaissance Imports, a beauty shop, Riley and McCormick, Bata Shoes, Laura Secord Chocolates, IGA, People's Credit Jewellers, and a dentist Dr. J.A. (Jack) Sherman.

Just a few blocks to the north Westminster Shopping Mall was going full bore, opening in 1970. In 1978, certainly one of the peak years for the strip mall, you could find the Bank of Nova Scotia, a Laundromat, Safeway, Captain Murphy's Fish and Chips, Fred's Bakery, Hoyt's Pro Home Centre, Addressograph, Bryan Wilson Photography, Storks Nest, One Hour Martinizing, Mr. Soft Drink, Les Toth Agencies, Westminster Drugs and Variety Fun Snacks.

With the old Westminster School gone, the shopping plaza opened with Westminster Drugs, Bank of Nova Scotia, One Hour Martinizing, a branch of the Lethbridge Public Library, Fred's Bakery, North Village Restaurant, the Rug Shoppe and where the school's front door once welcomed kids, North Side Shell took up residence. The Shell disappeared however, and in 1993, Tim Horton's moved onto the corner of the Westminster Mall property. Now, instead of readin', writin' and 'rithmatic, it's donuts, soup and sandwiches.

With IGA in Centre Village and Safeway (1970-1979) in Westminister Mall, and earlier Shop Easy opening up, the death knell was sounding for the remaining mom-and-pop groceries along the street.

The first major new-era food store to be built along 13th was Shop Easy, at 542 13th, right next to the old Sorokoski grocery. But for some reason or another, the large store has never really had a long-term resident, no matter what the business.

Shop Easy moved into the new store in 1956 but only lasted into 1959, making way for Jenkins Groceteria from 1960 through 1962. Tom Boy Store had a longer run, lasting until 1968 before seeing Econo-Mart Grocery take up residence at 542 13th. After a few years of sitting vacant Sidorsky's Furniture moved the food isles out, in 1973 and 1974, to be followed by Town and Country Furniture from 1975 through 1978. But once again the store was left behind as a business moved on, or out. From then on the store has had an even greater turnover, with Furniture World in for a while, followed by second hand sales and other retailers to where today Lethbridge Orthotic-Prosthetic Services Ltd. seems to have made a stable home.

But stores weren't the only thing changing the face of 13th Street.

In the early 1970s, about 1973-1974 in fact, a large new complex appeared at the north end of 13th Street, Bridge Villa Estates. It opened with 188 lots listed and today there are more than 320 sites, with the entrance at 23rd Avenue.

Many come-and-go businesses and establishments have appeared along 13th in its century-plus history. And as an aside I point out that even the Lethbridge Herald - where I laboured for 45 years - had a presence along 13th, albeit a very short one. The Herald had a north side office in a new building at 533 13th in 1958 and 1959, under supervision of Yvonne Schwitzer, and then it headed back south.

Before this, that area had homes, and one I remember from the earlier 1950s was at 531 where Mel and Walter Flathan lived with their mother Grace. Right next door was Doran Berlando and on the corner, across from Westminster School, was Sunny Service, operated by R.G. Rittenhouse.

*Through the Looking Glass*, written by Audrey (Cheswick) Swedish and George Watson Sr. said, in 1909 the east side of 13th, between 5th and 7th Avenues, had a series of four- acre plots, where the Kerr, Watson and Graham families homesteaded, with William Kerr, grandfather of George Watson Sr., at 531 13th. The Watson family was at 537.

## A Family Affair

Ted Petrunia came into Mihalik's one day and called tall, slim George Mihalik "Blondie", for his blonde hair, and the name stuck.

The little boy, who at age five was helping his father Andrew in Mihalik's grocery store in the late 1920s, went on to spend 62 years in the store, known to much of the north side as Blondie - and much of south Lethbridge, Diamond City, Coalhurst and Wilson Siding for that matter.

---

**Blonde Beauty**

Blondie fondly recalls a story of a wholesaler who was sent to Mihalik's and told to ask for Blondie, the buyer.

"He came in, about 8 a.m. and I saw him standing by the mirror in the dry goods section, combing his hair and fixing his tie," said Blondie with a big laugh. "He came up to me and asked, 'where can I find Blondie?' and I told him 'that's me.' Well, I sure spoiled his day. He took one look at me and his shoulders sagged. He thought he was going to meet a beautiful blonde."

---

Blondie wasn't the only Mihalik at Mihalik's, on 13th, just south of 7th Avenue. There were brothers Joe, the oldest, sisters Mary and Katie, and younger brother Ed. And, there was father Andrew, or Andy to his customers.

Andy Mihalik, born in Czechoslovakia, came to Lethbridge in 1920 as a young man. When he left home he stopped off for a while to work the coal mines of Pennsylvania, and it was there he learned of the opportunities in the coal industry in southern Alberta.

"He started work in Coleman and worked his way up to being a pit boss," said Blondie. He also worked in the Drumheller and Rosedale mines and then came to Lethbridge in 1920 and he worked in the No. 3, No. 6 and No. 8 mines for a time. While working in the mines he took a hair cutting course, working in the mines in the day and going to school at night. In 1921 dad opened a barber shop, in the little store across the parking lot from CFCN TV today. After a while he started to sell candy, chocolate bars and pop. By 1924 he turned the shop into a grocery store, Mihalik's."

It was while in Lethbridge he met and married Katie Hudak, a lady who had grown up in the same Czech village as Andy came from.

Lethbridge only had a couple thousand people when Andy opened his grocery store, only about a third of those on the north side. But they all had to eat, and Andy had the groceries. In the late '20s and early '30s butter was only 45 cents for two pounds and bread was six loaves for a quarter.

Andy died at age 91 in 1981, but by then the Mihalik name was indelibly linked to 13th Street North. Ironically there are no grandchildren to carry the Mihalik name into the 21st century.

"My dad used to say he'd give us boys $1,000 for the first grandson, and to this day there are still no boys with the Mihalik name," said Blondie. "My sisters had boys, but my older brother Joe had seven kids, all girls."

Andy and wife Mary had two daughters, Linda (Zook) and Debbie (Coyle), and now have four grandchildren, only one a boy. For Blondie and Mary's 50th anniversary in 2000, the grandchildren and children headed to Disneyland for a week.

Andy soon outgrew the narrow, but long original barber-shop-come grocery and was adding on, adding meats and produce to the grocery list. Finally he built a new, larger store in 1938, the CFCN building today. In 1952 he added an addition to the new store and in 1955 expanded the dry goods department by building an addition, which in 2002 was home to the Asian Market.

As a kid Blondie seemed destined for the grocery business, hanging out at the store at age five, pointing customers in the right direction down what seemed like ever-expanding aisles.

Blondie, born in 1921 in the Galt Hospital, received his schooling just a few blocks from the family home on 12th Street C North, at St. Basil's, and then headed south to St. Patrick's and Garbutt Business College, then in the Masonic Hall building. It was there Mrs. Bennett taught him all about business management - at least what he hadn't learned from his dad, brothers and sisters.

"She'd give me a list of numbers and I'd be right there with the answer. I could do rapid calculation in my head; I was always good at math," said Blondie.

While at St. Basil's one of his teachers was a young Steve Vaselenak, who went on to serve the community as an alderman and on the Separate School board, along with Blondie's father, Andrew Mihalik.

"Steve was a good teacher, and I remember one day he put a new nail in a bottle of cola and set it out for all to see," said Blondie. "Well, within a week that nail was gone and he told us to imagine what it did to your stomach. I never drank a coke again, to this day."

Blondie was also good at driving a horse and wagon.

Mihalik's had a solid clientele, most on the north side, but many in south Lethbridge as well, eventually as far out as the Green Acres Drive-In area, and even out of town. Mihalik's had a number of attractions, besides its quality products and family staff - the store delivered, and had a charge account set-up.

For many years the young Blondie was the delivery boy.

"I used to call on your dad and mother (Lily and Andy Allison) the Moores, and all those nice English people up Little Wigan, with our horse and buggy," said Blondie. "In later years we had five delivery trucks, but we started with a wagon and a single horse, north south and out to Wilson Siding. In those days the stores closed at 1 p.m. on Wednesdays and I'd hitch up and head for Coalhurst and Diamond City, mainly with bulk loads, like 100 pounds of potatoes and 100 pounds of flour. I'd leave at 1 p.m. and be back around 9 p.m."

Blondie and Mary Mihalik pose at the store's closing.

The deliveries were nice in those days of very few automobiles, but best of all Mihalik's ran a tab. You could charge your groceries, and even clothing, which carried many a miner and other workers through the Dirty '30s.

"My father would let the miners charge all summer long, and when they'd get work in the winter, when the mine started up again, they'd start paying their bill," recalled Blondie. "You know, when the Depression was over no one owed us money, they all paid up once they got on their feet."

Compassion like that earned Mihalik's many life-long customers, some staying with the store for four to six decades. The same could be said of Supina's, at the south end of the 13th Street business district, which like Mihalik's, offered groceries, meats and dry goods.

Despite being in the same business, with virtually the same service area, the two families did not consider either one the enemy.

"We were friends," said Blondie. "Nick (Supina) and my dad were friends, they came from the old country, they were both Slovaks and were real friends. There was no rivalry."

Both stores were very community minded, with Supina's best known for their soccer teams, while Mihalik's sponsored a Southern Alberta League hockey team from 1939 to 1942, a fastball team through the 1930s into 1950 and a bowling team from 1962 to 1979.

In 1942, through the end of the war, Andy Mihalik, F.A. Rogers, who owned the hardware at 13th Street and 6th Avenue North, and a handful of other business men, including George Kobal, used Mihalik's as a focal point for War Bond Drives. Signs - Pledge Your Savings to Hasten Victory - urged people to support the bond drive when in the store.

Blondie, a five decade member of the Miners' Library, was friends with many of the old Miners' baseball players, like best friend Fred Onofrychuk, and spent many an after-game hour at the Library, over a beer, discussing the game.

**North Side Who's Who worked for the Mihalik's**

Blondie still fondly remembers most of the store's staff through the years and many regulars will remember all the Mihalik family and folks like Alice Kennedy who was there for 45 years and wife Mary who worked by his side for 39 years, along with others like: Clarence and Margaret Sirouvak, Eugene Chollack, and delivery personnel and shelf stockers included George Petrunia, Mike Vaselenak, Jim Cattoni, Sonny Chollak, Andy Lengyl, Cecil Chumik, Reed Kenney, Johnny Ontko, Glen Bendall, Gordon McCarthur, Steve Motchyka, Ron Ponech, Bill Ponech, Ron Kazakoff, Danny Kazakoff, and Bert, Blair and Craig Nyrose.

And there were more, many more, the likes of Allan Wilkie, Allan Mikitka, Tom Allen, Dan Allen, Jim Campbell Jr., Rick Campbell, Duane Konynenbelt, Ed Wormley, Lyle Moore, Jerry Areshenko, Ron Opyr, Don Latham, Darrel Baceda, Brad Martin, Brian Kolibas, Ron Quapp, Greg Jarvie, John Hermanitz, Grant Pisko, Gerry Wilkie, and Jim, Brian and Tom Zook.

There were people like Wayne Weitz, Dennis Silbernagel, Mike Unser, Len Szves, Tim Secretan, Bill Gaehring, Larry Skidmore, Edward Pisko, Edwin George, Clarence Sirovyak Jr., Marty Sirovyak, Jan Nicolson, George Zuelke, Len Szucs, and Len Wigton.

Cashiers included Vi Donaldson, Millie Onofrychuk, Pauline Strong, Dorrie Asplund, Dollie Pozgooyi, Margaret Sirovyak, Masa Goshinmon, Eva Deringer, Delores La Fournie, Helen Dickson, Beverly Wallace, Ann Duval, Loretta Wilkie, Kay Groves, Helen Byrne, Pat Tobo, Rose Chollak, Mary Mihalik (Blondie's wife), Mary (Mihalik) Nicolson, Kay (Mihalik) Campbell, Helen Mihalik, Jeanie Mihalik, Roberta Mihalik, Linda Mihalik, Debbie Mihalik, Madeline (Mihalik) Toogood, Helen Zubach, Rena Quinton, Lorri Kimmet, Noreen Sanford, Crystal Nordin, Margaret Minor, Jean Wyrostok, Margaret Gazarek, Donna Hanke and Liz Ackroyd.

"We'd re-live the game after it ended," Blondie said with a laugh. "Because of the store I couldn't play, though I loved baseball. When the Miners' had a Sunday double-header I'd come to the store right from Mass because the store supplied cold cuts and cheese for both teams between the games. I'd carve up a 30-pound block of cheese and lay out 30 pounds of cold cuts.

"Both teams, even visiting teams like the House of David, and the guys from Picture Butte, the Watsons and the Haneys, would all go downstairs at the Library between the games for eats. Back then there were rugby teams too, like the Panthers and Maroons, with players like Louis Pavan and Steve Sousnar, who used to play at Adams' soccer pitch when the soccer wasn't on. It was just a short walk from the store to Adams for baseball, soccer or rugby."

One of the big boosts for Mihalik's came in 1952 when the decision was made to use radio advertising, and the ringing phone and "Good morning, Mihalik's" filled the air waves with CJOC's Bob Lang bringing the message of super deals to north and south side residents. Flyers, drawn up and printed by John Lawson at The Herald Printers, brought more customers to the store, and soon Mihalik's not only employed the family, but more than 30 other people as well at any one time.

Mihalik's had a number of specialties, from clothing, boots, hats and gloves for the working man to great baking, at one time whipped up by John Van Den Hengel - who later had his own bakery along 13th - and, of course its meats. Mihalik's meat cutters were well respected and included Joe and Eddie Mihalik, and others like Jimmy Tennant, Henry Piepgrass, Merlin Adams, Pete Pisko, George Luchanski, Fred Baceda, Bill Hleuka, Noah Barnaby, Harold Deal, Jim Campbell, Jim Toogood, Clarence Sirovyak, Frank Stewart, Steve Pisko, Albert Begalli, Dave Creighton, John Seaman, Al Levans, Jack McCall, and George Petras.

For years Mihalik's was open six days a week, never on Sunday, and closed Wednesday afternoons. Though Andy fought it, night shopping eventually came along, as did seven-day-a-week shopping.

In 1966 IGA bought out Mihalik's. Night shopping was here to stay and the Mihalik's charge accounts were closed. With Mihalik's sold, and Supina's closing the same year, shopping on 13th was undergoing a change. Andy was no longer in the store, wintering in Arizona instead. It was a time of change, with Blondie managing the new IGA. But one good thing about change is it is constant, and by 1971, Blondie Mihalik owned Mihalik's once again - and he maintained some special charge accounts for longtime customers' conveniences, like a city police chief and a couple of judges - with IGA moving to a new location.

But change raised its head again, and in 1986, after just about 60 years in the store, Blondie retired, selling the store, now known as Mihalik's Mayfair Foods Ltd., to young entrepreneur Dave Green, whose recycling business just across the street and down from Mihalik's was just starting to make an impact on 13th.

## Business Notes

You may argue that it was a housing development and thus people oriented, but the fact is, Rideau Court, which started construction about 1959, between 8th and 9th Avenues, between 20th and 23rd Streets North, was indeed a major business in north Lethbridge. When constructed, it contained 26 stand-alone buildings, six units to a building. Original rent was $38 a month for a small apartment and $43 per month for a larger, two-bedroomed affair.

The complex has changed owners a number of times through the years and in 2005 was known as Highland Park Townhouses, renting at $580 to $670 per month.

To bury their dead, the northsiders always went south, but in 1967 an alternative was offered when Martin Brothers established a funeral home on 13th Street, just south of the Miners' Library.

Martin Brothers had a long history in the city, buying out Flattery's funeral business about 1923.

* * *

In 1987, following the lead of Downtown LA, a Business Revitalization Zone was begun in north Lethbridge, with no less than 140 business license holders signing up, from 1st to 8th Avenues. Ed Parker with Bridge Appliances was the first chairman.

* * *

Smith's Color TV and Appliances actually began in 1930 as a John Deere dealership in Coaldale, by Herman Smith. But, since 1967 it has been a mainstay of 13th Street, sitting about where the old Supina's store stood.

When coloured television was introduced Smith's moved to Lethbridge, owned by Mike Miskulin, Ed Smith and Gerrard and Conrad Plettell. Today, Gerrard and his son operate the large Smith's Audio Video store.

Gerrard, with one of his earliest jobs in The Herald mailing room, started in the audio and visual business more than 30 years ago and is now the owner and manager of Smith's Audio Video, which celebrated its 30th anniversary in Lethbridge in 1998 at 236 13th Street, where it has been located since 1968.

* * *

In 1953 Western Plumbers (Leth) Ltd. and Western Heating built a large two- storey cement block building at 334 on the corner of 4th Avenue and 13th Street, and just across the avenue put up a small storage yard and sheds for their materials. Big as it was, it was gone by 1956 and the store sat vacant until Alberta Liquor Control Board Store No. 72 established itself on the corner. In 1966 Lethbridge Northern Irrigation District moved its offices to the top floor, and remains there to this day. However, the liquor store pulled out in 1980. Ironically, the Alberta Milk Control Board shared the same premises with the liquor people for a number of years in the 1970s, and in 2005 the tennant is the Old Antique Shoppe.

* * *

One of the enduring presences along 13th Street North through to the 1980s has been the availability of lumber, dating back to the Stacey Lumber Yard, prominent in many of the earliest photographs of 13th, just as you crossed the CPR tracks.

George Stacey ran the Stacey Lumber Yard for years, one of the first large businesses along 13th Street. It was there for many years before eventually giving way to Pioneer Lumber. Stacey, an avid gardener, was also a friend of Brigadier General Stewart for whom the Lethbridge Legion Branch is named. Stacey had a fleet of trucks, Internationals, and had one of the easiest phone numbers in town, 3421.

From 1913 through to 1929 Pioneer Lumber plied its trade at 245 13th. Advance Lumber moved into the same yard in 1929 but was headed south by 1933.

Bird Building Supplies and Bird Construction Co. Ltd. held sway at 200 and 202 13th from 1952 to 1972, when Bird flew across the street to 113 13th, where it remained until 1990. Certainly the best known man at Birds was the late Harry Hall, one of the most knowledgeable building men you could ever find.

Allan Builders went into the 1301 1st Avenue location in 1959 and stayed there until 1969. The gaping lot was still empty as the new millennium dawned.

* * *

In north Lethbridge Ted Feller has established himself as Mr. Outdoorsman. The lifelong outdoorsman, hunter, fisherman and target shooter and recipient of the Lethbridge Fish and Game Association's Earle Carr Award, is a businessman who owns and operates Marksman Guns and Sports Ltd. at 312 13th St. N.

Ted Feller

Before Feller moved into his own business, Precision Guns was established at the same address by Rick Kucheran back in 1974. "I bought Rick out and opened Marskman Guns and Sports in 1984," said Feller, who began his career in the fishing and hunting retail business in 1978 with Ken Kotaks, at Plainsman Sports, in downtown Lethbridge just south of the old Marquis Hotel. Marksman's is a true family business with Ted's father, Martin as a partner. Ted's daughter Michelle is now extensively involved in the business as is his son Mark, and both have followed their father's footsteps as hunters and photographers.

"Bob Voth has been with me about 18 years and Bill Lambert has been with the store for the past 10 years," said Feller, an award-winning target shooter, bird game and big game hunter and lately photographer. In 1998 Feller expanded his store right next door, into 314 13th, enabling him to expand his stock and offer a complete line of hunting, fishing, camping and other outdoor needs.

* * *

The banking industry has long been caring for the cash of north side workers, with the old Standard Bank likely the most noteworthy because it eventually gave way to the Bank of Commerce and then the Lealta Theatre when the Doughty family moved in back in 1942. From 1914 to 1917 the Standard Bank's address was 315 13th, then it moved to 258 until 1929, after it merged with the Bank of Commerce a year earlier.

Imperial Bank of Canada set up at 244 13th from 1952-1959, when Van Ree's Upholstery and Woodworks took over the building. The Imperial Bank of Canada, and later the Bank of Commerce after a merger in 1961, re-established itself at 515 13th, and is still there.

The Bank of Montreal was at 314 in 1959 and moved to 230 13th in 1972. In 1972 the Bank of Nova Scotia found itself part of the new Westminster Mall and is still there today along with a bowling alley, fish and chip and Chinese food restaurants and other smaller stores, including a liquor outlet and drug store.

In 1978 Lethbridge Central Savings and Credit Union took up residence along 13th, only to change its name to Southland Credit Union, which set up next to Gergley's Glass about 1981. The outlet then became First Choice Credit Union, and one of its first choices was to close the north side branch in 2001 because First Choice - which amalgamated St. Pat's and Southland - had the old St. Pat's building on 13th Street and 3rd Avenue South.

* * *

North Lethbridge's 13th Street is the home of one of the city's leading, and pioneer, proponents of recycling, Dave Green. Green, a hard-working self-made success, owns and operates Green's Pop Shop at 613 13th St. N. as well as GPS Recycling, which he started up about 1974 at 719 32nd St. N. In 1971 Green opened a little pop can recycling shop, calling it Green's Pop Shop, at 544 13th St., across the street and a little south of the present store, where a goldsmithing business now operates.

Below: Green's, a modern northside landmark.

"At first it was just a little depot and I also sold pop. . . . I gradually added on from there to where I sell pretty well everything now," said Green, who once worked as a delivery man for Percy Butler's Lethbridge Messenger Service, another business spawned on the north side in the late 1950s. Butler's business began out of his home on 5th Avenue A North, expanding to a small warehouse along 2nd Avenue and 12th Street C before moving to the south side.

About 1973 Green moved his pop shop next door, to 546 13th, right on the corner along 5th Avenue. By 1975 business was booming and he built his own store across the street, at 613 13th.

"I bought up three old houses, tore them down, and built the store," said Green, who employs about 50 people in his various endeavours. "When Mihalik (Blondie) retired I bought his store and operated the business for a while as Green's/Mayfair. It is now the Asian Market, a popular business, but I have no part of it."

Besides pioneering recycling in the city, and still operating Green's and GPS, Green has seen another branch of his business blossom. His bottled water business is delivering more than 2,000 large bottles of water a week throughout southern Alberta, far from his 13th Street base.

* * *

Alan Jarvie returned from World War II and set up a business in the Staffordville area, Jarvie's Superior Masonry, today known as LaFarge.

The twisting road, spiraling down into the Jarvie red shale pit was a favourite for many north side kids who were into the fine art of building go-carts. The carts became more and more elaborate, and the young drivers often wore old mine safety helmets as their only crash gear as they raced each other down the hill to the bottom, only having to tow the carts back to the top for another few seconds of speed.

Alan's son Jim Jarvie then operated Jarvie Red Shale in Coalhurst.

* * *

One of the fixtures along 13th Street, between 1st and 2nd Avenues, has been Southern Monument, dating back to the late 1950s. Now operated by Ted Anctil, who worked with the veteran's committee for the relocation of the Cenotaph to City Hall in 2000, the Anctil family has been designing and manufacturing memorials for almost half a century.

Just a few blocks to the north is another Lethbridge memorial manufacturer, Remco Memorials, located in a small strip mall, next to what used to be the north sides' only Saigonese Restaurant, where a former Shell Service Station once stood. Remco has a long tradition, dating back to 1924.

* * *

Many a shoemaker has called 13th home through the years, though none exist along the thoroughfare today.

In 1929 Harry Kilner had a shop at 408 13th, just up from the old Jack's Radio and TV store. Steve Mezei had a home on 13th for years, his shop ringing with the rat-a-tap-tap of the shoemaker's hammer and the fine smell of leather. I had many a shoe repaired by Steve in his shop, just up from McCaffrey's.

He did a super job of restoring dress shoes to cowboy boots, all for just a handful of change.

* * *

The old International Harvester Building, all five stories of it, is a provincial government building today, fully refurbished and loaded with offices of all sorts, at the heart of a busy intersection along 9th Street and 3rd Avenue North, where there's a continuous stream of vehicles.

But, in 1913 when the building was built for $125,000, it was more isolated than Galbraith School had been at the start. The building of the 9th Street Bridge gave the area a link to south Lethbridge, and reason for other buildings to go up along the artery. In 1959 the Alberta government bought the structure to house some of its offices.

When winter came along each year during the 1940s Adam Stickel would leave his job on the farms of southern Alberta and head for the city. In 1943 he worked in the International Harvester Building along 9th Street North.

"I was a first class diesel high-compression machinist when I worked at IHC," said Stickel, 92. "Our offices were on the fifth floor but we'd work on the main floor area when we were repairing the farm equipment. But I only did this work in the winter, because in the summer I was going back out on the farms to work."

In 1918 a tractor school was held at the IHC building, with more than 200 men in attendance. During the second World War, a number of men gathered to make use of farm machinery parts for the war effort.

* * *

Thomas McNabb, master mechanic with Alberta Railway and Irrigation Co., came to Lethbridge in 1884, living just west of the railway roundhouse. He was mayor of Lethbridge in 1894, the first north side resident to become mayor. The Pemmican Club's history book, Roundup, said McNabb's daughter, Alta, born in 1887, "was the first white girl to be born in Lethbridge that lived to any significant age".

Just back of the McNabb home was the Woolen Mill, with a brickyard, one of many in early Lethbridge, further to the north of the two-storey house.

One of those yards, Bruce's Brickyard, is shown on an 1890 map about the west end of 3rd Avenue. John Bruce and William Oliver operated the brickyard, and several structures built by the bricks produced here, are still standing in the city. Bruce arrived in the city in 1886, and operated the brickyard with his partner. A confirmed bachelor, Bruce died in 1924.

William Oliver was a mayor of the city from 1902-1905. He came to the city in 1886 and the next year linked up with Bruce to produce bricks. In 1890 he went into business for himself as a general building contractor. He died in 1937.

The men stopped work for the camera in this 1920s brickyard shot.

As a young boy Alfred Davis Jr., who lived at 3rd Avenue and 13th Street and was the only manager of the City Mine, worked in one of the brickyards. The location of the yard has been described as where the old road from north Lethbridge joined the No. 3 Highway, immediately north of Galt Mine No. 1, a road known to oldtimers as the Brickyard Coulee. Davis ran a donkey engine at the yard, pulling cars of clay from the clay bank to the pug mill, as well as cars loaded with finished bricks to the storage yard. He left the yard in 1908. Another of the young workers at the time was Albert Arnold.

During the same era there was a Woolen Mill just north of the tracks, between the round house and about where the 9th Street Bridge would be built. It was just north of the McNabb home.

* * *

Prior to 1914, at 1711 6th Ave. A North, you'd find Ritchie and Meredith Groceries and Provisions, run by Mickey Meredith and Allen Ritchie. Meredith settled in Lethbridge in 1906 and opened the store shortly after. He died in France in 1916, serving with the 20th Battery RCA of Lethbridge. Ritchie came to the city in 1886, at age seven, and started in the store in 1909. He stayed in business for 18 years.

* * *

Likely the first grocery store along 13th, in 1909, was located on the corner of 5th Avenue, just across from Westminster School. Even in those days, 5th, or McKay Avenue, was one of the few east-west through avenues in north Lethbridge - 9th Avenue was another.

In their paper *Through the Looking Glass*, George Watson and Audrey (Chiswick) Swedish point out that at the west end of 9th Avenue, and just a bit south, stood the No. 3 coal mine, going into production in 1889 and closing in 1924. In 1903 Sam Swedish opened a general store near the mine on 6th Street, just off 9th Avenue. It was a two storey building, home to the store and one of the first boarding homes for miners. After a tragic fire, the store was rebuilt just east

of its original site. The building had the only phone in the area - number 2756 - which was well used by families in the neighbourhood, many times in the middle of the night for fire, police or medical emergencies.

* * *

One of the city's true pioneers, druggist J.D. Higinbotham once owned a shop at 242 13th Street, near the original Labour Club. In 1930 Becky Robinson (Mrs. Carl Neilson) bought the building and operated a beauty shop there for more than 20 years.

* * *

Frache's Flower Shop may have been a downtown business, but its flowers came from north Lethbridge. The huge Frache's Greenhouse complex covered more than two square blocks along 6th Avenue and 21st Street North. The greenhouses, with their colour and sweet aroma, went up in 1911, under the name of the Terrill Greenhouse, and were torn down in 1975, making room for residential development.

Lynne (Easton) Davis and Bev Cranstoun in a sea of 'mums'.

Bill Reid was the florist and greenhouse manager for Terrill's from 1910 to 1955.

By the late 1950s, Lynne Easton (Davis) and Bev Cranstoun, were hard at work in what was then the Frache's Greenhouse, preparing for the annual I.O.D.E. Chrysanthemum Tea.

* * *

In 1961 a new store opened at 316 13th, Higa's Jewellery. It wasn't long however, before Higa's Jewellery and Men's Wear, with Francis Higa handling the jewellery and Harry Higa with the men's department downstairs, was located at 406 13th.

I bought many a shirt, pairs of pants and ties, sports coats and sweaters from Harry, but more significantly I bought Mary's engagement ring from Francis, back in 1962. I also returned there to purchase another ring for Mary, marking our 40th anniversary in 2003.

Both Harry and Francis are gone now, but Higa's Jewellery remains at 406 with an open lot on the south side of the building, still serving as a parking area for the store and other businesses along 13th.

* * *

You could always find a place to eat along 13th, or north Lethbridge in general.

In the very early times there was Pete's Restaurant, with Kate and Jim Jack and Mae Glidden, and they sold fruits, candies and tobacco as well.

Jim Wong, owner of the House of Wong, used to operate the Shangrila Cafe on 5th Street South, and set up a popular Chinese food outlet in the Westminster Mall when it opened in 1969.

The Dairy Queen has been a mainstay on 13th since 1955 and there were cafe-type establishments like Lou's Wonder Cafe on the corner of 5th Avenue, the various York Hotel restaurants and coffee shops through the years, Matt's, across from Adams, where the burgers were fine, and literally dozens of confectioneries for that needed pop and candy fix, on a daily basis.

The Dairy Queen

Travel down 13th today and you can get Italian, Saignonese, Chinese, Greek, and North American cuisine, and anything from hamburgers to donuts and soup, at a wide array of locations.

* * *

An early dump - or sanitary landfill as they call it today - was located in north Lethbridge, along the top of the Oldman River valley, about where the city yards now sit, then it moved out to a similar location across from Hardieville area, filling in the sloping coulees. Historian Irma Dogterom said the first city dump was about where The Lodge Hotel now sits, along Scenic Drive, close to downtown.

Another landfill, at the top end of what is now Stafford Drive, ran from east to west in the coulees and as a result often created a blizzard of paper and other flying debris every time a Chinook roared in, or even with a general wind. What other type of days does Lethbridge have?

The problem was solved in 1988, at least for north side residents downwind of the dump, with its blowing paper, sometimes smoke when burning was allowed, and of course the odour, when the landfill was moved to an area - again along the coulees - just east of the top end of 28th St. N., on the former Boulton property. It was well out of the way for most city residents.

A selection of my dad's photos from the Lethbridge and District Exhibition Parade of 1931 as they pass Hennesey & Wilson and The Peoples Drug stores. Viewed from Westminster School grounds, between 4th and 5th Avenue

# People
## of the
# North

People make a neighbourhood come to life, although 13th Street was the business core of the north side, the people were its heart. From the business owners and employees to the shoppers and homeowners along the three km street, it was people who made the street come alive.

And to get to 13th Street, to shop or play, most of the people came from the neighbourhoods of north Lethbridge, neighbourhoods full of people of all ages and from all walks of life.

Hey, on my paper route alone there were some real contributors to our society, including now retired Judge Clarence Yanosik, Roderick Mackenzie Patterson who started the Bonnie Doone Pipe Band back in the 1950s, with me as one of his drummers, along with others like Al Hudak and Mel Willis, and one piper I remember was my cousin Bev Allison (now Bev Paterson on the Chinook Health Region board). And how about the NHL, the north side also spawned the great Vic Stasiuk and later Doug Barkley, the Detroit standout who had his great career cut short by an eye injury, not to mention Autry Erickson of the Boston Bruins and Les Colwill who lived on 10th Ave. No. went to the New York Rangers.

Wilson Junior High School had a very talented singer, Delores O'Connell, who went on to sing in Las Vegas. And the north side spawned The Rockers, (later the Checkers) most of whom called the north side home, like Jerry Arnold, Wes Kucheran and Dennis Goshinmon. And of course we can't forget the great Lethbridge fiddler Eddie Dietrich.

North Lethbridge of my day was a melting pot of nationalities, and no one thought too much about it. We, as kids, accepted or rejected others on their personalities, nothing else as I remember. My neighbourhood was an ethnic treat.

Mabel Maloff's cooking was an experience not to be missed. She was a stupendous cook and her poppy seed buns were a treat to die for.

In the 1940s and 1950s rural southern Alberta still intruded into the city. My grandfather's neighbours, John and Mabel Maloff, whose son Pete was one of my best friends, had an old combine stored in the back yard, used by Mr. Maloff each fall to combine crops in the area. He simply drove it down the alley and out of town to the fields.

The Maloffs also kept a few chickens and it was a city boy's delight to watch them chop the heads off. It was from those experiences I learned what the old saying, running around "like a chicken with your head cut off," really meant.

My grandparents were Scots, and my grandmother would still make traditional Scottish dishes to her final days. But the one I really acquired a taste for was potted heed - or head cheese . . . At least until I found out what it was. I can't stand it today. She, and my father later, also made great scones. But they both made dishes few living people enjoy - blood sausage, tripe, and bread fried in blood sausage grease.

Kazo Sawata's mother, as I recall, didn't speak much English, and just down the street was Mrs. Glendenning, who was English as could be, and you couldn't understand her either. What is it they say, Englishmen and Canadians, separated by a common language? We often played at St. Basil's field, where many mainland Europeans enjoyed the same area, for soccer and the original form of beach volleyball - on turf, "Dobra" was a word I picked up real early while watching these volleyball matches, a term meaning good.

The north side was a melting pot, with streets containing names like Coates, Hepple, Hudak, Lee, Wong, Norman, Foster, Evdokimoff, Hildebrandt, Beddington and Withage.

Everyone has their own personal memories of the neighbourhood in which they grew up, and I'm no different. While everyone who grew up on the north side will have their own particular memories of 13th street and its people, I'm certain some of my memories will overlap with yours as I talk about the people I remember. My memories come in no particular order, or chronological setting, as you'll see.

I remember Maury Archibald, who had a small car lot on the corner of 13th and 2nd Avenue, where, on the urging of my father, I ventured in to buy my first car. It was a 1948 Dodge - this was in 1959 - and I purchased it for the princely sum of $130. I put exactly 13 miles on that car before it threw a rod and that works out to $10 a mile, cheap by today's airline rates perhaps, but certainly something a kid making $50 a week couldn't really handle. Apparently you were supposed to check the oil before you drove it.

While on the subject of cars, my next car was a 1941 Chevrolet business coupe, a two-tone green affair on which, assisted by Dan Guylai, I painted an awesome set of red and orange flames. On the corner of 7th Avenue and 13th sat a Texaco garage, Northway Service, operated by Morris Colin Whitlock, a great guy. He kept that old Chevy on the road for me, and would let us putter around in his shop when he wasn't busy. Colin and wife Patricia lived just a short walk from the station, at 1416 6th Ave. N. A good number of years later one of my neighbours on 4th Avenue, Clarence Radley, took over that little service station from Alex Kowalski, and ran it from 1964 to 1974 when he retired. By the mid-1980s the station was gone, leaving a handy turn-around area for those going to Green's Bottle Depot.

Isa and Johnny Dorren, left, with Lily and Andy Allison

Just a few steps north of Archibald's car lot, and just past the Labor Temple, was the home of my aunt and uncle, Jimmy and Georgina (Jean) Stewart. Uncle Jimmy was a coal miner, and Auntie was my grandmother's sister. From a very young age I can remember going to visit Auntie and Uncle in their cozy little home, always going in the back door, into the warm kitchen, and as my grandmother sipped tea, I received milk and cookies. In later years, as a newspaper carrier for The Herald, I'd often drop in prior to picking up my papers for a chat . . . but really for one of those homemade cookies. I think Auntie Jean knew that. Many people in north Lethbridge knew the Stewarts, especially the coal mining community.

Apparently Uncle Jimmy used to dress in his Scottish finest each Robbie Burns Day - Jan. 25 for those who aren't part of the chosen people - and head out to the Coalhurst Legion where he'd recite the poems of the immortal bard. With his death, his entire Scottish regalia, tartans, belts, vests, shirts, et al, were donated to the Sir Alexander Galt Museum and Archives in this city, and are carefully stored in the Galt collection.

Jimmy and wife Georgina - I called her Auntie Jean

or mostly just Auntie - had three boys, Jim, Alex and Andy and one daughter Isa (Dorren). I'm adding a little side note here to point out that Auntie Jean, as I've said, was my grandmother's sister, and in the tradition of the Scots the sisters continued the unadventurous tradition of selecting their children's names from a very limited list. Among the Allison sons was an Andy, Alec and Jim, and there was a sister Isa who died before the family came to Canada. That list of names sound familiar? How's that for imagination?

Jimmy, born Jan. 23, 1897 in Scotland, served in the First World War with the 61st Battery RCA before returning to work the coal mines of Lethbridge at war's end. Jim died, at age 76, April 13, 1963. His pallbearers were George McKillop, Cleve Hill, Jim Ruckman, Harry Unruh, Jake Rempel and Joe Nadornay.

Like everyone who read and collected comics as a kid, I had a number of key people where you'd go on a Saturday and trade comics. Among those on my route were Pete Maloff, Doug Sandberg, Bob Stevenson and Al Fraser. Al lived right across from the front door of Westminster School on 5th Avenue - I always envied him for being able to sleep in at least 15 minutes longer than anyone else because school was just across the street. This was the middle and late 1940s, when the comics included westerns like the "Ghost Rider" and heroes like Batman and Robin, Superman and the Green Hornet. It was also the heyday of the "Classic Comics", a thicker comic based on a classic novel. Those were prized books, not only for the good read, but in junior high school you could write a book review from just reading one - though the teachers pretended they didn't know - and it saved you from plowing through the entire book.

## The Lost cards

Speaking of trading, what boy wasn't into trading baseball cards during recess or before school at lunch time in the Westminster playground. I had quite a stack of cards, and like everyone else from that era am still trying to decide who to blame, my mother, grandmother or who could it be for throwing those cards away. It would cost me a fortune today. I had all the key cards, like Jackie Robinson, Minnie Minosso and Larry Doby, the first Black players in baseball, and others like Mickey Mantle, Pee Wee Reese and Duke Snider. Blair McNab was one of the people I remember trading with, though I'm sure there were many others.

Billy Wong, son of Jack Wong who ran the American Confectionary next to Lee Duck Cleaners, was a nice quiet kid I remember. In junior high Billy was a math whiz and often I copied his math homework, though that copying skill failed me drastically when test time came. Billy was a good athlete, starring on the basketball team at Wilson Junior High when it first opened. I always liked Billy, and not just for the fact his dad owned a candy store. It always made me wonder why I never saw him eating candy, chocolate bars or drinking pop. Put me in a store like that and my dad would have been bankrupt in a month. It has been many years since I've seen Billy, the last time being sometime in the 1980s at an elaborate Chinese Food-Hawaiian style restaurant in Edmonton. Billy was running the place and dropped by our table to say hello. He bought a round for the group, mine being a large pineapple juice.

Johnny Kobal lived just south of Billy's place on 13th, the son of a storekeeper. But Johnny was too far down the street, and we had to pass Jack's to get there, so Jack got all my change. Besides, Johnny was Catholic and went to different schools than our crowd attended. One of the families along 13th who did attend our school was the Barnaby family, with Carol and Jerry. Their dad had a butcher shop, and this was well before my barbecuing days so I seldom dropped in there, unless with my grandmother when she went shopping down 13th. In those days, the 1940s and 1950s, there was no need to go south to shop for food, the north side had it all, from bakeries like Credico's, stores like Johnson's Red and White, next to Barnaby's, meat markets of course, big food outlets like Mihalik's and Supina's - my grandmother favoured Mihalik's - and numerous confectionaries.

Then there was the wondrous Wonder Cafe, and Lou's burgers, for a mere 20 cents.

Once I was into junior high school the world of cars became a fascination. Each day on the way to school, I'd walk down 4th Avenue, cross 13th and go past Bolokoski's garage. In the back of the BA Service Station, Westminster Service as I recall, was Bolokoski's shop, and sitting outside that shop on most days - when it wasn't inside being worked on - was the 007 car of Alvin Bolokoski, who along with men like Ron Boyce and Roy Nelson, were the cream of the stock car racing scene in Lethbridge in the early 1950s. Alvin obviously had great foresight because this was well in advance of the James Bond movie era, and the 007 car had to mean he was a reader. I was a regular at the stock car track, despite the fact they were on the opposite end of the city, where the Lethbridge Community College now stands, just back of The Barn. Many a time a few of we neighbourhood kids would ride out to the races, in the back of 007 as it was being towed.

Just across from Bolokoski's and north a few yards was the Morrison Hardware, with boys Bud and Hugh. I'd see them from time to time, though they were older than I was, as you'd go to the hardware store. Theirs was a small family store compared to North Lethbridge Hardware, run by Pete Chumik, about a block to the south.

While not directly along 13th Street, the Lions swimming pool and Lion's outdoor skating rink, were magnets for north side kids. For me the walk was only a few blocks, down 4th Avenue, the same path I took to Wilson, past Bolokoski's, old Westminster School, Verna Gray's house, the home of Big Jim Culver a former prominent amateur boxer in the city and his daughter Patsy and son Jim, Frank Sherman's house

and to the pool or the rink. The pool, of course, was a summer attraction, with its balcony overlooking the swimming area and tempting more than one boy to leap from it into the water, at risk of not only splattering himself on the cement walkway, but immediate expulsion from the pool. The Lions served the north side alone, until 1985 when the indoor Stan Siwik Pool was built just east of Winston Churchill High School.

**Far from Home**

In 1997 I received a letter from Sydney, Australia, from Chuck Sava, who grew up in north Lethbridge. Though seven years older than I, we did share some of the same experiences as kids on the north side.

Chuck recalled how he and his pals would toboggan through the coulees just north of the CPR bridge, using an old grade which once carried an inclined railway to the top of the coulees from the coal mine below. That route today would pass right by the Helen Schuler Coulee Centre.

We used to toboggan just about where the Highway 3 bypass heads up the hill to Stafford Drive. Both were great runs, except when you hit a barbed wire fence like Doug Sandberg did once - I missed because I fell off before the collision.

Chuck also remembered placing .22 shells on the streetcar tracks, or empty 3.03 casings, filling them with match heads and crimping the ends. They centered their activities around the subway, where you got a bigger bang for your prank due to the echo. We used coins and chain links, saving the squashed results as tokens of our daring - I don't remember being as daring as Chuck though, with .22 shells.

"Summers usually found us going on overnight hikes and one of our favourites was taking a backpack, our .22s and going down to the river valley, crossing the river on the old suspension walkway under the high level bridge," wrote Chuck. "It used to be at the base of the pillars of the bridge. It was a real adventure to cross this, reaching up to the overhead hand-cable and walking gingerly on the 12-inch-wide foot-walk, watching the swirling waters below us as we crossed. Once on the west side, it was a further walk south to the site of the old Sheran mine, which in those days was still visible with its timbers and reinforced entrance. Mind you, it was all caved in by that time, so there was no temptation to wander into the drift. We would usually set up a camp, light a campfire, make coffee and eat. We also did a bit of plinking with our .22s. We'd also try to smoke some dried driftwood, then sleep the night in our bedrolls."

His buddies in those days included the likes of Don and Fred Standing, John Bodnaruk, Roger Gillette, Ken and Albert Halibert and Joe Shields.

Chuck recalled hunting gophers with .22s in the coulees along the Oldman River, a sport we also took part in, and I remember Pete Maloff having a number of traps as well to catch the wily varmints.

Sava would go into the coulees to the west of the

old International Harvester Building on 3rd Avenue and 9th Street North, now home of the John Howard Society which might be appropriate in some strange way.

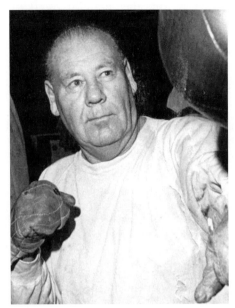

Big Jim Culver

"At the time it was bald-headed prairie and the nearest civilization was the Roman Catholic Cemetery and Staffordville, up there beside the site of the old No. 3 Mine," said Chuck. "The settlement then, however, was more commonly referred to as No. 3."

He went to Westminster School when Clarence Larsen was principal, but remembers Jim Wishart taking over. Like all of us in those days on the north side, leaving junior high meant heading for the LCI and the south side. Chuck was from the pre-tunnel era, under the CPR tracks about where the walking overpass now sits, so his group - and at times our group as well - walked up the hill over the tracks.

"You either had to walk up to 20th Street or go under the subway, but the most convenient was climbing the mesh fence and walking across the double tracks, regaining the street on the south side just east of Ellison Mills and the old Fefferman and Hyde Fur Company," Chuck said. "It is interesting to note how fast steam locomotives could accelerate under a load when some Proctor and Gamble Laundry Soap was rubbed on the rails while we crossed the tracks. The laboured chugging of the engine would suddenly increase in tempo as the big driver wheels lost their traction on the lubricated area."

Chuck went south when the LCI was still in the old Hamilton school building. But he also went to the new LCI, where D.S.A. (Sam) Kyle was king of the hill. Chuck was born in the Galt Hospital in 1934 and spent his first 20 years growing up in Lethbridge.

"I can recall attending, as a kid being led around by the hand by one of my parents, a fairly big air show at the old Municipal Airport, on what was then 9th Avenue and 20th Street North, which in those days was out in the sticks. I remember a single hangar in the northwest corner of the field and also, practically located, the high water tower just across the road to the north and east. To the south and east was the massive government grain storage elevator. Both were very conveniently placed to create formidable obstructions to the safe navigation of aircraft. Mind you, someone did have some thoughts, and placed a rotating beacon on top of the water tower as an aid to visual navigation."

Chuck recalled the war years, with a bit of a twist. "With World War II in full swing in the early 1940s, yellow training aircraft could be seen overhead every day. We also used to take the greatest pleasure in ridiculing the PoWs as they were driving past in trucks along 13th Street and 5th Avenue North, enroute to and from the PoW Camp in northeast Lethbridge. We would often pull our hair forward over our forehead, place little black mustaches under our nose and give the old Heil Hitler salute as they were driven past. Such was some of our entertainment.

"It was probably these early experiences and the fact so much wartime training took place around southern Alberta, that my interest in aviation was kindled. I decided very early in my life that I wished to pursue a career in aviation. I was fortunate enough to receive my private flying license, along with Mo Martin, Gerry Archer, Ron Peterson and Bob Richards. We also formed the Lethbridge Collegiate Pilots Association in about 1951 or 1952."

Chuck joined the Royal Canadian Air Force in 1953 and completed his initial training at Claresholm. From there he was transferred to Portage, Manitoba and flew T-33s, the type of plane on the pedestal sitting in front of the Lethbridge General Stewart Branch of the Royal Canadian Legion. After five years in the Air Force he became a bush pilot in northern Manitoba for three years, before returning to Winnipeg where he joined Australia's International Airline. He moved to Sydney in 1966.

## An Early Family

Jim Perry is a member of one of north Lethbridge's first families and wife Eva was a member of the city's historic Davies family. Jim's mother was Mary Perry, and the Perry home was along 9th Avenue North, at 1267, and the tiny house is still standing.

"My grandfather bought 40 acres in north Lethbridge, and it was four acres wide to the east and west and 10 acres long," said Jim, who was born in Hardieville in 1915. "I was the golden haired boy back then because I was the first grandson in both the Perry family and on my mother's side as well."

He didn't come to the Perry house until about 1920 though, spending his first five years along the Bow River with his grandparents. His grandmother instilled a strong work ethic in young Jim, even at that early age. Jim remembers a barn used to sit just along 13th Street, east of the old Perry home, and as a kid one of his chores was tending to the barn and feeding the chickens.

Jim spent his first 15 years growing up in north Lethbridge, becoming familiar with the people and the places. He remembers Matt Kropiniak opening the first store, just across from the Miner's Library, and then Joe George built a barber shop a door or so south of Matt's. Joe's brothers, Mikey and Johnny were midgets, and barbers as well. Joe was only slightly over five feet.

When he had his newspaper route Jim recalls thinking the Miner's Library was a "den of iniquity," perhaps because he was sent there by his mother from time to time, to tell dad to come home.

Jim Perry, shortly before his death in 2003, poses in front of a painting of his wife's original river valley home.

Jim always had a deep attachment to horses, so much so he even delivered the Lethbridge Herald on horseback at times.

"I think I was the youngest kid to ever deliver The Herald back then, being just 10 years old. My route went along 13 Street from 9th to 16th Avenue North, taking in Little Wigan, with the Mellings, Moores and the Sumners. All down 16th Avenue almost everyone was a Sumner or related to the Sumners. There were only two houses past 16th, Saxons and the Hackets. My uncle Alex married a Saxon. My sisters, Lettie and Clara helped me, and they usually did Little Wigan and I went over to 10th Street and even over to 6th Street, with about 60 customers. I got the route because I was helping a kid for eight months. He was 16 and one day he just blew his brains out - they did that in those days too - and The Herald asked me to do the route. My mother, being Irish, told them I was 12 and told them I was just small for my age."

His mother took over the role of Jim's bookkeeper, and the first day he had to cash-in (turn his collection money into The Herald) he was $1.25 short. He borrowed the money from his grandfather. He would have to go all the way downtown to The Herald, from his home at 1267 9th Ave. N., to not only cash in, but to pick up his newspapers as well.

"Jack Randle was at the Herald at that time and he took our money and he gave us our papers too, right at The Herald. I'd either ride over on horseback or take the streetcar there and back. It was too slow to deliver my route with the horse though . . . he couldn't climb fences like I could. I was a paper boy until I was

15 and then my brothers Bill and Jack took over. I'd get paid five cents for every quarter I turned in. The paper was 25 cents a week back then."

As a kid Jim didn't take much interest in sports like baseball or soccer. "If there were no horses involved, I wasn't much interested," he said.

Besides working for The Herald as a paper boy he also sold the Albertan on street corners downtown, in the days when the boys used to holler out the headlines or catch phrases. One such headline stated "King's Last Ball," - and Jim walked up and down his corner hollering "Castration of King!"

"I had some bad influences as a kid," Jim said with a smile. "I had seven bachelors on my route who were always saying to me, 'it's hot out boy, here, have a cold beer.' I learned to cover it up with Sen Sen (a breath sweetener)."

On the other end of the scale, Jim also knew John Torrence whose Hustler's Club was a boys' group within the First United Church. Jim only attended a few times, but got to know Torrence well. In later years he was on the west coast and had to phone home for some money, and Torrence made him a $20 loan. When he was back on his feet, and back in Lethbridge, Jim went down to pay Torrence the $20, and he refused the payment.

"He told me 'when you meet someone who really needs $20 then loan it to him' . . . Well I lived by that and I ended up paying out over $280," Jim said with a big laugh.

Jim and Eva, his wife of 60 years in 2001, met at a dance at the Burgman Hall, above McCaffery's Drug Store along 13th Street, and were married in the minister's home just back of the First United Church, along 5th Avenue.

"The minister looked at me and thought I was a $5 man, but I gave him $2 for the wedding," Jim said with a laugh. "The day we were married I went to work at 5 a.m. and Eva, a chambermaid at the Marquis Hotel, went to work at 7 a.m. It was a Wednesday and you'd get a half day off back then each Wednesday. I told my boss I wanted off at noon, but he told me to wait until Saturday to go out drinking. When I told him I was getting married, he laughed and said okay."

They owe their married life to Burgman's Dance Hall.

"As young people we'd go there on Thursday nights for the dances," said Eva, who turned 90 in 2002, and lived in the Oldman river valley before meeting Jim, often walking all the way in for the dances. "Usually one of the vehicles would take us in, my brother had an old farm truck and we'd go in with him and take a chance we'd get a ride home. Many a time we walked home though. Burgman was a brick layer by trade, and he was a boxer at times too. He ran a very clean dance hall. There was no cutting up or he'd throw you out on the streets. My first date with Jim was at that dance hall, and he took me home from the dance."

Jobs have been varied, and life never easy for the Perrys, but they look back and smile.

"I remember once I was watching them build the big government grain elevator from cement, standing in line waiting to be hired," Jim reminisced. "They were paying men 25 cents an hour to push carts of cement and dump them, with a foreman hollering at them all the time. If they didn't work hard enough he fired them on the spot and hired another guy. I just walked away. I didn't need that hollering.

"There were a lot of feathers in my life, but there was a little chicken every once in a while . . . but it was a good life."

At the time of his retirement in 1964, Jim was in the transport business and had 12 trucks. He was set up along 12th Street C North, between 2nd and 3rd Avenues, across from the old Scandinavian Hall. After that, he devoted his life entirely to horses, the animals he loved ever since he was a kid growing up in north Lethbridge.

## Some Talented Folks

North Lethbridge has had many famous alumni, not the least of which were the Alberta Ranch Boys way back in the late 1930s and 1940s.

It was an era when radio was king, and one of the most popular western groups on the Canadian air waves was Lethbridge's own Alberta Ranch Boys. Holding sway five shows a week, for four years (1939 through 1942) on CKWX out of Vancouver, were Joe Horhozer on accordion, Remo Baceda on drums or violin, Buck Waslovich on guitar, Curly Gurlock on the banjo and bull fiddle, and all-around Lou Gonzy on bass fiddle, clarinet, saxophone, violin and piano.

Remo was the group's tenor soloist and Curly, Buck and Remo made up the vocal trio, sometimes joined by Joe, renowned for his frog voice in the Smiley Burnett tradition. In fact, Burnett, the comic sidekick for Roy Rogers, Rogers himself and the other major cowboy singing movie star of the era, Gene Autry, were all backed-up by the Ranch Boys.

"We organized as the Southern Alberta Ranch Boys in 1937, but cut it down to the Alberta Ranch Boys," said Joe in 2002, when he was 82. "When we first started the group was made up of myself, Lou, Buck, Steve Voytko and Johnny Bolen and when we went to Vancouver in 1939 Remo joined the Ranch Boys. Steve left in September 1939 - he'd just gotten married - and Curly Gurlock had joined us in 1938. When we first began we also had a girl singer, Evelyn Nelson, who was only 16, so when we went somewhere her sister would travel with us as a chaperone."

In those initial years the band travelled with Steve Dobey who operated United Taxi. He drove his 1934 Tereplane around southern Alberta with the two girls, five band members, and all their instruments.

One of the Ranch Boys' first gigs was being part of the 1937 Lethbridge and District Exhibition parade. In fact, it was the parade which spurred the formation of the group, and with only two days practice and a six-song repertoire, they hit the streets for the big event.

Joe remembers their association in later years with the trio of cowboy stars the band performed with - Smiley Burnett the least likable of the three, but really enjoying Rogers' company. "Smiley was, well . . . a little different," said Joe with a laugh.

Roy Rogers, in light suit, with the Alberta Ranch Boys, from left, Remo Baceda, Joe Horhozer, Buck Waslovich, Curly Gurlock and Lou Gonzy.

"They had met Rogers in a restaurant across from the Beacon Theatre on Hastings Street in Vancouver. Rogers' big 1942 Buick station wagon and trailer was parked outside the restaurant. The five Ranch Boys went in, still wearing their cowboy suits from the band, and introduced themselves to the star and his manager. They were eating Chinese food and asked us to sit down after we introduced ourselves to him. We just got to talking. We all moved to a bigger booth and had a great time. Roy was doing four shows a day at the Beacon, and Trigger was in a special stall downstairs in the theatre. We ended up playing back-up for him during his afternoon shows. He was a very, very nice guy. You know, I never even got his autograph, or from the other two either. But Roy used to have a western store in California and for years he'd send up a catalogue each year."

The Ranch Boys used "Tumbling Tumbleweed" as their theme song, the same song made popular by Rogers when he was with the Sons of the Pioneers. Lou Gonzy told Rogers what they were doing and he gave the group permission to keep the song as their theme in Canada.

"He laughed and said it would help sell more records of the Pioneers' song," said Joe. It was a few years later, in 1946, when the Ranch boys played back-up for Gene Autry, this time at the Lethbridge Fair. They met Autry the night before the show at the Marquis Hotel, in downtown Lethbridge, and set up the program for the show at the Fair, which featured Autry. He entertained the returning military personnel and took part in the celebration of World War II's end.

"I liked Roy the best of all the ones we met, but it was a little different set up with him than it was with Gene," said Joe. "Roy was a wonderful man."

In Vancouver the Alberta Ranch Boys were on the air five days a week, and as well would do a Thursday evening live show, at various locations in the city, all with different sponsors. The popular group were featured cowboy entertainers at the Calgary Stampede during the same era and when the war years came were very active in promoting Canada war bond drives. As well, the members of the nationally-popular Happy Gang radio show were all friends of the band members, a friendship springing from a trip east.

"We never did record the Ranch Boys, though RCA Victor was talking with us at one time out in Vancouver," said Joe. "However, nothing came of it, and it's too bad now we didn't make at least one record. When we were down east, after the war, we were supposed to go to New York to do a radio show and a record, but Lou and Remo took ill, and that ended the group. That incident turned my life around. But, like my mother used to say, 'things always happen for the best'."

That spelled the end of the Ranch Boys. Joe turned to a working career, first as a butcher with Supina's, but owner Nick Supina fired Joe when Joe announced he was going to marry Nick's daughter, Everal. Enerson's had been one of the Alberta Ranch Boys sponsors, and

Mr. Enerson gave Joe a position in the parts department in 1949, where he remained until 1970 when he moved to Kirk's Tires for seven years. From 1977 to his retirement, Joe worked for Beny's, ironically the arch rivals of Enerson's where his career in the automotive industry had begun.

Joe was born up No. 3, in 1921, and came by his accordion playing honestly. His father had come from Hungary to New York when he was only 14, and moved on to Cleveland and then Saskatchewan before coming to Lethbridge in 1919.

"My father was quite a hockey player and played for seven years with the Esterhazy team while he was working for the CPR there," said Joe. "There were seven on the team and they used to travel to the next town for games on the old CPR handcarts. My dad was a beautiful skater and a great stick handler. We'd play with him and he'd stick handle right through us again and again; it made you want to cry. He also played baseball, and pitched for those early Miner's teams at Adams Park. He played accordion too and he went all the way to Chicago to buy it. My dad came to Lethbridge from Esterhazy and worked in the coal mines for much of his life, then with the city and finally having his own trucking business. He met my mother here and they married in 1920. She too had come from Hungary arriving in Lethbridge at age 13."

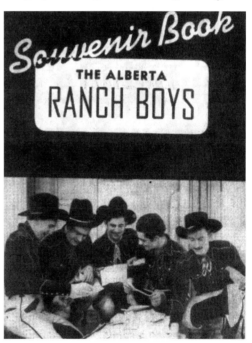

Alberta Ranch Boys souvenir program

One afternoon Joe and his father were downtown, with plans to take in a Lethbridge-Coleman hockey game later that evening at the old Arena, when they found themselves in the music department at Eaton's. His father struck a deal for a new accordion, for Joe, for $134.50, receiving $34.50 for his own accordion as a trade-in. Then they headed off for the hockey game, Joe in a state of near euphoria. Monday morning the big, dark blue Eaton's delivery van pulled up to the Horhozer door on 7th Street North with a brand new accordion, and a lifetime of music for 14-year-old Joe.

"I took lessons from Tony Niedermier," Joe said. "I first showed an interest in my dad's accordion one day when we were out at Mr. Les Chenger's ranch. My father left his accordion sitting there and while they were out I took it out and tried playing it. I heard them coming back, and tried to hide it under the quilt on the bed. My dad didn't say a word, but the next day he took me to Tony Niedermier."

Well into his 80s Joe was still lugging the big squeeze box, as a member of the Metros, with Bill Sikking, Joan Ward and Arlene Price, as they played in Lethbridge's hospitals, lodges, seniors centres and homes and the occasional dance, and even sometimes out to Coaldale.

"We still play a lot, (in 2002) about 100 to 120 times a year," he said, as he reminisced about how CJOC's Norm Botterill was once the assistant manager at CKWX in Vancouver, where the Alberta Ranch Boys starred from 1939 through 1942.

522 12th St. B. N. in 1915, from left are, Catherine McGowan, Mrs. John Kerr, Mr. and Mrs. J.K. McGowan Sr., John McGowan and Jim McGowan (seated).

The Second World War put an end to the four-year run of the Alberta Ranch Boys on Vancouver radio station CKWX. With the war under way the Ranch Boys headed back to southern Alberta to enlist. But fate stepped in. Ranch Boys Remo Baceda and Lou Gonzy had been severely injured in a Chilliwack car accident a few years earlier and Remo and Lou failed to pass the physical. Joe too was turned down, dating back to a smashed nose suffered on Joe Chenger's farm as a kid which left him unable to breath through his nose, to this day. Buck Waslovich and Curly Gurlock went into the army, Buck only staying nine months.

"In 1945 we went to Toronto, even though Curly was still in the army, playing our way all the way down east," said Joe. "We picked up Ameen "King" Ganom to replace Curly, but he was only with us until October. King later went on to have his own television show and be part of the Tommy Hunter Show for years.

"Down east we were on radio and were to go to New York when Remo and Lou both took ill and we had to come home."

That spelled the end of the Ranch Boys, but not Joe's accordion work.

In the later 1950s and early 1960s he was part of another superb country music group, the Country Capers, featuring Lethbridge's singing policeman Eddie Potts, his sisters Shirley, Sharon and Betty, Herb Urano, Don Petrak, and former Ranch Boy, Remo Baceda.

"I played with the Capers from 1957 through to the mid 1960s," said Joe. "I've had a good life in music and in the entertainment world. I got to know a lot of people from Roy Rogers and Gene Autry to the members of the Happy Gang and many others. From those days in Vancouver, when Bill Moyer of Red Deer did all our regular announcing, to playing for the seniors in the city now, it's been loads of fun."

Southern Alberta has produced two extremely talented and popular western groups, the Alberta Ranch Boys and the Country Capers, and Joe Horhozer and his accordion have been an integral part of both. Sixty years later, from dances at the Trianon, to Waterton, to radio in Vancouver and Toronto, and television in Lethbridge, there are still loads of fans who remember the western sounds of southern Alberta.

## My Family

My father, Andy Allison, came to Lethbridge in 1920, with his father and mother, Robert and Elizabeth Allison, his brothers Bob, Jim and Alec. His sister Margaret and Bertha and brother Stewart were born here in Lethbridge.

My grandfather had worked the coal mines in Falkirk, Scotland, though really a plasterer by trade. Upon arrival he set up home on 12 St. A North, later moving to 522 12th St. B, and worked in the No. 6 coal mine for a while. As an aside here, he would never let his sons work the mines.

"Dad always said he would walk all the way to Hardieville and then walk that far again underground in the mine," Andy said of his father.

As I was going through a photo and clipping collection of John Easton, I came across a picture from 1915. Six people, Catherine McGowan, Mrs. John Kerr from the Crowsnest Pass community of Passburg, Mr. and Mrs. J.K. McGowan Sr., John McGowan and Jim McGowan are all seated on a porch, at 522 12th Street B - my grandfather's house a few years later. The Robolgan house to the south isn't built yet and you can see right through to 12 St. A.

Andy (my dad) went to school at Westminster, as an 11-year-old when he arrived, but for some reason Bob was sent to Galbraith. In 1980 my father took part in a reunion of his 1925 Grade 8 class at Westminster, from the days when Herbert Bruce was the principal. At the reunion, held to celebrate Alberta's 75th anniversary, 19 of the original 39 kids in that class showed up - 13 of the class were dead by 1980.

The class turned out a number of teachers, including Olive Ross, Bill Rae, Hilda Robinson, Kathleen Frayne and the city schools' music supervisor for many, many years, Janet Larson. The class also turned out one of the city's fire chiefs, Wilf Russell and some former policemen attended the reunion, including Bob Parks, George Onofrychuk and Bill Kergan, Kergan later becoming the city schools' truant officer and a long-time alderman. Parks also operated Parks Chicken Inn for a number of years, behind the Dallas Hotel, where my father worked for 45 years.

Front, is my grandfather John Melling, me, and my grandfather Robert Allison. In back is my mother Lily Allison, father Andy and my grandmother Elizabeth Allison.

Some of the other well-known graduates at the reunion were Jim Marshalsay, who for many years ran the grocery store across from the front door of St. Michael's Hospital, Nina Seargeant, whose husband Neils Kloppenborg was a scientist at the Research Station and Lizzi Nicol, who farmed in the Kipp area and married classmate Bill Rae. Rounding out the 19 returning grads were Duncan McNabb, Laurie Davis - who for years worked as a city bus driver with my uncles Bob, Alec and Stew - Art Hostetter, Wilf Shreeves, Mary Bogusky Moore, Anne Fox Savage, Dave Birrell, who was once yardmaster for the CPR, Ernie Berent, Mercy Jones Rae, a longtime clerk at Supina's, and, of course, my dad.

On certain days my father would be out of school at 4 p.m. and "run like hell to a lot on 4th Avenue South" to play soccer in the city school league, against the south side schools. "We beat those schools in soccer, but we lost in baseball," he said with a smile. "Soccer was the north side game."

The field was adjacent to the original curling club, on that little cul-de-sac now midway along 4th Avenue coming off 13th Street South. The only way over south was shank's pony - your feet - but if you had money you could take the streetcar.

But who had money? Besides it was still a two or three block walk to the field. One week the north side schools would go south, and the following week the games were on the north side, all the way up at Adams Park, a long hike for the southsiders, though the streetcar did go right past the park.

"We'd be playing at Adams soccer pitch and the coal miner's would get off the bus as their shifts ended about the same time, and many would stay and watch us play, instead of going home or to the Miner's Library right away," said Andy. "Johnny Easton would often referee those games and George McKillop organized all the school league games back then; he was quite a sportsman."

My father married Lily Melling Sept. 7, 1937. Almost 10 years to the day, Sept. 8, 1947, she died.

## We Lived in Little Wigan

Growing up in Little Wigan I was one of few young people at the time, and one of my favourite people was Mrs. Riley, who lived in a tiny house at the back of 1220 13th St. Like all young kids who latch onto grandmother-types, I remember Mrs. Riley for her cookies and milk treats. It was from Mrs. Riley I first heard about the mysterious card game, whist. She was forever going to whist drives, a passion for many a card-player in the 1940s.

Mona LaValley was born right in Mrs. Ellen Riley's house (1604 14th Street), 67 years ago.

"My grandma (Ellen Riley) delivered me," Mona said with a laugh. "The doctor, a mine doctor, was in Waterton on vacation. My grandmother was just a little minute of a woman. She once lived in the big house out front of the property, right on the street, but when Annie and Jack Marsh moved into the big house, she moved into the little house, which we called a shack, out back my dad was raised in the big house. My grandmother used to work as a caretaker, a char woman really, at the telephone office and she drove a single horse and buggy back and forth to work. They had about four or five acres behind the house, so there was plenty of room for a horse."

Mrs. Riley's 85th birthday party.

Born in St. Helen's Lancashire, England in 1872, Ellen (Cassidy) Riley arrived in Lethbridge at age 22, after a journey alone across the Atlantic and Canada in order to join up with her husband William, whom she married the day after her arrival. She had to borrow a ring, until hers arrived from England, and drive by horse and carriage to Fort Macleod, fording the Oldman River, in order to get a marriage license.

Ellen Riley passed away April 1, 1958, at age 87.

Mona said her father was eight years old when his father was hit on the head with a bat during a fight in the midst of a baseball game at the Research Station. The family always said he died of the blow, but recent research shows he likely died about 15 years later in a hospital in Winnipeg.

Mona's father, Jim Riley, only eight years of age, soon went to work at the brickyard in an isolated area just north and west of the IHC building in order to earn money for the family. He later went to work in the coal mines.

"One time dad showed me all the different mines he worked in, No. 1 through 8 and Shaughnessy, Diamond City and Commerce as well," Mona said. "He left the mines because he had what they called black lung. We moved to Crystal Lake, where Sunnyside School is today. I have fond memories of Little Wigan, and the water pipe which was run by Mrs. Crombie. We hauled water from that pipe (on the corner of 18th Avenue and 13th Street). It was finally moved out in the late 1960s I believe. That Little Wigan area was mainly all families who came from the mining town of Wigan in England."

Mona's aunt and uncle were Belle and Bill Riley, who lived around 3rd Avenue North, near the Smeed family.

"Bill Riley was one of the last employees of the old No. 8 mine before it closed down," said Mona.

As for myself, another person from Little Wigan - though I really don't remember him too clearly - was an older kid I knew as Jimmy Cricket. His presence on 13th always put the fear of God in me, and I spent many a day avoiding a run-in with Jimmy Cricket who, it seems to me, lived up north of our house. There were other older boys, though not that much older, in the persons of Ken and Doug Wilkie who certainly were no threat to my livelihood, simply being great guys.

There were two coal mining families side by side in Little Wigan, the Tyrers and the Shermans. Sydney Sherman Sr. was the man who delivered coal to our little house right on 13th, dumping the coal out of the back of his truck right down the coal chute on the south side of the house, into the basement. Many years later, when I started work at The Herald in 1957, there was Frank Sherman, who would serve as one of my mentors in the Herald's composing room. It's funny how things have a way of coming around. Frank's mother Ada, another fine lady who gave me cake and cookies, passed away in 1992, well into her 90s.

Mavis (Harding) Standing remembers back to 1929 when the Peacock family had a fire alarm on a post outside their yard along 13th Street, just down from Little Wigan.

"If anyone had a fire in that area they had to run to that post and pull the alarm to report it," Mavis said.

The old Canadian Western Natural Gas yard and building is still along 13th Street, but gravel has replaced the lawn and flowers John Melling cared for in the 1940s.

The Allison house of my first five years in Little Wigan, was at 1806 13th St. N., on what is now 18th Avenue and 13th, and was right next to the water pipe on the corner. The water pump was a busy spot, as city residents and farmers from the area, used to come by regularly to fill their water trucks with the necessary liquid. The water shed, with its drop-down hose to fill the water tanks on the trucks, sat in a little island of sorts, creating an ideal turnaround spot for 13th Street traffic, mostly the city buses. It was neat because my mother and I just had to step out of our side gate and step onto the bus. The gate also proved handy as I had to run out sandwiches from time to time at lunch breaks to my uncles Bob and Alec who were city bus drivers. My mother also had tea and biscuits for some of the other drivers too, the likes of Bill Metcalfe, Bill Lee, Johnny Frouws and Johnny Walker.

Little Wigan derived its name from the people who settled in the area along 13th Street, from about 9th to 18th Avenues. The people who settled in the homes mainly came from the Wigan coal mining area of England, many of them worked above ground in the mines as technical people, machinists and cable splicers.

My grandfather, John Melling, lived just south of us, our house being on the corner of 13th Street and 18th Avenue, just a few houses down the street and past Moore's, when I was a kid. My grandfather was deaf, but it didn't slow him down a bit. He'd keep in touch with his hockey by sitting next to the radio, volume cranked to the fullest, alone in the kitchen while the rest of us sat in the living room, listening to the game through the closed door.

He also had a passion for sweet peas. I always remember his yard, with row after row of high, chicken-wired frames just loaded with sweet peas. Those were his favourite flowers, and he also grew flowers down 13th, about 12th Avenue, where Canadian Western Natural Gas Company, had a sub station set up. It was chain-link fencing, but inside was a nice lawn and a man-made rainbow of flowers and lawn. Now ATCO, this sub-station helps maintain the gas pressure for homes in the area, which is regulated down as it is fed into the city. The station itself requires little maintenance and is simply checked periodically to make certain there are no gas leaks. There is some lawn in the compound today, but mostly gravel, and certainly no flowers like in my grandfather's time.

My grandfather also looked after the grounds at Henderson Lake, when it was still a swimming hole and playground area, about where the Henderson swimming pool now sits.

Our house wasn't exactly on the corner; there was a water standpipe on the corner lot, which remained into the 1970s or 1980s. The standpipe, where farm and town water wagons filled up daily, used to stand on 14th Street in the 1920s, but was later moved up to the corner of 18th, in Little Wigan.

The Wilkie family lived right next to my grandfather Melling's sweet pea-filled yard, and they included father Spud - very few knew his first name was James - and wife Loretta and their family, Doug, Ken, Brian and Gerry. Ken went on to serve in the Canadian Army for three years, including a year with the United Nations in Egypt.

I lived up Little Wigan way, from 1941 through 1946 when my mother died. Much of my first five years were spent with my mother, my father being busy fighting overseas. One of the vivid memories of 13th Street, from a kid's point of view, was those little houses out back, the outhouse. These little buildings could be elaborate, with the siding to match the house, along with shingles; others were cold, drafty plain-boarded sheds. Some had one hole, most were two, one at a long-legged adult's level, the other for a child. Some had three holes, but why I just don't know. After all, use of the outhouse was not a community event.

As I recollect, there was an old fellow who came around every once in a while, up the back alley with a horse-drawn wagon, to clean out the basements of those little sheds. I wonder if he had many friends. The folks of the day knew those carts as the "Honey Wagon".

I was never a fan of the outhouse, especially in summer. That's right summer. They were hot, rather odorous and more often than not a garter snake would pop its head through the floor boards or skitter away as you opened the always sagging door. In winter it was cold, downright cold, which led to many a sleepless night contemplating that long walk out back early in the morning.

Come Halloween night, as often as not pranksters would tip one, or many, of those wee houses over. Hopefully when they were unoccupied. They must have done it to our wee hoose sometime during the war years because one of the first memories I have of my father, upon his return from overseas, was the Halloween of 1946 when he moved our outhouse a few yards into the back yard, and lightly covered over the hole, with a very weak cover. That Halloween night, some of the neighbourhood young folk came around to tip our outhouse, with its moon shaped window, over on its side. They came to an odorous end.

I wonder if it is just coincidence, or the way times are, but have you noticed now the outhouses are all gone, we no longer have mail-order catalogues delivered to our homes?

A wee hoose.

The only other memory I have of the outhouse era was the day I burst out of my grandfather Melling's wee hoose, breeks at half mast, and looking up because my cousin Lil Wright was shouting, "look at the parachutes". They weren't Axis invaders from the skies however, her husband Bill had simply blown into a large handful of dandelion puff balls and the hundreds of "parachutes" were snowing down.

## The Turtle Missed Matthew

In 1903 a new coal miner moved into north Lethbridge. But the day he moved in, Matthew Petras did not realize the significance of the move.

In 1902 Matthew, who worked the mines in the Fernie B.C. area, moved into Frank in the Crowsnest Pass to work in the Frank Mine.

"The family lived in a log cabin at the foot of Turtle Mountain, and rocks sometime fell from the mountain and hit the roof of the Petras house," wrote Matthew's great-granddaughter Marianne E. Croil. "Matthew had an argument, over mine safety issues, with the mine foreman (in mid-April) and was told to pack up his belongings, and Matthew moved his family to Lethbridge."

Two weeks later, at 4 a.m. April 29, 1903 the Frank Slide hit.

Turtle Mountain fell, leaving the cabins at the base of the mountain - including Matthew's former home - buried under tons of rock, and swept over much of the rest of the small mining town, filling the valley with 82 million tons of sandstone rocks, many larger than the houses themselves, killing an estimated 70 people.

"Three months later Matthew Petras' daughter Anna was born in Lethbridge," wrote Croil.

By 1911 five more children were born.

Matthew Petras was born Oct. 25, 1866 in northwest Slovakia, the son of a shepherd. His father was gored to death by a bull at age 45, in 1880 and when Matthew was 19 he headed for the United States, arriving at Ellis Island Dec. 8, 1885.

After clearing immigration he travelled west by train to Montana. The two brothers boarded a stagecoach to Fort Benton and on to Great Falls. They finally arrived in Lethbridge via a river barge moving up the Oldman River. There was a barge system which once serviced Medicine Hat and Lethbridge.

Matthew's granddaughter is Frances Kaupp and her mother was Anna, the newborn who would have also died in the Frank Slide had the family not moved to north Lethbridge.

"Just a few months prior to the trip across Montana there had been Indian uprisings in the area. From 1885 to 1887 Matthew worked the coal mines in the Coal Banks (Lethbridge) area," wrote Croil.

He headed back to the Pennsylvania and Ohio coal mines for two years, and sent for his wife-to-be, Anna Evancho. They married in 1889 in Leisering, Penn. And by 1890 the young couple had their first son.

Matthew kept traveling, and mining, working the coal in Indiana, Illinois, Belt, Montana and finally back in Lethbridge, before heading into Fernie.

After the trauma of the Frank Slide, Matthew had worked as a miner in the Taber area for a time and Lethbridge.

"His children attended St. Basil's School, and the family lived at 327 13th Street in 1911 while Matthew worked for the Federal Coal Company and the Grace Mine," said Kaupp. "In 1920 the family moved to Drumheller, and by 1922 had moved back to the United States."

Matthew Petras died at age 94, in 1960.

The Federal Mine was formerly the Sheran Mine.

## Nellie's Memories

Nellie Seaman was born, raised, worked and lived all her life in north Lethbridge, up to her death in January 2003. Her memories of 13th Street went back to the 1920s, and the names of the people rolled off her lips in an interview shortly before her death.

As a sales clerk in Mihalik's, where she worked after her schooling was finished selling groceries and dry goods like towels, pillow cases, table clothes and dish towels, Nellie remembered customers like the Chollack, Petrunia, Gardner and Allison families.

"Nick Ponech was just across the avenue from Mihalik's, and for many years he was a bookkeeper at Supina's," said Nellie. "Curly Baird was a butcher then for Mihalik's. And speaking of butchers, Adnitt had a butcher store on 13th near 4th Avenue and Fred Seaman worked there before going to Lingards.

He later bought into Value Village.

"There was a Roger's Hardware on 13th and 6th Avenue, right next door to Sorokoski's Grocery," said Nellie. "There was a big empty lot on 13th then between 5th and 6th and then there was Olander's Hardware."

Years later Miss Blanche Olander taught at the LCI. Nellie remembered when the original United Church stood where Martin Brothers funeral home is today, and how she went to Sunday School with Lil Wright. She had memories of Joe Mason delivering bread to the door with a horse and buggy, and how Lily Allison (my mother) put on a baby shower for her shortly before her mother's death. The shower included my mother's friends and neighbours like Marjorie Snowden and Mary and Amy Gilmore. Nellie also remembers Mike Petrunia and how his son Dennis has gone on to become a world-renowned doctor now residing in Vancouver.

Dancing was a passion for most back in the 1930 and 1940s and like most, Nellie went south to the Trianon, on the second floor of the Hudson's Bay Store which closed in 1929. The Trianon always seemed to be packed.

"There were dances at the Rainbow Hall (now the Moose Hall) on 5th Avenue, but my father wouldn't let me go there," said Nellie. "They called it the Bolshevik Hall back then and it was a place for Communists to hang out and the RCMP kept track of the people who went there. There was also Burgman's Hall, over McCaffrey's, but I never went up there. Lily (Allison) went to Burgman's, not for the dances but because she was a member of the Rebekah Lodge and that's where the Oddfellows Lodge met before they moved downtown. And speaking of McCaffrey's, Wilson's Dry Goods was right next door, and it was all clothing. My mother and I used to go there a lot, but the Wilsons moved downtown, with Imperial Women's Wear and then Juniors."

Nellie Seaman

Before the Wilsons moved south, they operated Hennesey and Wilson along 13th, in the old McCaffrey block area.

Nellie dedicated 56 years to the Rebekah's Lodge and was a member of the Legion's women's auxiliary for more than 50 years. Her life-long membership in St. Augustine's Church served her well through her life, and she in turn served the church equally as well.

## Lil's Views

Lil Wright (Saxon) was born in Little Wigan, her mother Clara dying when Lil was only six weeks old in 1924, and her father Harry taken by cancer when Lil was nine years old. She then lived with her grandparents, John and Isabella Melling, right in the heart of Little Wigan.

The Saxons' were long-time Little Wigan residents, living along 13th Street in an almost isolated area with a few open lots between their home and the next house on the corner of 18th Avenue, on the way to Hardieville.

"When I was a kid I recall some real big snowstorms," said Lil. "One time you could hear the coal trucks, loaded with coal from the No. 6 mine, coming down 13th, but you couldn't see them because of the snow drifts and plowed snow piled so high. You had to climb to the top, above most of the house roofs, to see the trucks go past."

In the winter, if the kids up Little Wigan wanted to skate in the late 1920s or early 1930s, they walked all the way over to 16th Street, just south of 5th Avenue to the open-air rink.

"We'd put our skates on at home and walk all that way, on the boardwalks, just to skate. Usually we were too tired to skate by the time we got there. There were kids from Hardieville, our gang and the Perry boys on 9th Avenue who would have to make that walk. Down 13th a bit, about 12th Avenue or so, there were some open lots, a wide open space with no houses, so we built our own skating rink right there, between the Milner house and the next home to the south. We cleared a patch, built a border around it, and the city would flood it for us all winter long. I was about 10 or 12 at the time."

In 1936 13th Street, near Little Wigan area, was socked in and isolated by drifted snow.

Lil attended Galbraith School, and one of her classmates was a lad named Thornton (Charlie) Tweed.

"His dad ran the airport over on the north side, and Thornton was the youngest kid to ever fly in Lethbridge," Lil recalled. "In 1935 (Oct. 2) he was 11 years old when he flew solo, after only just under seven hours of instruction from his father. He was in my class in Grade 6 at Galbraith, and one day I was out in our yard when a plane zoomed overhead and dropped a shower of crackers into our backyard. It had to be Thornton."

Right across 13th Street from Little Wigan was the Tiffin Farm, and after the Tiffin's did their summer fallowing she, her grandfather, and the neighbouring Wilkie kids would go across the street to look for mushrooms in the newly-ploughed soil. She remembers there being one small house, lived in by Pat and Primrose Low, between Little Wigan and Adams Park along the east side of 13th Street.

Lil's grandfather, John Melling, used to grow sweet peas, by the acre, in his back yard, and on a regular basis in the summer he and Lil would go by taxi all the way downtown to sell the sweet peas to Fred Edmundson at the Marquis Flower Shop. John Melling also looked after the gardens at Henderson Lake, and

maintained the lawn and flower beds at the CWNG pump house along 13th Street, at about 12th Avenue. He had been a coal miner for many years, at No. 6, but when deafness set in, Bill Hope, the city's gardener who ran the city greenhouses, got John the job at Henderson Lake.

Lil also remembers the war years, going with the Director of Activities for the service men to the huge PoW camp, and even eating a meal or two behind the wire in the guards' facility, and going out to the Bombing and Gunnery Training School at the new Kenyon Field south of town. Naturally there were dances, with many opportunities to meet the airmen.

"There was Burgman's Hall, above McCaffrey's, but I didn't go to too many dances there I thought it was a dump," Lil said. "We'd also go to dances at the Rainbow Hall, at the airport, Henderson Lake and the Trianon. I don't remember any problems with the dances at the Rainbow Hall; I thought it was a great place."

After the war, Lil Wright married returning sailor William David Charles Wright, on March 21, 1946. Bill's grandfather owned Wright's Bakery, along 13th Street, just south of 4th Avenue in the late 1930s. Bill's father, Dave Wright, drove truck for the bakery and Bill would run to the homes and businesses with deliveries of baked goods.

In later years, the late 1940s and early 1950s, the Wright family moved to 12th Street B, just off 4th Avenue. She and husband Bill would frequent the nearby Lealta Theatre on Friday and Saturday nights, and shop the southern part of 13th, instead of the northern end, where she missed the great hamburgers served at Matt's, kitty corner to Adams Park.

"Linda (Lil's oldest daughter) and Marnie Skelton were just little, but they'd often walk from our house on 12th St. B to Bill Skelton's pharmacy at the York Hotel," Lil said. "That meant crossing 13th, and they'd sure get in trouble for that. On the way they made sure they stopped and looked in the window at Credico's Bakery (just off the corner of 4th Avenue along 13th Street). They'd press their noses to the window, and stare in. Sure enough, Mr. Credico would come out and give them a bun or sweet roll."

## Hep

Alan Hepple came to Lethbridge from East Grinstad, England as a young boy. Born in 1941, Alan died at the young age of 56, but left an indelible mark on the north side history, growing up on 12th Street C, between 6th and 7th Avenues, and attending old Westminster and the new Wilson Junior High when it opened. He graduated Grade 12 at LCI, attending the south side school as all northsiders did if they wished to complete high school, before the advent of Winston Churchill High School.

Alan served in Canada's Armed Forces for 35 years and was Honourary Regimental Sergeant Major of the 18th Air Defence Regiment at the time of his death. He was also president of the auxiliary to the Lethbridge

Regional Hospital, an active member of York 119 Masonic Lodge and St. Augustine's Anglican Church. He was also a tireless worker with the Lethbridge Soup Kitchen, and with wife June was involved in many a Canada Day Committee function. His devotion to the betterment of Lethbridge earned him the 125th anniversary Canadian medal.

Hep, as we called him when we all patrolled the west side of 13th Street, was liked by everyone and will always be remembered for his self-produced motorized bicycle sounds and as a great comic book trader. In later years, this soft-spoken giant of a man overwhelmed most of us with his passion and his concern for others. Hep left a lasting impression not only on the youth of his north side days, but this city as a whole.

### June's Street

June (Glanville) Carpenter was raised between 5th and 6th Avenues North, along 12th Street A. Her father was Archie Glanville, her mother Fanny Louise.

"I was actually born on the next block, while my parents were waiting for their house to be built on 12th Street A," said June. "But I was raised on 12th Street A. My real name is Joan. I didn't change it to June, but at home they called me Joan and at school I was June, so I had a home and school name. To those outside the home I'm still June today."

As a little girl in the 1920s, June attended Westminster, with fond memories of having her hair done for school by the lady in the little house across the street from the school's front door. She married Jim Carpenter - her husband of 67 years with Jim's death - who went on to become one of Lethbridge's police chiefs, but not before he walked a beat on the north side and served as a Scout and Cub Master at First United Church in the 1940s.

"The minister, Rev. Whitmore, came to see Jim when we lived on 12th Street C and asked him if he'd set up something for the young boys, like the Tuxis program," said June. "Instead, Jim talked the minister into starting a Cub group. Jim had been Scout Master at St. Mary's and St. Andrew's too (farther along 13th Street) before he started the groups at First United. Bob Anderson was one of his Scout assistants at First United."

June grew up with her brothers and sisters, enjoying life in north Lethbridge. Her sister Vera, who married George Sinclair, was a well-known music teacher. Sister Iris married Tom Archibald and brother George became a Mountie. George was known to his friends, which included Horace Barrett and Addie Donaldson, as Hippy or Hip, before he left for a career in policing.

As a Mountie in Ottawa in 1942 George, who left north Lethbridge about 1930, posed for a photograph by the renowned Josef Karsh. Karsh photographed George in his full Mountie reds, astride a horse on a small knoll. The photo, in black and white and in colour, appeared for years on much of the promotional materials for the RCMP, from a small two-inch pocket knife - one of which June still has - to calendars, post cards, CPR menus and other sundry items, including the cover of Maclean's Magazine. During a 2004 antique show and sale in Lethbridge one of the calendars, a 1947 offering with a full colour print of George, was selling for $275.

"I believe George was the first Lethbridge person to earn a black belt," said June. "His certificate was signed in blood and came from Japan. George was born in 1907 and was about 23 when he enlisted in the Mounties. He died in 1992, at age 85."

George Glanville

There were other notable folks along that single block of 12th Street A where George and the rest of the Glanville family grew up. The Kergan family included June's friends Peggy and Anne, and their brother Bill. June's father was a trained singer, and June played piano all her life. It was little wonder music was always part of the home, including next door neighbour Dave Morris.

"He was Welsh and had a beautiful singing voice," said June a few months before she died in 2005. "For entertainment people would get together at our home. Mr. Gurr would come over and play the piano and he and I would play duets while Mr. Morris and my father sang. We always had music in our home, and I couldn't believe it when I found out not everyone did."

The street also include Mr. Redpath, with a tailor shop downtown, along with a family named Lorre, who had a daughter Annie. She was an early playmate of June's, but died at age four.

The street also included O.K. Davis, who worked in the CPR yard office, the Soady and Lothian families and the Barretts. Mr. Barrett was a magician with wedding cakes and other decorative cakes and his son Horace went on to become a prominent figure in the city.

Horace was founder of the Morris and Barrett Hardware, later becoming Barrett-Forrest Hardware Co. Horace came to the city from England in 1919 and his father, Charles, was a well-known city businessman as well.

Horace became a prominent Lethbridge businessman and was active in public service as well. He was manager of the Nikka Yuko Centennial Garden at the time of his death on May 28, 1967 at age 60.

He was also a past-president of the Chamber of Commerce, a Rotarian and president of the Lethbridge Musical Theatre. As well, he served for four years as chairman of the public school board and was a major contributor to the success and acceptance of the Nikka Yuko Centennial Garden.

Horace and wife Helen had one daughter, Elizabeth.

## Another Neighbourhood

As the second World War ended, 12th Street B, between 4th and 5th Avenues, included the Bissett family, the Sherman, Doe, King, Wardman, Kearny, Mucklow, Whitfield, Trenholm, Good and Hildebrandt families.

Phyllis (Bissett) Slovack remembers the Hildebrandts built a new home on a vacant lot about mid-block and the Wardmans building a new house on an open lot across the street. Joe Montgomery lived on the big house on the corner of 4th Avenue and 12th Street B, a home later bought by the Lee Duck family.

"When Hennesey and Wilson closed out I bought two black satin bathing suits for my boys. I bought them each two pair and that's what they wore all summer," said Phyllis, who also remembers Maude Heaton working at Hennesey and Wilson for many years.

On the west corner of 12 B and 4th Avenue was the Sherman home, once the site of Levellie's Livery Stable, but the domain of the Shermans since the late 1920s and early 1930s. Bette Sherman has some fond memories of the neighbourhood and 13th Street in particular.

"I remember my mother's friend, Isa Dorren (daughter of Jimmy and Jean Stewart) living in one of the houses along the block, across from the fire hall," said Bette (Sherman) Slovak. "Then of course, there was the York Hotel. I remember as a child going there with my parents, Walt and Nan Sherman, and getting a side-by-side double scoop ice cream cone. That would be in the 1930s. In the 1940s the York had a wonderful restaurant, and the meals were wonderful. Skelton's Pharmacy also was located there for awhile. On the west side of the street, I think next to Supina's, there was a house in which the Nakamuras lived. I remember Mrs. Nakamura did dress-making there, in the 1940s and maybe into the 1950s. Along in there too was the Hart Hardware. I think the Potts Family lived upstairs . . . Later this building became the Chinook Hardware and then it was a Second Hand Store.

"The Lealta Theatre was operated by the Doughty family and many a Saturday Matinee found the neighbourhood kids there. At the evening shows one could get dishes and eventually build up a fine dinner set. I still have some of mother's dishes."

Naturally Bette recalls stores like Henry Roelof's Tire Shop, and on the corner of 13th and 3rd Avenue a dress shop operated by Mrs. Binda, which later became Jack's Radio and Repair Shop. Back in the 1930s she recalls Swingler's Meat Market and then Kohal's Confectionary, and from the late 1930s and into the 1940s there was a Chinese Confectionary near the 4th Avenue corner, just east of the Sherman home on 12th Street B.

"I can't remember the name of it though," Bette said with a laugh, "but I do remember the store. He used to have a Chinese Lottery going on there. I don't know if it was legal or not but I remember punching out a number board. This board had about an eight or 10 inch surface and had paper numbers all over it. For 10 cents you got to punch out two or three numbers. I remember, as a tyke, winning $10 - I don't think I will ever forget the thrill of that. Can you imagine what $10 could buy in those days?

"Then I remember Greggy's Barber Shop and McCaffrey Drugs - a man named Paul (Pheirson) worked there and he used to tease a lot. Along the block, in the 1940s was a dress shop, Fay's Apparel. I believe it later moved downtown. Also there was Yip's Confectionary. I remember going there on a Saturday afternoon with my Saturday nickel and getting stocked up with a whole bag of candy before heading for the Lealta. In those days (late 1930s and into the 1940s) you could buy an all-day Lucky Sucker for a nickel and if you found a certain piece of paper inside that sucker, you got a free one . . . Hence the Lucky Sucker. I remember winning lots of Lucky Suckers! I believe the building that housed all of these businesses was called Burgman's Block. Upstairs used to be Burgman's Hall. Many a function, and of course, dances were held here. I was too young for the dances but I do remember my parents and aunts and uncles going to them."

In 1912 William Leviellie operated a livery along 4th Avenue North.

"On the corner of 5th Avenue, across from Westminster School, was the Wonder Cafe operated by Lou Hong," said Bette. "What a kind man he was! Many a Sunday found me there doing dishes for Lou. In those days all the dishes were done by hand and I used to love going up to help him. He used to give me chocolates for Christmas and of course, the occasional free sundae. I loved him and kept in touch for many years."

Bette remembers the John Martin family living in a little house just across the avenue, north of Westminster School, and on the southeast corner of 6th Avenue, the Tyrer family,

Across from Lou's, when Bette was a child, was the United Church Hall. "I went there as a child and could hardly wait to go to the 'Big Church' farther up 13th on the East side, where the adult church services were held," she said. "I never got there though because the 'Big Church' was sold to the Fraternal Order of Eagles and the adult services moved down to the Sunday School building, which was expanded."

"In the 1930s, and maybe the 1920s, there used to be a hardware store called Olanders. My father, Walter Sherman, along with his father, Ed and brother Frank, had a dray business. This is how they used to haul merchandise in those days. It was a large flat wagon or dray, pulled by two horses. At that time we had a big barn in our yard on 4th Ave. and 12th St. B., and we were in the 'draying business'. Anyway, during the early 1930s Olander's Hardware closed and my dad had the job of hauling off the excess goods. I remember this so well because his payment was a dray full of toys. What a Christmas we had that year, doll carriages, table and chairs, dishes, irons and ironing boards, dolls, etc. etc.! All a child could ever dream of! It didn't fill my parents pocket book, but did wonders for my sister and I."

This is Bette's world on 13th Street, she remembers, "Memory fails when I get north of 6th Avenue, but I know Mihalik's Grocery was further north. Occasionally I was sent there by my mom, but it seemed so far. This was our world in those days and what a wonderful busy street 13th was. I remember I was not to loiter there though, that was the rules in our home - Go do your business on 13th and get straight home."

South of Sherman's along 12th Street B included the Lee and Buttazoni families and 4th Avenue included the Waltons, Nora Jackson, the Skeltons, the Browns, the Garrets, Sloans, Withages, Chengers, Radley, Turcott, DeCoste and Kloppenborg families through the years.

"Another man we used to know as kids, along 12th Street B, was John Fossard, my friend Kathleen's father," said Phyllis (Bissett) Slovack. "He worked at city hall with my father, who also served on council in 1906. John Fossard was a Baptist, so naturally we kids all referred to him as John the Baptist."

## One Of A Kind

In 1989, the oldest surviving Canadian-born sailor, who served in both world wars was Aubrey Bissett. Aubrey was born Dec. 3, 1901 in Saint John and served with the Canadian Navy, in the First War as an early teen and the Second at an age where his nickname was "Gramps".

During his 42 years as a CP Rail conductor, before retiring to Cardston in 1989, Aubrey and his family lived in north Lethbridge, and for a time in Medicine Hat. His north Lethbridge home was an apartment along 13th Street, above Kobal's Grocery, before moving the family to 12th Street B North, just a few blocks west.

In 1914, when the First World War broke out, Aubrey was 14 and living in Nova Scotia. He ran away to join the army, but he was caught at Truro. Aubrey then got permission from his parents to join the navy as a boy seaman and he signed on as a Boy Seaman on a Canadian training ship called the EMCS Shearwater.

"There were 135 of us on that training ship," Aubrey said. "We patrolled all the West Indies islands and we were based in Bermuda. We had a lot of fun. I was just finishing Grade 11 when war broke out."

One of his early exploits was on Bras d'Or Lake in Nova Scotia, at Badeck, Alexander Graham Bell's hometown. The task was to recover submerged davits which belonged to Bell's nearby factory.

"He (Bell) would come out every morning to see how things were going," said Aubrey of the man who invented the telephone. "He gave all the boys $50 extra when we finished and he gave me $100 because I was in charge."

The Shearwater was both sail and steam powered and had three pound guns. The ship's role was to train novice sailors for duties on other ships. While it never saw direct action, the ship was involved in one of Canada's most infamous disasters, the Halifax Harbour Explosion of 1917.

116

"We just happened to be in port the day the explosion occurred," Aubrey said "We had started out of the harbour but were called back. We weren't hurt and there was no damage to our ship. But seven other ships were badly damaged. They figured later it was an act of sabotage. A ship loaded with ammunition was heading out and another was coming in with a partial load. The loaded ship rammed into the other. They exploded. We were at the north end of Halifax harbour about half a mile away. We sure could hear it and we felt the concussion. One started to blow and then another . . . the blast was so intense it blew up a school in Halifax proper, killing everyone. Over 2,000 people were killed."

---

**Tragedy Hits**

Tragedy hit the Shearwater in 1918, during an outbreak of influenza. The ship lost 65 of the 170 men on board, crew and officers, to the flu. Only three men were unaffected, including Aubrey.

"We kept the corpses in the hold of the ship and we had to stay up, with flashlights and a stick, to keep the rats from eating on the bodies," said Aubrey.

Some bodies were wrapped in canvas, with a heavy shell at top and bottom, and slipped over the side to be buried at sea. Others were kept on board and buried when the ship arrived back at Sydney, N.S.

---

Only 17, he was sent ashore to help with the injured, offering any type of assistance possible. As trainees, the young boys had first-aid knowledge and attended school aboard the ship. The crew stayed in Halifax only a few days assisting in the clean-up and rescue operations and then headed back to Bermuda where they were bound when the explosion occurred.

One of the roles for the ship while on patrol was to go ashore and quell a series of riots in the West Indies, which was under the control of the British Empire. He laughed as he talked about the ridiculousness of the situation, being put ashore with unloaded rifles, armed only with bayonets.

By the time the war ended, Aubrey was a chief petty officer, aged 19 with five years experience at sea, in war time.

After the war, in October, Aubrey married May, a girl from Manchester, England and spent the next 42 years with CP Rail, working his way up through the ranks to conductor on the Canadian, on a run from Medicine Hat to Calgary. When the Second World War broke out, Aubrey, then a Lethbridge resident, was on a trip to Calgary and took the opportunity to join the navy again.

It wasn't until he returned home, in uniform, any of the family knew he was headed to war again. He was 42 at the time and had two granddaughters. May was at home with six children, including two nephews the couple raised.

Aubrey completed an engineer's course at Esquimalt, B.C. and was posted to Saint John, N. B. and the destroyer Ottawa. The first trip out, from Saint John to Halifax, the sea was so rough three crewmen were washed overboard, one wasn't recovered. Aubrey was in charge of the stokers, a group of 27 young men who became a tightly knit group.

Aubrey Bissett

The Ottawa, a ship which would do 50 knots, made three trips to England, but the crew never got ashore. The Ottawa was refueled at sea immediately on arrival and set back across the North Atlantic.

"We sank four or five subs," said Aubrey with pride.

In 1945 the Ottawa was 12 miles out of Halifax when it was hit by a torpedo, taking 30 feet out of the front of the ship. The blast blew Aubrey through the air, bringing him down on another crewman. Aubrey told the bridge, via radio, the doors were jammed shut - later forced open when back in dry dock - and a young fellow was in bad shape, probably with appendicitis aggravated by the explosion. Word from the bridge was in form of a question, "Can you operate?"

Aubrey said he could try, but air vents and pipes were twisted so badly that surgical instruments couldn't be passed down to the engine room, so the operation was put off. They then asked Aubrey to start the boilers and give the ship 250 pounds of steam to get it back to harbour.

"I was burned from my neck to my knees by hot oil," said Aubrey. "I told them we'd have to hurry if we wanted to save this kid. I started up the boilers and got 300 pounds of steam and we headed in."

As the Ottawa arrived in port, Aubrey started up a ladder and on reaching the top passed out, falling flat on his face and breaking his nose. He woke up in hospital.

"I was laying on a table with nothing on and two or three nurses were gathered around piercing the blisters. . . I grabbed for a blanket and told them, we couldn't have this," laughed Aubrey.

With the war in Europe over, Aubrey signed up to fight the Japanese, but while waiting for orders, that theatre, too, ended. He and thousands of other Canadian men and women came home.

A major military tattoo in Calgary in 1985 set about to find the oldest Canadian-born sailor who served in the navy for Canada during both wars. They contacted Aubrey. He felt specially honoured by the notoriety, and it became a major memory in his life.

## Cherished Avenue

In the movie, "My Fair Lady", Jeremy Britt, as Freddie Lynsford-Hill, immortalized the song "On the Street Where You Live". Well, in 2000, Avice (Frayne) Anderson and her friend Mavis (Harding) Standing got together and took a look back. The two friends explored 4th Avenue North, between 13th and 15th Streets, remembering back to the 1920s, and how it was on the street where they lived.

If buildings could talk, what a story they'd tell. But buildings can't talk, so Mavis and Avice did the talking for them, recalling memories of their cherished childhood.

On the southwest of 4th Avenue they remembered the BA Service Station.

"It was here we could get a wet six-volt car battery re-charged. It wasn't for a car, but power for the battery-operated radio. Now we could listen to Jock Palmer (at CJOC) as he gave news, music, and stock quotations. Next to the lane was a tall house, and one morning, at about 9 a.m. we saw a couple dressed in evening attire, arriving home. In answer to our puzzled looks they told us they were just getting home from a dance, the Pemmican Ball," said Mavis.

"The Gilmore family had beehives in the country. It was at their home we saw our first honeycomb, and watched the honey being extracted. A little farther east was the home of Dr. R.B.C. Thomson. Jim, Homer, Ivan (Chick) and Bessie Thomson lived there, with their widower father. Bessie was raised by her Aunt . . . oops, Auntie. Bessie said ants were those little things that crawled on the ground. It was here, in the basement of the Thomson house, we learned the art of kite making. We had sticks of wood to which we pasted sheets of The Lethbridge Herald."

The next house was the home of Mrs. and E.A. Wilson of the Hennesey and Wilson store on 13th Street, right next to McCaffrey's second store. Their children were Herbert, Donald and Eleanor. Donald and wife Shirley later operated Imperial Women's Wear and Juniors downtown.

"The Hennesey and Wilson store sold shoes, ribbons and lace and things like that," said Avice. "When we'd have a school function at Westminster, we'd wear the school colours, mauve and gold, buying eight-inch strips of ribbon at the store. They sold shoes and would toss out all the old shoe boxes at the back and I'd get those boxes and make a bed for my dolls, and I'd put string through holes in one end and pull the box and doll along behind me, sort of a home-made carriage."

Then came 1414 4th Ave., where Arthur and Edith Frayne lived, with their children Elsie, Doris, Kathleen, George and Avice. Arthur arrived in Lethbridge in 1902 and started his business as a carpenter/house builder. He later became interested in city politics and was elected Alderman in both 1910 and 1911.

Upon his return from the First World War in 1919, he was appointed Librarian for the new Lethbridge Public Library. Arthur was also an avid gardener and planted a large lot with gladiolas year after year.

"The house on the corner of 4th Avenue and 15th Street had many tenants and owners over the years. At one time this was the home of Kathleen (Kay) Frayne, who taught for many years at Westminster School," the ladies recalled.

We take a few more steps and reach the house on the southwest corner in the 15th-16th block. It was here Mr. and Mrs. C.S. Donaldson and their children, Adam (Addy), Kathleen, Wilson and Chris lived. C.S. was financially connected with the Federal Coal Mine, formerly the Nick Sheran Mine. Mr. Donaldson later operated the coal mine at Shaughnessy.

"The newer house on the northwest corner of 4th Avenue and 15th Street was owned by the Pinchak's," the ladies stated. "This family, for many years, kept milk cows in the city. Morning and evening the milk from these cows was delivered, in syrup pails to customers. The father kept the cows, the mother milked them and their youngest daughter Anne had the delivery job and we often joined Anne, helping her carry the pails of milk from door to door. When Anne grew up she married John Kobal, and they operated Kobals store on 13th Street.

Kathleen and Avice Frayne (later Anderson) stand along 4th Avenue in 1924, with the Westminster Annex just back of the girls and the Hub Cigar and Greggy's at the end of the sidewalk.

"Next to the Pinchak house was the home of Verna Gray and her father. Verna taught home economics for many years at Westminster School. Near the fence of the Gray property was a V-shaped depression. Our parents told us that irrigation water had flowed down the v-shaped ditch in the early 1900s. It was still visible to us in the mid 1920s."

At 1401 4th Avenue they remembered the home of Charles and Barbara Harding and their family, Edina, Mavis and Fred. Charles came to Lethbridge in 1888 and became interested in city politics, serving City Council as an Alderman in 1905 and 1906. Charles Harding owned a considerable amount of land adjacent to his house and in 1905 he sold Lot No. 37 to the Lethbridge Public School Board for $225. Westminster School was built on the northwest corner of this property. The lot was about a city block square, from 13th to 14th Street, between 4th and 5th Avenues.

Westminster School opened its doors to the children of the area for 62 years, from 1906 to 1968.

## A Memory Filled Walk Down 13th

Avice (Frayne) Anderson was born Sept. 8, 1914, delivered by Dr. R.B.C. Thompson who lived just three houses down from the Frayne family on 4th Avenue North. Her entire youth was spent on that avenue, between 13th and 15th Streets.

June (Glanville) Carpenter was raised at 515 12th St. A N., and like Avice her house is still standing. June was really born a block over, in 1915, but spent most of her youth at 515. Naturally both girls would venture onto 13th, a thriving business street of the North Ward.

Avice's father, a former city alderman Arthur Frayne, used to drop in on a regular basis at the No. 2 Firehall to play cards with the firemen on night shift. Just north of the fire hall was Supina's, where Avice's sister Elsie worked for a time, in the 1930s after The Hudson Bay Co. had closed.

"You'd go into Supina's and to the right was the ladies wear and then down on the other side was the meat counter and the offices and the grocery area was at the back," said Avice. "They added a men's clothing department to the left in later years. North of Supina's was a building with apartments and a second hand store and Hart Hardware, which had been down between 4th and 5th Avenue, moved to that building 1935 or 1936. Hart helped me with a project I was working on. It was the era when hunters loaded their own shells and used little cardboard caps, and Hart sold only one size. I was a teacher in training in Calgary at the time, and I needed play money, nickels and dimes, whatever and he volunteered to cut different sizes of cardboard for me. Mr. Hart made my day for me."

The hardware was run by William Hart and Dave Patterson, going back to 1915, and made use of every inch of space. The long counters were piled high with hardware items, hoses hung along the front, and stock was piled or hung against and on the walls. Even the ceiling was jam packed, with buckets hanging down on hooks.

June said the Hart family used to live on 12th Street C, near Lou Gonzy. Hart Hardware turned into the Neely second hand store in the 1940s. The store later became Kerrison's Second Hand Store. Just north of those stores, and next to the old Lealta, Carpenter's daughter Lynn now operates GI Jen's, one of the more intriguing stores along 13th in the new century, reminiscent of stores of the past.

June also remembered a house, set back off 13th behind Supina's, at 242, where Becky Robinson had a hairdressing shop and gave the first permanent waves of any hairdresser in town. June was an early teen at the time and remembers seeing all the ladies hooked up to a big machine with electric wires holding their hair in place. June was happy she had naturally curly hair.

"I got my first perm there, in 1929 when I was about 15 years old," said Avice. "The hair was wound on rollers, some type of metal, with aluminum foil pads which included some type of chemical filling. The hair was dipped in water and clamped on each roller. They generated their own heat and sometimes you got 'hot spots', and the helper blew on them to cool them off. Oh, what tortures we put our hair through to get those curly locks!"

A curling machine like this greeted customers at Becky Robinson's shop.

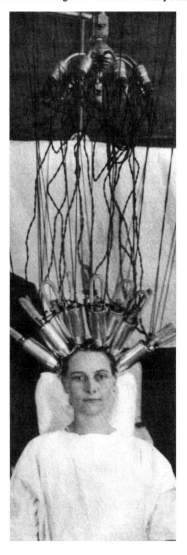

She said the building, operated as a beauty shop, beginning in 1930, by Robinson (later Mrs. Carl Neilson) for more than 20 years, once belonged to Lethbridge pioneer druggist John D. Higinbotham.

Avice also recalls the Wallwork house, built in 1886, being located just north of the old Stacey Lumber Yard on the east side of 13th, just as you entered the north side. Further north, on the west side, was the old No. 2 Fire Hall, where she recalls the Alford family - with daughters Miriam and Nellie, living in the second floor apartments.

"There was a bank on the corner of 3rd Avenue, the Standard Bank, later the Lealta Theatre," said Avice. "I did a lot of my parents' banking for them and I'd go into that bank and the tellers were in barred cages, locked in so no one could get at the money. Just before the bank was the Moose Lodge. They built that hall, but they weren't in it for long. Our church group, from St. Mary's, used to put on plays in that building, about 1925 or 1926. I'll never forget one play. I was a grandpa, and I had a false beard and I was supposed to eat something. I put it, and the beard right in my mouth, and the audience just roared."

June remembered what she called a Kiltie Band practising in the basement of the bank once a week when she was just a kid. "Margaret Leech, Peggy Kergan and I would sit on a bench and listen to them practice . . . it was a wonder we all weren't deaf with all that bagpipe music."

Scotty Armitt believes the pipe band practising downstairs used to be the Lethbridge Caledonian Pipe Band, one of the first pipe bands in the city. It included the likes of Jimmy Stewart, Jim Goldie, Joe Patterson, Alec McCord and Johnny Martin and Roderick Patterson drums. "These were all north side guys, and then Roddy Patterson started up the Bonnie Doone Pipe Band in the 1950s, with Bev (Allison) Paterson, Gordon Cargill, Bev Plomp as pipers and drummers included Al Hudak, Mel Willis and Garry (Allison). They used to practice at his house and at Westminster School."

Mavis (Harding) Standing remembers the bank for another reason. "I had an account at the Standard Bank," she said. "I had a little bank book and you could deposit 25 cents at a time. I was about eight years old and it was 1922. When the Nazarene Church was raising money for its building fund I wanted to help and I asked my dad to help me write a cheque for $1 out of my bank account to give to the fund."

Avice went to Westminster, right through Grade 8 and remembers Jean Jackson as an early teacher. She said early Westminster principal H.H. Bruce lived between 2nd and 3rd Avenue along 13th. In later years, the 1940s, Avice's sister Kathleen was teaching, at the same time as Mary Kadlac, who in her more than 30 years teaching at Westminster never missed a day of school.

"You've got to remember, a lot of north Lethbridge is undermined with coal mine shafts, and I believe that is why the first McCaffrey building was condemned and torn down because it was undermined, just south of where the drugstore moved to, and that new building still stands," Avice said.

Bev (Allison) Paterson

June said Burgman's Dance Hall was above McCaffrey's new building, and has some memories of the owner, though her mother never allowed her to go to the dances in the hall. "My dad knew Burgman, who was a great big, tall man and was a wrestler. He wrestled in a lot of the big cities back in that era. He had what I'd call a gaunt face and he'd scare us kids, though I think he was a very nice man. My dad was in those old Minstrel Shows of the era . . . something you're not allowed to do now, with characters like Mr. Interlocutor. My dad would put on black face and his white gloves and do the shows at club meetings, in halls like Burgman's and other spots on the north side, and the south side as well."

Being a girl, Avice was not one to frequent barber shops, but she did know where Greggy's was located, right at the top of 4th Avenue, as it jogged, next to the original McCaffrey building. It was 1928 and she was 12 to 14 when she used to frequent Greggy's, not for a haircut but to pick up a plug of tobacco and a little box of matches for her father at the smoke shop portion of the store operated by someone else. She'd just step in the door and there was a counter.

Avice and June also had memories of Pete's Bakery and Gurr's Butcher Shop, which closed down when the Gurr boys joined the war effort. The shop was run by Alfie Gurr and was always sparkling white and squeaky clean.

Norman Gurr also ran the Hub Cigar Store, in the same building Greggy's Barber Shop later moved into.

"There was a pool hall, south across the avenue from Credico's Bakery and I hated to go past there," said June. "I'd be about 12 and all those guys would be leaning against the outside window, and it was scary. That pool hall later became Lee Duck Cleaners. South of the pool hall was the Bing Wo Confectionary and a Chinese family lived in the store. My middle name is Winnifred and he couldn't say it, so he called me Windy. They used to sell those licorice pipes for a penny."

South again was the hardware store and a building where Kobal's was later located. Then came a hairdresser and Mrs. Lucas had a millinery shop and apartment where she was busy bringing up her orphaned nieces.

"She made beautiful hats, and they lived in the back of the store," June recalled. "South again, was Swingler's Meat Market, and the family lived in a little house right next door to the butcher shop. The shop had sawdust on the floor and there were four Swingler boys, Joe, William, Harris and Cecil. Jim's (June's husband late city police chief Jim Carpenter) dad Harry was a salesman for Swift's Canada and he used to go to Swingler's all the time. He'd tell us Mr. Swingler had a gall bladder or appendices in a glass jar on the parlour mantle, and he'd see it every time he went in."

North side kids play back of the H.G. Kilner Shoe Shop in 1937, from left are: Ed Pike, Phyllis Bissett (later Slovack), Alvin Bissett, Darlene Douglas, Audrey Bissett (later Kesler) and George Bissett.

Avice said Swingler's always had freshly-spread sawdust shavings on the floor each morning and it wasn't uncommon to see a side of beef hanging on a peg just inside the door. Mr. Swingler usually didn't have time to get that side of beef into his large walk-in cold room in the early morning," said Avice. "I always marvelled at the little red light that came on when the cold room door opened."

"Mrs. Swingler did some cooking for the shop, and often made faggots . . . large meat balls. Whenever I found out she had made some I dashed home to get a syrup pail (complete with handle) and got permission to buy some faggots. Sometimes Mrs. Swingler would take me into her kitchen and put some of the cooking broth into the pail."

South of Swingler's June remembered the Kilner Shoe Repair shop and later Van Rees Upholstery, who not only made furniture for Jim and June Carpenter but was later a member of their stamp club.

Avice recalls the bakery run by Pete Credico on the corner of 4th Avenue, with its baked goods and penny licorice plugs, pipes and cigars. She also enjoyed ice cream seated on the fancy metal ice cream chairs. "At one time the Gurr brothers operated a butcher shop next to the bakery. But, WWII broke out and all the able-bodied men were called up and their meat market was closed."

Avice said Bill Gregoski (Greggy) ran a barber shop just to the north of the bakery and also sold tobacco in a small compressed package, which had to be cut in fine strips by the user. "Many times, as a 12-year-old, I would be sent to Greggy's to buy a plug of tobacco, two nickel stinkers (cigars) and a small box of matches. The clerk who waited on me was Winnie Gurr.

During the 1920s when a young June would venture onto 13th there was Ontkean's Ladies Wear, across from the United Church - Lou's Wonder Cafe, had yet to arrive. Another vacant lot put the J and A Johnson Red and White Store a fair piece from the corner, and there was another vacant lot to the south of the store.

"Behind the store was a stable where they kept their horse and buggy for deliveries," said June. "The two Marshalsay boys, Jim and George and their half brother would deliver for Johnson's. They'd come out to your house in the morning, get your order and then bring it that afternoon. Talk about service."

On the east side of 13th, between 5th and 6th Avenue were large homes, for the likes of the Watson, Kerr, and Shorthouse families. Further north along 13th Street was Orlander's Hardware, and Avice remembers it as quite a store in the pre-war era.

"I don't know how long the store operated but the house was still there in 1937," she said.

June recalled O'Sullivan's Garage on the east side of 13th, between 3rd and 4th Avenues. "When radio first came in my dad would take me to their house and we'd hear the radio, over earphones. I thought it was magic to be able to listen to music coming out of a box like that." Years later June's first job was high atop the Marquis Hotel as a secretary for CJOC.

## Talented Folk

To be sure north Lethbridge had a lot of interesting folk through the years. The city's third mayor, Thomas McNabb, once resided along the west side of 13th Street in 1909.

Many-time world champion long drive champion, from the world of golf, Jason Zuback, was a northsider and you'll find him honoured in the Winston Churchill Hall of Fame. Churchill spawned a lot of notable northsiders, not the least of which was a teacher there, Bob Tarleck, who became Mayor of Lethbridge in 2001 after a distinguished career as an alderman. As well, the Sir Alexander Galt Museum and Archives displays are lovingly and artistically created by former Winston Bulldog football star Brad Brown. Yes, he's one of the Browns from 12th St. C, whose father Jimmy was one of this city's most likeable milkmen and a fixture on the Miner's Library Board.

There were many Petrunias contributing to the north side through the years, on sports teams and at work. In 1986 Ted Petrunia was honoured with a Memorial Park. The son of John and Ilona Petrunia served on the Miner's Library Board for years and was an active sportsman so its appropriate the super lawn bowling greens between Churchill and the Blue Sky Manor are named in his honour.

One of my boyhood chums was Rick Steadman, at least a two-time Canadian junior badminton champion. When he smashed those heavy feathered birds just right he literally drove them through the net.

Hey, on my paper route alone there were some real contributors to our society, including now retired Judge Clarence Yanosik and Roderick Mackenzie Patterson. Roddy started the Bonnie Doone Pipe Band back in the 1950s, with me as one of his drummers.

And speaking of the NHL, the north side also spawned the great Vic Stasiuk and later Doug Barkley with Les Colwill. Aut Erickson, who scored the first penalty shot in history for the Boston Bruins, was also a northsider and lived along my paper route.

Frank and Evelyn Leffingwell, northsiders for much of their lives, were a true championship couple in the 1960s and 1970s. Frank was one of Canada's top rifle shooters before his death and earned more than a dozen Canadian titles in bench rest and other disciplines and once recorded a perfect score at the Ponoka Rifleman's Rodeo. He earned the Gold Shield five times from the Canadian Shooting Federation. Evelyn is a former Canadian champion bench rest shooter and holder of four provincial target championships.

Frank and Evelyn Leffingwell.

Between the two of them they had more than 250 medals and 180 trophies by the time of Frank's passing. Ev has been target shooting since she first met Frank, who died in 1991 at age 61.

"I took up shooting because Frank did it, I started the sport with him," said Ev. "He was always at the range and if I wanted to be with him I had to join him there, so I did." They also helped others.

> Evelyn and Frank distinguished themselves not only on the rifle range but as instructors. Both have been honoured for their long service with the Green Acres Kiwanis junior shooters, which has spawned a number of Pan Am and Commonwealth Games shooters. Few people attain the success Evelyn and Frank Leffingwell have gained in a sport.

Evelyn's most memorable moment in her sport came when she opened the mail and found a gold medal in it.

"I didn't know I had won the Canadian women's .22 championship until I received the gold medal in the mail," she said. "Don't ask me what my score was, it was a long time ago, 1968, and I don't remember. Not only was it my most memorable achievement but it was also my biggest surprise. We would shoot .22 targets, 12 prone, four kneeling and four standing, and then send the targets in to the Canadian federation, and they tallied the results."

The couple are among the most respected scorers and shooting officials in Alberta, and Frank was chosen to be one of the official scorers at the Commonwealth Games in Edmonton in 1978.

Frank always felt his most memorable moment on the range occurred at the Ponoka Rifleman's Rodeo in 1975, where he recorded a perfect score. The record he broke was 47 out of 50, a score he had recorded a few years earlier. The perfect score was recorded against pop-up animal targets, simulated game animals. One target is moving and the other four pop up for four seconds. A shooter never knows which one will pop up, and the targets are set at different ranges, from 100 to 325 yards.

Frank shot competitively for well over 25 years, in virtually every target shooting discipline. He won the Willow Valley and Cardston grand aggregate three times and the Lethbridge Fish and Game aggregate twice. The Frank Leffingwell Memorial Shoot is now held each summer in Lethbridge, keeping alive the memory of this great shooting champion, and his contributions to the sport of target shooting.

"Frank dedicated his life to safe gun handling and shooting and taught a junior program for 20 years in this city," said Evelyn. Among those he taught was my son Jason, now a wildlife biologist and a former Southern Alberta Summer Games smallbore target competitor, thanks to Evelyn's urging.

Evelyn, after a few years off when Frank died, then returned to the sport, not only running the smallbore events at the Alberta Summer Games, but competing as well, shooting .22 and largebore.

She was the top female shooter at Fort Saskatchewan, Ponoka, Lethbridge and numerous other rifle rodeos and has also won the Lethbridge aggregate title, for both male and female shooters.

Evelyn and Frank were the forces behind the fact smallbore shooting has been a part of the Southern Alberta Summer Games since the Games inception more than 30 years ago. Evelyn continues to volunteer for Games smallbore events in the rural communities of southern Alberta chosen to host the Games each year. At Cardston, in 2001, she won two gold medals in the smallbore event.

She is a strong supporter of the Fish and Game movement in Alberta and in 2001 was honoured as a life member of the Lethbridge club.

Husband Frank was awarded a life membership in the Lethbridge Fish and Game club as well. Evelyn has been part of the Fish and Game scene for 40 years.

## Ice Cream and the Chief

My neighbourhood was an ethnic treat, with streets containing names like Hepple, Mogus, Hudak, Lee, Wong, Norman, Grotollo, Foster, Evdokomoff, Hildebrandt, Wardman, Beddington and Withage, all of whom enjoyed the new ice cream treats of the day.

About 1956 the north side Dairy Queen opened its doors, right next to First United Church. North of the church and later the Dairy Queen location lived the Rae family. The father was a herbalist and son Bill went on to teach at the LCI and became one of the city's top curlers. As things turned out the new Dairy Queen was a real pain for the church, and for Lou's Wonder Cafe, as well, at least as far as receiving kids' money was concerned. Ice cream cones, usually bought at Lou's were now being bought at the Dairy Queen, and why not, they had that new fangled soft ice cream, and it only cost a nickel. That nickel also impacted the church's collection plate. Most of us were given a dime for the collection plate each Sunday, and after the Dairy Queen opened most of us felt the Lord certainly deserved at least 50 per cent of that dime - the Dairy Queen, and our stomachs, deserved the other five cents.

Such was the drain on the Sunday School collection the church officially stepped in. Through a petition to city council the Dairy Queen's hours were adjusted on Sunday, the ice cream shop not opening until at least an hour after church let out. From then on, the Good Lord received his full 10 cents.

One of the key figures at First United in the 1950s was Jim Carpenter, who would move on to become the city's police chief, from 1957 to 1971. Carpenter, who lived just around the corner from the church, along 12th St. C, was very active with the youth, serving as Scout Master for many years.

From 1940 to 1971, Carpenter's life centered on police work. Carpenter went into the Lethbridge City Police as a rookie constable and came out as Chief of

Police, a position he held from 1957 until his retirement. The one constant through his 31 years on the force was the fact Jim Carpenter enjoyed the job.

"I enjoyed it, the people, the beat work, everything," said Carpenter, who died in 2001. "It was fun then; we used to get a lot of laughs out of many of the things we did."

In 1941 the city police only had one vehicle and walking was the way the city was patrolled. Occasionally, if a policeman found a lost or stolen bicycle on his beat he wouldn't be adverse to riding it as he took it back to the station. Carpenter said he enjoyed walking a beat, something not done by police in the city any longer, except on special occasions. He said two men always walked the downtown beat and foot patrol police went into the entire business district, checking doors nightly on stores and warehouses downtown, to the eastern edge of town and all along 13 Street North and the entire railyard and freight shed area.

Police Chief - James H. (Jim) Carpenter.

Jim stated: "The longest beat was the north side beat, 8 p.m. to 5 a.m. We left the police station, walked in a zig zag pattern through the warehouse beat, under the subway to the freight sheds and yards, then west to check the warehouses north of the CPR tracks and back again before going north on 13th street to the last store. To cover it twice during the shift we walked a total of 23 miles. It was the quietest beat and in winter, after midnight, cold and lonely with only two places to get warm, the fire hall and the York Hotel; sometimes if we were lucky we could also warm up at a poker game going in Greggy's Barber Shop or Matt Kropiniak's store."

Jim recalled stopping in at Greggy's on occasion on Saturdays to watch a poker game in progress. Poker was generally frowned on, but Greggy's was a friendly game. The more discreet and serious gamblers played poker at the Chinook Club. Under its charter through the Northwest Territories Act the Chinook Club allowed gambling and even liquor during prohibition.

"I was proud to be able to look east down 3rd Avenue and north from 13th Street and be able to tell my beat was secure," said Carpenter. "I enjoyed the beat I'd walk 23 miles a night. I enjoyed being able to stop at Pete Chumik's Hardware and help take stock for a while, or if I was downtown go into Lethbridge Ironworks and many a time I helped the guys at Ellison's bag flour."

He and wife June had five children, daughters Lee, Joan and Lynn, and sons Brian and David - the latter went on to serve as the mayor of Lethbridge from 1986 to 2002, the first north side-born mayor in the city's history.

One of Police Chief Carpenter's more memorable moments occurred on the north side. "I was going off shift one night, in the 1940s, and Charlie Wilson was coming on. We were both in civilian clothes when a call came in from Galbraith School Principal Clarence Larsen about a shooting. We took a car and drove over north. When we got there Larsen said 'there's a man in that house over there and he just shot a woman.' Wilson and I started over. The house was a good two blocks north of the school in the prairie (in what was to be the Dominion Square development). Half way there Wilson asked me, 'You got your gun Jim?' I said no. He didn't have his either."

The two policemen kept walking though and when they reached the house it was decided Carpenter would go in the front door, on the floor and Wilson the back, also on the floor. The two policemen charged into the house.

"There was this fellow, lying dead on the floor between us. He shot this woman and then shot himself. The man had been a civilian guard at the PoW camp in north Lethbridge," Jim said.

The incident was the late chief's one memory of Dominion Square, though he vaguely remembered a circus or two visiting the city and setting up in that section of town years earlier, well before he joined the police force. The shooting incident occurred during the early years of the Second World War, and only a few houses existed in the Dominion Square area. Not much of a development from the grand dream of 1912.

"My worst experience was with a woman," Jim said. "We got a call on 11 Street, Alex Porteous and I, and it was an upstairs suite."

The two policemen went into the hallway of the house and Carpenter started up the stairs. There, at the top, with a .38 pistol pointing right at him, stood the woman. "You don't think of a gun barrel as being that big," Carpenter said with a laugh as he put his thumbs and forefinger together. The two policemen were on the stairs, Porteous in behind Carpenter. I kept talking to her as I edged up the stairs. Luckily she just threw the gun at us and ran for her room, where it turns out she had two shotguns laying on the bed. I chased

her and wrestled her down before she reached them. She was drunk of course. She was going to shoot her husband; she wasn't really interested in shooting two policemen. It was a frightening experience. Porteus told me later he went home that night and had two stiff drinks."

Besides serving the community as a policeman, Carpenter was also active in the Optimist Club and, at age 18, was the youngest commissioned Boy Scout Master in the city. He, Roy Nelson and Bob Anderson, ran the 11th Lethbridge Troop at First United Church. He was also honoured by the Lethbridge Community College and is in their Hall of Fame.

Jim wrote a history of the city police force, *The Badge and the Blotter*, published by the Historical Society in 1974. He also served as treasurer of the historical society for a time and was named the Member of the Year. The society has honoured Jim's memory by naming the Community Meeting Room in the Lethbridge police station, opened in 2000, in his name.

Jacob and Emily Walton, the parents of Jake Walton, in 1898.

# Places
## and
# Spaces

There is no way you can write about 13th Street North and not venture off a time or two for a look at some other key north side places and spaces.

Naturally there are far too many of these off-13th areas to talk about in this book, but I felt some were certainly worthy of mention, and at the same time realize I've missed a number of others.

## Air History

As the Post Master of the first sub-station Post Office in Lethbridge, in McCaffrey's People's Drug Store, it is only fitting William Henry McCaffrey played a small role in the city's first Air Mail shipment. Knowing the city was about to fly in its first shipment of Air Mail, McCaffrey wrote letters to each of his children, Jack, Dorothy and Betty, and had the letters mailed, for the first flight into Lethbridge.

"The letters came here on the first Air Mail Flight, Jan. 15, 1931," said Gwen McCaffrey who also has the mint-like envelope which carried her husband Jack's letter, from his father. "The air mail came into the old city airport, in North Lethbridge, near the old water tower and the government grain elevators in the background."

The airport's boundaries were south of 5th Avenue between 22nd and 28th Streets North, an area of 50.6 hectares. The field was unimproved except for some levelling, with no paved runways. The first airfield in the city had been the infield area of the Lethbridge and District Exhibition's race track, back in 1911, but due to its restrictive size, and other obvious problems, a new airfield was created about 1919.

By 1928 the "Lethbridge flying field" was the registered port of entry for planes coming north from the United States.

As far back as the 1920s, Jock Palmer and Harry Fitzsimmons had undertaken a test flight as a mail carrier, in a plane they called Jenny. Things went well until a landing at Minot, North Dakota went wrong, severely damaging their plane, forcing the flight to terminate short of its destination. However, by June 1928 an air service between Salt Lake City, Great Falls and Lethbridge was inaugurated. Also in 1928, the building of a hangar, or airdrome, was the next goal, to facilitate storage, repairs and plane servicing.

George Davies, a Royal Air Force WWI veteran, said Lethbridge had "one of the finest fields for landing and taking off in Canada" in the late 1920s. One of the key figures in local flying in that era was George Ross, who was seeking to form a local flying club.

Late Lethbridge historian Alex Johnston said Emil G. Sick, in 1928-29 - of the Sick's Lethbridge Breweries - realized aviation was developing into a viable industry. He started to pursue the commercial possibilities of air and service. Charles B. Elliott's Southern Alberta Airlines Ltd. pestered city council with requests to lease the airport, to install telephones and complete other badly-needed improvements.

To this day, Jock Palmer and Harry Fitzsimmons, still find their aircraft featured on the label of Pilsner beer. "Emil Sick, of the Sick's Lethbridge Brewery, included the image of their famous Jenny on the label when he introduced his new beer in 1928, Lethbridge Pilsner," says Lethbridge historian Carly Stewart. "Molson Breweries bought out Sick in 1958, and in 2005 continues with the Jenny as part of their label for Old Style Pilsner."

In September 1930, the National Air Tour, at great cost and sponsored by the Board of Trade, was talked into returning to the city, something it had been doing since 1925. In came 18 high-powered, high-speed aircraft which drew more than 10,000 people for the one-day show. They roared approval as the planes swooped down onto the airport landing field. There was a Waco biplane, a Goodrich Silvertown, a De Forest-Crosley, called a flying radio station, and the Independence Monarch Ford. A highlight was daredevil Captain Frank Hawks and his Travel Air Mystery Ship, which had recorded a record-setting transcontinental trip from Los Angeles to New York. Hawks had flown from Calgary to Lethbridge in just 35 minutes. At 2 p.m. the planes took off for their next show, in Great Falls, Montana.

Another significant day for the north side airport was Jan. 15, 1930, when the Postmaster General approved Lethbridge as a point of call on the Trans-Prairie Air Mail service. As a result of these pressures, council okayed a $20,000 expenditure for a floodlight, fences and construction of a hangar at the airport. As well, a meteorological station and beacon were installed by the Department of Transport. Air Mail service began Jan. 15, 1931, when Herbert Hollick-Kenyon landed a Canadian Airways Limited Fokker monoplane at the floodlighted Lethbridge Municipal Airport. More than 4,000 people were on hand, including W.H. McCaffrey, to welcome the first Air Mail flight, with its historic letters.

First Air Mail Letter sent from Lethbridge.

The first air mail flight out of the city came the next day, Jan. 16, at 2:30 p.m. on a Boeing B-40. One of the letters on that flight was from John Easton, his seven cent stamp carrying a letter to his cousin Bert Paterson in Stewartfield House, Broxburn Limlithgowshire, Scotland.

There was a water tower, or standpipe as they were called, at the airport, a large metal one, but it never held water after it was built in 1912, well before the airfield which didn't move in until the very late teens. The water tower was painted with yellow and black diagonal stripes so pilots would be able to see it. Through its entire useless life, the tower's placement at an air field was always a source of wonder.

The tower finally went up for sale in August 1952, after what The Herald dubbed as "a 40-year history of uselessness". The 135-foot high tower was a technical blunder. The pressure required to get water up the tank would have burst the old wooden mains, and, if the tower had ever been filled, it would have caused other standpipes in the city to overflow.

"We used to climb that old standpipe as kids, up the outside right to the top," said Scotty Armitt. "We'd get way up there and then we were afraid to climb down because it was so high and the fire department had to come and get us down."

Margaret Schile remembers Charlie Tweed as an old bush pilot who was set up at the north side airport.

"From our house we saw everything that went on at the airport, and we'd go to the air shows there," said Florence Seager, who lived along 21st Street, between 4th and 5th Avenue North. Born in 1912, she came to Lethbridge in time to attended Galbraith school in Grades 6 to 8, graduating with honours.

"We saw the air shows, but most of them from outside the fence from our car because we couldn't afford to go in," she said. "A lot of times we just stayed at home in our yard and watched. Living way out there we'd have to walk all the way to 13th Street just to catch a streetcar, even in the winter. When we got to the stop in the winter, the streetcar driver would let us warm our feet on the little fire box he had right inside the car, next to his feet. It was a little coal-burning warmer and sure felt good."

During the Second World War it was thought the tower could supply water to the huge PoW camp not too many blocks to the north. But the 110,000 gallon tower was found to have holes in the pipe leading from the ground to the tank.

In 1944 a huge, square water storage tank was built along 5th Avenue North, just about a kilometre west of the main gates of the PoW camp. Records indicate this tank wasn't used either and the huge cement structure, 80 per cent underground, was later purchased by Bill Bickman. A warehouse structure was built on the site in the 1950s, with the concrete tank serving as a basement. By 2002 the building was still being used, as a home for Liquidation Warehouse, a huge discount store.

Below: - The unused water tower overlooks the activities of the 1930s air show.

In place of the airport tower, the city built a new standpipe just down the road, a block or so south, on the south side of the tracks, in the 1960s. It always reminded Herald cartoonists of a curling rock - without the handle. In 2004 the water tower was refurbished and opened as Ric's Grill, a two-tiered top-end restaurant and lounge.

The old airport water tower was sold to a farmer who used it as a granary for years, without the leg supports of course. The tower-granary is still to be seen along Highway 62 a few miles west of Skiff, Alberta.

In 1931 a quiet north side Sunday was shattered on Feb. 2, when Donald McKenzie, the 18-year-old son of W.L. McKenzie, and Dr. R.B.C. Thompson's 19-year-old son Ivan were killed in a plane crash. The plane, a Tiger Moth, crashed to earth at 3 p.m. in an open area just north of the International Harvester building.

There was a Sunday afternoon ball game on the open prairie near the crash site, so the fatal crash wasn't without witnesses. Most say the pilot was attempting to make a flat turn, without banking, when the plane came down.

Above - This north side airplane crash took the lives of two teens in 1931.

Right - This 1914 photo of Arthur Harding and his wife shows the blacksmith shop of Philip Harding in the background, on what became the Westminster School yard. The lettering on the shop states: Plow Work by Sharp; Buggy & Delivery Wagons; Auto Springs & Bodies.

The boys had taken off at the north side field, young Thompson at the controls, and circled Henderson Lake and the Duff Addition before turning north. It was only three minutes into the flight when they crashed. The Herald said a huge crowd quickly gathered at the site, and the Mounties had to rope off the crash scene. Eye witnesses said the plane was only 300 to 400 feet up when it went into a spin after attempting a flat turn, striking the ground with such force the crash was heard in many sections of the city.

"Dr. Thompson owned the BA Garage on the corner of 4th Avenue and 13th," said Mavis (Harding) Standing. "He bought it for his boys, Jim, Homer and Ivan. Homer was killed overseas in the war and Ivan was killed in the plane crash. Jim moved away and later became mayor of Helena, Montana. They also had a daughter Bessie. As kids we'd always catch pollywogs at the frog pond by the Catelli factory, and feed them to Dr. Thompson's chickens. The service station was a great place for playing cards. In later years it became the Bolokoski Garage."

As a nine or 10 year old, Scotty Armitt used to go to Thompson's Garage, on the corner of 13th Street and 4th Avenue, to take flying lessons, or at least to pretend to take lessons. After all the owner of the garage was Dr. Thompson, whose teenage son Ivan had an interest in flight and even had his pilot's license. His grandson Robert is in charge of the Western Canadian Aviation Museum in Winnipeg.

Dr. Robert Thompson graduated from the University of Manitoba in 1900 and began practicing in Lethbridge about 1903. He retired from medicine in 1944.

The young boys would also go out to the airport to watch the planes and to dream of flying. But, 19-year-old Ivan went flying with his buddy Donald and their Tiger Moth, piloted by Ivan, crashed in the open prairie north of International Harvester, just before 3 p.m., killing both boys.

Herald photographer Joe Hunter was out for a walk the Sunday afternoon the accident occurred, apparently as the teenage pilot tried to make a turn keeping the wings flat without going into a bank. Hunter, always at the ready with his camera, took the pictures for The Herald.

## An Era Passes

Just across the alley from Lee Duck Dry Cleaners was one of the last blacksmith shops in the city, run by Harold Perkins. Jack Lee was among the many people who used to drop in and watch Perkins ply his trade.

"He lived at the back of the building, and he'd do some of his cooking on the fire place, the forge, at noon times," Jack said with a laugh. "He was a real nice guy though and didn't mind anyone watching him. One time I smashed up a bike, and it wasn't mine, and he fixed up the front wheel, replacing the spokes and straightening the forks. He was nice that way."

After the blacksmith shop closed, Jimmy Lee bought the lot and built a home for his family, on the avenue where he lived much of his life, and just across the alley from the back door of Lee Duck Dry Cleaners. Talk about a short walk to work. Jimmy also served as president of the Chinese National League in 1972.

Sitting along 4th Avenue, just a building's length off 13th, blacksmith Harold Perkins held sway - though I didn't know his name at the time. He ran his shop from the late 1920s through the early 1950s. In 1927 Harold Perkins was an employee with Lethbridge Sales Co. and living on the south side. By 1928 he had seen the light and moved north, opening a blacksmith shop at 1268 4th Avenue. Perkins would remain in his shop, and the attached living quarters, with wife Gratia at the same address until 1956, when the shop closed and an era ended.

"I remember my dad taking his carpenter's hand saws over to Perkins to sharpen, in the late 1940s or early 1950s," said Carly Stewart, a past-president of the Lethbridge Historical Society. "Mr. Perkins showed us a wood carving he'd made from a single piece of wood. It was a ball carved inside a quad helix. It made about a half turn on its length and the ball travelled down the helix as the carving rotated end to end."

Blacksmith - Harold Perkins.

There were other blacksmiths on the north side through the years, though none located on 13th Street itself. You'd find smithies like Barclay and Sons on 16th Street, near 4th Avenue, in 1912 but they were gone by 1917, and in 1917 Wm. Brown had a shop on 6th Avenue A North and Philip A. Harding was set up at 1409 4th Ave. He was still there in 1940. In 1925 Roger Dolan was at 727 12th St. N.

"My brother, Phil Harding, had a blacksmith shop on what would later become the east end of Westminster school grounds, about 1946," said Mavis (Harding) Standing. "The kids always used to come into his shop and he'd allow them to pump the large bellows on his forge. He could make just about anything with that forge and his hammer."

All are gone now, closing a special era in city history. Other old traditions are gone as well.

I moved onto 4th Avenue in 1949, and one of my regular stops was visiting the blacksmith shop, an old barn-like building complete with fire, bellows and anvil. There were still a few of the horse-drawn milk wagons around back then, and Perkins did shoe the occasional horse.

The blacksmith would allow us to stand by his door and watch him as he pounded out a wagon wheel rim or prepared a horseshoe. The shop always had a warm feel and an odour of coal, horses, sweat and coal oil. Every time I visit the blacksmith shop at Heritage Park in Calgary, those short visits to a real, honest-to-goodness smithy just a block from my home always come to mind.

## Chilly Past

Gone are the days when we used to see all the horse-drawn delivery wagons frequent the north side. While living on 12th St. B, at 522, my grandmother's house was on the route for the milk wagon and the 4X bread wagon which my uncle, Jim Allison, used to drive. The ice man also cometh, via Van Horne's ice wagon, with those big tongs and big blocks of ice carried in on his broad shoulder, and a Chinese man, Ian Yee who also had routes on the south side, delivered vegetables. The drivers used to leave the wagons unattended, the horses stopped only by a big iron weight on a rope, attached to the halter. We'd pick up the weight, set it on the wagon step and set the horses on their way. The vegetable man in particular failed to see the humour in this. The milkman's horses, on the other hand, seldom moved.

C.H. (Charlie) Van Horne and his Lethbridge Ice Co. brought the ice north in small horse-drawn wagons, one still on display at the Remington Carriage Museum in Cardston. Van Horne started up in 1922 and supplied ice for the city's ice boxes for 31 years, finally falling prey to electricity and the refrigerator.

Charles Herbert Van Horne, who died at age 82 in 1957, joined with William McAdoo at the turn of the century to form a company specializing in cartage, home moving, and ice and coal. Before the city waterworks were completed in 1906, Van Horne's company was also delivering water door-to-door, their water wagons service filling family's water barrels.

Van Horne managed the Lethbridge Ice Co. from 1922 to 1953 when he serviced his final customer. By 1948 he was the last of three ice companies still in operation in the city. In the end he only had 150 customers, as refrigerators were the rage of the day. Just a few years earlier, in 1949, he delivered 4,500 tons of ice to his 1,500 customers, the ice cut in the winter from the Oldman River and stored in huge ice sheds, insulated with sawdust and hay bales. George Niedermier's picture appeared in The Herald in 1930, one of a crew of men manning the ice saws.

Ross Van Horne, who was killed overseas during W.W.II, was one of the ice delivery men in the 1930s.

One of the icemen of the era was a friend of my father's, Eddie Masson. Ed was a longtime northsider born in 1918 to Bill and Mary Ann Masson. Ed's father was cutting and delivering ice in 1914 and was joined by his son when Eddie was just 14 writes Charlie Watmough in *The Bend*, a history book about west Lethbridge.

Western Transfer Co., one of the large draying outfits, was owned by Tom and Oliver Long and had 12 ice houses throughout the city.

Much of the ice was cut from the Oldman River, just below where the university now sits, though in warmer years when the river wasn't stable, ice was taken from lakes and reservoirs. It was cut and stored in the ice houses, with walls 16 inches apart and the gap filled with sawdust for insulation.

"The inner wall was made of two-inch material to withstand the battering when the ice blocks were slid into place," writes Charlie. "It would remain cold in there all through the summer and into the fall. Some of those ice houses had a capacity of about 700 tons or more."

The ice harvest usually began when the ice was 18 inches thick. A scraper removed the top two inches, clearing off most dirt and debris. Eddie Masson and his father would drive a team of horses over the ice, pulling the scraper.

As to how the ice was cut and harvested, I'm leaving it to Charlie to tell you, just as he wrote it in *The Bend*: "The big operators had a slick way of harvesting ice and yet there was lots of work to it. In the early days it had to be horse power because the gasoline engines of that day didn't do too well at 20 below zero and that was the right time to put up ice. The run usually started as soon as the ice was about eighteen inches thick, often late in December and lasted about six weeks. The scrapers were pulled with a team of large horses with good sharp calks in their shoes. Having cleared a large surface thusly a 'marker' was pulled with a team making a straight line in the ice about two inches deep. A guide was then set two feet off to one side of the marker to follow this line on the next trip, thus making a series of marks two feet apart over a large area.

"Then they did the same thing at a right angle to the first marks but this time they were three feet apart making a neat grid design on the ice with each block marked out two by three feet. The purpose of this was they could be cut into six, one-foot squares when delivered to the customer.

"When the area was marked out two inches deep another machine, an ice plow, also pulled with horses, which was like a huge saw with heavy duty teeth and plow handles on the back deepened the marks to eight inches. The narrow cuts ran parallel with the flow of the river and then another cut was made off to the side. This one was cut at an angle with an ice saw so that these narrow blocks could be pushed down under the ice to drift away. When this was cut the full length of the area it was continued another thirty or forty feet and another cut parallel to it to make a trench a little wider than the blocks and down stream from the end. A ramp with steel rails and guide rails was then set into this trench to slide the blocks onto a platform.

"The next operation was loading. The ramp made this very simple. The eight inch marks made a good head start to saw out the first four individual blocks at a right angle to the trench. Then they used a 'splitter', (quite like our present day ice scrapers, for sidewalks with the heavy wooden handle) to split the blocks off and let them float into the trench. They next cut off four blocks in one slab to act as a 'pusher' and let that float into the trench behind the four singles. A device called a 'monkey', consisting of a short steel frame with two strong hooks to reach over the back of the pusher block, two spurs on the under side to hold it straight, an upright handle on the top and a cable on the front was laid on the back end of the pusher. The cable on the front of the monkey was laid on top of the pusher as well as on the four individual blocks floating in the trench, up the ramp, over the platform and right past the dray to a team in front.

"When the team pulled the cable, the pusher and the four blocks were loaded right onto the wagon and moved over by hand to make room for the second batch. The second batch of eight completed the load, 16 blocks at 300 lbs. each, 4,800 pounds. That was a big load for one team on the old Laundry Hill, (6th Avenue South) and they made about four trips a day with each team. The blocks were unloaded one at a time with a horse-operated hoist," Charlie concluded.

Delivery was not easy either. Commercial customers took 100-pound blocks of ice and the driver used a canvas to cover the ice while he was delivering. Housewives generally took blocks weighing 40-50 lbs., three times a week. The cost was $3 a month.

When the new refrigerators came on the market Ed left the business, mainly because there wasn't any business any more, and went to work for Hudson's Bay Wholesale in 1947.

## One Man's Scrap is . . .

As kids we used to scrounge copper wire, lead or other metal parts we could find and head for National Salvage, along 2nd Ave. North, usually on a Saturday morning as we headed over the 9th Street Bridge to the morning matinee and the afternoon shows. George Varzari would dole out a handful of change for our booty and off we'd go.

"We used to have a lot of kids stop in, but now we buy that stuff by the ton," said George, whose son Glenn is now president of National Salvage Ltd., at 206 33rd Street in the Industrial Park. "Back in those years we were lucky to get 100 to 200 pounds of stuff at a time simply because there wasn't that much scrap around. The thing I liked most about the business was you were into everyone else's business . . . no matter who phoned you you'd buy it. It was the kind of business then when you could buy anything. I don't think Glenn buys the kind of stuff we used to buy."

George Varzari started up on the south side, with one shop next to the old Palm Dairy (on 7th Avenue South, between 5th and 6th Streets). By the early 1950s he had moved his National Salvage junk and scrap yard to 2nd Avenue North, creating a vast gathering point for scrap metal of all types. By 1953 he had created an entire yard and in 1955 the yard was shipping 1,200 tons of scrap a month.

"We must have had about three acres there," said George. "My brother was next door to us with Varzari Iron and then there was Dominion Salvage. AGT had a yard in there too, with all their poles and stuff. When I started the business up it was a time when you couldn't get a job."

> **No parking**
>
> "That whole area has really changed from when we were in there; there's not much left from what there used to be," George said with a chuckle. "You know you could always buy a lot of buildings along 13th Street, and generally pretty cheap because there was never any parking."

George said he looked around, realized who had all the money and set about becoming a scrap dealer, starting off as we kids did - only he was doing this in the 1930s - by scrounging copper wire and pipe, brass and anything else found in alleys and byways and selling it to existing dealers.

"As kids we'd sell to people like Joe Green's dad and other places on the south side, right downtown," said George. "Once we set up we were in the steel business, and we used to take in a lot of old cars and sell them to Al Davis, set up just about where the city stores are west of 9th Street along the coulee tops. We'd take 100 or 200 cars over at a time and he'd buy them and bail them. We had model T Fords, old steam engines which we'd sell most of to a guy in Great Falls. We used to operate an old steam crane for a number of years as well. I wish I still had that. One day I had a guy stop by from Cranbrook, with an old Model T

Ford truck he was taking to Saskatchewan. It took me three hours to talk him out of that. In those days you could get that for $300 to $400."

About 1970 the city began clearing out the strip from 13th through to 9th Street, with an eye to a shopping mall and further expansion after. George headed for the Industrial Park.

Aerial photos in 1969 show the sprawling freight sheds and their miles of spur lines - though along 13th there was a stretch of lawn and some fairly large trees which provided a nice rest stop on walks to and from downtown - with the fenced-in yards, and their piles of scrap metal, covering the area about where the old frog pond once was a source of enjoyment.

The photos also show the large commercial complex which had sprung up between 13th, the railway tracks and even up to 3rd Avenue, right over to the 9th Street Bridge, - with the exception of a row of houses on 12th St. C, one of them belonging to the Stewarts.

Now son Glenn is established as a second-generation Varzari with the National Salvage name and what used to be junk is now called recycling. Someday George hopes to see the business become a three-generation affair.

## The Lions Step In

The Lions complex was the one place where all north side kids came together, leaving behind the community neighbourhoods, within whose boundaries they usually stayed.

The outdoor hockey rink - one of a number in north Lethbridge in those early years - was a special treat in the 1950s, with its ice surface cared for by Ab Paskuski's father, John, and its warm changing shack. Hockey ruled the surface much of the time, and for a poor skater like myself, goaltending became the way to be on the ice and get in the games. Problem was, it meant facing the booming shots of guys like Garth Hughes, Freddie "Turk" Perkins, Brent Seely, Al Willis and Fred "Ziggy" Zasadny and the great Jim "the Rocket" Culver. You haven't lived until you've had Hughes rattle a slap shot off your "can".

Another hockey great, Vic Stasiuk, happily was on the outdoor ice before my time, and Irma Dogterom remembers how Vic would always be shooting a puck at the girls' skates as they glided around the ice.

Those outdoor hockey games often went well beyond the five skaters to a side idea, with kids showing up and simply moving onto the ice with one team or the other - the super stars like the aforementioned however were always on opposing teams.

One of the times you left your neighbourhood was for school, or for recreation. The Lion's swimming pool and the outdoor skating rink in the winter, were magnets which drew kids from all over the north side to one central location. It was at the rink or pool where you'd freely mix with the kids from other areas, like Tom Wheeler and his sister Marilyn from up 12th

Street A, or Mel Willis, Gordon Briosi or Al Hepple from 12th Street C, or the 16th Street people like Gord Burns or Frank Tuttle.

Vic Stasiuk

Construction of the Lion's Pool came after a true community fund-raising project in the mid-1940s. At the time you weren't allowed to run a raffle for a big-ticket item, but the Lions came up with a plan for a draw, for a house.

The Lions built a luxury home along 13th Street South, on the corner of 5th Avenue, with Sven Sandberg, a northsider, as the contractor. It was valued at $11,000 - how times have changed! They set about seeking donations for the home, with the idea that all those who made a donation would have their name entered in a draw - for the home.

In May 1945 the draw was made, and a Calgary man, who had just completed building a new home in the cowtown, won the draw. He had the choice of the house or $10,000 and he opted for the cash. The house was subsequently bought by the Beny family, and the Lions went away smiling with a $15,000 windfall, and the pool was under construction and opened the following year. Former Herald photographer Lloyd Knight was at the opening and took a shot of Fred Standing diving into the pool, a keepsake he still cherishes.

The Lion's complex, between 4th and 5th Avenues on 16th Street North, included the pool and to the south and east, the old outdoor skating rink which was the fun spot of the winter season.

On top of this, when the new Wilson Junior High School opened, the Lion's Pool and rink would both be right on the school grounds. What more could a kid ask for? What the pool meant was, as members of the new Wilson Junior High, our phys-ed classes would not only include hockey in the winter but swimming in the summer. If memory serves, and it usually doesn't, about the time I entered Grade 8 we began to have phys-ed at the pool and the rink. Our class then included the likes of Doug Rusk, Freddie 'Turk' Perkins, Lloyd 'Slugger' Potter, Hank Schippers, Howard Norlin, Jack Dietzen, Blair McNab, Johnny

Potts and Reg Arnold on the male side and girls included Lois Styner, Sharon Belliveau, Donna Berglund, Wendy Large, Nancy Dedels, Barbara Walker, Betty Field and many others. Our home room teacher was Miss Simmonds.

It seems to me the phys-ed people ran the swim classes. And just knowing you were the only school class in the city - at least that's what we thought, although some south side schools had swimming as well - made the phys-ed class bearable for a change. Skinny little me - that's right skinny - hated phys-ed. I was at least a year younger than those in my class and I didn't like physical exertion, even then. To me classes like tumbling and gymnastics should have been outlawed.

Through the years the Lion's pool has served the north side well. The high diving board was a test of courage, and the real dare devils leapt from the balcony into the pool - after a quick scout around to see if the lifeguards were watching. They always were.

## Ethnic Societies

In March of 2002, the Italian Canadian Cultural Centre celebrated its 25th year at 1511 St. Edwards Blvd. North, but the club had been around for many decades prior to that. The Italians had come together in the early 1920s, as a support organization for the men working in the coal mines of Lethbridge and area. By the mid-1950s however, it was almost strictly a social organization.

For years the club bounced around from building to building, but in the 1976 members got together and decided a permanent home was needed.

Members not only financed the project, but built the club themselves, with their own sweat doing everything from pouring concrete to walling and painting. Eight years after opening the club was debt free. John Mazzuca, who has been a member of the club since 1957, took over as president in 1975.

### Sick-Aid Society

In 1937, members of the original Sick-Aid Society included Andy Androkovich, Charles Peta, Joe Urban, Joseph Szarko, Joe Horhozer, Steve Voytko, Gabor Szakacs, Louis Revesz, Ethel Gall, Mary Toth, Margaret Poche, Rose Oslanski, John Lottus, Victor Fuszy, Irene Zubric, Julia Kaszas, Helen Lengyel, Helen Kaszas, Frank Tarnocsi, Paul Gaejci, Steve Veleti, Albert Godrulo, Andy Ducs, John Hanzel, Louis Sipos, Peter Nagy, John Buga, Sandor Revesz, Joe Thomas, John Toth Sr. and George Szarko. Other member-family names on the north side at the time included Tomie, Balasz, Buga, Chenger, Sonyi, Mikia, Istok, Gonzy and Horvath.

Oct. 6, 1901 the First Hungarian Sick-Aid Society was formed in the city, and some time later, on May 1, 1927, received its charter. On charter day, the members gathered at the city's first Hungarian Hall, along the

800 block on 7th Street North. By 1937, with a growing membership, a new hall was built along 9th Avenue, where the Japanese United Church now sits. Eventually the Sick-Aid Society and the Hungarian Oldtimers amalgamated.

One of the most intriguing events in the city, though it received little press attention at the time, was the fact two of the city's ethnic clubs were closed, by police order. In June 1940 Police Chief T. Nicholls issued orders to close the Ukrainian Labor Temple on 5th Avenue North and the Hungarian Hall, on 9th Avenue North. The orders came under the Defence of Canada Regulations and both premises were closed, the windows boarded over and doors padlocked.

Both memberships adhered to the ruling, and understood police action would be taken against individual members if any meetings were held.

In 2001 the Polish Hall, at 745 13th Street, celebrated its 50th anniversary, despite the fact the Polish people had played a role in the coal mines and settlement of the north side many decades earlier.

The Canadian Polish Association of Lethbridge really sprang up after World War II, when a large number of Poles settled in north Lethbridge, under the Displaced Persons program. There were Polish immigrants earlier, but not in the numbers north Lethbridge witnessed after the war.

The north side also had a Caledonian Society, that had its own pipe band, back in the 1920s through 1940s. The club met in the basement of the Standard Bank - later the Lealta Theatre - from 1925 to 1929.

"My grandmother, Helen Campbell, was president of the Caledonian Society for a while, but I really don't know how long it lasted, likely to the end of the 1930s or the early 1940s," said Cammie Randle. "They used to have banquets each Robbie Burns Day (Jan. 25) and they'd have little Scottish teas in the afternoons, and they'd sing the old Scottish songs.

"I remember too going over to the Empress Theatre downtown to see and hear Harry Lauder, and he greeted us with it's 'a braw bricht moonlit nicht ye ken' . . . We also saw Gracie Fields here in Lethbridge, always using her scarf as a prop when she performed. I remember the pipe band included the McColl brothers playing the pipes and drums, and they practiced downstairs of the old Standard Bank. James Moore was also a piper, and I think he ran the band at one time."

In the early 1920s, a slain Alberta Provincial Policeman was honoured with a large funeral procession. His body was carried on a horse-drawn funeral carriage across the barren prairie from his widow's home near Fort Macleod, to the Presbyterian Church in Macleod and then on to the cemetery, it was led by the Caledonian Pipe Band. Pipers included Jim Cameron, a CPR section foreman and father of Marie Sorgard later to become a well-known Picture Butte and area historian, and Jock Kennedy, a Lethbridge policeman.

The German-Canadian Club, on the corner of 9th Avenue and 6th Street North first saw the light of day in 1958.

The club Haus, where I've enjoyed a few Herald functions and a magnificent walleye barbecue with Frank Bishop, Lorne Fitch and some of the fisheries biologists, came about when the Edelweiss Club, founded by John Liebe in 1954, and the Lethbridge Bombers Soccer Club amalgamated.

The Bombers passed beyond the boundary of German nationality, and to this day the membership of the German-Canadian Club is not restricted, open to all nationalities.

---

**Bombers Soccer Club of '58**

The Bombers of 1958, who became the provincial senior men's soccer champions, included Mario Petri, Eddie Ruff, John Husch, Erich Gast, Adam Rath, Alec Kogler, player-coach Willie Becht, Willie Hahn, Karl Phillips, Arnold Jauerneck, Frank DeJong in goal along with Ray Mercer, Walter Hoffman, Joe Paragut, Steve Mezei and John VanderHeide. It certainly was not an all-German club. The team lost its first two games of the year in the finals for the Western Canadian championships to a pro team out of New Westminster, B.C.

---

In forming the German-Canadian Club the goal was to preserve the German heritage, and one of the projects in 1968 was creation of a language school, where school children could learn to speak, read and write German.

Among the longtime members of the club were Irma Strafehl-Horn, Ernest Horn, Conrad Weiler, Rudy Wermuth, John Liebe, Otto Wagner, most of the Bombers and Hans Bohnert, chairman of the building committee.

The club opened its new $46,000 building in 1966 with a grand banquet and 200 participants, enjoying speeches, fine food and polkas. Special guests included Mayor Frank Sherring and Dr. Wilhelm Theonnes, German consul in Edmonton.

The club has played host to many functions through the years, including Oktoberfest, a Kinderweihnachts Fest for children at Christmas and Saengerball, a traditional song and dance fest. Club members have also participated in the city's Heritage Days and Canada Days activities, supported school scholarship programs, and earned a fine reputation for its quality male choir, dating back to its formation in 1971.

## Lodges

The Eagles, Independent Order of Foresters, Oddfellows and Moose Lodges all found homes at one time or another in north Lethbridge, the Oddfellows soon heading south however. The Oddfellows met in the old Burgman's Dance Hall for a spell until building their permanent home in the heart of downtown, the corner of 5th Street and 4th Avenue. Mizpha Lodge No. 72 of the IOOF was situated at 418 13th Street as far back as 1917.

The Moose Lodge began back in 1911, with 50 members, and after years where the lodge reached upwards of 500 members, it still exists at 1401 5th Avenue North, with about 70 members. The Loyal Order of Moose dates back to 1888 when Dr. John Henry Wilson of Louisville, Ky. gathered a group of friends together, forming a fraternal order to assist in community service projects. The Lethbridge lodge has made donations through the years to community facilities like the Regional Hospital, and other organizations such as the DARE program, Alzheimer's Society, Streets Alive, the Cancer Society and Salvation Army.

The Eagles Hall sits along 13th Street, on the corner of 6th Avenue A.

## The Forgotten Place

Cemeteries are closely connected with the history of any city, and unfortunately a cemetery is often one of the first necessary institutions in a new community.

One of the first burial grounds established in north Lethbridge was known as St. Patrick's Cemetery, and at other times the Pioneer or Miner's Cemetery.

The 15-acre fenced grounds, on the extreme end of 6th Avenue across Stafford Drive, is truly the city's forgotten cemetery today.

The final resting spot of many early north side residents is bordered by laughter and games, with a soccer pitch, skateboard park, fastball diamond and the Dave Elton Little League complex all directly south of this hallowed place. Ironically the immediate area also contains two juvenile detention centres and a Christian school.

There are no records for the combined Protestant, Catholic and Chinese cemetery prior to 1920, as to who is buried where, and they are sketchy even into the 1950s. It seems all the early records were kept in the old St. Patrick's Church in south Lethbridge, which burned to the ground in 1920.

A view of St. Patrick's Cemetery

Land for the cemetery had been donated by the North Western Coal and Navigation Co., and in the very beginning in 1886 was reserved for Catholic burials.

"A lot of plots may look empty today, but then again they may not be," said Belinda Crowson, a cemetery afficionado and visitors co-ordinator with the Sir Alexander Galt Museum and Archives. Even though the land was surveyed and set out in lots, people selected their own locations for burials, and many graves were put in the wrong places, some even on dividing roads. Cattle broke through the fence around the cemetery to graze, trampling grave sites and mounds. Also, the location of the cemetery was not well chosen. The cemetery was right between shafts 1 and 3, of No. 3 mine and cave-ins were a possibility. Slack and dirt were also dumped around the area, making it unsightly."

St. Patrick's was first surveyed in December 1886. Burial prior to that in Lethbridge was done quickly, and most likely recorded inaccurately. It was common at one time in those very early days to bury people virtually where they died. It was also common for people to die at a much younger age.

The cemetery was built beside the Galt No. 3 mine, and the closest settlement was the Village of Stafford. St. Patrick's was originally designed as two separate blocks, separated by prairie. The westerly block was Roman Catholic and the easterly for Protestants (Methodists, Presbyterian, and Anglicans). The cemetery was associated with St. Patrick's Parish, the first Catholic Parish in this region, and the Roman Catholic portion was consecrated in June 1889. The Protestant portion of the cemetery was taken over by the city in the same year. The Roman Catholic portion was not taken over by the city until 1953.

St. Pat's dates back to 1886, and until 1901 it was the only burial place in Lethbridge, except for a small cemetery in the Oldman River valley, started by the Stafford family. The river valley cemetery was used as the local burial grounds from August 1883 until December 1896, when St. Patrick's was surveyed.

"Southsiders immediately complained about the location of St. Patrick's cemetery," said Crowson. "They claimed it was too far out of the way, and that it could never be irrigated and cared for. Ironically, today St. Pat's has a complete underground irrigation system, while Mountain View Cemetery on the south side is still watered by above ground sprinklers.

"St. Pat's was once located between two coal mines, No. 3 and No. 6, and the city fenced it off in 1880, not only cutting off miners' shortcuts to work, but keeping cattle from grazing in the area. It was not the best possible site for a cemetery. Many complaints about the distance came from the south side of town. There were calls as early as the 1890's for a new cemetery to be developed in south Lethbridge, and in 1901, the Anglican Church developed their own cemetery south of the tracks, now the north-east corner of Mountain View Cemetery. In 1905, an undertaker named Moore started a company and operated a cemetery beside the

Anglican one. This cemetery was soon taken over by the city and became the public cemetery. The city took over the Anglican Cemetery in the 1920s and in 1947 amalgamated these areas, and some additional land, into Mountain View Cemetery.

Archmount Memorial Gardens in West Lethbridge, didn't come along until 1950.

"The disputes between Mountain View and St. Patrick's can also be seen as a conflict between the north and south sides of Lethbridge. It is one of those things you think would have diminished with time, but there are still differences in the ways people view the two communities," said Crowson.

Despite the early age of St. Patrick's, none of the city's early so-called wheelers and dealers, like Galt, Stafford, Magrath or Houk, are buried there. Most of those early city leaders saw their bodies sent back to their homeland, or buried on the south side at Mountain View.

However, you will find the Sheran name.

The Sheran name is well known in the city, honouring Nicholas with a city park and a school. He operated the first coal mine in the city but was drowned in the Oldman River near the stagecoach crossing at the Halfway House, 20 kilometres west of Lethbridge.

"Family members operated the mine until it was sold," said Avice (Frayne) Anderson. "James Sheran Sr. was buried in St. Patrick's Cemetery in May 1924. His wife Kate (Catherine) Sheran was buried there Jan. 14, 1930. Kate's brother, Ben McGovern, was also buried in St. Patrick's, on Aug. 30, 1925."

There is a section set aside for Catholic Nuns, with about 10 plots being used, in Section 6.

---

**Memorials**

At the centre of the north section of the cemetery there is a memorial rock set up by he Pemmican Club, in 1961, assisted by Hamilton Junior High students, in remembrance of those laid to rest prior to 1910. There's another monument near the children's section remembering four unmarked graves, with four new name plates attached.

---

Coalhurst mine disaster graves in St. Pat's and the funeral procession with the multiple caskets.

St. Patrick's is still active as a cemetery - if indeed, you can use that term in regards to a cemetery - in the sense that, if someone owns a pre-paid plot they may choose to be buried there, even today. No new plots are for sale, however.

The cemetery is broken into a series of distinct areas readily visible to visitors. One particularly isolated area is the northwest corner, a section which slopes dramatically down towards the coulee, just a 100 or so metres off busy North Scenic Drive. There are few markers, some with children's names, one has a tiny iron rail fence.

"Over that edge is where the unbaptized babies were buried, but there was a big furor about that in the 1970s because the area was not being kept up," said Crowson. "Since the city took over operation of the cemetery in 1980, that area has been well maintained. This area, where unbaptized children were buried, was originally outside the cemetery because these children could not be buried in consecrated ground. The area became overgrown with grass and was uncared for. People became very concerned about the condition of the graves of these unbaptized. It was believed by many Catholics these children were in limbo, the abode of souls barred from Heaven through no fault of their own. This was why their graves were in a remote corner, and purposely neglected. The graves were over the side of the coulee as far down the slope as possible and overlooked unsightly soil banks and clay diggings. In 1982 the city took over the care of this neglected area, ensuring it was watered and the grass mowed. There are no records for this area and while it is cared for, it is left undisturbed."

These graves were buried in weeds, some simply mere mounds of ungrassed earth, some with broken markers, others with bent or demolished fences when citizens began to raise concerns in the 1970s. It was in stark contrast to the well-cared-for trim lawns of the other sections of the main cemetery. The area was considered outside the cemetery proper when the city assumed responsibility for the grounds in 1957 and there were very limited records as to who was buried there.

The Catholic belief was children were supposed to be baptized within a month of birth. Parents were considered at fault if they neglected a baptism beyond that time. The church wrestled with the question of these unbaptized burials, but cited the Bible as teaching "except a man be born again of water and the spirit, he can not enter Heaven".

In those early days unbaptized infants were buried and left to the mercy of God to achieve their destiny.

In a Herald article in 1973, Father J.A. Carroll, Parish Priest of St. Patrick's Catholic Church said: "Today, conditions are different. Priests conduct regular funeral services for stillborns and young infants and the babies are buried alongside the rest of the cemetery. In the early 1900s infant mortality was high and a third of all deaths were children. Baby sections were very common in cemeteries. The purpose of these

sections though, was economic not spiritual. By having all of the smaller graves in one area, it lowered the cost of the graves and made them cheaper."

Crowson also said suicide burials are not recorded nor graves marked. At one time those committing suicide were buried outside the cemetery's fences.

The Chinese section of the cemetery is the closest to the eastern fence line, to the north of the main gate. "With the Chinese, because it was never said they were buried in St. Pat's, but rather that they had simply gone to No. 3., as in coal mine," said Crowson.

At one time the remains of the Chinese dead in St. Pat's were dug up and returned to China for re-burial, once the family could afford it. The bodies would actually be stockpiled at Vancouver while all the paper work was completed for their return home to China. There's an unproven story of one Chinese man having his body held up in Vancouver because he had a missing finger. The entire skeleton had to be in place before the shipment to China could be completed.

Crowson said a search of the records back in Lethbridge showed the man had lost his finger in a mine accident, and once that was verified the body was sent back to China.

"Around 1930 the practice was halted due to the Communist Chinese takeover in China and inability for families to raise the money during the Depression era," Crowson said. "There were other problems with Chinese burials in those early days because the Chinese would leave offerings of money and food on the graves. After dark, kids would sneak into the cemetery and steal these offerings."

> As you walk through the cemetery, you will find tombstones in Hungarian, Chinese, Italian, Polish, and other languages. The north side was where most immigrants, coming to work the coal mines, settled.

The north side cemetery has many prominent headstones, along with many, many unmarked graves. Among the concrete and marble markers there are still two wooden crosses, though they are illegible.

Crowson also points out the many symbols found in the cemetery, with a lamb meaning a child - sadly, virtually all the small marble lambs have had their heads snapped off - or a cut-off tree meaning a life ended far too soon. There are also the Gates of Paradise, many flower symbols including the Scottish thistle, and even a finger pointing upwards, indicating which direction the deceased went.

Between 1882 and 1900 the main causes of death were accident, illness, and drowning. The first burial in St. Patrick's Cemetery was 25-year-old Frank Greer. He died of consumption and was buried Dec. 15, 1886.

Walking through the cemetery many markers jump out at you, some with interesting stories behind them. One such marker concerns an 11-year-old girl.

"Peachie, the daughter of Mr. and Mrs. D.H. Cox died July 25, 1904 at age 11 years, 10 months, and 13 days," said Crowson. "She had been riding in the back of a loaded hay wagon on the family ranch near Grassy Lake when the wagon's wheel hit a badger hole and Peachie fell forward. Two wheels ran over her back. Her brother and two sisters drove her into Grassy Lake but the railroad wouldn't transfer the body to Lethbridge without a doctor's certificate. These three youngsters drove the horse and wagon all night to bring her body to Lethbridge for burial - the same wagon that had run over the girl. At the time, the father was in Winnipeg and the mother was deceased."

While walking in the well-treed, quiet cemetery, with its strong ethnic mix, emblematic of the north side itself, it is not uncommon to see headstones with both English and the language of the homeland.

As you walk through the manicured grounds today you'll find the marker for Thomas Peter Kilkenny, the only city fire chief to die as a result of a fire. Kilkenny passed away from pneumonia, about a month after battling the blaze at the Balmoral Hotel on 5th Street South, in minus 40 degree weather in January 1911.

One of the prominent memorials in the cemetery is the Coalhurst Coal Mine Disaster Monument of 1935, identical to one in Mountain View Cemetery. Ten miners are buried in St. Patrick's and six are buried in Mountain View. There is the larger marker, with five of the men's names on it, and smaller headstone in front, remembering Andrew Prokop, Lou Gossul, Evaristo Rota, Angelo Ermagora and Albina Simoni, who all died Dec. 9, 1935.

As you walk, you find the Gorog tombstones, for Jozseg, age 13, and Gyorgy, 10. The tombstone is in both Hungarian and English.

"The two boys were caught in a freak snowstorm trying to bring a flock of sheep home to shelter," said Crowson. "The father searched for three days, after he had reached home safely with the youngest son."

In Section A, as you enter the gate, you find, in row 20, the Bodnaruks. All four were killed by a train as they came back from visiting on their mother's farm.

"They were sisters-in-law, with one son each," said Crowson. "Two other children survived the accident, which occurred in September 1944 near Tempest."

Row after row you see the familiar north side names: Pupko, Burkette, Ondrik, Devernichuk, Dorin, White, Koshman, Demers, McAllion, Peta, Stanko, Cunningham, Leoni, McDermott and Luciani, Joseph and Lena. Joseph was a caretaker at the Garden Hotel and Lena, a clerk at Supina's Mercantile.

There's the Sawchuk marker, a large concrete one, virtually flush against a huge tree. And in another section the Perry family has a younger tree growing between the marker and the concrete covering on the grave site. As you walk through the Chinese section many markers are in Chinese script, but there are many familiar names - Hong, Yip, Nuck, Ng, Lamb, Chow, Fong, Wong, Leong and Dong.

The ethnic mix continues, with Popovich, Macdonald, McLean, Morris, Homulos, Bolokoski, Petrunia, Krekosky, Tennant, Maloney, Seaman, Stasiuk, Rath, Tedesco, Chenger, Yanosik, Chollak, Coyle, Mudrak, Wyrostok . . .

And the list goes on and on, including the Pavans, Joseph and Maria, who once operated Pavan Dairies just north of Hardieville. Pavan Park is named in their memory.

Above - The Perry house still stands along 9th Avenue North.

Below - The house at 522 12th St. B N. as it looked in 2004.

# My Last Glance

Well, there you have it, I hope you have enjoyed it. To me, north Lethbridge will always be home. It's where I was born and raised, it's where I first met my wife, Mary Smith. It's where I spent nine years of my 10 years of schooling. The north side is where my grandfather and his family settled when they arrived from Scotland in 1918, and where my dad, his four brothers and two sisters grew up.

As I look back, I see many visions of North Lethbridge, it's people, stores, schools and sports venues and even some of my heroes.

Here's a last glance back over my shoulder:

Fred and Joan Wardman.

My mother Lily (Melling) Allison

The Snowdens, Roland and Marjorie and sons George and Robert, lived between Little Wigan and Staffordville, about a block west of 13th Street.

137

Above - There were two sets of 3-generation families who had or were attending Galbraith School when it celebrated it's 50th Anniversary in 1963: Left, Clifford Heaton who was in grade one in 1913 when the school opened, along with daughter, Joy Penny and her three children: Douglas, Dennis and little Susan. At Right: Sarah Fraser with her daughter, Edna Malacko with her children Lynette, Calvin and Jimmy.

Right - Lil (Saxon) Wright, niece of my mother and wife of my good friend Bill.

Below - Elizabeth (Cook) Zsovan of 12th St C North provided this 1927 photo of the Lethbridge First Hungarian Sick-Aid Society, formed Oct. 6, 1901 and chartered May 1, 1927. This charter-day photo was taken in front the first Hungarian Hall, in the 800 block of 7th Street North. With a growing membership, a new hall was built on 9th Avenue North in 1937, which today is the home of the Japanese United Church. The hall was sold when the sick-aid society and Hungarian Oldtimers merged. Some of the people in the photo are unknown or only partial names, but, as Elizabeth and friends' memories go, here they are: Front row are the officers and executive, from the left: Andy Androkovich, (?) Lengyel, Charles Peta, (?) Tomie, (?) Balasz, (?) Kaszas, (?) Buga, (?) Poche, (?) Gall, Joe Urban, (?) Locszo, and Joseph Szarko. Second row, from left: Joe Horhozer, Steve Voytko, Gabor (Szakacs) Cook, (?) Matizs, (?), (?) Istok, Louis Revesz, (?) Chenger, (?), (?) Voytko Sr., (?), (?) Sonyij, and (?) Mikla. Top row, standard bearers, from left: Ethel Gall, Mary Toth, Margaret Poche, Rose Oslanski, John Lottus, Victor Fuszy, Irene Zubric, Julia Kaszas, Helen Lengyel and Helen Kaszas. Others in the photo include: Frank Tarnocsi, (?) Horvath, Paul Gaejci, Steve Veleti, (?) Gonzy, Albert Godrulo, Andy Dues, John Hanzel, Louis Sipos, (?) Szarko Jr., Peter Nagy, (?) Boros, John Buga, Sandor Revesz, Joe Thomas, John Toth Sr., and George Szarko.

Dianne (Pedersen) Violini is the daughter of Steve and Berthella Pedersen. Steve was a fine bowler, but Dianne surpassed his achievements attaining national and international recognition.

Joyce and Greta Sandberg, sisters of my good friend Doug.

Strange as it seems, all four of these beauties lived on the same street - my street.

Dorothy Wardman wife of Fred Wardman.

John Credico operated a 13th Street pool hall and barber shop for decades.

Above - The Anderson sisters, a famous dance band troupe that played many a night at various Southern Alberta venues. They did however own the Rainbow Hall at 1327 5th Avenue North during the 1940s where they played to a regular crowd.

Below - The Lethbridge Caledonian Pipe Band. Members names have long since been lost, this image was lifted from the early pages of the Lethbridge Herald.

Above - North Lethbridge Hardware where Pete Chumik reigned as king of carload sales of home appliances. He was "Carload Pete" during the 1950 and 1960s.

Above right - Long standing York Hotel has had many owners and a few other names but it still stands it's ground at 3rd Ave. and 13th.

Right - Mo-Tires, a longtime fixture along 13th Street North as North Lethbridge Motors.

Below - The first Lions Swimming Pool at the corner of 16th Street and 5th Ave. N. ca 1952. A newer pool now stand on the same corner operated by a neighbourhood association.

Above - Author, Garry Allison and his first grade teacher, Erla (Keyes) Sanderson reminisce and look over the release of Garry's 2005 publication *People of the Mines*.

Rear - Spud Wilkie, John Melling, Lil (Saxon) Wright. Front - Ken Wilkie and me, Garry Allison.

Bert Randle was the first mail man in North Lethbridge.

My grandparents, Robert and Elizabeth Allison celebrate their 50th Wedding Anniversary. Their wedding photograph is in the background.

This ae
1945) I
from th
permiss

This is a fold-out page:

Above - The Polish Hall on the corner of 13th Street and 8h Avenue North.

Right - Bonnie Doone Pipe Band drummer and my friend, Mel Willis

In the late 1930s the camera caught a bunch of north side kids, who will forever remain northsiders at heart. While some are unknown, we see, from left, Brian Wardman, Donnie Good, Buddy McClean, and an unknown girl, Don Kearney at rear, Lamar Kearney, Phyllis Montgomery, Shirley Ann Montgomery, Joan Wardman, Kathleen Gruenwald, Bobby Gruenwald, names of the four people centred in the rear row are lost to memory, but from the right working left are: Audrey Bissett (later Kesler), Bob Montgomery, Ted Washbrook and Joe Montgomery.

Undoubtedly before this book comes off the press I will have remembered a few other things and people that I could have and should have included. But, I guess that's another story.

No one ever really leaves north Lethbridge; it remains an important aspect of your life, and although I've lived in Coalhurst for the past 30 or so years, north Lethbridge will always be *My Side of Town*.

# Where They Were

I have included below, randomly selected portions from along 13th Street North (Westminster Road), taken from 1909 and 1975 Henderson Directories. It lists many of the businesses and people from over those years. Henderson used various abbreviations including es for east side; ws for west side.

**1909 Henderson Directory**
es Stacey Lumber Co
es Johnson Peter
es Tuff Joseph.
Helen Street Intersects
es Scott John
es Harvey Edwin G
es Vacant
es Negry George
es McNulty Thomas J
es Nimmons Robert
es Fryer William G
es Pioneer Lumber Co
ws Matthews Wm
ws Bellevue & Supina
ws Supina Mike
ws McKeown Alfred G
ws Alexander W P J drugs
ws Restaurant
es Lytle Rev A A
Rachel Street Intersects
es Watson William
ws Perock Mike grocer
ws Lee Wong restaurant
ws Brook Silas M gen store
ws Johnston J and A grocers
ws Methodist Church (North Ward)
es North Ward School
McKay Street Intersects
es Kerr William
es Kerr Allan
es Watson Robert
Niven Street Intersects
es Norman John
es Forsman Charles
es Norman Street begins
es Vacant
MeBeth Street Intersects
Luckhurst Street Intersects
Galbraith Street Intersects
es Anglican Church
ws Rosaine Herman
ws Rosaine Mrs John
ws Heaton Thomas
ws Holik John
ws Turner Peter
ws Crook Jan Wm
ws Talbot John
ws McNabb Thomas
ws Peacock Charles
ws Foster John
ws Hirst James
ws Watmough John
ws Riley Mrs Wm
 McLeary Stewart
ws Moore John
ws Sumner James
ws Sumner J R
ws Saxton Robert

ws Leadbeter Timothy
ws Hopkins Frederick
No. 5 and No. 6 Mines here

**1913 Henderson Directory**
East Side
201 Scott, Jno., owner.
217 Odney, Mrs. C. C., tenant.
221 Tirvey, Alf, tenant.
225 Negrey, Geo., owner.
237 Nimmons, Robt., owner.
245 Pioneer Lumber Co., owner.
261 Vacant.
303 Ingraw, A. J., tenant.
309 Rissiter, E. & Co., tenant.
313 Hart Patterson Hardware Co
 tenant.
327 Petras, Matt. owner.
519 Kerr, Andrew, tenant,
531 Kerr, A. owner.
537 Watson, R. W., owner.
609 Hyssop, Abe, owner.
613 Kilner, Henry, tenant.
619 Hartley, Jesse, tenant.
627 Finley, Thos., owner
635 MacDonald, J. R., tenant.
639 Hazen, L., tenant.
St. Andrew's Church, owner.
West Side
140 Fire Hall No. 2.
224 Matthews, Wm, owner
230 Church Hall
234 Supina, M., owner
236 Vacant
240 People's Drug Store, owner
242 Success Meat Market, owner
246 Williams, A., owner
248 McCarty & Co., Grocers,
 tenants
250 Monarch Theatre, owner
310 Westminster Meat Market
318 Vacant
328 Hong Lee Restaurant, tenant
402 Brooks, S.M., owner
404 Cooksley, Miss C, A., tenant
406 Palace Meat Market, owner
408 Kennedy, Russell, owner
408a Central Realty Co., tenants
414 North Lethbridge Realty Co.,
 owner
414a Gilmore, Jno., Store, tenant
416 Wilson Furniture Co., owner
420 Parsons, Ernest, tenant
426 North Ward Grocery, J. & A.
 Johnston, owner
502 Westminster Methodist
 Church
522-524 Olander, C. G., owner
526 Morden & Bennett, owner

546 North Lethbridge
Co-operative store, owner

**1914 Henderson Directory**
West Side
Columbia Flouring Mills Co Ltd
Fire Hall No 2
Western Transfer Co Ltd
CPR Freight Sheds
Second Avenue Intersects
2nd Avenue A Intersects
224 Mathews Wm
230 Vacant
234 Supina Mike
236 Vacant
210 Peoples Drug Store
212 Pacific Fish Market
246 Williamson Andw clothier
246 Williamson Block
248 Lang Robt F grocer
250 Monarch Theatre
Third Avenue Intersects
308 Swingler Fred
310 Westminster Meat Market
318 McMeekin Mrs Margaret
318 Vacant
320 Royal Cafe
328 North Ward Restaurant
Fourth Ave Intersects
402 Brook Silas M gen store
402 Globeshoe and Gen Store
Holmes Street Intersects
404 Cooksley Charlotte A. milliner
406 Palace Meat Market
408 Kennedy Russell barber
408 Simm Frank
408 Central Realty Co
414 Shaw Wallace confr
414 North Lethbridge Realty Co
416 Donaldson Block
 1-2 Vacant
 3 Anderson Peter
 4 Vacant
416 Wilson Furniture Co
418 Vacant store
418 Burgman Block
418 Mizpah Lodge 10 Q F No 72
420 Kwong Sam restaurant
426 North Lethbridge Grocery
Fifth Avenue Intersects
502 Westminster Methodist
 Church
512 Kilner Harry G shoemkr
522 Olander Carl G
524 Olander Carl G hdw
526 Morden Robt B gen store
544 Moody & Frayn herbal store
546 Vacant store
546 Ritson Wm

6th through to 9th Avenue
Intersects
East Side
131 Pankhurst Chas
Second Avenue Intersects
201 Scott John
205 Vacant store
217 Vacant
221 Ingram Alfred J
225 Negrey Geo
229 Vacant
237 Nimmons Robt
245 Pioneer Lumber Co Ltd
261 New building (under const.)
Third Avenue Intersects
303 Pilchak John N
309 Jackson Henry grocer
313 Hart Patterson & Co hdw
315 Standard Bank of Canada
317 Pilchak John N barber
327 Petras Mat
Fourth Avenue Intersects
Westminster School
Fifht Avenue Intersects
619 Kerr Andrew
531 Kerr Allan
537 Watson Robt W
Sixth Avenue Intersects
609 Hyssop Abraham
613 Vacant
619 Parsons Thos
Sixth Avenue A Intersects
635 Vacant
7th Avenue Intersects
St Andrew's Presbyterian Church
707 Bryan Rev Andrew C

**1917 Henderson Directory**
West Side
Columbia Flouring Mills Co Ltd
 (closed)
Fire Hall No 2
Western Transfer Co Ltd.
CPR Freight Sheds
Second Avenue Intersects
Second Avenue A Intersects
224 Matthews Win
230 Supina & Son
234 Supina Mike
236 Vacant
240 Peoples Drug Store
242 North Meat Market
244 Johnston John S
246 Williamson Andw clothier
246 Williamson Block
248 Vacant store
248 Midby Elmer A
250 Vacant

Third Avenue Intersects
308 Swingler Fredk
310 Westminster Meat Market
318 McMeekin Mrs Margaret mlnr
320 Bing Wo groc
328 Lee Wong
Fourth Avenue Intersects
402 Vacant
404 Vacant
406 Hopkins Mrs Edith R
406 Palace Meat Market
Holmes St intersects
408 Kennedy J Russell barber
408 Crowe John
410 Kennedy Thos shoe repr
414 Kilner Harry G
414 Grist John
414 Daldson Block
416 Hennesey & Wilson
418 Hart Hardware Co
418 Burgman Block
418 Miziah Lodge IOOF No 72
420 Kwong Sam restaurant
426 Johnston J & A ,
Fifth Avenue Intersects
Westminster Methodist Church
    (closed)
522 Olander Carl G
524 Olander Carl G hdwre
526 Morden Robt B gen store
544 Aloody & Frayn herbal store
546 Rogers F A
Sixth through Ninth Avenues
    Intersect
946 Rosaine Herman
950 Heaton Thos
1106 Thomas Edw
1116 Hoose David
1122 Vacant
1124 Ralston James
1127 Jamesfield Frank
1128 Crook John W
1130 Ashcroft Robt
1122 Talbot Chas
1140 Clark Thos
Greek Orthodox Church
1202 Peacock Chas
1206 Foster John A
1210 Hurst James
1214 Melling John
1224 Riley Mrs Ellen
1222 Steele James
1232 Vacant
1240 Moore Geo
Victoria Avenue Begins
1304 Smith Fred
1308 Holland Thos
1510 Saxon Robt
1606 Diggory Richd
1610 Vacant
1612 Vacant
1614 Degaust Danl
East Side
131 Pankhurst Chas
Second Avenue Intersects
201 Scott John
205 Vacant store
217 Ingram Alfd J
221 Vacant
225 Negrey Geo
229 Vacant
237 Williams Fred
239 Vacant
245 Pioneer Lumber Co Ltd.
Third Avenue Intersects
303 Hodgson John E
309 Lee Duck tailor
313 Vacant

315 Vacant
327 Petras Matthew
Fourth Avenue Intersects
Westminster School
Fifth Avenue Intersects
519 Kerr Andw
531 Kerr Allan
537 Watson Robt W
Sixth Avenue Intersects
609 Hyssop Abraham
613 Parsons Thos
619 Roberts Thos
Sixth Avenue Intersects
635 Rae John
Seventh Avenue Intersects
St Andrew's Presbyterian Church
707 Kinneburgh James

**1921 Henderson Directory**
West Side
CPR Freight Sheds
Western Transfer Co Ltd
Second Avenue Intersects
Fire Hall No 2
Second Avenue A Intersects
224 McMorrow Wm
230 Supina & Son
234 Supina Michael
236 Vacant
240 Carter Jens shoemkr
242 Dodd Walter A tailor
244 Johnston John S
246 Williamson Block
    Williamson Andw clothier
    Vacant
258 Pilchak John M barber
258 Standard Bank
Third Avenue Intersects
308 Swingler Fredk
310 Westminster Meat Market
318 McMeekin Mrs Margaret mlnr
320 Bing Wo grocer
328 Brunton Dave meats
Fourth Avenue Intersects
402 Lee Duck tailor
404 North Lethbridge Bkry
406 Hopkins Mrs Edith R
406 Burns P & Co br
408 Laychen Charlie grocer
410 Kennedy Thos barber
414 Donaldson Block
414 Peoples Drug Store
416 Hennessey & Wilson
418 Burgman Block
418 Hart Hardware Co
418 Mizpah Lodge 1 0 0 F No 72
420 North Ward Transfer
420 Kilner Harry G shoe mkr
426 Johnston J & A
Fifth Avenue Intersects
Westminster Methodist Church
    (closed)
524 Olander Carl G hdwre
526 Morden Robt B gen store
532 Olander Carl G
544 Frayne A
546 Rogers F A furniture
Sixth Avenue Intersects
Sixth Avenue A Intersects
Seventh Avenue Intersects
706 Scott
Ninth Avenue Intersects
946 Rosaine Herman
950 Heaton Thas,
954 Greek Orthodox Church
1106 Thomas Edw
1114 McIlvena James
1116 Hoose David

1120 Worthington Thos
1124 Ralston James
1126 Lamesfelder Frank
1128 Crook John W
1130 Ashcroft Robt
1132 Talbot Chas
1140 Clark Thos
Twelfth Avenue Begins
1202 Peacock Chas
1206 Foster John A
1210 Hurst James
1210 (rear) King Sam, D
1214 Melling John
1214 King Saml
1200 Riley Mrs E1 1 len
1222 Wilson John
1224 Morton Thos
1232 Vacant
1240 Moore Geo
Thirteenth Avenue Begins
1304 Vacant
1308 Melling John
1308 Holland Thos
Fourteenth Avenue Begins
Fifteenth Avenue Begins
1510 Saxon Robt
1606 Diggory Richd
1612 Cook Albt A
1614 Vacant
East Side
131 Pankhurst Chas
Second Avenue Intersects
201 Scott John
205 Bethany Hall
217 Ingram
225 Negrey Geo
237 Williams Fred
239 Vacant
245 Pioneer Lumber Co Ltd
Third Avenue Intersects
303 Smith Fred H
309 Jackson Edw A
313 Vacant
315 Vacant
317 Vacant
327 Petras Matthew
Fourth Avenue Intersects
Westminster School
Fifth Avenue Intersects
519 Kerr Andw
531 Kerr Allan
537 Watson Robt W
Sixth Avenue Intersects
609 Hyssop Abraham
613 Parsons Thos
619 McIntosh Alex C
Sixth Avenue A Intersects
635 Soady Edw
Seventh Avenue Intersects
United Church North Lethbridge
707 Rae John
Eighth Avenue Intersects

**1925 Henderson Directory**
West Side
CPR Freight Sheds
Western Transfer Co Ltd
Second Avenue Intersects
Fire Hall No 2
Second Avenue A Intersects
224 Piko John
230 Supina Mercantile Co
234 Supina Michael
236 Vacant
240 Lethbridge Labor Temple
240 Roberts Music Store
240 Sloan James
240 Vacant

244 Bruce Herbert H
246 Williamson Block
246 Williamson Andrew
246 Sinclair Harry
246 Sheffield A W
246 Williamson Andrew clothier
250 Vacant
258 Standard Bank
258 Cripps W T H
258 Caledonian Club
258 Lockwood Thornton
Third Avenue Intersects
306 Kilner Harry G shoermkr
308 Swingler Frederick
310 Westminster Meat Market
318 Munro Millinery
318 Munro Mrs Daisy
320 Bing Wo grocer
328 Lee Wong restr
330 Jooreas John C barber and
    billiards
344 Jooreas John C
Fourth Avenue Intersects
402 Lee Duck tailor
404 Canadian Union Bakery
406 Palace Meat Market
408 Lee Hop grocer
408 (over) Vacant
410 Hub Cigar Store
410a Ryan Katherine minr
414 McCaffrey Block
414 PO No 1
414 Knibbs Mrs M
414 Neilson David
414 Peoples Drug Store
416 Hennesey & Wilson
418 Burgman Block
418 Hart Hardware
418 Mizpah Lodge IOOF No 72
420 Edwards Alfred see hand dlr
426 Johnston J & A
432 Ontkean's dry goods
Fifth Avenue Intersects
502 United Church Hall
522 Olander Carl G
524 Olander Carl G hdwre
526 Gust (The) S Estores Ltd
544 Sorokoski Bros grocers
546 Rogers F A
Sixth Avenue Intersects
646 Central Meat Market
Sixth Avenue A Intersects
Seventh Avenue Intersects
706 Dayman Arthur
740 Kropinak Matt confy
Eighth Avenue Intersects
Ninth Avenue Intersects
946 Rosaine Mrs Ellen
950 Heaton Thomas
954 Greek Orthodox Church
1104 Grisak John
1104 (rear) Grisak John L
1020 new house
1026 Jossul Mrs Barbara
1114 McNealy E A
1116 Hoose David
1120 Worthington Thomas
1124 Ralston James
1108 Richmond James A
1130 Ashcroft Robert
1132 Talbot Charles
1140 Wolstoncroft Robert
Twelfth Avenue Begins
1202 Peacock Charles
1206 Foster John A
1210 Hurst James
1210 (rear) Vacant
1210 (rear)Wolstencroft John

1212 (rear) vacant
1214 Green John
1220 Riley Mrs Ellen
1222 Vacant
1224 Ditchfield Thomas
1232 Draper Robert
1240 Sherman Sidney express
Thirteenth Avenue Begins
1304 Baird Thomas
1308 Melling John
1320 Moore George
Fourteenth Avenue Begins
1404 Leadbeater Timothy
Fifteenth Avenue Begins
1510 Saxon Robert
1606 Hackett Thomas
1612 Marsh John
1614 Salahub Steve
East Side
131 Jones Robert
131 Holbertson Elias J
Second Avenue Intersects
201 Scott John
217 Binning Mrs Ellen
221 Binning George
225 Negrey George
229 Vacant
237 Bruchet George A
239 Vacant
245 Pioneer Lumber Co Ltd
259 Kings Hotel
Third Avenue Intersects
303 Vacant
309 Dodd Walter A tailor
313-317 North Lethbridge Garage
327 Scott James
Fourth Avenue Intersects
Westminster School
Fifth Avenue Intersects
519 Kerr Andrew
519 Shorthouse David
531 Kerr Allan
537 Watson Robert W
Sixth Avenue Intersects
609 Dunlop Peter A
613 Milner George H
619 Hurst Wm T
Sixth Avenue A Intersects
635 Garrett John
Seventh Avenue Intersects
701 United Church of North
    (Lethbridge)
707 Rae John
733 Lethbridge Miners Library
    Club
733 Kotch Steve
735 Briosi Peter
Eighth Avenue Intersects
Adams Park

**1927 Henderson Directory**
West Side
CPR Freight Sheds
Western Transfer Co Ltd
Second Avenue Intersects
Fire Hall No 2
Second Avenue A Intersects
224 Trowhill John
230 Supina Mercantile
234 Supina Michael
236 Vacant
240 Lethbridge Labor Temple
240 Roberts Music Store
240 Roberts Thomas
240 Sloan James
244 Bruce Herbert H
246 Williamson Block
246 Williamson Andrew

246 Gawthorpe E
246 Williamson Andrew clothier
250 Moose Hall
258 Standard Bank
258 Cripps W T H
258 Caledonian Club
258 Lockwood Thornton
Third Avenue Intersects
306 Kilner Harry G shoemkr
308 Swingler Frederick
310 Westminster Meat Market
318 Lucas Mrs Laura
320 Bing Wo grocer
328 Lee Wong restr
330 Briosi Pete
Fourth Avenue Intersects
402 Lee Duck tailor
404 Canadian Union Bakery
406 Palace Meat Market
408 Lee Hop grocer
408 (over) Vacant
410 Hub Cigar Store
410a Jooreas John C
414 McCaffrey Block
414 PO No 1
414 Ritson Wm
414 Neilson David
414 Peoples Drug Store
416 Hennesey & Wilson
419 Burgman Block
418 Hart Hardware
418 Mizpah Lodge IOOF No 72
420 Edwards Alfred secondhand
    dlr
426 Johnston J & A
432 Ontkean's dry goods
Fifth Avenue Intersects
502 United Church Hall
522 Olander Carl G
524 Olander Carl G hdwre
526 Gust (The) S Estores Ltd
544 Sorokoskl Bros grocers
546 Rogers F A
Sixth Avenue Intersects
630 Mihalik Andrew
646 Central Meat Market
Sixth Avenue A Intersects
Seventh Avenue Intersects
706 Vacant
740 Kropinak Matt confy
Eighth Avenue Intersects
Ninth Avenue Intersects
946 Rosaine Herman
950 Heaton Thomas
954 Greek Orthodox Church
1104 Grisak John
1114 McIlvena James
1116 Hoose David
1120 Worthington Thomas
1124 Ralston James
1128 Richmond James A
1130 Ascroft Robert
1132 Talbot Charles
1140 Wolstoncroft Robert
Twelfth Avenue Begins
1202 Peacock Charles
1206 Foster John A
1210 Hurst James
1210 (rear) Vacant
1210 (rear)Wolstencroft John
1210 (rear) Monks Wm H
1214 Green John
1220 Riley Mrs Ellen
1222 Vacant
1224 Ditchfield Thomas
1232 Sherman Sidney F express
1240 Shrives Charles
Thirteenth Avenue Begins

1304 Baird Thomas
1308 Melling John
1320 Moore George
Fourteenth Avenue Begins
1404 Leadbeater Timothy
Fifteenth Avenue Begins
1510 Saxon Robert
1606 Hackett'Thomas
1612 Marsh John
1614 Gray Mrs Mary
East Side
131 Jones Robert
131 Holbertson Elias J
Second Avenue Intersects
201 Scott John
217 Binning Mrs Ellen
221 Binning George
225 Negrey George
229 Vacant
237 Bruchet George A
239 Vacant
245 Pioneer Lumber Co Ltd
259 Kings Hotel
Third Ave Intersects
303 Vacant
309 Dodd Walter A tailor
313-317 North Lethbridge Garage
327 Scott Wm
Fourth Avenue Intersects
Westminster School
Fifth Avenue Intersects
519 Kerr Andrew
519 Shorthouse David
531 Kerr Allan
537 Watson Robert W
Sixth Avenue Intersects
609 Dunlop Peter A
613 Milner George H
619 Hurst Wm T
Sixth Avenue A Intersects
635 Garrett John
Seventh Ave N intersects
701 United Church of North
Lethbridge
707 Rae John
733 Lethbridge Miners Library
    Club
733 Kotch Steve
735 Briosi Peter
Eighth Avenue Intersects
Adams Park

**1929 Henderson Directory**
West Side
CPR Freight Sheds
Western Transfer Co Ltd
Second Avenue Intersects
Fire Hall No 2
Second Avenue A Intersects
224 Jones Benj
230 Supina Mercantile Co
234 Supina Michael
236 Vacant
240 Lethbridge Labor Temple
240 Appleton Stanley
242 Roberts Music Store
242 Roberts Thomas
244 Bruce Herbert H
246 Langridge Ernest
246 Hall Charles
246 Bastram Mrs M C
246 Marshall H R clothier
246 Williamson Block
248 Vandervoot Albt shoes
250 Moose Hall
258 Can Bank of Commerce
258 Veale Mortimer C
258 Clay Rev A

258 Caledonian Club
Third Avenue Intersects
306 Kilner Harry G shoemkr
308 Swingler Frederick
310 Westminster Meat Market
318 Lucas Mrs Laura
318 Popular Hat Shop
320 Vacant
328 Lee Wong restr
330 North Lethbridge Pool Room
330 North Lethbridge Beauty
    Parlor
Fourth Avenue Intersects
402 Duck Lee tailor
404 Canadian Union Bakery
406 Palace Meat Market
408 Peakesidney J
408 Guise David
408 Wadeking Wm F
410 Hub Cigar Store
410a Jooreas John C
414 McCaffrey Block
414 PO No 1
414 Beveridge David
414 Knibbs Mrs M
414 Peoples Drug Store
416 Hennesey & Wilson
418 Burgman Block
418 Hart Harvey G hdwre
418 Mizpah Lodge IOOF No 72
420 Edward Alfred secondhand
    dealer
426 Johnston J & A
432 Vacant
Fifth Avenue Intersects
502 United Church Hall
522 Olander Carl G
524 Olander Carl G hdwre
526 Twentieth Century Store
544 Sorokoski Michael grocers
546 Rogers F A
Sixth Avenue Intersects
630 Mihalik Andrew (groc)
646 Central Meat Market
Sixth Avenue A Intersects
Seventh Avenue Intersects
706 Ponach Fred
732 Crystal Palace conf
732 Chollak George
740 Matts Taxi
740 Kropinak Matt confy
Eighth Avenue Intersects
Ninth Avenue Intersects
946 Rosaine Herman
950 Heaton Thomas
954 Greek Orthodox Church
1104 Grisak John
1114 McIlvena James
1116 Hoose David
1120 Worthington Thomas
1124 Ralston James
1128 Richmond James A
1130 Ascroft Robert
1132 Talbot Charles
1140 Wolstoncroft Robert
Twelfth Avenue Begins
1202 Peacock Charles
1206 Foster John A
1210 Hurst James
1210 (rear) Vacant
1210 (rear)Wolstencroft John
1210 (rear) Monks Wm H
1214 Green John
1220 Riley Mrs Ellen
1222 Vacant
1224 Ditchfield Thomas
1232 Sherman Sidney F express
1240 Shrives Charles

Thirteenth Avenue Begins
1304 Baird Thomas
1308 Melling John
1320 Moore George
Fourteenth Avenue Begins
1404 Leadbeater Timothy
Fifteenth Avenue Begins
1510 Saxon Robert
1606 Hackett'Thomas
1612 Marsh John
1614 Gray Mrs Mary
East Side
131 Appleton John
Second Avenue Intersects
201 Scott John
205 Plymouth Bros Mission
217 Tarleton James
221 Stewart James
225 Negrey George
229 Galenkemp Walter
237 Mills Frederick
245 Advance Lumber Co Ltd
259 Kings Hotel
Third Avenue Intersects
303 Dante George
309 Dodd Walter, Taylor
313-317 North Lethbridge Garage
327 Nettleton George
Fourth Avenue Intersects
Westminster School
Fifth Avenue Intersects
519 Kerr Andrew
519 Shorthouse David
531 Kerr Allan
537 Watson Robert W
Sixth Avenue Intersects
609 Dunlop Peter A
613 Milner George H
619 Hurst Wm T
Sixth Avenue A Intersects
635 Garrett John
Seventh Ave Intersects
701 United Church of North
Lethbridge
707 Rae John
733 Lethbridge Miners Library
Club
733 Kotch Steve
735 Briosi Peter
Eighth Avenue Intersects
Adams Park

**1933 Henderson Directory**
West Side
CPR Freight Sheds
Western Transfer Co Ltd
Second Avenue Intersects
Fire Hall No 2
Second Avenue A Intersects
224 Pachman Adolph
230 Supina Mercantile Co
234 Supina Michael
240 Lethbridge Labor Temple
240 Appleton Stanley
242 Vacant
244 Vacant
246 Beaumont Stan
246 Stobie James
246 Birkett Saml
246 Park Arthur E
246 Robinson Edith hairdrsr
246 Robinson Wm. A
246 O'Brian Fredk
246 Greenhorn Alex
246 Hart Hardware
246 Williamson Block
250 Woods Exchange
258 Can Bank of Commerce

258 Dennis Floyd C
258 Patterson Allan
Third Avenue Intersects
306 Kilner Harry G shoemkr
308 Swingler Frederick
310 Westminster Meat Market
318 Wonder Beauty Shop
318 Bilderbeek Mrs M
318 Calder Nathaniel
320 Murray Mrs Betty
328 Lee Wong restr
328 Lee Wong Block
330 Wrights Bakery
Fourth Avenue Intersects
402 Lee Duck tailor
404 Canadian Union Bakery
406 Palace Meat Market
408 Kennedy Block
408 McLenn Thos
408 Andorsson Andw
408 Olsen John
408 Olsen Alfd
408 Kregosky Wm barber
410 Hub Cigar Store
410a Jooreas John C
414 McCaffrey Block
414 PO No 1
414 Dunbar Robt
414 Watson Mrs Isabel
414 Knibbs Fredk G
414 Knibbs Mrs Martha
414 Peoples Drug Store
416 Hennesey & Wilson
418 Burgman Block
418 Mizpah Lodge IOOF No 72
420 Glover Robt M
426 Johnston J & A
432 Westminster Grocery
Fifth Avenue Intersects
502 United Church Hall
522 Olander Carl G
524 Olander Carl G hdwre
514 Sorokoski Michael grocer
546 Rogers F A
Sixth Avenue Intersects
630 Mihalik Andrew groc
646 Central Meat Market
Sixth Avenue A Intersects
Seventh Avenue Intersects
708 Ponech Fred
732 Crystal Palace conf
732 Valerio Louis
734 George Joe
740 Matts Taxi
740 Kropnak Matt
Eighth Avenue Intersects
Ninth Avenue Intersects
946 Mihalik John
946 (rear) Ferenz Joe
950 Heaton Thomas
954 Greek Orthodox Church
1004 Grisak John A
1004 (rear) Grisak John L
1020 Tomie Andrew
1026 Comei S
1114 Green John
1116 Hoose David
1120 Worthington Thomas
1124 Ralston James
1128 Richmond James A
1130 Ascroft Robert
1132 Talbot 'Mrs Mary
1140 Gurr Albert
1140 Watson Mrs Jane,
Twelfth Avenue Begins
1202 Peacock Charles
1206 Foster John A
1208 Wolstencroft John

1210 Hurst James
1210 Milner Geo H
1212 McCallum Robt C
1214 Sneddon Robt
1220 Riley Mrs Ellen
1222 Hogg John
1224 Hyssop Ralph
1232 Tyrer Edw
1232 Tyrer Harold
1240 Sherman Sidney express
Thirteenth Avenue Begins
1304 Johnstone Geo
1308 Melling John
1320 Moore George
1320 Baines Arthur
Fourteenth Avenue Begins
1404 Wolstoncroft Robt
Fifteenth Avenue Begins
1510 Smith Harold
1606 Hackett 'Thomas
1612 Baptist Louis
1614 Noss Ole
1714 King Wm
1716 Robuliak Harry
East Side
131 Stitt Marshall D
Second Avenue Intersects
201 Carnill Walter H
205 Plymouth Brethren Mission
217 Joule Mrs Isabella
221 Stewart James
225 Rawleigh's Products
225 Frank Alfd H
225 Wheeler Geo
229 Galenkemp Mrs Walter
229 (rear) Lethbridge Box &
Furniture Co
237 Mills Frederick
237 Dietrich Albt
237 North Ward Auction
259 Kings Hotel
Third Avenue Intersects
303 Dante George
309 Dodd Walter, A Taylor
313-217 North Lethbridge Auto
Wrecking
319 Morfitt & Minty
327 Nettleton George
335 Westminster Service Station
Fourth Avenue Intersects
Westminster School
Fifth Avenue Intersects
519 Kerr Andrew
519 Shorthouse David
531 Murphy Geo
537 Watson Robert W
Sixth Avenue Intersects
603 Binning Geo H
609 Triska Win
613 Kolesar John
619 Crowe Mrs Jessie
Sixth Avenue A Intersects
635 Garrett John
Seventh Avenue Intersects
701 First United Church
707 Rae John
733 Lethbridge Miners Library
733 Walker Charles
735 Briosi Peter
Eighth Avenue Intersects
Adams Park

**1936 Henderson Directory**
West Side
CPR Freight Sheds
Western Transfer Co Ltd
Second Avenue Intersects
Fire Hall No 2

Second Avenue A North Intersects
224 Kurzaba Steve
230 Supina Mercantile Co
234 Supina Michael
240 Lethbridge Labor Temple
240 Appleton Stanley
242 Robinson Edith hairdrsr
242 Robinson Wm A
244 Christie Thos
246 O'Brian Fred
246 Pyke Ernest
246 Greenwood AV
246 Joule Mrs Isabel
246 Moorhouse Fredk
246 Hart Hardware
246 Williamson Block
250 Vacant
258 Can Bank of Commerce
258 Galin K W
Third Avenue Intersects
306 Kilner Harry G shoemkr
308 Swingler Frederick
310 Westminster Meat Market
318 Douglas Beauty Shop
318 Douglas Mrs Grace
320 La Marr Win
320 Bissett Aubrey
328 Lee Wong restr
328 Baceda Mrs Eliz
328 Whitson Norman
328 Yorho John
328 Lee Wong Block
330 Wright's Bakery
Fourth Avenue Intersects
402 Lee Duck tailor
404 Canadian Union Bakery
406 Central Meat Market
408 Kennedy Block
408 Ingoldsby B
408 Lawson James M
410 Hub Cigar Store
410a Kregosky Wm barber
414 McCaffrey Block
414 PO No 1
414 Jongkind J
414 Edmonds Philip
414 Peoples Drug Store
416 Hennesey & Wilson
418 Burgman Block
418 Mizpah Lodge IOOF No 72
420 Triska Nick
426 Johnston J & A
432 Pisko Steve
Fifth Avenue Intersects
502 United Church Hall
522 Olander Carl G
524 Olander Carl G hdwre
526 Galenkamp W
544 Sorokoski Michael grocer
546 Rogers F A
Sixth Avenue Intersects
630 Mihalik Andrew groc
646 City Meat Market
Sixth Avenue A Intersects
Seventh Avenue Intersects
708 Ponech Fred
732 Vacant
732 (rear) Cartwright Mrs Ida
734 George Joe
740 Matts Taxi
740 Kropinak Matt
Eighth Avenue Intersects
Ninth Avenue Intersects
946 Mihalik John
946 (rear) Kovach John
950 Heaton Thomas
950 La Roche Mrs Clara
954 Greek Orthodox Church

1004 Grisak John A
1020 Tomie Andrew
1026 Comai S
1110 Lowe Douglas
1114 Milner George H
1116 Hoose David
1120 Coutts George
1124 Ralston James
1128 Valerio Louis
1130 Ascroft Robert
1132 Talbot Mrs Mary
1140 Gurr Albert
1140 Watson Mrs Jane,
Twelfth Avenue Begins
1202 Peacock Mrs Susan
1206 Foster John A
1208 Clark John
1210 Hurst James
1212 Petrunia Peter
1214 Gardiner Randolph R
1218 Green John
1220 Riley Mrs Ellen
1222 Mabley Larry
1224 Nemis J
1232 Boyd Earl G
1240 Sherman Sidney
Thirteenth Avenue Begins
1304 Walden John
1304 Love Edw J
1308 Melling John
1320 Moore George
Fourteenth Avenue Begins
1404 Vacant
Fifteenth Avenue Begins
1510 Rollorchuk Win
1606 Mills Harold
1606 Andrew John
1612 Baptist Louis
1614 Noss Ole
1706 Robuliak Harry
1714 Hall H L
East Side
131 Stitt Marshall D
Second Avenue Intersects
201 Fix Rudolph
201 Fix Transport
205 Plymouth Brethren Mission
217 Dancosine Mrs Mildred
217 McNulty Hugh
221 Stewart James
215 Rawleigh's Products
225 Frank Alfd H
229 Galenkemp Mrs Walter
237 Mills Frederick
237 (rear) Armour Douglas
259 Kings Hotel (closed)
Third Avenue Intersects
303 Dante Angelina 309 Dodd
    Walter
313 O'Sullivan Frank
313-317 North Lethbridge Auto
    Wrecking
319 Vacant
327 Potts Ralph
335 Westminster Servicestation
335 Westminster Repair Shop
Fourth Avenue Intersects
Westminster School
Fifth Avenue Intersects
519 Kerr James
519 Shorthouse David
531 Murphy Geo
537 Watson Robert W
Sixth Avenue Intersects
603 Szarko Joseph
609 Tabacchi Steve
613 Nettleton Geo
619 Spencer Mrs Esther

Sixth Avenue A Intersects
635 Vacant
Seventh Avenue Intersects
701 First United Church
707 Rae Mrs Jennie M
733 Lethbridge Miners Library
733 Gonczy Louis
735 Briosi Peter
Eighth Avenue Intersects
Adams Park


**1938 Henderson Directory**
West Side
CPR Freight Sheds
Can Pac Cartage
Western Transfer Co Ltd
Second Avenue Intersects
Fire Hall No 2
Second Avenue A Intersects
230 Supina Mercantile Co
234 Supina Michael
240 Lethbridge Labor Temple
240 Walker Andw
242 Robinson Mrs Edith hairdrsr
242 Robinson Wm A
244 Christie Thos
246 Smith Thos
246 Ferguson Duncan
246 Ramage John
246 Greenwood W
246 Hart Hardware
246 Williamson Block
250 Lealta Theatre
258 Can Bank of Commerce
258 Galin K W
Third Avenue Intersects
306 Kilner Harry G shoemaker
308 Swingler Frederick
310 Westminster Meat Market
318 Douglas Beauty Shop
318 Douglas Mrs Grace
320 Hales Wm shoe repr .
320 Bissett Aubrey
328 Lee Wong restr
328 McNulty Hugh
328 Whitson Norman
328 Warner John
328 Lee Wong Block
330 Wright's Bakery
Fourth Avenue Intersects
402 Lee Duck tailor
404 Canadian Union Bakery
406 Central Meat Market
408 Kennedy Block
408 Adams Lloyd
408 Barnes Mrs G
408 Smelke James
410 Hub Cigar Store
410a Kregosky Wm barber
414 McCaffrey Block
414 Appleton Mrs A
414 Pyke Mrs F
414 Cheeseman Mrs J
414 PO No 1
414 Peoples Drug Store
416 Hennesey & Wilson
418 Burgman Block
418 Mizpah Lodge IOOF No 72
420 Canada Cafe
426 Johnston J & A
432 Ed's Coffeeshop
Fifth Avenue Intersects
502 United Church Hall
522 Olander Carl
524 Olander Carl G hdwre
526 Galenkamp W
544 Sorokoski Michael grocer

546 Rogers F A
Sixth Avenue Intersects
630 Rebar & Son
646 City Meat Market
646 Liptok Joseph
Sixth Avenue A Intersects
Seventh Avenue Intersects
708 Ponech Fred
732 Lethbridge Co-operative
    Miners Assn
732 (rear) Cartwright Mrs Ida
734 George Joe Jr
740 Matts Taxi
740 Kropinak Matt
Eighth Avenue Intersects
Ninth Avenue Intersects
946 Mihalik John
946 (rear) Challak Pete
950 Heaton Thomas
950 (rear) Heaton Harold
950 La Roche Mrs Clara
954 Greek Orthodox Church
1004 Grisak John A
1004 (rear) Grisak Geo
1004a Grisak John L
1020 Tomie Andrew
1026 Comai S
1110 Lowe Mrs Isabella M
1114 Milner Geo H
1116 Hoose David
1120 Coutts Geo
1124 Brown John
1128 Valerio Louis
1130 Ascroft Robert
1130 (rear) Ascroft Thos
1132 Talbot Mrs Mary
1140 Gurr Albert
1140 Watson Mrs Jane
Twelfth Avenue Begins
1202 Peacock Hector
1206 Foster John A
1208 Smedon Win
1210 James Hurst
1212 Willetts Ernest
1214 Hargreaves Mrs K
1218 Green John
1220 Riley Mrs Ellen
1222 Johnson Joseph
1224 Gildford Chas S
1232 Hill Sydney T
1240 Sherman Sidney F
Thirteenth Avenue Begins
1304 Wilkie James
1308 Melling John
1308 Holland Thos
1320 Moore George
Fourteenth Avenue Begins
1402 Allison Andrew
Fifteenth Avenue Begins
1510 Rae Wm
1606 Baptist Verne
1612 Baptist Louise
1614 Noss Ole
1706 Robuliak Harry
East Side
131 Stitt Marshall D
Second Avenue Intersects
201 Terry's Tire & Auto Shop
201 Ingoldsby B
205 Plymouth Brethren Mission
217 Crabb Jesse
221 Stewart James
225 Rawleigh's Products
225 Frank Alfd H
229 Galenkemp Mrs Walter
237 (rear) Schuler Norman
259 Kings Hotel (closed)
Third Avenue Intersects

303 Dante Margaret
303 Susnar Steve
309 Dodd Walter A
313-317 North Lethbridge Motors
    & Auto Wrecking
319 Lethbridge Technical High
    School
327 Potts Ralph
335 Westminster Servicestation
335 Westminster Repair Shop
Fourth Avenue Intersects
Westminster School
Fifth Avenue Intersects
519 Kerr James
519 Shorthouse David
531 Love Ernest J
531 Gillingwater Mrs W
531 Nillson Ivan
537 Watson Robert W
Sixth Avenue Intersects
603 Szarka Joseph
609 Schagel Geo
609 Stewart James
609 White James
613 Nettleton Geo
619 Spencer Mrs Esther
Sixth Avenue A Intersects
635 Campbell Thos
Seventh Avenue Intersects
701 First United Church
707 Rae Mrs Jeanie M
733 Lethbridge Miners Library
733 Gonczy Louis
735 Pallett Fred
Eighth Avenue Intersects
Adams Park


**1940 Henderson Directory**
West Side
CPR Freight Sheds
Can Par Cartage
Second Avenue Intersects
Fire Hall No 2
Second Avenue A Intersects
230 Supina Mercantile Co
234 Supina Michael
240 Lethbridge Labor Temple
240 Walker Andw
242 Robinson Mrs Edith hairdrsr
242 Robinson Wm A
244 Christie Thos
246 Hart Hardware
246 Williamson Block
1 Bennett Frank
2 Lothian K
3 Smith Thos
4 Potts Ralph
5 Ramage John
248 McIntosh John tinsmith
250 Lealta Theatre
258 Canadian Bank of Commerce
258 Pineau W P
Third Avenue Intersects
306 Kilner Harry G shoemkr
308 Swingler Mrs Margt C
310 Westminster Meat Market
318 Hales Wm shoe repair
320 Dolly's Beauty Salon
320 Bissett Aubrey
328 Lee Wong restr
328 Lee Wong Block
    A Watson Wm
    B Percseley Alex
    C Warnock John
    2 McNulty Hugh
    6 Gray Jessie
330 Numaid Bakery

147

404 Canadian Union Bakery
406 Central Meat Market
408 Kennedy Block
408 Adams Lloyd
408 Whitson Win
408 Barton Frank
408 Britespot Confy
408 Cyr Lawrence J
410 Hub Cigar Store
410a Greggy's Barber Shop
414 McCaffrey Block
414 Appleton Mrs L
414 Joule Mrs Isabel
414 PO No 1
414 Peoples Drug Store
416 Hennesey & Wilson
418 Burgman Block
418 Mizpah Lodge IOOF No 72
420 Canada Cafe
426 Johnston J
432 Wonder Cafe
Fifth Avenue Intersects
502 United Church Hall
522 McDougall Mrs W
522 Jones John C
524 Vacant
526 Galenkamp Walter Sr
544 Sorokoski Michael grocer
546 Rogers F A
Sixth Avenue Intersects
630 Rebar & Son
642 Mihalik Andw grocer
646 Liptok Mrs Annie
Sixth Avenue A Intersects
Seventh Avenue Intersects
708 Ponech Fred
722 Lethbridge Co-operative
    Miners Assn
732 (rear) Cartwright Mrs. Ida
734 George Joe Jr
740 Kropinak Mrs Mary confy
Eighth Avenue Intersects
Ninth Avenue Intersects
946 Mihalik John
946 (rear) Toogood Saml J
950 Coutts Geo
950 (rear) Heaton Harold
1004 Grisak John A
1004 (rear) Grisak Geo
1004a, Grisak John L
1018 Heaton Clifford
1020 Tomie Andrew
1026 Comai Silvio
1110 Lowe Mrs Isabella M
1114 Milner Geo H
1116 Hoose David
1120 Vacant
1124 Brown John
1128 Valerio Louis
1130 Ascroft Robert
1130a Ascroft Thos
1132 Talbot Mrs Mary
1132a Talbot Geo
1140 Gurr Albert
Twelfth Avenue Begins
1202 Hanson Mrs M
1206 Foster John A
1208 Hogg David
1210 Hurst James
1212 Hackett John W
1214 Hargreaves Mrs K
1218 Green John
1220 Riley Mrs Ellen
1222 Johnson Joseph
1224 Gildford Chas S
1232 Hill Sydney T
1240 Sherman Sidney F
Thirteenth Avenue Begins

1304 Wilkie James
1308 Melling John
1308 Holland Thos
1320 Moore George
Fourteenth Avenue Begins
1402 Allison Andrew
Fifteenth Avenue Begins
1510 Rae Wm
1606 Garrow Fred
1612 Baptist Lewis
1614 Noss Ole
1704 Rubuliak Harry
East Side
131 Stitt Marshall D
Second Avenue Intersects
201 Terry's Tire & Auto Shop
201 Ingoldsby B
205 Gospel Hall
217 Barton George
221 Stewart James
225 McCrae John
225 Tatton Victor A
229 Galenkamp Mrs Walter
237 Mills Fred S
237 (rear) Schafer Adolph
259 Modern Beauty Shop
259 York Coffeeshop
259 York Hotel
259 Inkster Mrs Anna confy
Third Avenue Intersects
303 Dante Margaret
303 Susnar Steve
309 Dodd Walter A
311-317 North Lethbridge Motors
    Auto Wrecking
319 Lethbridge Technical High
    School
327 Fisher R A
335 Westminster Servicestation
335 Westminster Repair Shop
Fourth Avenue Intersects
Westminster School
Fifth Avenue Intersects
519 Vacant
531 Love Ernest J
531 Gillingwater Mrs W
537 Watson Mrs Jessie
Sixth Avenue Intersects
603 Szarka Joseph
609 Schagel Mrs G
609 Stewart L
609 Whyte James
613 Nettleton Geo
619 Spencer Mrs Esther
Sixth Avenue A Intersects
635 Cederberg C Richd
635 Piepgrass Henry
Seventh Avenue Intersects
701 Vacant
707 Rae Mrs Jeanie M
733 Lethbridge Miners Library
733 Gonczy Louis
735 Pallett Fred
Eighth Avenue Intersects
Adams Park

## 1942 Henderson Directory
West Side
CPR Freight Sheds
Can Pacific cartage
Second Avenue Intersects
Fire Hall No 2
Second Avenue A Intersects
230 Supina Co
234 Supina John
240 Lethbridge Labor Temple
240 Walker Andw
242 Robinson's Beauty Shoppe

242 Robinson Wm A
244 Christie Thos
246 Hart Hardware
246 Williamson Block
    Paterson Rodk M
    Smith Thomas
    Potts Ralph
    Ramage John
248 Vacant
250-258 Lealta Theatre,
Third Avenue Intersects
306 Kilner Harry G shoermkr
308 Swingler Mrs Margt
310 Jahrig Mrs E R
318 Hales Wm shoe repair
320 Vacant
328 Lee Wong restr
328 Lee Wong Block
    Dougan Wm H
    Ryan
    Warnock John
    McNulty Hugh
    Gray Jessie
330 Chisholm R J
Fourth Avenue Intersects
402 Lee Duck tailor
404 Canadian Union Bakery
406 Central Meat Market
408 Kennedy Block
408 Papp Joe
408 Trentini Carl
408 Berlanda Mrs A
408 Kerrison's Second Hand Store
410 Modern Beauty Shop
410a Greggy's Barber Shop
414 McCaffrey Block
414 Royle Mrs J J
414 Adamson Merlin
414 Joule Mrs Isabel
414 PO No I
414 McCaffrey's Drug Store
416 Hennesy and Wilson
418 Burgman Block
418 Mizpah Lodge IOOF No 72
420 Canada Cafe
426 Johnston J & A
432 Wonder Cafe
Fifth Avenue Intersects
502 First United Church
522 Richardson Norman
522 Bruchet Irvine
524 Vacant
526 Galenkamp Walter Sr
544 Sorokoski Michael grocer
546 Rogers F A
Sixth Avenue Intersects
610 North Home Grocery
642 Mihaik Andw grocer
646 Liptok Mrs Annie
Sixth Avenue A Intersects
Seventh Avenue Intersects
708 Ponech Fred
732 Lethbridge Co-oper Miners
    Assn
734 George Joe Jr
740 Kropinak Mrs Mary confy
Eighth Avenue Intersects
Ninth Avenue Intersects
946 Mihalik John
946 (rear) Toogood Sam
950 Coutts Geo
1004 Grisak John A
1004 (rear) Grisak Geo
1004a, Grisak John L
1018 Heaton Clifford
1020 Tomie Andrew
1026 Comai Silvio
1110 Lowe Mrs Isabela, M

1114 Milner Geo H
1116 Hoose David
1120 Smerek Wm
1124 Brown John
1128 Valerio Louis
1130 Ascroft Robert
1130a Ascroft Thos
1132 Talbot Mrs Mary
1132a Talbot Geo
1140 Gurr Albert
Twelfth Avenue Begins
1202 Hanson Mrs M
1206 Foster John A
1208 Hogg David
1210 Hurst James
1212 Hackett John W
1214 Hargreaves Mrs K
1218 Green John
1220 Riley Mrs Ellen
1222 Johnson Mrs Joseph
1224 Gildford Chas S
1232 Hill Sydney T
1240 Sherman Sidney F
Thirteenth Avenue Begins
1304 Wilkie James
1308 Holland Thos
1320 Moore George
Fourteenth Avenue Begins
1402 Allison Andrew
Fifteenth Avenue Begins
1510 Rea Wm
1606 Baptist Verne L
1612 Baptist Lewis
1614 Noss Ole
1706 Robuliak Harry
East Side
131 Stitt Marshall D
Second Avenue Intersects
201 Terry's Tire & Auto Shop
201 Ingoldsby B
205 Gospel Hall
217 Barton George
221 Stewart James
225 Tatton Victor A
229 Galenkemp Mrs Walter
237 Mills Fred S
237 (rear) Hughes Hubert
255 Big Cone (The)
259 York Coffeeshop
259 York Hotel
Third Avenue Intersects
303 Dante Margaret
303 Susnar Steve
309 Dodd Walter A
311-317 North Lethbridge Motors
    & Auto Wrecking
319 Lethbridge Technical High
    School
327 Fisher R A
335 Westminster Service Station
Fourth Avenue Intersects
Westminster School
Fifth Avenue Intersects
519 Vacant
531 Vacant
537 Watson Mrs Jessie
Sixth Avenue Intersects
603 Nelson Mrs C O
609 Schagel Mrs G
613 Nettleton Ceo
619 Spencer Mrs Esther
Sixth Avenue A Intersects
635 Hagblad Theo
Seventh Avenue Intersects
701 Vacant
707 Rae Mrs Jeanie M
733 Lethbridge Miners Library
733 Baceda Joseph

733 Lethbridge Miners Library
733 Baceda Joseph
735 Pallett Fred
Eighth Avenue Intersects
Adams Park

## 1944 Henderson Directory
West Side
CPR Freight Sheds
Can Pacific Cartage
Second Avenue Intersects
Fire Hall No 2
    Hutton Mrs E
    Alford E. W.
    Campbell Mrs W J
Second Avenue A Intersects
230 Supina Mercantile Co
234 Supina John
240 Lethbridge Labor Temple
240 Morrison Douglas
242 Robinson's Beauty Shoppe
242 Robinson Wm A
244 Vaselenak Mrs Catherine
244 Flexal Cyril
246 Hart Hardware
246 Williamson Block
    Paterson Rodk M
    Smith Thomas
    Potts Ralph
    Ramage John
250 Kerrison's Second Hand Store
250 Kerrison Thomas
250 Lealta Theatre
Third Avenue Intersects
306 Moss B tinsmith
308 Swinger Mrs Margt C
310 Jahrig Mrs E R
318 Hales Wm shoe repr
320 Kobal Geo grocer
320a Wood Olive
320a Werling Mrs Fox
328 Lee Wong restr
328 A B Confectionery
328 Lee Wong Block
Davis Albt
Warnock John
McNulty Hugh
Gray Jessie
330 Chisholm R J
Fourth Avenue Intersects
402 Lee Duck tailor
404 Canadian Union Bakery
406 Vacant
408 Kennedy Block
408 Hill Mrs Justin
408 Trentini Carl
408 Berlanda Mrs A
408 Adamson Merlin
410 Modern Shoe Repair
410a Greggy's Barber Shop
414 McCaffrey Block
414 Mills Otto
414 Sedgewick Roy
414 Joule Mrs Isabel
414 PO No 1
414 McCaffrey's Drug Store
416 Hennesey & Wilson
418 Burgman Block
418 Mizpah Lodge IOOF No 72
418 Farmers Market
420 Canada Cafe
426 Johnston J & A
432 Wonder Cafe
Fifth Avenue intersects
502 First United Church
522 Kennedy Mrs Alice
522 Hume Mrs A
524 Vacant

526 Galenkamp Walter Sr
544 Sorokoski Michael grocer
546 Rogers F A
Sixth Avenue Intersects
630 North Home Grocery
642 Mihalik Andw grocer
646 Ukrainian Canadian Assn
Sixth Avenue A Intersects
Seventh Avenue Intersects
708 Ponech Fred
732 Milian Mrs D E
732 Godsalve Chas
734 George Joe Jr
740 Kropinak Mrs Mary confy
Eighth Avenue Intersects
Ninth Avenue Intersects
946 Mihalik John
946 (rear) Toogood Saml J
950 Coutts Geo
1004 Grisak John A
1004 (rear) Grisak Geo
1004a Grisak John L
1016 Watt Mrs Phyllis
1018 Heaton Clifford
1020 Tomie Andrew
1022 Bolokoski Wm
1024 Crawford Mrs M M
1026 Comai Silvio
1026 (rear) Kannel Mrs J
1036 Hopkins Roy
1110 Kast Mrs A
1114 Joevenazzo Joseph
1116 Hoose Mrs D
1120 Zimmerman Clifford
1124 Bergland Oliver
1128 Valerio Louis
1132 Talbot Mrs Mary
1132 Romanchuk Nicholas
1140 Osborne James H
Twelfth Avenue Begins
1202 Sherman S Frank
1206 Foster John A
1208 Hogg David
1210 Hurst James
1212 Williams Mrs W W
1214 Troyanek Rudolph
1218 Burton Mrs A
1220 Riley Mrs Ellen
1222 Vacant
1224 Marsh W
1232 Ness Wilbert
1240 Tyrer Edward
Thirteenth Avenue Begins
1304 Wilkie James
1308 Melling John
1320 Moore George
Fourteenth Avenue Begins
1404 Allison Andrew
1412 Grovis, Fred
Fifteenth Avenue Begins
1510 George John
1606 Babtist Verne L
1612 Hebert Henry
1614 Noss Ole
1706 Robuliak Harry
East Side
131 Stitt Marshall D
Second Avenue Intersects
201 Terry's Tire & Auto Shop
201 Ingoldsby B
205 Gospel Hall
217 Beckner Everett G
221 Stewart James
225 Pethevrach Joseph
229 Galenkemp Mrs Walter
237 Hall Harry S
237 (rear) Marshall Angus
255 Vacant

259 York Coffeeshop
259 York Hotel
Third Avenue Intersects
303 Vacant
309 Dodd Walter A
311-317 North Lethbridge Motors
    & Auto Wrecking
319 Lethbridge Technical High
    School
327 Fisher R A
335 Westminster Servicestation
Fourth Avenue Intersects
Westminster School
Fifth Avenue Intersects
507 Olagos John
519 Berlanda Mrs M
531 Hollett James
537 Watson Mrs Jessie
Sixth Avenue Intersects
603 Nelson Mrs
609 Stewart James
609 Chenger Leslie
611 Nettleton Geo
619 Spencer Mrs Esther
Sixth Avenue A Intersects
635 Hagblad Theo
Seventh Avenue Intersects
701 Eagles Hall
707 Bakos Steve
707 Yackulic Mike
733 Lethbridge Miners Library
733 Baceda Joseph
735 Pallett Fred
Eighth Avenue Intersects
Adams Park

## 1946 Henderson Directory
West Side
CPR Freight Sheds
Can Pacific Cartage
Second Avenue Intersects
Fire Hall No 2
    Hutton Mrs E
    Alford E W
    Campbell Mrs W J
Second Avenue A Intersects
230 Supina Mercantile Co
234 Barkley Mrs Dorothy
234 Hanisko Mrs Anne
240 Lethbridge Labor Temple
240 Morrison Douglas
242 Robinson's Beauty Shoppe
242 Robinson Wm A
244 Quast John
244 Jahrig Mrs C R
244 Hoye B
246 Hart Hardware
246 Williamson Block
    Sylvester Mrs Ethel
    Bannerman Wm S
    Zelinsky Fred
    Potts Mrs R
    Wall Mrs A T
    Ramage John
    Dorren John
250 Kerrison's Second Hand Store
250 Kerrison Thomas
250 Lealta Theatre
Third Avenue Intersects
304 La Kay's Ladies Wear
306 Moss B tinsmith
308 Leismister
310 Swingler Mrs Margt C
310 Gifts Unlimited
310 Jones Fred W
318 Hales Wm shoe repr
320 Kobal Geo grocer
320a Smith James

328 Simon Joseph
328 A B Confectionery
328 Lee Wong Block
    Miller Bertha
    Davis Albt
    Warnock John
    McNulty Hugh
    Burnaby Roy
    Gray Jessie
330 Lee Duck Cleaners
Fourth Avenue Intersects
402 Peter Morris
404 North Lethbridge Bakery
406 Berent Arthur
406 Lakose R
406 Adams M
408 Kennedy Block
    Neilly Morris
    Ward Fred
    Oddie Robt
    Migneault Philip
    Hatcher Harold
    Powell A J
    Seeley Frank
408 Fred's Barber Shop
408 Vogup Beauty Parlor
410 Modern Shoe Repair
410a Greggy's Barber Shop
414 McCaffrey Block
414 Smerek Percy
414 Sedgewick Roy
414 Joule Mrs Isabel
414 PO No 1
414 McCaffrey's Drug Store
416 Model Dress Shop
418 Burgman Block
418 North Lethbridge Hardware
418 Simons Pool Room
420 Canada Cafe
426 Johnston J A
432 Wonder Cafe
Fifth Avenue Intersects
502 First United Church
522 Kennedy Robt
522 Hume Allan
524 Quality Meat Market
526 Galenkamp Walter Sr
544 Sorokoski Michael grocer
546 Rogers F A
Sixth Avenue Intersects
630 North Home Grocery
642 Mihalik Andw grocer
646 Morrison Hugh
Sixth Avenue A Intersects
Seventh Avenue Intersects
708 Ponech Fred
732 Vath Donald
732 Godsalve Harry
734 George Joe Jr
740 Kropinak Mrs Mary confy
Eighth Avenue Intersects
Ninth Avenue Intersects
946 Mihalik John
946 (rear) Morgan Carl
950 Coutts Geo
950a Dewhurst Walter
1004 Grisak John A
1004 (rear) Grisak Geo
1004a Grisak John L
1016 Taylor John J
1018 Heaton Clifford
1020 Tomie Andrew
1022 Bolokoski Wm
1024 Crawford Mrs M M
1026 Comai Silvio
1026 (rear) Kannel Mrs J
1036 Hopkins Roy
1114 Joevenazzo Joseph

1116 Hoose Mrs
1120 Zimmerman Clifford
1124 Rigo Andrew
1128 Valerio Louis
1132 Talbot Mrs Mary
1140 Skinner George
Twelfth Avenue begins
1202 Sherman S Frank
1206 Foster John A
1208 Hogg David
1210 Hurst
1212 Occupied
1214 Williams Wm R
1218 Burton Mrs
1220 Hebert Henry
1222 Riley Mrs Ellen
1224 Marsh
1232 Ness Wilbert
1240 Tyrer Edward
Thirteenth Avenue Begins
1304 Wilkie James
1308 Melling John
1320 Moore George
Fourteenth Avenue Begins
1404 Allison Andrew
1412 Visser John
Fifteenth Avenue Begins
1510 Leishner Ted
1606 Marsh John
1612 Irwin Douglas
1614 Troyanek Rudolph W
1706 Robuliak Harry
East Side
131 March Albt
131 Makley W G
139 Gordie's Service & Auto Parts
Second Avenue Intersects
201 Terry's Tire & Auto Shop
201 Ingoldsby B
205 Trades & Labour Council Hall
217 Dunbar David
221 Stewart James
225 Hughes Albt
229 Galenkemp Mrs Antonia
237 Hall Harry S
237 (rear) Elder James
255 Southern Alberta Distributors
259 York Coffeeshop
265 York Hotel
Third Avenue Intersects
311-317 North Lethbridge Motors
    & Auto Wrecking
319 Lethbridge Technical High
    School
327 Fisher R A
335 Westminster Servicestation
Fourth Avenue Intersects
Westminster School
Fifth Avenue Intersects
519 Berlanda Mrs M
531 Hollett James
531 Rosine Chas
537 Watson Mrs Jessie
Sixth Avenue Intersects
603 Crabb Danl J
609 Whyte James
609 Stewart Forrest
609 Supina John
609 Chenger Leslie
613 Nettleton Geo
619 Spencer Mrs Esther
Sixth Avenue North Intersects
635 Kuck Emil
Seventh Avenue Intersects
701 Eagles Hall
707 Bakos Steve
707 Culler Chas
707 Valendorf Fred

707 Robinson Joseph
733 Lethbridge Miners Library
733 Baceda Joseph
735 Pallett Fred
Eighth Avenue Intersects
Adams Park

**1948 Henderson Directory**
West Side
CPR Freight Sheds
Cdn Pacific Cartage
Second Avenue Intersects
Fire Hall No 2
    Hutton Mrs E.
    Alford E W
    Campbell Mrs W J
Second Avenue A Intersects
230 Supina Mercantile Co
234 Nakamura Mrs C.
240 Lethbridge Labor Temple
240 Morrison Douglas
242 Lucille's Beauty Shop
242 Rossetti Lucille
244 Moss B tinsmith
246 Acme Billiard
246 Williamson Block
    Sylvester George
    Bannerman Wm S
    Jones Fred
    Potts Mrs R
    Wall Alfred
    Ramage John
    Persely Alex
250 Kerrison's Second Hand Store
250 Kerrison Thomas
250 Lealta Theatre
Third Avenue Intersects
302 Jack's Radio Shop
302 Heibert Wm
304 La Kay's Ladies Wear
306 Pete's Taxi
306 Pete's Coffeeshop
306 Peterson Morris
308 Swingler Mrs Margt C
310 Mike's Confectionery
318 Hales Wm shoe repr
320 Kobal's Grocery
320 Kobal Mrs Anne
320a Smith James
324 North Lethbridge Hardware
328 Simon Joseph
328 A B Confectionery
328 Lee Wong Block
    Lindseth Arth
    Davis Albt
    Franz Lorne
    McNulty Hugh
    Farris Robt
    Gray Jessie
330 Lee Duck Cleaners
Fourth Avenue Intersects
402 Nagy's Shoe Repair
404 Canadian Union Bakery &
    Confy
406 Berent Arthur
406 Cockburn Chas
408 Kennedy Block
    Ward Fred
    Neilly Morris
    Thorburn John
    Migneault Philip
    Hatcher Harold
    Silzer Harold
    McIntosh R G
    Seeley Frank
408 Fred's Barber Shop
408 Vogue Beauty Parlor
410 Modern Shoe Repair

410a Greggy's Barber Shop
414 McCaffrey Block
414 Ascroft George
414 Sedgewick Roy
414 Joule Mrs Isabel
416 Model Dress Shop
418 Burgman Block
418 McCaffrey's Drug Store
418 Sub PO No 1
420 Lethbridge Fish & Chips
420 Lapp Albert I
422 Parker J Murray
426 Johnson A L
432 Wonder Cafe
Fifth Avenue Intersects
502 First United Church
522 Kennedy Robt
522 Cook Larry
524 Quality Meat Market
526 Galenkamp Walter Sr
544 Sorokoski Michael grocer
546 Rogers F A
Sixth Avenue Intersects
630 North Home Grocery
642 Mihalik Andw grocer
646 Morrison Hugh
Sixth Avenue A Intersects
Seventh Avenue Intersects
708 Ponech Fred
732 Vath Donald
734 George Joe Jr
740 Pisko Andw grocer
Eighth Avenue Intersects
Ninth Avenue Intersects
946 Toogood Saml J
946 (rear) Mihalik John Jr
950 Coutts Geo
950a Dewhurst Walter
1004 Grisak Annie
1004a Grisak Geo
1016 Taylor John J
1018 Heaton Clifford
1020 Tomie Andrew
1022 Bolokoski Wm
1024 Brown Geo
1026 Comai Silvio
1026 (rear) Kannel Mrs J
1032 Dodd Sidney G
1036 Robertson Eliz E K
1036 Hopkins Roy
1040 Noss Merle
1114 Joevenazzo Joseph
1116 Hoose Mrs Edith
1120 Zimmerman Clifford
1124 Rigo Andrew
1128 Valerio Louis
1120 Talbot Geo
1132 Talbot Mrs Mary
1136 Barnett Cyril
1136 Matheson Alex
1140 Skinner George
Twelfth Avenue Begins
1202 Sherman S Frank
1206 Foster John A
1208 Hogg David
1210 Hurst Mrs M A
1212 Cartwright Arth
1214 Williams Wm R
1220 Hebert Henry
1222 Riley Mrs Ellen
1224 Marsh John
1232 Ness Wilbert
1240 Tyrer Edward
Thirteenth Avenue Begins
1304 Wilkie James
1308 Sillito Wm
1320 Moore George
1320 Crombie Mrs Evelyn

Fourteenth Avenue Begins
1404 Skretting Hans
1412 Visser John
Fifteenth Avenue Begins
1510 Leishner Ted
1606 Cutler Chas
1606 (rear) Gittel Saml
1612 Bobinec Mike
1614 Troyanek Rudolph W
1706 Robuliak Harry
East Side
131 Benekritis Chris
135 Christie's Auto Body Works
139 Gordie's Service & Auto Parts
Second Avenue Intersects
201 Terry's Tire & Auto Shop
201 Ingoldsby Barney
205 Trades & Labour Council Hall
217 Dunbar David
221 Stewart James
225 Hughes Albt
229 Galenkemp Mrs Antonia
237 Hall Harry S
237 (rear) Hardy Jack
255 York Pharmacy
257 Lo'Riel Beauty Shoppe
259 York Coffeeshop
265 York Hotel
Third Avenue Intersects
311-317 North Lethbridge Motors
    & Auto Wrecking
319 Lethbridge Technical High
    School
327 Fisher Ralph A
335 Westminster Servicestation
Fourth Avenue Intersects
Westminster School
Fifth Avenue Intersects
519 Berlando Roy
531 Hollett James
531a Flathen Mrs Grace
537 Watson Mrs Jessie
Sixth Avenue Intersects
603 Crabb Danl
609 Whyte James
609 Whyte James T
609 Zanoni E V
609 Supina John
613 Nettleton Geo
619 Housley Henry
Sixth Avenue A Intersects
635 Groel Nick
Seventh Avenue Intersects
701 Eagles Hall
707 Nernedy Alex
733 Lethbridge Miners Library
733 Baceda Joseph
735 Pallett Fred
Eighth Avenue Intersects
Adams Park

**1950 Henderson Directory**
West Side
CPR Freight Sheds
104 Catelli Food Products Ltd
Second Avenue Intersects
CPR Cartage
Fire Hall No 2
    Hutton Mrs Eliz
    Alford E W
    Campbell Mrs Susan
Second Avenue A Intersects
230 Supina Mercantile Co
234 Nakamura Mrs C
240 McNabb Roofing & Siding Ltd
240 Davis Ernest
240 (up) Lybbert Thos M
242 Robinson's Beauty Shop

242 Robinison Win A Sr
244 Vacant
246 Acme Billiards
246 Williamson Block
   Persely Alex
   Bannerman Wm S
   Polyson Michl J
   Shaw Reynolds
   Jones Fred W
   Hopkins Roy,
250 Kerrison's Second Hand Store
250 Kerrison Thos
258 Lealta Theatre
Third Avenue Intersects
302 Jack's Radio Shop
302 Heibert Wm
304 La Kay's Ladies Wear
306 Pete's Taxi
306 Dilly Del
306 Peterson Morris
308 Swingler Mrs Margt C
310 North Lethbridge Jewellers
310 Guest H D
318 Billy's Shoe Repair
318 Hales Mrs Annie
320 Kobal's Grocery
320 Kobal Mrs Annie
320a Smith James T
324 North Lethbridge Hardware
328 Sly Robt W
328 A B Confectionery
328 Lee Wong Block
   Lindseth Arth
   Hart Gordon R
   Franz Lorne
   Gray Jessie
330 Lee Duck Cleaners
Fourth Avenue Intersects
404 Can Union Bakery & Confy
406 Boehr John W
406 (rear) Sawatsky Jacob
406 (up) Czech John
408 Kennedy Block
   Neilly Morris
   Thorburn John
   Migneault Philip
   Silzer James
   Ponech Mrs Eva
   Walker Raymond
   Ward Fred H
408 Fred's Barber Shop
410 Modern Shoe Repair
410a Greggy's Barber Shop
414 McCaffrey Block
414 Morrison Hardware
414 Morrison Hugh
414 McMurren Henry A
414 Joule Mrs Isabel
416 Model Dress Shop
418 Burgman Block
418 McCaffrey's Drug Store
418 Sub PO No 1
418 Garbutt Business College Ltd
420 Pete's Men's Wear
420 Koshman Peter P
426 Johnston J and A Grocery
430 Mezei's Shoe Repair
432 Hong Lou
432 Wonder Caf,
Fifth Avenue Intersects
502 First United Church
522 Kennedy Block
522 (up) Carlyle P Douglas
524 Quality Meat market
526 Chalmers Duncan cabt mkr
544 Sorokoski's Grocery
544 (rear) Dvernichuck Mrs Dora
546 Rogers F N gen merchant

Sixth Avenue Intersects
630 North Home Confectionery
630 Gow Lee
642 Mihalik Andrew grocer
646 Pawlyshyn Alex
Sixth Avenue A Intersects
Seventh Avenue Intersects
708 Ponech Fred
712 Vath Donald
734 John's Confectionery
734 (rear) Sakatch Mike
740 Matt's Confectionery
740 Kropinak Mrs Mary
Eighth Avenue Intersects
Ninth Avenue Intersects
946 Toogood Saml
946 (rear) Mihalik John Jr
950 Coutts Geo
950a Wolfe Patk
1004 Grisak Mrs Annie
1004a Grisak Geo
1016 Taylor John
1018 Heaton Clifford
1020 Tomie Andw
1022 Bolokoski Wm
1024 Brown Geo
1026 Comai Sylvio
1026 (rear) Travaglia Giovanni
1032 Dodd Sidney G
1036 Vacant
1040 Noss Merle
1046 McIntyre Kenneth
1110 Wojtowicz Joseph
1110 Watson A R A
1114 Joevenazzo Joseph
1116 Hoose Mrs Edith
1120 Kinnell Alex
1124 Rigo Andw Sr
1128 Valerio Louis
1130 Talbot Mrs Mary
1132 Hurkens G
1136 Holowka. James
1140 Skinner Geo
Twelfth Avenue Begins
1202 Sherman S Frank
1206 Foster John A
1208 Hogg David
1210 Hurst Mrs Mary A
1212 Cartwright Arth
1214 Williams Wm R Sr
1220 Hebert Henry
1222 Riley Mrs. Ellen
1224 Marsh John
1232 Ness Wilbert
1240 Anderson Thos
Thirteenth Avenue Begins
1304 Wilkie James
1308 Sillito Wm
1320 Moore Geo
1320 Crombie Mrs Evelyn
Fourteenth Avenue Begins
1404 Skretting Hans
1412 Visser John
East Side
131 Benekritis Chris
135 Christie's Auto Body Works
139 Gordie's Service and Auto Parts
Second Avenue Intersects
201 Terry's Tire & Auto Shop
201 Ingoldsby Barney
207 Trades & Labour Council Hall
207 Knights of Pythias
217 Gale Joneph P
221 Stewart James
225 York Pharmacy
257 Lo'Reil Beauty Salon
259 York Coffee Shop
259 York Hotel

Third Avenue Intersects
301-317 North Lehbridge Motors
   and Auto Wreckers
319 Lethbridge Technical High
   School
335 Westminster Service Station
Fourth Avenue Intersects
Westminster School
Fifth Avenue Intersects
519 Burlando, Roy
534 Hollett James
531a, Flathen Mrs Grace
537 Watson Mrs Jessie
Sixth Avenue Intersects
603 Harrington Rev M A
609 Husar Frank
609 Whyte James T
609 Zanoni E V
613 Lesson Steve
619 Housley Henry
Sixth Avenue A Intersects
635 Garrett Delbert A
Seventh Avenue Intersects
701 Eagles Hall
707 Horvat John
733 Lethbridge Miners Library
733 Baceda Joseph
735 Pallett Fred
Eighth Ave Intersects
Adams Park

**1952 Henderson Directory**
West Side
CPR Freight Sheds
104 Catelli Food Products Ltd
Second Avenue Intersects
200 Bird Building Supplies
CPR Cartage
Fire Hall No 2
   Hutton Mrs Eliz
   Alford E W
   Campbell Mrs Susan
Second Avenue A Intersects
230 Supina Mercantile Co
234 Nakamura Toyosaburo
240 vacant
240 Davis Ernest
240 (up) Dick Henry
242 North Lethbridge Furniture
   Ltd
244 Imperial Bank of Canada
246 Acme Billiards
246 Williamson Block
   Persely Alex
   Bannerman Wm S
   Potts Mrs Jenny
   Shaw Reynolds
   Fitzpatrick Dave
   Hopkins Gordon
   Adams Lloyd
   Jones Fred W
248 Douglas Plumbing
250 Kerrison's Second Hand Store
250 Kerrison Thos
258 Lealta Theatre
Third Avenue Intersects
302 Jack's Radio Shop
302 Heibert Wm
304 La Kay's Ladies Wear
306 Pete's Taxi
306 Dilly Del
306 Peterson Morris
308 Swingler Mrs Margt C
310 North Lethbridge Jewellers
318 Ed's Barber Shop
318 Joy's Beauty Shop
318 Hales Mrs Annie
320 Kobal's Grocery

320 Kobal Mrs Annie
320a Smith James
324 North Lethbridge Hardware
328 A B Confectionery
328 Lee Wong Block
   Lindseth Arth
   Woo Gow
   Berkhauk Sidney
   Gray Jessie
330 Lee Duck Cleaners
Fourth Avenue Intersects
404 Western Canada Plumbers Ltd
406 Boehr John W
406 Fraser Mrs Mary
408 Kennedy Block
   Neilly Morris
   McIntosh James
   Johnson E W
   Ponech Mrs Eva
   Quintin Laurent
   Kiesner Ina
   Migneault Phillip
408 Fred's Barber Shop
410 Modern Shoe Repair
410a Greggy's Barber Shop
414 UN Confectionery
414 Lamb G K
414 Sou Wong
414 Higa James
416 Morrison Hardware
416 Morrison Hugh
418 Burgman Block
418 McCaffrey's Drug Store
418 Sub PO No 1
418 Garbutt Business College Ltd
420 Pete's Men's Wear
420 Koshman Peter P
426 Johnston J and A Grocery
430 Mezei's Shoe Repair
430 Collier H J
432 Hong Lou
432 Wonder Caf,
Fifth Avenue Intersects
502 First United Church
522 Hall Wm
522 (up) Carlyle P Douglas
524 Quality Meat market
526 General Woodworker and
Cabinet Makers
544 Sorokoski's Grocery
544 (rear) Dvernichuck Mrs Dora
546 Rogers F N gen merchant
Sixth Avenue Intersects
St, Basil's Catholic Church
620 North Home Confectionery
630 Gow Lee
642 Mihalik Andrew grocer
Sixth Avenue A Intersects
Seventh Avenue Intersects
708 Ponech Fred
712 Vath Donald
734 John's Confectionery
734 Brown J B, barber
740 Matt's Confectionery
740 Kropinak Mrs Mary
Eighth Avenue Intersects
East Side
121 Lethbridgesheet Metal
131 Benekritis Chris
135 Christie's Auto Body Works
139 Gordie's Service and Auto Parts
Second Avenue Intersects
201 Terry's Tire & Auto Shop
201 Ingoldsby Barney
207 Labor Temple
207 Trades & Labour Council Hall
207 Knights of Pythias
217 Gale Joseph P

221 Stewart James
225 Petkewech Jospeh
237 Hall Harry S
255 York Pharmacy
259 York Coffeeshop
259 York Hotel
Third Avenue Intersects
301-317 North Lethbridge Motors
    and Auto Wreckers
319 Victory Equipment Ltd
327 Baillie E G
335 Westminster Service Station
Fourth Avenue Intersects
Westminster School
Fifth Avenue Intersects
519 Burlando, Roy
531 Hollett James
531a Flathen Mrs Grace
537 Watson Mrs Jessie
Sixth Avenue Intersects
603 Baczuk Wm
609 Husar Frank
609 Whyte James T
609 Zanoni E V
613 Lesson Steve
619 Housley Henry
Sixth Avenue A Intersects
635 Garrett Delbert A
637 Greek Orthodox Church
Seventh Avenue Intersects
701 Eagles Hall
707 Horvat John
733 Lethbridge Miners Library
733 Baceda Joseph
735 Vacant
Eighth Ave Intersects
Adams Park

## 1954 Henderson Directory
West Side
CPR Freight Sheds
104 Catelli Food Products Ltd
106 Dench of Canada Ltd
Second Avenue Intersects
200 Bird Construction Co Ltd
200 Bird Building Supplies
CPR Cartage
220 Fire Hall No 2
    Hutton Mrs Eliz
    Campbell Mrs Susan
Second Avenue A Intersects
230 Supina Mercantile Co
234 Nakamura Toyosaburo
240 Dyck Henry
240 Sorensen's Barber Shop
240 North Side Beauty Salon
240 (up) Travalia Romano
242 North Lethbridge
    Furniturestore
244 Imperial Bank of Canada
246 City Snooker
246 Williamson Block
    Persley Alex
    Bannerman Wm S
    Colby Joseph
    Smith And
    Fitzpatrick Dave
    Leuck Nick
248 Vacant
250 Kerrison's Second Hand Store
250 Kerrison Thos
258 Lealta Theatre
258 Doughty C F
Third Avenue Intersects
302 Jack's Radio Sales & Service
304 Bel-Aire Beauty Salon
306 Grey Wm
306 Grey's Shoe Repair Shop

308 Ainsworth Wm
310 Al's Meat Market
312 LaKay's Ladies Wear
318 Ed's Barber Shop,
318 Joy's Beauty Shop
318 Hales Mrs Annie
320 Kobal's Grocery
320 Kobal Mrs Anne
320a Smith James
324 North Lethbridge Hardware
328 Wong Jack
328 American Confectionery
328 Lee Wong Block
    Lindseth Arth
    Woo Gow
    Berkhauk Sidney
    Gray Jessie
330 Lee Duck Cleaners
334 Western Plumbers
    (Lethbridge) Ltd
334 Western Heating Ltd
334 Dry Wall Taping Co Ltd
Fourth Avenue Intersects
406 Quinton Laurent
406 Boehr John W
408 Kennedy Block
    Williams W R
    Harris Fred
    Melsness Walter
    Robinson Stewart
    Migneault Phillip
408 Fred's Barber Shop
408 Fred's Second Hand Store
410 Modern Shoe Repair
410a Greggy's Barber Shop,
414 Lamb G K
414 Higa James
414 UN Confectionery
416 Morrison Hardware
416 Morrison Hugh
418 McCaffrey Block
418 McCaffrey Drug Store
418 Sub PO No 1
418 Garbutt Business College Ltd
420 Pete's Men's Wear
420 Koshman Peter
426 Johnston J & A Grocery
430 Mezei's Shoe Repair
430 North Lethbridge Realty
430 Collier Harry
432 Hong Lou
432 Wonder Cafe
Fifth Avenue Intersects
502 First United Church
522 Hawley Gordon
522 (up) Steinhauer Hans
526 General Woodworker &
    Cabinet Makers
544 Sorokoski's Grocery
546 Paul's Plumbing
Sixth Avenue Intersects
St Basil's Catholic Church
604 Volgyesy Father John
620 North Home Confectionery
630 Gow Lee
642 Mihalik's General Store
Sixth Avenue Intersects
Seventh Avenue Intersects
732 Schiebout John
734 John's Confectionery
740 Matt's Confectionery
740 Smerek Mike
746 City Service
Eighth Avenue Intersects
East Side
121 Lethbridgesheet Metal
131 Benekritis Chris
135 Christie's Auto Body Works

139 Gordie's Service & Auto Parts
Second Avenue Intersects
201 Terry's Tire & Auto Shop
201 Ingoldsby Barney
207 Labor Temple
207 Trades & Labor Council Hall
207 Knights of Pythias
217 Gale Joseph
221 Stewart James
225 Vacant
237 Hall Harry S
255 York Pharmacy
259 York Coffeeshop
265 York Hotel
Third Avenue Intersects
301-317 North Lethbridge Motors
    & Auto Wreckers
321 Victory Equipment Ltd
327 Baille E G
335 Westminster Servicestation
Fourth Avenue Intersects
Westminster School
Fifth Avenue Intersects
519 Berlando Doran
531 Flathen Mrs Grace
531a Vacant
537 Watson Mrs Jessie
Sixth Avenue Intersects
603 Vacant
609 Huszar Frank
613 Lesson Steve
619 Housley Henry
Sixth Avenue A Intersects
635 Garrett Delbert
637 Greek Orthodox Church
Seventh Avenue Intersects
701 Eagles Hall
707 Dimnik Steve
733 Lethbridge Miners Library
733 Baceda Joseph
735 Kochanski Edw
Eighth Avenue Intersects
Adams Park

## 1956 Henderson Directory
West Side
CPR Freight Sheds
104 Catelli Food Products Ltd
Dench of Canada Ltd
CPR Cartage Dept
Second Avenue Intersects
200 Bird Construction Co Ltd
200 Bird Building Supplies
220 Fire Hall No 2
    McIntosh Mrs Hazel
    Campbell Mrs Susan
Second Avenue A Intersects
230 Supina Mercantile Co
234 Nakamura Toyosaburo
240 Nugent Electric
240 (up) McKenna Gilbert
240 (rear), Hamilton Gordon
242 North Lethbridge Furn Store
244 Imperial Bank of Canada
246 City Snooker
246 Williamson Block
    Persley Alex
    Bannerman Wm S
    Smith Andw
248 The Mart
250 Kerrison's Second Hand Store
252 Paul's Plumbing
258 Lealta Theatre
258 Doughty C F
Third Avenue Intersects
302 Jack's Radio & TV Sales &
    Service
304 Paulyne's Style Centre

306 Grey's Shoe Repair Shop
306 Higa's Jewellery
306 Grey Wm
308 Adachi Kiichiro
310 Al's Meat Market
312 La Kay's Ladies Wear
318 Ed's Barber Shop
318 Bel-Aire. Beauty Salon
318 Hales Mrs Annie
320 Kobal's Grocery
320 Davies Mrs Ann
322 Coby's Beauty Salon
324 North Lethbridge Hardware
328 Wong Jack
328 American Confectionery
328 Lee Wong Block
    Lindseth Arth
    Zaliplun Steve
    Grey Jessie
330 Lee Duck Dry Cleaners
334 Vacant
Fourth Avenue Intersects
406 Quinton Eugene
406 Mauryko John
406 (rear) Traichel Mrs Maria
408 Kennedy Block
    Shaffer Mrs Florence
    Robinson Stewart
    Desroshers Mrs Josephine
    Migneault Mrs Betty
408 Frcd's Barber Shop
408 F'red's Second Hand Store
410 Modern Shoe Repair
410a Greggy's Barber Shop
414 Lamb G K
414 Rees Lucille
414 UN Confectionery
416 Morrison Hardware
416 Morrison Hugh
418 McCaffrey Block
418 McCaffrey Drug Store
418 Sub PO No 1
418 Garbutt Business College Ltd
420 Lethbridge Public Library
    (North Branch Childrens
    Dept)
422 Quality Meat & Grocery
426 City Electric
430 Mezei's Shoe Repair
430 Schroeder's Sausage & Deli
432 Wonder Confectionery
432 Hong Lou
Fifth Avenue Intersects
502 First United Church
516 Dairy Queen
542 Shop-Easy Food Fair
544 Sorokoski's Grocery
546 Karl's Plumbing & Heating
Sixth Avenue Intersects
604 St Basil's Catholic Church
604 Killen Father J Q
630 North Home Grocy & Confy
630 Hong Jong
642 Milhalik's Food & Dry Goods
    Store
Seventh Avenue Intersects
708 Ponech Mrs Zena
732 Acme TV Service
734 Joe's Confectionery
740 Matt's Confectionery
740 Smerek Mike
742 Polish Hall
746 City Servicestation
Eighth Avenue Intersects
East Side
121 Lethbridge Sheet Metal
125 Jehovah Witnesses Kingdom
    Hall

131 Krushniruk Gene
135 Christie's Auto Body Works
Second Avenue Intersects
201 Terry's Tire & Auto Shop
201 Ingoldsby Barney
207 Labor Temple
207 Trades & Labor Council Hall
207 Knights of Pythias
217 Herter Ben
221 Stewart James
225 Wyszynski M
237 Hall Mrs Katherine
255 York Pharmacy
259 York Coffeeshop
265 York Hotel
265 Kikinday Dr L
Third Avenue Intersects
301-317 North Lethbridge Motors
    & Auto Wreckers
321 Victory Equipment Ltd
335 Westminster Servicestation
Fourth Avenue Intersects
Westminster School
Fifth Avenue Intersects
505 Sunny Service
519 Potvin Romeo
531 Flathen Mrs Grace
531a Halsey Mrs Grace
537 Watson Jesse
Sixth Avenue Intersects
603 Christie Roy
609 Huszar Frank
613 Lesson Steve
619 Housley Henry
Sixth Avenue A Intersects
635 Garrett Delbert A
637 Greek Orthodox Church
Seventh Avenue Intersects
701 Eagles Hall
707 Dimnik Joseph
715 St Vladimir's Ukrainian
    Catholic Church
715 Chehovsky Father Stephen
733 Lethbridge Miners Library
733 Baceda Joseph
735 Joevenazzo Arth
745 Polish Hall
Eighth Avenue Intersects
Adams Park

**1959 Henderson Directory**
West Side
104 Catelli Food Prods Ltd
CPR Freight Office & Sheds
Can Freight Assn
Dench of Canada Ltd
CPR Cartage Dept
Second Avenue Intersects
200 Bird Constn Co Ltd
200 Bird Building Supplies
220 Fire Hall No 2
    McIntosh Mrs Hazel
    Campbell Mrs Susan
Second Avenue A Intersects
230 Supina Mercantile Co
234 Nakamura T
240 Marvan Building Supplies
240 (up) McKenna, Gilbt
240 (rear) Hamilton Gord
242 Medhurst Realty
244 Van Ree's Upholstery &
    Woodwork
246 City Snooker
246 Maranne Apts
    Fredrick Lloyd
    Daignault Arth
    Rohsler Frank
    Duda John

248 Tom's Trading Post
250 Kerrison's Second Hand Store
252 Paul's Plumbing
258 Lealta Theatre
258 Doughty C F
Third Avenue Intersects
302 Jack's Radio & TV Sales &
    Service
304 Higas Jewellery
306 Grey's Shoe Repair Shop
306 Grey Wm
308 Adachi K
310 Jubilee Gospel Supplies
312 La Kay's Ladies Wear
314 Bank of Montreal
318 Ed's Barber Shop
318 Bel Aire Beauty Salon
318 Hales Mrs Annie
320 Kobal's Grocery
320 Davies Lloyd
320 (up) Smith James
322 Coby's Beauty Salon
322 Tiny Tots
324 North Lethbridge Hardware
328 Wong Jack
328 American Confy
328 Lee Wong Block
    Wong Lee Buck
    Grey Jessie
    Lindseth Arth
330 Lee Duck Dry Cleaners
334 Alberta Liquor Control Board
    Store
Fourth Avenue Intersects
406 Marutkyn John
406 Bourassa Mrs Alma
408 Kennedy Block
    Wutzke Mrs Verna
408 Fred's Barber Shop
408 Fred's Second Hand Store
408 (rear) Ward Fred H
410 Modern Shoe Repair
410a Greggy's Barber Shop
414 UN Confectionery
414 Suites
    Arik Ungene
    Lamb Geo
416 Morrison Hardware
418 McCaffrey Block
418 McCaffrey Drug Store
418 Sub PO No 1
420 Mezei's Shoe Repair
422 Lethbridge Public Library (No
    Branch Children's Dept)
426 City Electric
428 North Side Bakery
428 North Side Restaurant
430 Mueller's Sausage &
    Delicatessen
430 Pruegger's Accordion College
    Ltd
432 Wonder Confectionery
432 Hong Lou
Fifth Avenue Intersects
502 First United Church
516 Dairy Queen
542 Shop-Easy Food Fair
544 Sorokoski's Grocery
546 Karl's Plumbing & Heating Ltd
546 (up) Wierzbowsk i Mike
Sixth Avenue Intersects
604 St Basil's Catholic Church
604 Killen Rt Rev Monsignor James
Sixth Avenue A Begins
630 New Confectionery
630 Young York
642 Mihalik's Food & Dry Goods
    Store

Seventh Avenue Intersects
708 Ponech Mrs Zena
730 John's Barber Shop
730 Pastime Billiard Parlour
732 Credico John
734 Joe's Confectionery
734 (rear) Wesko John
740 Matt's Confectionery
740 Smerek Mike
746 City Servicestation
Eighth Avenue Intersects
East Side
121 Lethbridgesheet Metal
125 Jehovah Witnesses Kingdom
    Hall
131 Kushniruk Gene
135 Christie's Auto Body Works
139 Archibald Motors
Second Avenue Intersects
201 Terry's Tire & Auto Shop
201 Ingoldsby Barney
207 Labor Temple
207 United Brotherhood of
    Carpenters (Local 84G)
207 Lethbridge Labor Council
207 Internatl Hod Carriers Building
    & Common Laborers Union
217 Logan Chas
221 Stewart James
225 Wyszynski M
237 Hall Mrs Katherine
255 York Pharmacy
259 York Coffeeshop
265 York Holel
265 Kikinday Dr. phys
Third Avenue Intersects
301 North Lethbridge Motors
313 Vacant
331 Northside Shell Serv
Third Avenue A Begins
335 Westminster Serv Stn
335 (rear) Bolokoski Serv
Fourth Avenue Intersects
Westminster School
Fifth Avenue Intersects
505 Sunny Service
513 Imperial Bk of Canada
519 Potvin Romeo
519 (down) Johnson Frank
Fifth Avenue A Begins
531. Flathen Mr. Grace
531a Jolliffe
533 Retail Credit Co
533 Lethbridge Herald Co Ltd (Br)
535 Appliance Discount Centre
535 Acme Television Ltd
537 Watson Jesse
Sixth Avenue Intersects
605 Northway Service
609 Huszar Frank
609 Renter Carl
609 (down) Lazar Joe
613 Lesson Steve
619 Housley Henry
Sixth Avenue A Begins
635 Garrett Delbert
637 Greek Orthodox Church
Seventh Avenue Intersects
701 Eagles Hall
707 Nuchel Geo
715 St Vladimir's Ukrainian
    Catholic Church
715 Diadio Rev Father Nicholas
733 Lethbridge Miners Library
735 Filgas Dave
745 Polish Hall
Eighth Avenue Intersects
Adams Park

**1962 Henderson Directory**
Odd numbers East Side
104 Catelli Food Products Ltd
121 Lethbridge Sheet Metal Ltd
125 Jehovah Witnesses Kingdom
    Hall
131 Fawcett Ronald D
135 Christie's Auto Body Works
139 Hermas Auto Service
CPR Merchandise Service
CPR Pensioners Club
Second Avenue North Intersects
200 Bird Building Supplies
202 Bird Construction Co Ltd
207 Labor Temple
207 United Brotherhood of
Carpenters Local 846
207 Lethbridge Trades & Labor
    Council
207 Intnatl Hod Carriers Bldg &
    Comn Laborers Union of Amer
    Local 627
217 Van Lieshout Peter
221 Stewart James
Second Avenue A Intersects
225 Wyszynski Marion
230 Howards Furniture Ltd
230 Lethbridge Rugs & Carpets
234 Nakamura Toyosaburo
236 Canadian Electronics Ltd
237 Simons Peter
237 Simons P Brick Block & Tile
    Contractors
238 Cottrell Jack Dr phys & surg
238 Sequoia Central Systems
    (Leth) Ltd
240 Marvan Building Supplies &
    Cabinet Works
242 Under construction
244 Oscar's TV Service
246 Acmesnooker
246 Maranne Apartments
248 Tom's Trading Post
250 York Pharmacy (Leth) Ltd
252 Paul's Plumbing & Heating
254 No return
256 Lealta Building Supplies
256 Modrzejewski Constn Ltd
250 Lealta Theatre
258 Doughty C F
259 York Hotel Cafe
265 York Hotel Ltd
265 Kikinday L phys & surg
265 York Hotel Barber Shop
Third Avenue Intersects
301 North Lethbridge Motors &
    Auto Wreckers
302 Jack's Radio & TV Sales &
    Service
304 Van Ree's Upholstery &
    Woodwork
306 Grey Wm shoe repr
308 Adachi Kichio
310 Richards Electrical Repair
    Centre
312 La Kay's Ladies Wear
314 Bank of Montreal
316 Higa's Jewellery & Men's Wear
318 Beauty Salon
318 Hales Annie Mrs
320 Kobal's Grocery
320 Davies Lloyd
320 Smith James
321 Northsideshell Service
Third Avenue A Begins
322 Coby's Beauty Salon
322 Lethbridge Beauty School
324 North Leth Hdw (1961) Ltd

324 North Lethbridge Appliance
328 American Confectionery
328 Wong Jack
328 Lee Wong Block
    Grey Jessie
    Lindseth Arth
330 Lee Duck Dry Cleaners
334 Alta Liquor Control Board Store
    No 72
335 Westminster Servicesta
Fourth Avenue Intersects
es Westminster School
406 Marutkyn John
408 Sonalta Real Estate
408 Ritt Agencies (Genl Ins)
408 Ritt Heating
410 Bel-Aire Beauty Salon
410 Greggy's Barber Shop
412 Riethman & Hudson
    Decorating Ltd
416 No return
418 McCaffrey Block
418 McCaffrey Drug Store
418 Sub PO No 1
420 Mezei's Shoe Repair
422 Lethbridge Public Library
    (North Branch)
424 Muellers (Hugo) Sausage
424 Old Country Sausageshop
426 Knit King of Lethbridge
428 North Side Bakery
428 City Elec (Leth) Ltd
430 Pruegger's Accordion College
430 North Lethbridge Ladies &
    Gents Tailoring
432 Kearney Glen W
Fifth Avenue Intersects
502 First United Church
505 Sunny Service
513 Cdn Imperial Bk of Com
516 Grismer's Dairy Queen
519 Potvin Romeo
Fifth Avenue A Begins
531 Birdie Mrs
531 Wong Bing
533 Easy Way Cleaning Supplies &
    Services Ltd
533 Southwest Hdw & Machy Ltd
535 Acme Television Ltd
535 Artistic Beauty Salon
535 Smith Bryce G chtd acct
535 Pippet Kingston barr
535 Bel-Air School of Dancing
535 Delmar Coffeeshop
537 Watson Jessie
542 Jenkins Groceteria
544 Marlene's Fish & Chips
546 Progressive Roofing & Bldg
    Supplies
Sixth Avenue Intersects
604 Killen Jas Rt Rev Monsignor
604 St Basil's Catholic Church
605 Northway Service
609 Huszar Frank
610 Karl's Plumbing Ltd
610 Shirley's Beauty Shop
612 K I P Heating Ltd
613 Lesson Steve
614 Buzy-B Dry Cleaning
616 Steed D J dentist
618 North Plaza Florist
619 Housley Henry
620 Van Den Hengels Pastry
622 Thriftway Drug
624 Dean's Fabric Land
626 McLean F J phys
Sixth Avenue A Begins
630 New Confectionery

635 Garrett Delbert A
637 Greek Orthodox Church
642 Mihalik's Food & Dry Goods
Seventh Avenue Intersects
701 Eagles Hall
707 Triebwasser Albt
708 Ponech Zena Mrs
715 Vladimir's Ukrainian Catholic
    Church
715 Hurko Tiofil Rev
730 John's Barber Shop
730 Pastime Billiard Parlour
732 Credico John
733 Lethbridge Miners Library
734 Joe's Confectionery
735 Massey Ronald
740 Matt's Confectionery
740 Smerek Mike
745 Polish Hall
746 City Servicestation

**1964 Henderson Directory**
Odd Numbers are East Side
104 Catelli Food Products Ltd
106 CPR Pensioners Club
121 Lethbridgesht MtI Ltd
125 Jehovah Witnesses Kingdom
    Hall
131 Vacant
135 Christie's Sharp Shop Subway
    Auto Reprs
139 Herman's Auto Serv gas
Second Avenue A Intersects
Fire Hall No 2
220 Bird Bldg Supplies
202 Bird Construction Ltd
207 Labour Temple
    United Brotherhood of
    Carpenters Local 846
    Lethbridge & Dist Labour
    Council
    Labour Club of Lethbridge
    Internatl Hod Carriers Bldg &
    Comn Laborers Union of Am
    Local 6Z7
    Nation Union of Public
    Employees
217 Vacant
221A Stewart James
Second Avenue A Intersects
225 No return
230 Howards Furniture Ltd
234 Nakamura Toyosaburo
236 Cdn Electronics Ltd
237 Vacant
238 Campbell Clinic
240 Marvan Building Supplies &
    Cabinet Works
242 Vancell Confectionery
244 Oscar's TV Service
244 Nowicki Anthony
246 Acmesnooker
248 Tom's Trading Post
250 Draffin's North Drugs
252 Paul's Plmb & Htg Ltd
254 House of Wong restr
256 Lealta Building Supplies
    Modrzejewski Constn Ltd
258 Doughty C F
265 Royer Hotels Ltd
    Kikinday Dr Ladislaus phys
    York Hotel Cafe
Third Avenue Intersects
302 Jack's Radio & TV Sales & Serv
304 Vacant
305A North Lethbridge Mtrs &
    Auto
306 Grey Wm Shoe Reprs

308 Vacant
310 Vacant
312 La Kay's Ladies Wear
314 Bank of Montreal
316 Higa's Jewellery & Higa's Men's
    Wear
318 Hales Annie Mrs
    Ed's Barber Shop
    North Lethbridge Ladies &
    Gentleman Tailor Shop
320 Kobal's Grocery
    Davies Lloyd W
    Smith James L
    Smith Jean R
321 Northsideshell Serv
Third Avenue A Intersects
322 Coby's Beauty Salon
    Lethbridge Beauty Sch
324 Hoyt's North Lethbridge Hdw
328 American Confectionery,
    Wong Jack
328 Lee Wong Block
    Gray Jessie Mrs
    Lindseth Arth
330 Lee Duck Dry Clns
334 Alta Liquor Control Bd
335 Westminster Serv Sta
Fourth Avenue Intersects
406 Marutkyn Ian
408 Sonalta Real Est
    Jubilee Homes contr
408 Ritt Agencies Ltd Ins
    Ritt Heating
410 Bel-Aire Beauty Salon
410 Greggy's Barber Shop
412 Riethman & Hudson
    Decorating
416 Lyle's Hdw
418 McCaffrey Block
    McCaffrey's Drug Store
    Sub PO No 1
420 Mezei's Shoe Repr
422 Lethbridge Public Library
    (North Branch)
424 Old Country Sausageshop
426 Vacant
428 North Side Bakery
428 City Elec (Lethbridge) Ltd
    contrs
430 Pruegger's Accordion College
    Ltd
432 Kearney Glen W
436 Wonder Cafe
Fifth Avenue Intersects
502 First United Church
505 Sunny Service
515 Cdn Imperial Bank of Com
516 Grismer's Dairy Queen
519 Cunningham Archie
    Wick N
    Jennings Norton
5th Avenue A Intersects
531 Wong Bing J
533 Easy Way Cleaning Supplies &
Services Ltd
    Southwest Hdw & Machy Ltd
    Cavalier Barber Shop
535 Acme Television Ltd
    Artistic Beauty Salon
    Pippet Kingston barr
    Bridge Booster Co publ.
    Astaire Fred Dancestudio
    Preston Fredk T phys
535 Delmar Coffeeshop restr
537 Watson Jessie
542 Tom Boy Grocery Store
544 Vacant
546 K & K Clothing & Shoe Ltd

Sixth Avenue Intersects
603 North Way Service gas sta
604 Killen James Q Rev
    St Basil's Roman Catholic
    Church
609 Huszar Frank
610 Karl's Plumbing & Heating Ltd
    North Plaza Millinery
610 Ann's Beauty Parlor
612 K I P Heating Ltd
613 Lesson Steve
614 Buzy-B Coin Operated Dry
    Cleaning
616 Steed David J dentist
618 North Plaza Florist
619 Housley Henry
620 Van den Hengels Pastry Shop
622 Thrift-Way Drugs
624 Yardstick dry goods
626 McLean Fred J phys
Sixth Avenue Intersects
630 New Confectionery
635 Garrett Delbert A
637 Greek Orthodox Church
642 Mihalik A genl mdse
Seventh Avenue Intersects
701 Eagles Hall
707 Triebwasser Albert
708 Ponech Zena Mrs
715 Vladimir's Ukrainian Catholic
    Church
715 Hurko Tiofil Rev
730 John's Barber Shop & Pastime
    Billiard Parlour
732 Credico John
733 Lethbridge Miners Library
    Club Inc
734 Joe's Confectionery
735 Vacant
740 Matt's Confectionery
    Smerek Michl
742 Norbridge Royalite
745 Canadian Polish Hall

**1966 Henderson Directory**
Odd numbers East Side
104 Catelli Food Products Ltd
CPR Mdse Service
106 CPR Pensioners Club
123 Vacant
125 Jehovah Witnesses Kingdom
    Hall
131 Fawcett Ronald D
135 Furnasman Ltd
    Subway Auto Reprs
139 Herman's Auto Serv gas sta
Second Avenue A Intersects
Fire Hall No 2
200 Bird Bldg Supplies
202 Bird Construction Ltd
207 Labour Temple
    United Brotherhood of
    Carpenters Local 846
    Lethbridge & Dist Labour
    Council
    Labour Club of Lethbridge
    United Packinghouse Wkrs of
    Am
    Cdn Union of Pub Emps
221 Stewart Georgina Mrs
Second Avenue Intersects
225 Schramm Horst
230 Howard's Furniture Ltd
234 Nakamura Toyosaburo
236 Cdn Electronics Ltd equip
237 Simons Peter H
    Simons & Son Masonry Constn
238 Campbell Clinic

240 Marvan Building Supplies &
	Cabinet Works
242 Vancell Confectionery
	Joe's Coffee Bar
244 Smith's Color TV Stereo Centre
244 Nowiki Anthony
246 Acmesnooker billiards
248 Tom's Trading Post
250 Draffin's North Drugs
252 Paul's Plmb & Htg Ltd
254 House of Wong restr
256 Lealta Building Supplies
	Modrzejewski Constn Ltd
258 Vacant
265 Royer Hotels Ltd
	Kikinday Dr Ladislaus phys
	York Hotel Cafe restr
	York Hotel Barber Shop
Third Avenue Intersects
302 Jack's Radio & TV Sls & Serv
304 Van Rees Upholstery & Furn
305 North Lethbridge Mtrs
306 Chinook Stationers Ltd
308 Vacant
310 Richard's Electrical Repair
	Centre contrs
312 La Kay's Ladies Wear Ltd
314 Bank of Montreal
316 Higa's Jewellery
	Higa's Men's & Boy's Wear
318 Ed's Barber Shop
320 Kobal's Grocery
	Davies Lloyd W
321 Northsideshell Serv
Third Avenue A Intersects
322 Coby's Beauty Salon
	Lethbridge Beauty Sch
324 Hoyt's North Lethbridge hdw
328 American Confectionery
	Wong Jack
328 Wong Apartments
	Zelipula Peter
	Wong B Lee
	Lee David
330 Lee Duck Dry Cleaners
334 Alta Liquor Control Bd Store
	No 72
	Lethbridge Northern Irrigation
335 Westminster Service
Fourth Avenue Intersects
406 Marutkyn Ivan J
408 Sonalta Real Est
410 Bel-Aire Beauty Salon
410 Greggy's Barber Shop
412 Riethman & Hudson
	Decorating Ltd
413 Hudson Agencies Ltd real est
416 Lyle's Hdw
418 McCaffrey Block
	McCaffrey's Drug Store
	Sub PO No 1
420 Mezei's Shoe Repr
422 Lethbridge Public Library
	(North Branch)
424 Old Country Sausageshop
426 Norbridge Farmers Mart
	producers
428 North Side Bakery
428 Alberta Floor Coverings
430 Vacant
432 Wonder Cafe
Fifth Avenue Intersects
502 First United Church
505 Sunny Service gas sta.
515 Cdn Imperial Bank of Com
516 Grismer's Dairy Queen
519 Cunningham Archie
Fifth Avenue A Intersects

531 Kearney Pat M Mrs
535 Acme Television Ltd reprs
	Scholdra. Roman law ofc
	Artistic Beauty Salon
	Astaire Fred Dancestudio
	S & 0 Realty Ltd
535 Dehner Coffeeshop
537 Watson Jessie
542 Tom Boy Store
544 Johnny's Barber Shop
546 K & K Clothing & Shoe Ltd
	Rozycki Konstanty
Sixth Avenue Intersects
603 North Way Service gas sta
604 St Basil's Roman Catholic
	Church
609 Huszar Frank
610 Karl's Plumbing & Heating Ltd
	North Plaza Millinery
610 Pruegger's Accordion College
610 No Return
612 K I P Heating Ltd
613 Lesson Steve
614 Buzy-B Coin Operated Dry
	Cleaning
616 Steed David J dentist
619 Housley Henry
620 Van den Hengels' Pastry Shop
622 North Plaza Ladies and
	Children's Wear
624 Yardstick dry goods
626 McLean Fred J phys
	Dudley Chiropractic Clinic
Sixth Avenue A Intersects
630 New Confectionery
631 Eagles Hall
635 Garrett Delbert An
637 Greek Orthodox Church of
	Holy Trinity
642 Mihalik A genl mdse
Seventh Avenue Intersects
701 vacant
707 Triebwasser Albert
708 Ponech Zena Mrs
715 Ukrainian Catholic St
	Vladimir's Church
	Syvenkey Ludornyr Rev
724 McLean Fred J phys
730 John's Barber Shop
	Pastime Billiard Parlour
732 Credico John
733 Lethbridge Miners Library
	Club Inc
734 Joe's Confectionery
735 Lapierre Phil
738 Fanci Full Beauty Salon
740 Matt's Confectionery
	Smerek Michl
742 Norbridge Royalite gas sta
745 Canadian Polish Hall

**1968 Henderson Directory**
Odd numbers East side
104 Catelli Food Products Ltd
	CPR Merchandiseserv
106 CPR Pensioners Club
121 Southern Monument Co
125 Jehovah Witnesses Kingdom
	Hall
131 Orich Wm M
135 Furnasman Ltd
	Crusader Whol Htg & Plmb
	Ltd
	Agor Sheet Metal
139 Texaco Serv
Second Avenue A Intersects
Fire Hall No 2
200 Bird Bldg Supplies

202 Bird Construction Co Ltd
207 Labour Temple
	United Brotherhood of
	Carpenters Local 846
	Lethbridge & Dist Labour
	Council
	Labour Club of Lethbridge
	United Packinghouse Wkrs of
	Am
	Cdn Union of Pub Emps
221 Stewart Georgina Mrs
Second Avenue Intersects
225 Kolibar Steven
230 No Return
234 Nakamura Toyosaburo
236 Smiths Color Television
237 Simons Peter H
	Simons P & Sons
238 The Kings Inn
240 Marvan Building Supplies &
	Cabinet Works
242 Vancell Confectionery
	Joe's Coffee Bar
244 Vacant
244 Nowiki Anthony
246 Acme Snooker Billiards
248 Tom's Trading Post
250 Draffin's North Drugs
252 Paul's Plmb & Htg Ltd
254 House of Wong restr
256 Lealta Building Supplies
	Modrzejewski Constn Ltd
258 Vacant
265 Royer Hotels Ltd
	Kikinday Ladislaus phys
	York Hotel Cafe
	York Hotel Barber Shop
	York Hotel
	York Coffeeshop
Third Avenue Intersects
302 Jack's Radio & TV Sls & Serv
304 Van Rees' Upholstery & Furn
305 North Lethbridge Mtrs
306 Chinook Stationers Ltd
308 No Return
310 Under Constn
312 La Kay's Ladies Wear Ltd
313 Northside 66 Serv Sta
314 Bank of Montreal
316 National Cash Register Co of
	Can Ltd
318 Ed's Barber Shop
320 Kobal's Grocery
	Davies Lloyd W
324 Northsideshell Service
Third Avenue A Intersects
322 Coby's Beauty Salon
	Tiny Tot Shop
	Lethbridge Beauty Sch.
324 Hoyt's (North Lethbridge)
	hdw
328 American Confectionery
328 Wong Jack
328 Wong Apartments
	Unreiner Peter
330 Lee Duck Dry Clns
334 Alta Liquor Control Bd Store
	#72
	Lethbridge Northern Irrigation
335 Westminster BA Serv Sta
Fourth Avenue Intersects
406 Higa's Mens & Boy Wear
	Higa's Jewellery
408 Sonalta Real Est
	New To You Shop
410 Bel-Aire Beauty Salon
410 Greggy's Barber Shop
412 Riethman & Hudson

	Decorating Ltd
413 Hudson Agencies Ltd real est
414 Lyle's Hdw & Furn Ltd
416 Lyle's Hdw dlrs
418 McCaffrey Block
	McCaffrey's Drug Store
	PO Sub PO #1
420 Mezei's Shoe Repr
422 Lethbridge Public Library
	(North Branch)
424 Old Country Sausageshop
426 Lyles Furniture
428 Musicland
428 North Side Bakery
430 Filter Queen Sls & Servs
432 Wonder Caf,
Fifth Avenue Intersects
502 First United Church
503 South Alta Japanese United
	Church.
505 Sunny Service gas sta
515 Cdn Imperial Bank of Corn
516 Dairy Queen
519 Cvetko John
Fifth Avenue A Intersects
531 Kearney Pat M Mrs
533 McAras Health Center
535 Acme Television Ltd reprs
	Scholdra Roman law ofc
	Murray Arth Sch. of Dancing
	S & 0 Realty Ltd
	Hoyte Martin barr
	Diversified Incomesecurities
	Ltd
535 Foothills Mrs
537 Matson Jessie
542 Gordons Tomboy
544 Johnny's Barber Salon
544 Italia Importers
546 K & K Clothing & Shoe Ltd
Sixth Avenue Intersects
603 North Way Service gas sta
604 St Basil's Roman Catholic
	Church
609 Huszar Frank
610 Karl's Plumbing Ltd
	Prueggers Accordion College
610a North Plaza Beauty Salon
612 K I P Heating Ltd
613 Lesson Steve
614 Buzy-B Coin Operated Dry
	Cleaning
616 Steed & Selk dentists
618 North Plaza Florist
619 Housley Henry
620 Van den Hengels' Pastry Shop
622 Sommers Ladies Wear
624 Baker's Yardstick
626 Dudley Chiropractic Clinic
Sixth Avenue A Intersects
630 Sakumoto Confectionery
631 Eagles Hall
635 Garrett Delbert A
637 Greek Orthodox Church of
	Holy Trinity
642 Mihaliks IGA
Seventh Avenue Intersects
702 Thriftway Drugs
707 Triebwasser Albert Savage
	Peter
708 Ponech Zena Mrs
714 Under Constn
715 Ukrainian Catholic St
	Vladimir's Church - Syvenkey
	Ludomyr Rev
716 Okamura Yashiyuki phys
718 Okamura T dentist
720 Under Constn

155

722 Bennett R phys
724 McLean Fredk J pbys
730 John's Barber Shop
    Pastime Billiard Parlour
732 Credico John
733 Lethbridge Miners Library
    Club
734 Joe's Confectionery
735 Smith Robt S
736 Sue's Coffee Bar &
    Confectionery
738 Fanci Full Beauty Salon
740 Matt's Confectionery
    Smerek Helen Mrs
742 Norbridge Royalite gas sta
745 Canadian Polish Hall

## 1972 Henderson Directory
Odd numbers East Side
104 Catelli Ltd food products mfrs
106 Under Constn
113 Bird Bldg Sups
121 Southern Monument Co
125 Jehovah Witnesses Kingdom
    Hall
131 McDonald Margt Mrs
135 No Return
    Alberta Brewer's Agents
139 Stop & Save Petroleums gas sta
Second Avenue A Intersects
200 Vacant
202 Vacant
207 Labour Temple
    United Brotherhood of
    Carpenters Local 846
    Lethbridge & Dist Labour
    Council
    Labour Club of Lethbridge
    Genl Constn Wkrs
    Cdn Union of Pub Emps
221 Stewart Georgina Mrs
Second Avenue Intersects
225 No Return
230 Bank of Montreal
234 McDougald Anna Mrs
236 Smith's Color TV & Appliances
    Ltd
237 Simons Peter H
    Simons P & Sons Constn Ltd
    mason contrs
240 Marvan Bldg Sups & Cabt Wks
    Simpson Sears Auto Motive
    Centre
242 Vancell Confectionery
    Joe's Coffee Bar
244 Yesterday's Appliance used
    appliances
244a Nowicki Mary Mrs
246 Acme Billiards
248 Tom's Trading Post
250 Looker C A Ofc Equip
252 Red Lantern Room
254 House of Wong restr
256 Victoria Confectionery gro
    store
258 Vacant
265 York Hotel
    York Hotel Barber Shop
    York Hotel Coffeeshop
279 Vacant
Third Avenue Intersects
302 Jack's Radio & TV Sls & Serv
304 Van Ree's Upholstery & Furn
305 North Lethbridge Mo Tires Ltd
306 Chinook Stationers Ltd
308 Chudobiak Don
310 North Leth Barber Shop
312 La Kay's Ladies Wear

313 Northside 66 Serv
314 Capri Carpets Ltd
316 National Cash Register Co of
    Can Ltd
318 Vacant
320 Kobal's Grocery
    Davies Lloyd W
321 Vacant
Third Avenue A Intersects
322 Coby's Beauty Salon
324 Hoyt's North Lethbridge hdw
328 American Confectionery
    Wong Jack
    Wong Apartments
    Dietrich Frank
    Ternowsky Wm
330 Lee Duck Dry Cleaners
334 Alta Liquor Control Bd Store
    No 72
    Lethbridge Northern Irrigation
    Dist
354 Gergely's Glass
Fourth Avenue Intersects
406 Higa's Men's & Boys' Wear
    Higa's Jewellery
408 Sonalta Real Est
    City Plmb (Lethbridge)
410 Bel-Aire Beauty Salon
410a Greggy's Barber Shop
412 Riethman & Hudson
    Decorating Ltd contrs
    Hudson Kenneth E
418 McCaffrey Block
    McCaffrey's Drug Store
    Sub PO No 1
422 Alan W Dudley chiro
424 Old Country Sausageshop
425 Westminster Shopping Plaza
    Westminster Drugs
    Bank of Nova Scotia
    One Hour Martinizing
    Leth Pub Library (N Br)
    Northsideshell Serv
    Fred's Bakery
    North Village Restr
    Rug Shoppe The
426 Baker's Fabric Centre dry
    goods
428 Trifles & Treasures Antiques
430 Mezei's Shoe Reprs
430A Up Your Alley
432 Vacant
Fifth Avenue Intersects
502 First United Church
505 Sunny Esso Serv gas sta
515 Cdn Impl Bank of Com
516 North Dairy Queen
519 Cvetko John
Fifth Avenue A Intersects
531 De Georgio Kathy Mrs
533 Club 40
535 Acme Telev Sls & serv
    Scholdra Roman barr
    Monte Carlo Dance Academy
    Northside Taxi
    Foothills Mus
537 Watson Jesse
542 Vacant
544 Green's Pop Shop
546 Paola's Italian Restr
Sixth Avenue Intersects
603 North Way Texaco Serv gas sta
604 St Basil's Roman Catholic
    Church
    Marien Gaston A Rev
609 Huszar Frank
610 North Side Bakery
    North Plaza Beauty Salon

612 KIP Heating contrs
613 Lesson Steve
    Fantin Matilda Mrs
614 North Plaza Koin-O-Mat
616 Steed, Selk & Strong dentists
618 North Plaza Florist
619 Housley Ellen Mrs
620 Chinook Ofc Machs
622 Queen's Pizza restr
624 E-J New & Used clo
626 Stewart & Taylor phys
Sixth Avenue A Intersects
630 1waasa Confectionery
631 Eagles Hall
635 Malatesta Attilio P
637 Greek Orthodox Church of
    Holy Trinity
642 Mihalik's Mayfair Foods
Seventh Avenue Intersects
702 Thriftway Drugs
703 Martin Bros Ltd
707 Eftoda Margt Mrs
708 Ponech Zena E Mrs
714 Vacant
715 Ukrainian Catholic St
    Vladimir's Church
    Syvenkey Ludomyr Rev
716-724 North Lethbridge Med
    Bldg ofcs
716 Okamura Yoshiyuki phys
718 Okamura Takeshi dentist
720 Vacant
722 Bennett Ronald phys
724 McLean Fredk J phys
730 John's Barber Shop
    Pastime Billiard Parlour
732 Credico John
733 Lethbridge Miners Library
    Club Inc
734 Joe's Confectionery
735 No Return
736 Sue's Coffee Bar &
    Confectionery
738 Fanci-Full Beauty Salon
740 Matt's Confectionery
    Smerek Helen Mrs
742 Matts Econo Serv gas sta
745 Canadian Polish Hall

## 1975 Henderson Directory
Odd Numbers East Side
104 Catelli Ltd food products mfrs
113 Bird Building Supplies building
121 Southern Monument & Tile Co
Ltd material building a
121a Sign Rite Lettering Studios
125 Jehovah Witnesses Kingdom
    Hall
131 Under Constn
135 Alberta Brewers' Agents Ltd
    brewers
139 John's Turbo Service gas sta
Second Avenue Intersects
207 Canadian Food & Allied
    Workers
    Local P740 organization
    Cdn Union of Public
    Employees
    Labour Club of Lethbridge
    Labour Temple labour union
    Lethbridge Building &
    Construction Trades Council
    Lethbridge & District Labour
    Council
    United Brotherhood Of
    Carpenters Local 846
221 Parking Lot
Second Avenue A Intersects

225 Moser Doris Mrs
    Chernuka Ken
230 Bank Of Montreal
234 Vacant
236 Smith's Color T V & Appliances
    Ltd
237 Simons P & Sons Construction
Ltd mason contra
    Simons Peter H
240 Smith's Color T V & Appliances
    Ltd storage
242 Pearl River Restaurant
244 Yesterday's Appliances whse
    Nowicki Mary Mrs
246-248 Tom's Trading Post
250 Looker Office Equipment
    (1972) Ltd
252 Red Lantern Room restr
254 House Of Wong restr
256 Jimmie's Food Fair gro
258 Neptune Coring Ltd horizontal
    drilling contra
258a Orr Karatestudio karate judo
258b Lethbridge Figuresalon
265 York Hotel
    York Hotel Barber Shop
    York Hotel Cafe
    Northside Taxi 4
Third Avenue Intersects
302 Jack's Radio & T V Sales &
    Service
304 Van Ree's Upholstery &
    Furniture furn
305 North Lethbridge Mo-Tires Ltd
306 Luigi's Pizza & Steak House
308 Vacant
310 Vacant
312 Vacant
313 Northside 66 Service gas sta
314 Vacant
314a Walter Kurt Ceramic Tile Ltd
    ceramic tile
316 National Cash Register Canada
    Ltd
318 Vacant
320 Kobal's Grocery gro
    Davies Lloyd W
321 Apollo Muffler Centres Ltd
    Install & Repair
Third Avenue A Intersects
322 Coby's Beauty Salon
323 Vacant
324 Rug & Drapery Shoppe
324a Professional Carpet Care Ltd
328 Wallocha Hans Apartments
    Monroe John
    Johnson Charles
    Klaassen Ole
    Oezku H J
    Flower Pot The
    Briosi Ross
330 Lee Duck Dry Cleaners
334 Lethbridge Northern Irrigation
    District
    Alberta Milk Control Board
    Alberta Liquor Control Board
354 Gergely's Glass glass
Fourth Avenue Intersects
406 Higa's Men's Wear
    Higa's Jewelry
408 City Plumbing (Lethbridge)
    Ltd
    Roto-Rooter Sewer Service
410 Woman's World Beauty Salon
410a Gus Barber Shop
412 Riethman & Hudson
    Decorating Ltd
    Hudson Kenneth E6

414 Sadler J T S phys
  Alexander Archibald phys
  Melling Michl T phys
416 Lilley E R Photography photo
  Book Exchange The
418 McCaffrey Block
  PO Sub No 1
  McCaffrey's Drug Store
422 Dudley Alan W chiropractor
424 Old Country Sausageshop
425 Westminster Shopping Plaza
  Astro Realty Ltd real est
  Bank of Nova Scotia The
  Canada Safeway
  Cotter Brian C chiropractor
  Nook The kitchen bathroom
  accessories
426 Bridge City Cabinets Ltd
  cabinets
425 Fred's Bakery
  Krahn Homes Ltd bldg contr
  Hoyt's Pro Home Centr
  Hobby Wine & Brew Centre
  Northsideshell Service
  One Hour Martinizing
  Vantas Ranchland Meats
  Toth Les Agencies ins and
  accounting
  Westminster Drugs retail
  drugs
  Variety Fabrics drygds

426 Alladins Lamps Boutique
  Easy Sweep Building Cleaning
  Ever-Lite Electric Ltd
428 A-1 Cabinet & Crafts cabtmkrs
  Trifles & Treasures Antiques
430a Bridge Appliancesales & Serv
430 Mezei's Shoe Repair
432 Elsie's Confectionery
  Brassard Eug A
Fifth Avenue Intersects
502 First United Church
515 Canadian Imperial Bank of
  Commerce
516 North Dairy Queen
519 Cvetko John
  Anderson Debbie
Fifth Avenue A Intersects
531a Vacant
633 Club 40 health club
535 Vauxhall Foods Ltd
  Chipper Foods mkt french fry
  mix
  Growers Supply farm pts &
  servs
  Pak-Well Produce Ltd
  201 Walters J D & Associates
  Scholdra Roman barr
  Whittick Mechanical
  Contractors Ltd
  Hilder's T V Service
537 Watson Andrew K

541 Seven Eleven
542 Towne & Country Furniture
544 Lethbridge Watch & Repair
  Green's Pop Shop Ltd
Sixth Avenue Intersects
603 Westminster Texaco Service
604 St Basil's Church
  Marien Gaston A Rev a
  St Basil's Rectory
609 Dietzen Trucilia
610 North Plaza Books
610a Northside Bakery
612 K I P Heating Ltd
613 Lesson Steven
614 North Plaza Koin-O-Mat
616 North Plaza Beauty Salon
618 North Plaza Florist
619 Vishloff Pete
620 Chinook Office Machines
622 Queen's Pizza & Spaghetti
House
624 Remus Television
626 Vacant
  Martin Dalton A & Associates
Sixth Avenue A Intersects
630 Asahi Gift & Confectionery
  Ablonczy Elsie H
631 Fraternal Order of Eagles
635 Plomp Wm J
637 Greek Orthodox Church of
  Holy Trinity

640 CFCN Television
642 Mihalik's Mayfair Foods
Seventh Avenue Intersects
702 Thriftway Drugs
703 Martin Bros Ltd Memorial
  Chapel
708 Ponech Zena E Mrs
714 Com-Serv Association South
  Alberta
715 Ukrainian Catholic Parish of St
  Vladimirs
  Syvenkey Ludomyr Rev a
716 North Lethbridge Medical Bldg
716 Okamura Yoshiyuki phys
718 Takeshi Okamura dentists
720 Vanda Beauty Counselor
722 Bennett Ronald phys
724 Mc Lean Fredk J phys
730 John's Barber Shop Pastime
  Billiard Parlour
732 Credico John
733 Lethbridge Miner's Library
  Club
734 Joe's Confectionery
736 Kelly's Confectionery
738 Fanci-Full Beauty Salon
740 Vacant
742 Matts Turbo Service gas sta
745 Canadian Polish Hall

Other Lethbridge Historical Society publications in print in 2005 available from the Society or through local outlets.

**The Butcher, The Baker, The Candy Maker 1870 - 1920**

**Sterndale Bennett - A Man for All Theatre**

**Sweetgrass Hills - A Natural and Cultural History**

**Prairie prisoners - POWs in Lethbridge during two world conflicts**

**Where Was It? A Guide to Early Lethbridge Buildings**

**Railways in Southern Alberta**

**C. P. Rail High Level Bridge at Lethbridge**

**Last Great (Intertribal) Indian Battle**

**Boats and Barges on the Belly (Oldman River)**

**The Whoop-Up Trail**

**Rocky Mountain Rangers**

**Plants and the Blackfoot**

Other publications written by author Garry Allison (available through the publishers).

**People of the Mines (2005)**

**100 Years: A History of the Lethbridge & District Exhibition**

The Author
## *Garry Allison*

Garry Lawrence Allison was born December 10, 1941 at 1806 13th Street North in Little Wigan, a predominantly Scottish community stretching from 18th to 26th Avenues. Garry always dreamed of becoming the Sports Editor for The Lethbridge Herald. He not only attained that dream, but he changed the way high school, amateur and women's sports, as well as rodeo, were covered by the newspaper in southern Alberta. He also served as The Herald's District Editor, City Editor and at the end of his career in 2003, he was the Outdoors Editor. After spending 1957 to 1974 as a typesetter/printer, Garry moved into The Herald's sports department full-time in 1974. He had however, started covering rodeo, boxing and other sports back in 1962 for both The Herald and the Ad-Viser. He raised the level of news coverage given to high school and amateur sports, and gave women's sports equal billing as men's.

An avid rodeo fan, Garry covered that sport, in amateur, native, college, high school and professional levels. He also attended the first 10 Canadian Finals Rodeos as well as numerous Calgary Stampedes and North American Amateur rodeo championships in Denver, Colorado and El Paso, Texas. Amateur sports also received Garry's attention as he covered the Southern Alberta Summer Games from its inception in 1970 until 2001.

Garry earned Thomson Newspaper national and regional awards for outstanding editorial achievement. National awards and local awards for his extensive coverage of rodeo, high school sports and the outdoors. In 1979, he won the Max Bell Memorial Award for outstanding coverage of amateur sports in the province. The award included membership in the Alberta Sports Hall of Fame. As well, he was inducted into the Lethbridge Sports Hall of Fame in May, 2003. He has received the Canadian Professional Rodeo Cowboys Association's Jimmy Brown Award for rodeo coverage in Canada. He has been honoured by Ducks Unlimited Canada, on a national and local level and in March 2005 was named to the Ducks Unlimited Hall of Fame. Also honoured by the Alberta and Lethbridge Fish and Game Associations, as well as Trout Unlimited Canada's Lethbridge chapter.

In non-sports fields the General Stewart Branch #4 of the Royal Canadian Legion, Korea War Veterans Association, the Great Canadian Plains Railway Society and the town of Coalhurst have honoured him. In 1984 he was named Parent of the Year by Coalhurst High School. Garry was given a special Blackfoot name, Eagle Wing, by the Peigan Nation through Head-Smashed-In Buffalo Jump Interpretive Centre in 1996. He is a member of the Headdress Society of the Kainai Nation and in 2000 was honoured by the National Aboriginal Day program at Fort Whoop-Up. In 2002 Garry received the Queen's Golden Jubilee Medal and in 2003 was the Honourary Parade Marshall of the Lethbridge Exhibition's Whoop-Up Days parade.

Garry also spent 10 years coaching high school girls basketball, nine years at Coalhurst and one at Winston Churchill High School, he coached senior girls soccer for eight years, winning the city championship once with his Coalhurst team.

Since retiring in 2002, Garry has continued writing, initially for the Rocky Mountain Turf Club and then completing two books: a history of north Lethbridge "My Side of Town" slated for release in late 2005 by the Lethbridge Historical Society, and "the People of the Mines", for the No. 8 Mine Society, published in April of 2005. He has also completed "The 100-Year history of the Lethbridge Exhibition," published in 1999 and an unpublished manuscript about rodeo cowboy Reg Kesler.

Garry also has a completed manuscript entitled: "The Prairie Boys", about the numerous men and women he had interviewed throughout the years about their exploits during the many wars Canadians have been involved in. He is presently seeking a publisher. Garry and Mary are also members of the Lethbridge Historical Society.

Garry and wife Mary have been married 42 years, together they have seven children: Kathy, Shannon, Jason, Jackie, T-Jay, Cheyenne and Melissa and 17 grandchildren. Garry and Mary have cared for 76 foster children, three of which are still in their care, Kyle, Nathan and Jayden.